Nineteenth-Century Poetry ar

Nineteenth-Century Poetry and Literary Celebrity

Eric Eisner

palgrave
macmillan

Softcover reprint of the hardcover 1st edition 2009 978-0-230-22815-3

First published 2009 by
PALGRAVE MACMILLAN

Palgrave Macmillan in the UK is an imprint of Macmillan Publishers Limited, registered in England, company number 785998, of Houndmills, Basingstoke, Hampshire RG21 6XS.

Palgrave Macmillan in the US is a division of St Martin's Press LLC, 175 Fifth Avenue, New York, NY 10010.

Palgrave Macmillan is the global academic imprint of the above companies and has companies and representatives throughout the world.

ISBN 978-1-349-31001-2 ISBN 978-0-230-25084-0 (eBook)
DOI 10.1057/9780230250840

A catalogue record for this book is available from the British Library.

Library of Congress Cataloging-in-Publication Data

Eisner, Eric, 1971-
Nineteenth-century poetry and literary celebrity / Eric Eisner.
p. cm.
Includes bibliographical references and index.

1. English poetry—19th century—History and criticism. 2. Authors and readers—Great Britain—History—19th century. 3. Authorship—Social aspects—Great Britain—History—19th century. 4. Fame—History—19th century. 5. Fans (Persons)—Great Britain—History—19th century. 6. Popular culture and literature—Great Britain—History—19th century. I. Title.

PR585.A89E57 2009
821'.809355—dc22 2009013625

10 9 8 7 6 5 4 3 2 1
18 17 16 15 14 13 12 11 10 09

Contents

Acknowledgments

An earlier version of Chapter 3 appeared in *Prisms: Essays on Romanticism* 11 (2003) 7–36, and a version of Chapter 6 in *Victorian Review* 33: 2 (2007) 85–102. I thank the editors for permission to use this material here.

I am grateful to many people for their help in sustaining and cheering my work on this book. Barbara Johnson, Marjorie Garber and Ann Wierda Rowland, terrific teachers and readers, supervised the first stages of this project with patience and care. Leo Damrosch and James Engell gave helpful comments on early versions of some of these chapters. In graduate school and since, it's been my great luck to count Jesse Matz as a teacher, mentor and friend. Earlier on, Nancy Armstrong, Susan Bernstein, Ellen Rooney and the late Roger Henkle first made me think I'd like to be in this profession. To their extraordinary and dedicated teaching goes a good part of the credit, or the blame, for the path I've taken. Mai-Lin Cheng has been a comrade-in-arms since Providence. Meeting Claire Lewis and Sarah Kareem in graduate school was an era in my existence. Sarah read the earliest and the latest drafts of many of these chapters. It is hard to imagine having written this book without her as an interlocutor.

While I was first formulating this project, Susan Wolfson, Deborah Elise White, and Karen Swann gave me crucial guidance. I've had the chance to try out parts of this book on various audiences over the years; for responses, challenges, suggestions and conversation on those occasions, I'm grateful to Patrick O'Malley, Jason Goldsmith, Tom Mole, David Higgins, Michele Martinez, Kirstie Blair, Jason Rudy, Alison Chapman, Sarah Zimmerman, Anne Frey, Marjorie Stone and William Galperin. Lisa Surridge's sharp editorial eye improved the material that became Chapter 6. Joan W. Scott's reading helped me think about this project as a book. I would also like to acknowledge the very thoughtful reports of my anonymous readers; this is a far better book for their suggestions.

This book was completed at George Mason University, where I have joined an amazingly friendly, welcoming, and accommodating department. Among many great colleagues, I would like to thank in particular, for friendship and wise counsel, my chairs, Deborah Kaplan and Robert Matz; for all kinds of help in navigating teaching and writing, Zofia Burr, Alok Yadav, Devon Hodges, Rosemary Jann, Denise Albanese, David Kaufmann, Roger Lathbury, Tamara Harvey, Kristin Samuelian, Mark Sample, and Jessica Scarlata; and with special notice for their hospitality, Michael Malouf and Kristina Olson. Devon and Rosemary generously read portions of this manuscript. Research on this book was completed with the assistance of a Summer Research Grant from the Provost's Office and the Terry Comito fellowship from the English Department. Much of the research was carried out at the New York Public Library; I am especially grateful to the knowledgeable staff of the Pforzheimer Collection for their assistance.

I would like to thank the Keats-Shelley Association of America for organizing its mentorship program, and especially for pairing me with the unfailingly generous Judith Pascoe, who has gone way beyond the call of duty in shepherding this project along.

Finally, I would like to express my gratitude to my family, Eisners and Scotts, for their many forms of support and encouragement. Most of all, I want to thank Lizzie, Henry and Nadia. Henry and Nadia have put up with my working on this book their whole lives, and Lizzie for what must now feel like a lifetime. They have made space and time for the book with characteristic grace and good humor. This book is for Lizzie, without whose trust, love and partnership this book would not have gotten written, and for Henry and Nadia, romantics and realists both.

Introduction

Poets writing in Britain in the nineteenth century participated in a burgeoning culture of literary celebrity in which readers responded to writers with powerful feelings of fascination, desire, love or horror. Besotted readers wrote fan letters, sought autographs and souvenirs, adopted the clothes and style of their literary heroes, and elevated the "homes and haunts" of famous writers into pilgrimage sites. Portraits of contemporary authors became a hot commodity, while from country fairs to fancy emporiums, one could purchase curios featuring images of famous dead poets: busts of Shakespeare or Chatterton handkerchiefs.[1] A memoir-mad public devoured the gossip about writers' private lives retailed not just in autobiographies and reminiscences but in reviews, *romans-à-clef*, and newspaper notices, and some adoring readers schemed to see in person, to get to know, even to sleep with the poets they idolized. This book connects the literary experimentation of nineteenth-century poets with the exchanges between these poets and their passionate readers (many of them writers themselves) in this culture of celebrity. Though critical treatments of the period often characterize the era's most artistically ambitious poets as distancing themselves from a supposedly debased, commercialized culture of mass-mediated celebrity, a sophisticated, strategic and fascinated engagement with new modes of fame and new kinds of fandom turns out to have been central to these poets' experiments with literary form.[2] Nineteenth-century poetry was crucially shaped by the practices of its star-struck readers and by the affective relationships between reader and writer those practices served to mediate.[3]

In our understanding of nineteenth-century poetry, though, we tend to view mass-mediated celebrity as categorically distinct from the intimacy of the genre for which the period is best known, the lyric. Public, market-oriented and corporeal, fueled by sensation and scandal, the dynamics of celebrity seem far removed from the scene of lyric reading, often imagined as the psychological encounter of the reader with the disembodied "voice" of the text—an encounter that occurs in the privacy of the reader's study, and in the privacy of the reader's mind.[4] When poets do achieve popular celebrity, we tend to see them or their popularizers as capitalizing on, or selling out, the privacy and prestige of the lyric; we see the apparatus of celebrity as aggressively dismantling structured relations between publication and the private self the lyric aims to manage in a more controlled fashion. Similarly, scholarly discourse often seeks to draw a firm line between its own motivations and investments and more popular forms of admiration and curiosity, forms seen as exaggerated, naïve, or tainted by crass commercialism.[5] This book revisits these habitual critical oppositions in order to suggest that they elide important aspects of the practice of the poets we read, as well as of our own critical practice and its history.

My study's central claim is that in nineteenth-century poetry the resources and resistances of poetic language themselves intersect with the mechanisms and structures of the public world of popular celebrity. Poets not only explore the ways local effects of language reinforce the reader's emotional investment in the writer's personality—a projected sense of essential character or unique, embodied subjectivity. They also find the very structures of mass-mediated celebrity mimed by the impersonality of linguistic or figurative systems, and exploit this congruence. Focusing on the affective dimension of celebrity rather than on a history of critical pronouncements about fame or an analysis of "fame discourse," the readings in this book link the performative operation of language in poetic practice with the array of novel cultural practices and technologies through which celebrity is created and sustained. Neither a traditional reception study nor a study of poetic form to which reception is only ancillary, my analysis aims to show how deeply related are the tropological and cultural processes that shape our experience of poetry.

I use the term "literary celebrity" in a capacious sense that embraces various kinds of public notice, including both adulation and notoriety, in which both the writer's personality and the writer's body take on a public significance and a market value of their own. In nineteenth-century usage, "celebrity" is a term in flux, taking on new meaning as something a person can be, rather than a quality a person, book, place or event can possess—"no longer something you had, but something you were," in Tom Mole's nice formulation ("fan" in its modern sense takes longer to appear; its first recorded use is in American sports reporting in the 1880s).[6] The celebrity, that is, emerges over the course of the nineteenth century as a new social category, a new kind of public person. As a description of a phenomenon, the term "celebrity" offers the signal advantage of a simultaneous reference to individual and shared affect and to mass mediation. The concept of celebrity connects the social and experiential terrain on which individual writers and individual readers encounter one another with the abstract, institutional structures informing writer-reader transactions. Celebrity in this sense is not necessarily equivalent to popularity or prestige, and it is distinct from classical rhetorics of fame stressing virtue and achievement through heroic action. I understand literary celebrity not simply as one possible version of authorship but rather as a historically determinate form of the relationship between readers and writers.

Most recent accounts of reader-writer relationships in the nineteenth century, including recent accounts of celebrity, stress the growing separation between writers and their audiences as an older, patronage-based model of authorship gives way to one much more dependent on an ever-expanding literary market.[7] It is certainly true that, as Bertrand Bronson writes, "the gradual detachment, through print, of the writer from a present and familiar audience is one of the most far-reaching influences of modern times in our western civilization."[8] But this received history tells only half the story. Nineteenth-century writers and readers also found themselves paradoxically growing closer, disturbingly present to one another physically as well as psychologically. As account after account testifies, celebrity writers were safe from their admirers—and detractors—neither at home nor abroad. "Think of my being found out by American tourists in Dove's Nest!" reported the celebrated poet Felicia Hemans to a friend in 1830. "The young ladies, as I feared, brought an Album concealed in their shawls, and it was levelled at me like a pocket-pistol before all was over."[9] The violence was not always figurative. Thomas Medwin claimed that Percy Bysshe Shelley was at the Post Office in Pisa asking for his letters, one day in 1819, when a stranger cried out "What! are you that damned atheist, Shelley?"

and "without more preamble, being a tall powerful man, struck him a blow which felled him to the ground and stunned him."[10] Medwin's story (even if apocryphal or at least exaggerated) suggests how the seductively intimate voice often conjured by nineteenth-century poets in writing might uneasily parallel these poets' real interactions with an embodied audience at once familiar and unfamiliar, sometimes distant and sometimes aggressively present, violent both in the love and the horror with which it responds to authorial personality.

Live encounters between author and audience were also, of course, a vital and often well-planned part of the business of achieving literary celebrity. Celebrity authorship was staged in fashionable drawing rooms and salons, in lecture halls and at dinner parties, before crowds or in front of acquaintances one could count on to publicize the experience. Maria Jane Jewsbury's 1825 sketch "The Young Author" brilliantly satirizes the requisite forms of performance: her hero, an aspirant to celebrity, launches his career by quoting "whole lines of Moore, and half lines of Byron, during the intervals of a ball supper" before moving on to "pale and languid looks in public" and just enough of a cough to indicate "consumptive tendencies," prompting "the declarations of the young ladies, that he is 'more inter*est*ing than ever!'"[11] Engaged by such performances, nineteenth-century readers were both determined and inventive in pursuit of writers who sparked their curiosity. Think of Caroline Lamb reading *Childe Harold's Pilgrimage* (1812) and writing fan mail to its author, leading to their disastrous and very public affair; or the adventurer and proto-groupie Edward John Trelawny's going off to Italy to insinuate himself into the lives of Byron and the Shelleys; or Elizabeth Barrett Browning declaring of her own literary idol, "I won't die, if I can help it, without seeing George Sand!"[12] When Byron stops in Dover on his way out of the country in the wake of the separation scandal in 1816, Lady Byron is told by her confidant Dr. Lushington, "the curiosity to see him was so great that many ladies accoutred themselves as chambermaids for the purpose of obtaining under that disguise a nearer inspection whilst he continued at the inn."[13] Such voracious pursuit of writers may have begun with eighteenth-century celebrities, but in the nineteenth century these forms of fandom had become virtually institutionalized: by the Victorian era, Wordsworth found curious tourists regularly making off with his shrubbery, and even dead poets weren't immune—mediums kept the ghost of Shelley busy.[14]

A modern, mass-mediated, and transitory form, celebrity attracted anxieties that paralleled those attached to literary works in an era of literature's increasing commercialization: fears about the slippage between aesthetic response and consumer demand, about the value of popular judgment, about the dangers of media saturation, about the possibility of lasting fame in an age seemingly overrun by the ephemeral.[15] Like celebrity in our own cultural moment, public notice in the late eighteenth and early nineteenth centuries was bound up with scandal. In what Coleridge called "the Age of PERSONALITY," the most intimate (real or fictional) details of writers' lives and bodies were broadcast to the public, circulating by word of mouth, in newspaper and magazine writing, in fiction and in poetry, in caricatures and even pornographic fantasies, and—especially after Boswell's *Life* of Johnson—through immensely popular tell-all biographies that made writers' lives, in Annette Cafarelli's nice phrase, "irretrievably public."[16] The close association of fame and scandalous sexuality made celebrity especially risky for women writers—witness the devastating effects of William Godwin's memoir of Mary Wollstonecraft (1798), or the intrusive curiosity later faced by writers like Letitia Landon, Caroline Norton, and Harriet Martineau—but public curiosity was equally inflamed by the gossip constantly swirling around male poets like Byron and Shelley.

At once individual and collective, the feelings incited by celebrity are properly neither public nor private, but help organize through a sense of shared emotional experience a new kind of public space in which deeply private meanings find display.[17] Writers in this culture are often fans too, of course, and so know the experience from the inside. Byron was obsessed not only with world-famous figures like Napoleon but also with figures of more local renown—boxers, theater personalities, the fashionable and the eccentric; Keats thought deeply not only about the kinds of fame available to writers but also about the audience appeal of actors like Kean or the political organizer "Orator" Henry Hunt; Shelley was haunted by personalities of the past, like Beatrice Cenci, who still held a grip on the popular imagination; Landon's poetry transmutes the bewitching power of Byron; and Barrett Browning, a Byron-worshipper in her youth, wrote frequently of her own "impulses to lionizing."[18] The mechanisms of celebrity fascinate these writers not only because they have ambitions for fame, but also because they recognize both mass-mediated charisma and mass-mediated fandom as new, powerful and mysterious phenomena. Why do some personalities exert a special kind of hold on us, they ask? How is such charismatic force like or different from the seductive power of works of art?

To spell out how the reader-writer interactions I am describing worked in practice, it may be helpful to look at a concrete example: Thomas De Quincey's extraordinary narrative of the progress of his feelings for his literary idol, William Wordsworth. In a series of essays first written for *Tait's* in 1834 and 1839–40 known as the "Lake Reminiscences," De Quincey reconstructs his "discovery" of the *Lyrical Ballads* as an initiation into a new world of feeling.[19] The discovery of their poems is nothing less, he reports, than "the greatest event in the unfolding of my mind": "at a period when neither the one nor the other writer was valued by the public [...] I found in their poems 'the ray of a new morning' and an absolute revelation of untrodden worlds teeming with power and beauty as yet unsuspected amongst men" (p. 1). De Quincey's marked and unmarked quotation from the *Lyrical Ballads* here seems meant to suggest that what he experienced was not just a conversion to Wordsworth but a Wordsworthian conversion—that the specific form of such transformative reading is authorized by the Wordsworthian text.[20]

Yet in this first encounter, the identities of the poets are a secret to him; too reverential to give into base curiosity about their names, it is two years (he claims) before he finds out. Seized then with the irrepressible desire to see Wordsworth in the flesh, he writes to Wordsworth to introduce himself in 1803, but does not meet the poet until 1807. In the interval, he haunts Grasmere like Frankenstein's monster outside the De Laceys' cottage—too intimidated to present himself, he keeps getting close and running away:

> Twice [...] did I advance as far as the lake of Coniston; which is about eight miles from the church of Grasmere, and once I absolutely went forwards from Coniston to the very gorge of Hammerscar, from which the whole Vale of Grasmere suddenly breaks upon the view in a style of almost theatrical surprise [...]. Catching one hasty glimpse of this loveliest of landscapes, I retreated like a guilty thing, for fear I might be surprised by Wordsworth, and then returned faintheartedly to Coniston, and so to Oxford, *re infectâ*.
>
> (pp. 88–9)

Already seduced into a relationship of veneration to Wordsworth, the source of textual power, De Quincey is looking for something more (something more reciprocal) than the distanced relationship of reader and writer mediated by the text. By meeting Wordsworth "face to face," he hopes to "form personal ties which would forever connect" the two: from De Quincey's self-presentation, it is unclear how much of this is the typical fan's dream about the hero, how much is a lonely young man's desire for a father figure, and how much is a canny decision to associate himself with a star he believes is rising.[21] The complications of this relationship are again indicated through quotation: punning on Wordsworth's appropriation in the "Immortality" ode ("like a guilty Thing surprised") of the description of Hamlet's father's ghost (who "started, like a guilty thing / Upon a fearful summons" [*Hamlet* 1.1.148–9]), De Quincey dramatizes his desire to see Wordsworth through a simultaneous displacement and repossession of haunted, and haunting, paternal authority.

When De Quincey does finally make it to Wordsworth's cottage as chaperone to Coleridge's wife and children, his anticipation of at last meeting the great man in the flesh nearly overwhelms him:

> Never before or since can I reproach myself with having trembled at the approaching presence of any creature that is born of woman, excepting only, for once or twice in my life, woman herself; now, however, I *did* tremble; and I forgot, what in no other circumstances I could have forgotten, to stop for the coming up of the chaise, that I might be ready to hand Mrs. Coleridge out. Had Charlemagne and all his Peerage been behind me, or Caesar and his equipage, or Death on his pale horse, I should have forgotten them at that moment of intense expectation, and of eyes fascinated to what lay before me, or what might in a moment appear. Through the little gate I pressed forward; ten steps beyond it lay the principal door of the house. To this, no longer clearly conscious of my own feelings, I passed on rapidly; I heard a step, a voice, and, like a flash of lightning, I saw the figure of a tallish man, who held out his hand, and saluted me with the most cordial manner, and the warmest expression of friendly welcome that it is possible to imagine.
>
> (pp. 93–4)

In this literally liminal encounter, Wordsworth's appearance in the potentially apocalyptic "flash of lightning" magically transmutes the idol—the ghostly source of sublime textual power (a "step" and a disembodied "voice") and a figure who inspires the same kind of "trembling" in De Quincey as, once or twice, "woman herself"—into a warm and welcoming, fully embodied friend.[22] Indeed, Charles Rzepka argues, "Wordsworth's very presence was healing":[23] De Quincey had so long held himself "almost [in] self-contempt, at my own want of courage to face the man whom of all since the Flood I most yearned to behold" that his very temperament had begun to change, acquiring a character of "eternal self-dissatisfaction" that vanishes only, but entirely, in the first night of conversation with Wordsworth himself (De Quincey, p. 164).

Though one of De Quincey's clear reference points in scripting this encounter is Boswell's narration of his introduction to Johnson (where Hamlet's encounter with his father's ghost is also quoted), his *Reminiscence* is no literary hagiography. By the time De Quincey writes this, Wordsworth the man no longer exercises the same power over him, and he elsewhere frankly tells the reader of his feelings of disillusionment and resentment toward the poet (he discovers Wordsworth to be petty, overly controlling, self-idolizing, and an inconstant friend). But in reproducing the encounter through the sublime build-up of narrative tension—a moment of ultimate anticipation, self-loss and safe recovery (almost in the arms of the poet)—De Quincey relives and reproduces, for himself and for the reader, the deeply pleasurable affective intensity generated by the manipulation of the distance between the seduced reader and the authorial body he so desperately desires to approach. Even after he finally encounters Wordsworth, he delays the actual meeting:

> The chaise, however, drawing up to the gate at that moment, he (and there needed no Roman nomenclator to tell me that this *he* was Wordsworth) felt himself summoned to advance and receive Mrs. Coleridge. I, therefore, stunned almost with the actual accomplishment of a catastrophe so long anticipated and so long postponed, mechanically went forward into the house.
>
> (p. 94)

With our author impelled mechanically from the masculine scenario of the sublime encounter into the feminine domestic space of the cottage, several pages of description of the interior of the cottage and of Dorothy and Sara Wordsworth follow before De Quincey again comes face to face with (and begins to describe) the poet himself.

The active manipulation of distance is all the more visible when read against the Johnson-Boswell encounter, in which Johnson merely happens upon Boswell in the back of a bookseller's shop.[24] In the *Life* (1791), Boswell does not hide the commercial location of his encounter with Johnson, and the theatricality of the scene combines with Johnson's very ordinary there-ness to deprive the encounter of the uncanny effect that would surely characterize a Romantic version of Johnson's "aweful approach" as the ghostly father.[25] What's salient here is not the increased distance between writer and reader in the early nineteenth century as compared with the mid-eighteenth, but the fact that De Quincey requires a sensation of that distance—indeed, in a way exacerbates it—in order to produce the peculiarly intense closeness of his relationship to Wordsworth.

As idiosyncratic and overdetermined as De Quincey's reaction to Wordsworth may be, he seems to want to make its intensity a culturally normative way of reading. To a great degree, my study argues, it was. The kind of feeling Wordsworth compels is one "peculiar" to literary creators, De Quincey asserts. Though we may stand in awe of "a great philosopher, a great mathematician, or a great reformer," he claims, this admiration is different from the "burning interest which settles on the great poets who have made themselves necessary to the human heart," such as Shakespeare and now Wordsworth (p. 107). This fascination speaks to the way the great poet at once becomes a vital part of the reader's emotional world and recedes into mystery, the workings of such creative power unfathomable by the ordinary reader. But De Quincey's argument about the "burning interest" compelled by literary creators also serves to justify the very commercial ends of his own writing. De Quincey wrote these articles about the Lakers for *Tait's* because he needed the money, and the magazine published them because De Quincey's popularity as the English Opium-Eater, and the reputation of the Lakers he wrote about, helped the magazine's appeal to the lower-middle-class and working-class groups it sought to attract. The families of Wordsworth and Coleridge saw the essays as a violation of trust.[26] De Quincey's essays, then, embody a central cultural contradiction: even as the unique subjectivity of the author is being elevated into a position of transcendence, authorial personality is increasingly visible as a commercial product.

The literary culture in which De Quincey writes is in fact marked by the competition between two models of authorial personality. The charismatic author is often seen as an object of wonder: a special, unique being whose power over readers is viewed with awe and sometimes suspicion. Such a perception of authorship builds on the cultural resonance of Romantic concepts of genius, individuality and original creativity; it takes up the legacy of post-Revolutionary charisma embodied in epochal figures like Napoleon, and reflects the *frisson* attached to literary celebrity following the sensational success of figures like Radcliffe, Scott, Moore and Byron.[27] This emphasis on the singular, transcendent personality of the author increasingly overlaps, however, with a perception of authorial identity as the impermanent product of a set of impersonal market structures—what Harriet Martineau called, in an 1839 essay in the *London and Westminster Review*, a "system" of "literary lionism."[28] In this system, authors are subjected to an oxymoronic form of public anonymity: cutting off "the retreat of literary persons into the great body of human beings," the system of lionism marks them out as a professionalized class and puts them permanently on display, so that "they can no longer take refuge from their toils and their publicity in ordinary life."[29]

In this star system view of authorship, fame is so widespread and so easily available that everyone can have it for a moment, but no one can have it for long. In *Don Juan* Canto XI (composed 1822), Byron wryly described the contemporary London literary scene, from which he claims the distinction of self-exile, as a galaxy of ephemeral luminaries. At fashionable soirées, Juan hobnobs with "ten thousand living authors," along with the "eighty 'greatest living poets', / As every paltry magazine can show *it's*" (11: 154).[30] Popular adulation passes from one star to another, making lordship of the "realms of rhyme" a kind of rotating position: Byron himself reigned for a time, he tells us, and "Sir Walter reigned before me, Moore and Campbell / Before and after" (11: 157). Such representations of the literary scene as a series of quickly rising and even more quickly falling stars become common in the 1820s and 1830s. In Martineau's essay, for instance, the lion knows he is the toast of the town only until "a rival brings out a still diviner poem, and seems 'destined to work a still mightier change' in those human affairs to which he is, in truth, only the fly on the wheel."[31]

These representations of the ephemerality of literary celebrity reflect important structural changes in the literary market, and contradictions in the market for poetry in particular. In the early nineteenth century, the sales achieved by such poets as Scott, Moore and Byron proved, as Richard Altick observes, that poetry could be marketed as a high-priced luxury item to a very wide audience.[32] The scale of their success reflects the modernization of the publishing industry, including the sophisticated coordination of marketing, promotion and distribution.[33] But such a powerful publishing apparatus also makes more obvious the commodity-status of volumes of poetry and of the writer's proper name. Indeed, the way both Scott and Byron could exploit forms of serial publication seems to identify literary production itself with the rhythm of consumption, blurring the line between aesthetic response and consumer demand. The popularity of Byron, Scott, Moore and later Hemans, however, overshadows a market in which the vast majority of poets do not experience anything like it.[34] Slowly shedding its earlier associations with aristocratic patronage and aristocratic leisure, literary writing is emerging as a middle-class profession, and thronging with new talent, but for most poets there is no way to make an income simply from publishing volumes of poetry. Poets must generally either rely on patronage (as did Wordsworth), private income (as did Shelley), or editorial and reviewing work for periodicals and literary annuals (as did Landon).[35]

The periodical reviews would themselves become, by the 1810s and 1820s, powerful players in the shaping of literary celebrity. For most of the reading public in the early nineteenth century, encounters with the work of leading poets came primarily through reviews (which often printed lengthy excerpts), or through magazine publication of poetry.[36] The reviews evolved a highly reflexive and self-aware commentary on the personalities of authors, maintained both through discussions of individual works and through surveys of the literary scene, and through a particular delight in gossip about writers (including, of course, fellow periodical writers). Especially in the politically charged climate of the 1810s and early 1820s, reviews dealt regularly in what was called "personality," or viciously personal attacks: the series of articles on the "Cockney School" in *Blackwood's* (1817–19), signed "Z.," is perhaps the most flagrant and best-known example.[37] While some reviewers establish a firm boundary between the professional interest of the literary critic and judgment on a writer's character, politics or private life, many periodical writers refused the very distinction: "In reviewing, in particular, what can be done without personality? Nothing, nothing," asserted Christopher North, the fictional editor of *Blackwood's* "Noctes Ambrosianae," in 1822.[38] By the early 1820s, in *Blackwood's*, the *London Magazine* and elsewhere, magazine writers are not only commenting on the lives of celebrities, but also—as in the case of De Quincey's "Opium-Eater" persona, for example—inventing new and complex forms of celebrity for themselves, through a very sophisticated interplay of anonymity, fictionality, self-reflexivity, and embodiment.[39]

At the same time, periodical publications began to offer a particular view of literary culture, a vision of what Pierre Bourdieu terms "the literary field" as an array of names whose significance is primarily relational: these are all stars of the moment, "in" by comparison with those who were "in" but are now "out," or on their way "out" by comparison with those who are now "in."[40] The model of the "star system" is embodied in publications like the popular "Gallery of Illustrious Literary Characters" which appeared serially in *Fraser's* from 1830 to 1838. In each of the 81 installments, readers were presented with a sketch of an illustrious character or group, along with a reproduced signature and a brief commentary. Tellingly, the series begins with editors (William Jerdan) before moving on to authors: what is on display is "literary culture" as much as the individual author.[41] Bourdieu's description of the field of cultural production as a relatively autonomous zone defined by competition for "the monopoly of literary legitimacy" maps convincingly onto the discourse of celebrity in the period.[42] I find useful both Bourdieu's notion of the literary field as a relational structure and his insistence that we attempt to understand "works of art as a *manifestation* of the field as a whole, in which all the powers of the field, and all the determinisms inherent in its structure and functioning, are concentrated."[43] But the economic terms of his analysis, I find, are not especially effective in accounting either for the affective dimension of the writer-reader relationship or for the ways in which the very mechanisms of prestige, in this period, seem to render celebrity a mere cliché: in the *Fraser's* series, for example, each personality is just this month's installment of eighty-one names.[44]

The poets I examine in this book are transitional figures in the shift I have been describing from an understanding of celebrity as a mark of distinctive personality to an understanding of celebrity as the product and sign of impersonal systems. We traditionally associate Romantic lyric poetry with the claims of subjectivity, the privatization of the aesthetic, and a resistance to the depersonalizing powers of marketplace or linguistic machineries. But I propose that second-generation Romantic and early Victorian poets and their readers identify—and seek to exploit—a significant overlap in the ways literary works and market structures conjure seductive forms of poetic presence. If in its earlier Romantic incarnations in the writing of Smith or Wordsworth a poetics of presence evolved as a way to investigate forms of interiority, in the writing I examine in this study a poetics of presence in fact thrives on forms of impersonality. Poems and market institutions both work through essentially impersonal mechanisms to create forms of presence that are at once compelling and ephemeral, and that exercise power by virtue of being, in fact, mere system-effects. Like lyric poetry itself, the poet's charisma depends on an impossible intimacy, where what seduces us is a presence we know is not really there.[45]

There are methodological consequences attendant on viewing reader-writer relationships in the terms I have advanced. If we abstract a generalized "reader" from the particular individuals who conferred celebrity on writers, or if we abstract the responses of readers to writers into the ideologies of artistic production for which they may be seen as symptoms, we miss important information about what it meant to read and what it meant to write in this culture, information that changes the terms through which we view the texts this culture produced.[46] At the same time, recourse to the individual psychology of particular writers and readers cannot fully account for the actual eccentricity with which writers and readers responded to one another, because that eccentricity itself is embedded within cultural practices and cultural systems that must be seen as institutional.

Studies of reader-writer relationships may employ any of several approaches.[47] Critics may construe "the reader" as a rhetorical function of the text (an implied or ideal reader), for example, or they may consider a writer's rhetorical appeal to specific audiences. "Reader response" may be adduced from the opinions of professional readers, such as reviewers, or from evidence of the ways "ordinary" historical readers read, or from the experiences of present-day readers, possibly the critic himself or herself.[48] Critics may survey representations of a writer or canvass discourse about reading and readers.[49] In order to talk on the one hand about the relationship between literary form and something so elusive and subjective as readerly feeling, and to talk on the other hand about the relationship between literary form and something so vast and abstract as the system of mass-mediated celebrity, I have found it necessary (like many critics) to move among these various approaches, and individual chapters in this study may emphasize one or another approach more strongly (as I outline below). I have found useful models in the poststructuralist narratology of Ross Chambers, with its attention to readerly desire, and Garrett Stewart's analysis of the phenomenology of what he calls the "event" of reading, working as Stewart does at the level of textual activity or "the marked textualization of response."[50] But while the approaches of both Chambers and Stewart have an important historical component, the actual "historical reader" hardly makes an appearance (this is Kate Flint's term for readers situated within individual histories and within wider historical contexts), and the empirical author is similarly absent.[51] Where Stewart views the event of reading in terms of the text's address to an unspecified reader, I am interested in what happens when we shift our analysis of textual activity to include both the performance of authorship within particular institutions of reading and the experiences and practices of actual individual readers within determinate histories. If the act of reading itself can be construed in terms of historically varying, learned practices (for example, reading piecemeal for information or choice passages, or reading for sustained absorption in a narrative) the act of reading a poem is also continuous with a whole series of other cultural practices (for example, writing fan mail, touring the homes of writers, reading about writers in magazines, collecting autographs, and so on). I situate the texts I read in the context of these practices and institutions of reading, as well as the contexts of publication history and public discourse about the author, in order to describe the connection between literary form and historically specific forms of feeling for writers.[52]

This book thus participates in a turn in the field to what Leah Price has described as alternatives "to a tradition of reception studies that focuses on the content of readers' opinions [...] to the exclusion of the form that those opinions take and the institutions that generated them in the first place."[53] I argue that the structure of mass-mediated celebrity is a formal problematic of the works I discuss, not simply a condition of their reception. The reader should not expect here primarily a discussion of writers' reputations (construed in terms of sales figures or evidence of shifting public tastes), nor a catalog of the way the public images of particular writers were fashioned, though of course I have something to say here about both. What this book offers instead is an analysis of the interaction of literary form with an evolving celebrity "system," a system coordinating particular cultural practices, literary and market institutions, and print networks, and involving the participation of poets themselves, their fascinated readers, publishers, booksellers, journalists, biographers, critics, collectors and fans.

The individual chapters in this book demonstrate the significance of new forms of celebrity and fandom to the work and reception of a wide array of Romantic and early Victorian writers, from Byron, Landon, and Barrett Browning—wildly popular poets in their day—to Keats and Shelley, who famously claimed to refuse a suspect contemporary popularity. Each of these poets constructed a type of high-cultural authority by at once critically examining and strategically appropriating newly available "celebrity effects." I examine how the careers of Romantic-era poets operated to crystallize and shatter models of celebrity with eighteenth-century roots, and how writers and readers who grew up in the Romantics' wake adapted and reconceived models of poetic celebrity in the different context of a Victorian literary scene in which literary fandom had become more routinized. This grouping of writers, then, tracks across traditional period boundaries. By considering the work of celebrity women writers alongside the work of male contemporaries now more securely canonized, I also show how a gendered culture of fame created rewards and perils for writers of either sex, though experiences of both fame and fandom played differently for men and women within nineteenth-century culture.[54]

Chapter 1, "Systems of Literary Lionism," develops the claims of this Introduction by discussing the example of Byron, who adjusts to new modes of fame that he helps to create, but that are also forecasted by the scandalous celebrity of earlier women writers, such as the actress, poet, novelist and polemicist Mary Robinson. I focus on Byron's lyric "Fare Thee Well!" (1816), addressed to his wife at their separation, and I connect the operation of performative language in the poem with the poem's status as public event. Circulated by Byron and his associates, pirated, reprinted, and replied to by various readers, the poem follows a dizzying social itinerary that maps and remaps the relationships between the charismatic author and his publics. This process continues in the writing and reception of *Don Juan* (1819–24), a poem that becomes in many ways an epic retrospective on Byron's own fame.

In my subsequent chapters, I explain how the different modes of lyric presence conjured by Keats, Shelley, Landon and Barrett Browning each represent a distinctive response to the way reader-writer relationships shift in Byron's wake. Though criticism tends to read Keats from the perspective of his supposed orientation toward posterity, for example, I argue in Chapter 2, "Keats, Lyric and the Culture of Celebrity," that the allure of such posthumous address occludes Keats's real investment in an immediately available celebrity like that of what he calls the "three literary kings in our time—Scott—Byron—and then the Scotch novels."[55] I look closely at Keats's early *Sleep and Poetry* (1817) and his late fragment *The Fall of Hyperion* (composed 1819, published 1857). Both poems pose as a formal problem, and a source of poetic capital, the question of the relationship of life and text, the poet's body and the poem, and they do so with a formal awareness of conditions of market abstraction on which Keats learns to capitalize.

Chapter 3, "*The Cenci*'s Celebrity," turns to the 1819 drama Shelley thought could win him a popular audience and looks more thematically at the problem of authorial charisma. I show how Shelley's portrayal of the female subject's relation to language and history grounds an interrogation of the conditions of Shelley's own charisma and authority in a literary market dominated by the reviewing system's circulation of scandalous personality. Notorious during his lifetime, Shelley is awarded a different kind of fame in the Victorian period. Chapter 4, "Shelley's Glamour," looks at the way Victorian readers negotiate Shelley's personal magnetism in the context of the celebrity industry that emerges around the poet. Matthew Arnold's influential discussions of Shelley in his essays "The Study of Poetry" (1880) and "Shelley" (1888) form the core of a case-study in reader response. I show how Arnold and other nineteenth-century writers on Shelley, such as E. J. Trelawny, share with Shelley's own poetics a concern with the impersonal structures—whether the movement of tropes or the technology of the literary market—that underlie poetic subjectivity.

By the end of the Regency, as the market appears to be not just the medium but the essence of literary culture, the publishing scene acquires a kind of glamour in its own right. Chapter 5, "The Atmosphere of Authorship," situates Landon's career in this context to examine the problematic conjunction of gender, professional authorship and celebrity in the 1820s and 1830s. One of the greatest literary stars of these decades, Landon mobilizes the resources of Byronic romance and of Byronic fandom to probe the gendered relations of spectator and spectacle in which she works, and to forge a public identity as a literary professional. But I also locate moments in her poetry in which feeling spins loose of subjectivity to become more problematically impersonal, interrupting the circuit of feeling that links writer and reader and opening up new possibilities for poetic subjectivity. My final chapter, "Elizabeth Barrett Browning and the Energies of Fandom," discusses Barrett Browning's "novel-poem" *Aurora Leigh* (1856) in the context of the author's own history of extravagant fandom and in the context of the "mania" the poem itself generated, as Barrett Browning reports. Though *Aurora Leigh* tells the story of a famous poet and her passionate readers, there has been until now little critical discussion of the poem in terms of cultures of celebrity and fandom. Understanding Barrett Browning as a participant in an emerging culture of fandom can productively revise our sense of Barrett Browning as an author, putting into new perspective the formal mechanisms through which *Aurora Leigh* engages and resists the kinds of passionate, idealizing reading it describes and in fact produced.

As is clear from this outline, I do not concentrate exclusively on the genre of the lyric, but all of the poets I discuss are strongly identified, at least in the course of their reception, as lyric poets. As the lyric becomes more and more *the* genre of poetry, lyric collects to itself and renders newly prestigious effects of intimacy that once had a more promiscuous generic identification, associated as closely with the epistolary novel, for example, as with poetry. I set my understanding of what I call lyric intimacy against two different but ultimately overlapping accounts of reader-writer intimacy prevalent in recent critical work on poetry. The first such account connects the desire for an intimate bond with the celebrity author to the alienation produced by contemporary market conditions, as in Andrew Elfenbein's suggestion that the apparatus of celebrity reflects the desire to replace a "person-to-person contact between producer and consumer with a person-to-'personality' contact between consumer and fetishized subjectivity."[56] Though my readings corroborate such studies to a degree, I want to make clear an important difference in emphasis. Accounts focusing on a rhetorical relation between writer and audience risk hypostasizing highly fluid relationships that involved live interaction as well as print mediation, and whose affective force crucially involved an awareness of the impersonality of the literary and market systems through which personality was disseminated and readerly response was organized. The argument that lyric intimacy counters the alienating effects of mass-mediated, consumer society, I believe, cannot fully explain the exaggerated, intense forms of feeling some poets incite in their readers. I understand lyric intimacy as in fact continuous with the myriad and novel forms of actual contact occurring between celebrities and audiences in the period. Lyric intimacy then describes a zone of unstable contact, of readers' tactics and writers' ruses, at once individual and social. Where nineteenth-century lyric poetry is traditionally connected with the privatization of the aesthetic, this study links lyric and publicity.

"Lyric intimacy" continues to operate in contemporary theories of reading as a powerful trope that merges a type of readerly experience with an imaginary form of address, linking the reader's sensation of closeness to the solitary speaker with the desire for relation or connection motivating the lyric. In her recent book *Invisible Listeners: Lyric Intimacy in Herbert, Whitman, and Ashbery*, for example, Helen Vendler focuses on a particular intensification of such intimacy that she proposes occurs when poets unable to find a corresponding sensibility within available social structures are forced to reach out to an ideal listener displaced into the future, the past or an invisible realm, in the process redefining the social norms that render such connection impossible in actuality.[57] What makes lyrics lyric, to Vendler, is the dream of a reciprocal response that is never actually allowed to disturb the perfect loneliness of the lyric speaker. Vendler's lyric intimacy is constitutive of the lyric across time, and turns, necessarily, on the privacy of both poet-speaker and reader: lyric from this perspective is a kind of shelter from the social. By stressing the connections as well as disjunctions between effects of intimacy and the public scene of literary celebrity, my study spins the concept of lyric intimacy in quite a different direction, out to the social site of the variously mediated interaction between the celebrity poet and a mass audience of live, embodied readers and (potential) consumers.

Attending to nineteenth-century poetry in these terms might ultimately lead us to think in new ways about the process of cultural transmission more generally.[58] We might come to account differently for the role of institutions and practices of reading beyond individual relationships of influence or discursive acts of legitimation or exclusion. Such thinking might also lead us to address in different terms the potentially troubling and rewarding question of the place of fandom in our own professional experience, our own classroom practice, and in contemporary constructions of cultural "inheritance." The structures of readerly desire I examine still inform the reception of nineteenth-century poetry, in a submerged way in scholarly discourse, and in a more explicit way in the tourist attractions and memorabilia shops built around the homes of writers, or in the enduring allure of the life stories of these poets. How might we connect, for example, the experience of Keats, who visited Burns's cottage only to be mortified by the garrulous presence of a "mahogany faced old Jackass who knew Burns," with today's Burns "Heritage Park," where Robert Burns "is brought to life through a mixture of modern technology and unique authentic locations and artefacts"?[59] How do we connect these experiences with how Keats and Burns are read and taught in the schools? How might we understand the cultural meaning of the Armstrong Browning Library at Baylor University in Waco, Texas—an astounding resource for scholars of the Brownings, and a temple to the Brownings, complete with stained-glass windows featuring scenes from Robert Browning's poems and a recreation of the Brownings' Florentine living room?[60] It makes as little sense to dismiss these afterlives as pure sentimentality or kitsch as it does to embrace them uncritically. Rather, they are resources for thinking about the transferential pleasures and desires that shape our relationship to the literary works of the past, and our continuing belief in the idea of the author.

1
Systems of Literary Lionism

The publication of the first two cantos of *Childe Harold's Pilgrimage* on 10 March 1812 notoriously sparked a sensation. Even before the poem was officially offered to the public, advance copies stirred excitement about the dashing young noble freshly returned from his exotic travels.[1] As Byron's friend Thomas Moore recalled (or re-imagined) the scene from a vantage point almost two decades later, Byron's effect on British audiences had been immediately "electric": "young Byron stood forth alone, unanswered by either praise or promise—the representative of an ancient house, whose name, long lost in the gloomy solitudes of Newstead, seemed to have just awakened from the sleep of half a century in his person."[2] Despite the campy, B-movie Gothicism, Moore is astute in observing that this figure exotically out of time had arrived perfectly on time to take advantage of the modern "taste for strong excitement" in a public captivated and fatigued by Napoleon. After the first edition of 500 copies of *Childe Harold* sold out in a mere three days, fan letters began pouring in from readers who had fallen hard for the writer whose own sensibility they imagined they recognized in the fashionably melancholic Harold. Byron found himself the darling of Whig high society, "the only topic almost of conversation—the men jealous of him, the women of each other," as the Duchess of Devonshire informed her son overseas.[3]

The sudden fame Byron experienced is indicative of a culture already primed for this kind of celebrity, on the lookout for stars. In many ways, the discourse of Byronic singularity so evident in Moore's remarks obscures how much Byron's celebrity owed to a thriving celebrity culture, and to the example of celebrity poets—especially female poets—who preceded him in blurring life and art in an emotional appeal to readers.[4] The experience of Mary Robinson (1758–1800) is a case in point. A stage sensation as a teenager, Robinson's notoriety was sealed when, at 21, she began an affair with the young Prince of Wales, who had seen her acting the part of Perdita in *The Winter's Tale*. During the scandal's heyday, Robinson found it difficult to move around the city without being physically surrounded by gawking crowds:

> Whenever I appeared in public, I was overwhelmed by the gazing of the multitude. I was frequently obliged to quit Ranelagh, owing to the crowd which staring curiosity had assembled round my box; and, even in the streets of the metropolis I scarcely ventured to enter a shop without experiencing the greatest inconvenience. Many hours have I waited till the crowd dispersed which surrounded my carriage, in expectation of my quitting the shop.[5]

Robinson's experience demonstrates how the late-eighteenth-century public had emerged not just as an abstraction but also as a spectatorial body—a "gazing [...] multitude"—produced by an accelerating set of technologies of publicity. The particular sites through which Robinson encounters the gawking crowds—the public gardens and the shop—indicate how Robinson's celebrity is tied to practices of consumption, fashion, and performance.[6] During the scandal and in its aftermath, Robinson's image and story were reproduced for the fascinated public in a variety of media, from caricatures like James Gillray's group portraits of Robinson and her reputed lovers and rivals to society portraits by Gainsborough, Romney and Reynolds, from overheated journalistic commentary to pornographic fantasy.[7] As Elizabeth Fay notes, Robinson's own careful attention to self-staging kept her in the public eye, her social appearances, her liaisons, and her fashion choices provoking gossipy newspaper notice.[8]

Robinson's scandalous celebrity was also the platform for a brilliant literary career as a leading poet, a prolific novelist, and poetry editor of the *Morning Post*, where many of her poems were published. By recasting her exposure to the public gaze in terms of a relationship of emotional intimacy with the individual reader, Robinson was able to capitalize on her notoriety. As Jacqueline Labbe observes, "her love poems were immensely popular, their pathos enhanced by Robinson's strategic self-placement as a bereaved woman made all the more attractive by her bereavement."[9] Attracted to ambitious, famous and powerful men and women, she forged friendships with figures as diverse as Marie Antoinette, Charles Fox, Mary Wollstonecraft, William Godwin, and the young Coleridge. In her extraordinary Wollstonecraftian *Letter to the Women of England on the Injustice of Mental Subordination,* Robinson's political radicalism coalesces with her fascination with fame, celebrity and public applause.[10] Discussing the performances of various celebrated or sensational women, from Sappho to Marie Antoinette and Charlotte Corday, Robinson makes the case not only that British women deserve lasting fame for literary accomplishments, but that they deserve the material trappings of celebrity, fame's outward show: "[W]e hear of no national honours, no public marks of popular applause, no rank, no title, no liberal and splendid recompense bestowed on British literary women!," she observes, complaining that talented women of England "must fly to foreign countries for celebrity, where talents are admitted to be of no SEX."[11] Robinson, who initially published the *Letter* under the pseudonym Anne Frances Randall, appended to her *Letter* a "List of British Female Literary Characters Living in the Eighteenth Century," including of course herself.[12]

Robinson shuttles among a raft of pseudonyms and a variety of genres in her writing. That the "real" Mary Robinson seems so easily to disappear, in her textual self-representation, into the performance of literary or theatrical character ("Perdita") has prompted some critics to describe Robinson as having "consciously created what we now call a 'postmodernist' subjectivity, a concept of the self as entirely fluid, unstable and performative."[13] This "postmodernist" subjectivity involves, I would argue, a typically Romantic confusion among real persons, literary characters, theatrical characters, and commodities, all of which could present, to the reader or viewer, forms of subjectivity that might call up virtually identical affective response. Robinson plays on this not to withdraw the self from the reader by disguising it as staged character, but to induce an emotional response: she asks her reader to sympathize and to purchase, to feel and to buy. Such a conjunction is underlined by the commendation that closes a mostly positive review of Robinson's *Poems* (1791): "The work is elegantly printed on superfine paper, exhibits a numerous list of subscribers from the first ranks of title and fashion, and is decorated with a copper-plate of the fair author, from an original painting by Sir Joshua Reynolds."[14] Anticipating one part of the appeal of Byronic celebrity, Robinson's reviewer makes it impossible to separate fashionable celebrity from literary value, the seductiveness of the material book from the seductiveness of the writer's person.

If Byronic celebrity is anticipated by careers such as Robinson's, however, the phenomenon of Byron also transformed what literary celebrity could mean, refashioning both the poet as public figure and poetry's publics. With an aura of transgression licensed and heightened by his nobility and his facility with classic literary codes, Byron exercised a new kind of charismatic sway over enthralled readers fascinated by the blending of his poetry and his personality.[15] Byron changes the terms of celebrity not only because of the sheer scale of his commanding popularity but also because of the intensity of the transferential relationship that develops between the public and the poet, the deep and complicated involvement of each in the emotional life of the other. This involvement was both the effect of and the impetus for what Peter Manning and Jerome Christensen have shown to be a new kind of literary and commercial system, a system "collaboratively organized in the second decade of the nineteenth century by coding the residual affective charge that still clung to the paraphernalia of aristocracy in order to reproduce it in commodities that could be vended to a reading public avid for glamor."[16] This system involved the interaction of Byron himself, his publisher, market-savvy literary advisors, sympathetic and hostile reviewers, writers, portraitists, illustrators, pirates, booksellers and consumers, each of whom had a hand in producing, refining, reproducing and disseminating a charismatic image of Byron.[17] Especially key in this process is the way in which serial publication permits Byron and the public taste to adjust to one another.[18] In the serial iterations of versions of Byron and the Byronic hero, readers recognized both an appealing and a dangerous symbol of the strength of individual personality and, at the same time, a symbol of the power of ultimately impersonal and abstracting literary and market systems to fashion, reproduce and capitalize on sensational personality.

The comparison of Robinson's career and Byron's reveals how, in a gendered culture of fame, similar gestures may have radically different effects depending on the sex of the writer. When a writer like Robinson, or, later, like Letitia Landon, multiplies personae or identifications, reception registers this either as an exaggerated performativity or as absorption into type. In Byron's case, as we will see, similar identity play tends to consolidate or confirm Byronic singularity, the distinctiveness of the poet's personality marked by the adjective "Byronic" itself. Similarly, where the critical reception of commercially successful female writers tends (then and now) to conflate these writers with their popularity, Byron and Byronizing readers have more room to separate the author from his popularity, which is assigned to the responsibility of an infatuated public, and particularly, infatuated female readers. These kinds of distinctions, however, were far from firm, but rather subject to anxious negotiation by Byron and his readers, as this chapter explores.

This chapter concentrates on one crucial episode in the shaping of Byron's celebrity—the scandal surrounding his separation from Lady Byron in 1816—using the scandal as a lens through which to explain and test the thesis of my study: that nineteenth-century culture saw the forging of intimate alliances among the performative operation of language in poetic texts, the cultural systems through which celebrity is staged, and the affectively charged reader-writer interactions celebrity describes. If the separation scandal strained relationships between Byron and his audiences—and forced Byron into exile—it also knotted Byron and his publics more closely together. I will begin by focusing on Byron's lyric "Fare Thee Well!," which emerges from a crisis in his marriage to cause a crisis in his relationship with his reading public. I then turn to *Don Juan*, which makes this crisis central to its critical reflection on Byron's own celebrity and on British culture generally. I will treat the poems I discuss in this chapter not simply as literary texts but, like Robinson's affair with the future King George IV, as public events: as texts whose meaning depends on their public life, and as texts whose circulation constitutes a real event in the shaping of the public's sense of itself as a public.[19] "Fare Thee Well!" and its reception demonstrate that scandalous celebrity is not lyric intimacy's opposite but rather its very ground.[20]

Byron married Annabella Milbanke at the start of 1815. By the end of the year, the marriage had fallen apart under the pressure of Byron's mounting financial difficulties, his periodic rages, and the disastrous incompatibility of the couple; Lady Byron increasingly believed him mad. In January 1816 Lady Byron (apparently acting in part on Byron's advice) decamped for her parents' home in Leicestershire, bringing with her the couple's month-old daughter Ada, while Byron remained in the couple's expensive lodgings in Piccadilly Terrace. By early February, Lady Byron's family had formally begun separation proceedings. As news of the separation spread, so too did rumors about what lay behind it: Byron's supposed insanity, his drinking, and, darkly hinted, incest, sodomy, cruelty, even a murder in his past. Writing to Lord Holland in late February, Byron noted that the unfolding separation had already become "so public & violent a topic of discussion" that it was impossible for him to imagine anyone in society had not heard news of it.[21]

Byron drafted "Fare Thee Well!" on 18 March, the day after agreeing to formal terms of separation. Soon after, he sent the poem, with a brief note, to Lady Byron; whether the poem was an attempt to win Lady Byron back, an attempt at self-vindication, or an attempt to land a punch is difficult to decide.[22] Circulating the poem in manuscript, Byron demonstrates his use of poetry to conduct a kind of spin control on his reputation, showing the poet as not just the hurt party but also the *feeling* party. As David V. Erdman stresses, both Byron and Lady Byron early on recognized the separation proceedings as a battle for public opinion, and both anxiously tracked and sought to manipulate public sentiment.[23] Indeed, Lady Byron recognized "Fare Thee Well!" as effective enough that she considered retaliating with newspaper publication of her own "Declaration," characterized by Erdman as "an equivocal document in which she denied responsibility for spreading injurious rumors against Byron yet refrained from denying their truth."[24] By early April, Byron had Murray print 50 copies for private distribution of both "Fare Thee Well!" and "A Sketch from Private Life," a vicious satire he had written on Lady Byron's maid (and former nurse) Mary Jane Clermont, whom he suspected of turning his wife against him. Murray reported to Byron on 13 April that "except during a walk to my banker I have not had a moment uninterrupted by incessant visits for the farewell."[25]

Given the heated and politically charged climate of rumor that swirled around the separation, it should come as little surprise that the game soon spun out of anyone's control. On Sunday 14 April, John Scott's newspaper *The Champion* printed (under the title "Lord Byron's Poems On His Own Domestic Circumstances") both "Fare Thee Well!" and "A Sketch," appending a denunciation of Byron's morals and conduct.[26] As other periodicals quickly piled on, "Fare Thee Well!" became a central text in the scandal now in full steam.[27] Byron and Augusta were cut in fashionable society. After signing the deed of separation on 21 April, Byron departed for the Continent, leaving England for good, and leaving the manuscripts of his recently written poems with his friend John Cam Hobhouse and Murray. With "Fare Thee Well!" already in wide unauthorized circulation, Murray and Hobhouse brought out their own "official" version of Byron's *Poems*, including "Fare Thee Well!" (now with an epigraph from Coleridge's *Christabel*) together with several of Byron's love lyrics (including verses addressed to Augusta) and a series of Byron's pro-Napoleonic poems, most of which had originally been published anonymously but which were also in wide circulation as Byron's.

In his important discussion of "Fare Thee Well!," Jerome McGann shows how the shifting public and private contexts of the poem pose a challenge for readings of the poem not attentive to its material and social situations.[28] In McGann's argument, each appearance of the poem—the poem Lady Byron receives, the poem Byron privately distributes, the poem as published in *The Champion*, the poem as published in *Poems*—needs to be seen as a different object. McGann thus counters the critical idealization of a single poem abstracted from its material contexts.[29] I take McGann's point but push it in a different direction, advancing an argument toward a different theoretical problem—the performative subjectivity at work in this lyric. Whether or not Byron as he wrote anticipated the poem's mutation from intimate address between husband and wife to very public document, I argue, this mutation can be seen as the playing out by social actors of contradictions internal to the logic of address in the poem itself. Rather than seeing the publication context determining the poetic "object," we might see the poem as a performative utterance that at once tries to erase its own context and that necessarily exceeds any context.

The poem is performative in two senses. It makes a series of promises:

> Fare thee well! and if for ever—
>   Still for ever, fare *thee well*—
> Even though unforgiving, never
>   'Gainst thee shall my heart rebel.—
>
> (1–4)

All my hopes—where'er thou goest—
Wither—yet with *thee* they go.—

(47–8)

Moreover, it seeks to create—to call into being, in almost incantatory fashion—the relationship between the "I" and the addressee it describes. As Paul Elledge stresses, the poem seeks to overcome the very distance between speaker and reader it inscribes, insisting that the speaker and reader are bound together in feeling even as it marks their physical separation.[30] The poem coordinates the speaker's heart with the reader's, with "heart" recurring at the start, middle, and end of the poem, shifting from Byron's heart to his reader's and back to his own: "never / 'Gainst thee shall my heart rebel" (3–4); "But by sudden wrench, believe not, / Hearts can thus be torn away" (23–4); "Then thy heart will softly tremble / With a pulse yet true to me" (43–4); "Seared in heart—and lone—and blighted— / More than this, I scarce can die" (59–60). The dynamics the poem sets up between speaker and reader can be understood not just in relation to the psychology of Byron's separation but also in relation to the problem of address in all writing. Like the ghostly speaker in Keats's eerie fragment "This living hand, now warm and capable," discussed in my next chapter, Byron's poem hauntingly describes the way his spirit will from a distance haunt the reader's heart (Byron says he might as well be addressing Lady Byron from beyond the grave in any case).

The poem projects a scene of impossibly intimate reading that the voice of the poem tries to approximate in the intensity of its presence:

Would that breast were bared before thee
  Where thy head so oft hath lain,
While that placid sleep came o'er thee
  Which thou ne'er canst know again:
Would that breast, by thee glanc'd over,
  Every inmost thought could show!
Then thou woulds't at last discover
  'Twas not well to spurn it so.—

(5–12)

This threatening tone becomes more concrete as Byron insists, in fact, that there *is* no separation:

> Yet—oh, yet—thyself deceive not—
>   Love may sink by slow decay,
> But by sudden wrench, believe not,
>   Hearts can thus be torn away;
>
> [...]
>
> These are words of deeper sorrow
>   Than the wail above the dead,
> Both shall live—but every morrow
>   Wake us from a widowed bed.—
>
> (21–4; 29–32)

This latter quatrain evokes the curious image of a husband and wife dead to each other but twinned in the single figure of the "widow'd bed." If the poem seeks to measure (or insist upon) the distance of the separation, then, it also insists on how present the speaker is to the reader—it collapses the distance between the reader and the speaking "I" whose felt presence to the reader depends on its performance of absence.

The intimacy the poem strives for is social from the beginning, not just in fact (the poem gestures toward the "world" of readers of the break-up in Stanza 4) but rhetorically, since any performative utterance has an implicitly public dimension. Self-divided, the poem's rhetoric of address renders its intimacy precariously public. This precariousness is played out in the iterability of the poem's performative utterance, an iterability the poem at once depends on and elides (though it is gestured toward in the repetition of the phrase "fare thee well" itself, and the way the poem's images of ceaseless mourning are built up out of repetitive actions—"every morrow / Wake us"). The poem is split between performative action and commemoration: it wants both to *be* the separation and to memorialize the separation that gives rise to it; to *be* the connection between the speaker and the reader and to predict it (all the figures within the poem, not least their child Ada, function in a similarly dual way). It is split because it always wants to enclose a prior context that gives rise to it. The iterability of its utterance means that the poem is caught in a loop of self-commemoration, always memorializing the originary moment it claims to be.

Many readers have pointed out the way Byron equivocates on his feeling through the poem's grammatical tricks, such as the undecidability, in the first stanza, of whose heart is "unforgiving"—is it Byron's or Lady Byron's? But the performative dimension of the poem also gives rise to a series of temporal catachreses that make so many of its figures difficult to decide. When Byron wishes that the "breast, by thee glanc'd over / Every inmost thought could show," for example, "glanc'd" contains not just a pun on looked at/struck a blow, but a temporal pun: "by thee glanc'd over" in the past or in the future moment he imagines? Or consider the last lines of the poem:

Every feeling hath been shaken,
  Pride—which not a world could bow—
Bows to thee—by thee forsaken
  Even my soul forsakes me now.—
But 'tis done—all words are idle —
  Words from me are vainer still;
But the thoughts we cannot bridle
  Force their way without the will.—
Fare thee well! - thus disunited—
  Torn from every nearer tie—
Seared in heart—and lone—and blighted—
  More than this I scarce can die.

(49–60)

The poem conjures an effect of immediacy by rhetorically conflating the feeling the poem describes with the time and action of the poem: "'tis done" refers both to the irreversible fact of the separation that precedes the poem and makes words "idle" *and* to the waning of the spasm of "unwilled" emotion that gives rise to the poem. Byron's pronouncement "'tis done" hides the performative aspiration of his own poem (the pronouncement rivals the legal accomplishment of the separation) and announces the conclusion of the poem whose words hold the reader and speaker together as long as the reader is reading (so that the poem's conclusion is the real farewell). The final lines hints that Byron's own declaration of farewell is what disunites the couple: the poem insists that this is all Lady Byron's fault and at the same time arrogates to its own (disunited) words the power to make the separation, so that the final lines are at once a performance of weakness and strength. Though "me" and "my" are scattered through the poem, it is only in the climactic final line that the pronoun "I" appears: disunited, the "I" nonetheless claims from the "thee" it addresses both the rhetorical focus and the last word. Yet what is it that has really left the "I" "seared at heart—and lone—and blighted"—Lady Byron's unfeelingness, or the spasm of feeling that the "I" enacts?

The iterability of performative utterance might be said to predict, though of course it does not necessitate, the iteration of "Fare Thee Well!" in its different contexts, an iteration that illuminates the social conditions through which Byronic personality is produced. The inability of the poem to master the iterability of its rhetoric of intimate feeling does not pose a crisis for Byronic performance, but rather points to what might be seen as its enabling condition. That is, it is the performative dimension of the utterance of feeling—the way Byron's lyric performance strives to call up the feeling it describes—that allows Byron in any instance of performance both to enact "real" emotion and to revise his relationship to the emotion he claims to have felt. Byron's lyric performances stage Byronic personality itself as a dialectic between the flexibility of the performing persona—which can be picked up, dropped or revised at will—and the irrevocability of the "real life" gaps that are said to generate the feeling being performed: the relationship between the narrator and the character of Childe Harold acts out this dialectic, and so does the relationship between the "I" of the poem and the actual events of Byron's life. Byron's performances of feeling always evoke a fissure or gap that calls them up (exile, separation, loss), and always in a way seek to write over, and so to undo, the singularity of the event to which they respond. From this perspective, the irony that famously explodes in *Don Juan* is simply the repressed condition of Byronic performance all along.

While some readers found "Fare Thee Well!" a deeply affecting work that confirmed Byron's noble sensibility, others saw in it pure hypocrisy, confirmation of Byron's unfeeling nature. Annabella herself seems to have pegged the mix of genuine hurt, bitter aggression, self-delusion, bravura and despair driving Byron's composition in her response to his letters earlier that month: "Lord B. particularly piques himself on a talent for equivocation which renders it impossible to discover the real sense of his words [...] according to the disposition of the reader, Love, Pride, or Cunning may be supposed the dominant motive."[31] For our purposes, it is less important where public opinion ultimately came down than that the public became involved in the drama of the separation in the way it did. Readers did more than denounce or defend Byron's character; they demonstrated not just idle curiosity but an emotional stake in the matter, taking sides by identifying with one or both parties. One indication of this process is the slew of poetic replies generated by "Fare Thee Well!," some of them, like *Lady Byron's Responsive Fare Thee Well!* (1816), pretending to adopt Lady Byron's voice, others, like the *Reply to Lord Byron's "Fare Thee Well!"* (1817) signed C. and attributed to Mary Cockle, weighing in on her behalf.[32] *Lady Byron's Responsive Fare Thee Well!* imagines Lady Byron as still loving, holding out hope the couple will reunite once he gives up his "cherish'd madness."[33] The poem quotes with equal and alarming frequency from Byron and from the Bible, hyping its religious authority and Byronic literary credentials at once. Cockle's *Reply* raises alarms about the vulnerability of feeling to Byronic manipulation, arguing that he turns the devices of sensibility against Lady Byron and, more deviously, their daughter. Cockle's *Reply* and her *Lines Addressed to Lady Byron* (1817) paint Lady Byron and Ada as sentimentalized figures of "suffering virtue," and Byron as tearing apart the domestic ties that should be most "sacred."[34] Cockle's *Reply* opens by making Byron both the exponent and the enemy of the gestures of sensibility Cockle herself deploys, so that she and Byron essentially compete, and collaborate, as authors of the feeling in question:

> Oh stay thy dang'rous pen,—nor seek to move,
> With the false pleadings of repentant love!
> Wake not again the retrospective sigh,
> Or the wild tear of trembling agony,
> Taught by THY hand in bitterness to flow
> From the FULL chalice of *domestic woe*![35]

In her *Lines* to Lady Byron, Cockle acknowledges not only the public's claim to share in her feelings, but a more particular identification:[36]

> Ask *where's* the heart, that is not prompt to share
> The wife's chaste sorrow, and the mother's care?

> Or *where* the breast, that is not quick to prove
> Its genuine sympathy with wounded love?
> But ah! if sympathy alone can claim
> The sigh, the tear that trembles at thy name,
> Ask what *that stronger* sympathy must be
> From one, who *suffers—mourns and weeps, like Thee,*
> O'er marriage vows, dissolv'd as soon as tied—
> *Like thine* dissolv'd ere scarcely ratified[37]

Cockle here herself wakes again "the retrospective sigh" and trembling tear to point out how she and Lady Byron are united not only by their shared situation but also by their shared feeling. Lady Byron, *her* "name" like her husband's now inspiring sighs and trembling, becomes an iconic figure of domestic affection—"the wife's chaste sorrow, and the mother's care"—defined through a shared experience of suffering. Such an image was reinforced by caricature prints like Isaac Robert Cruikshank's "The Separation, a Sketch from the Private Life of Lord Iron," showing Byron "in the act of abandoning his wife and child, supposedly to run off with the well-known actress Charlotte Mardyn."[38]

While some onlookers, like Cockle, described their relief that Annabella was now safe from her supposedly deranged and depraved husband, a good number professed a desire for a reconciliation. Among these was the anonymous author of *A Narrative of the Circumstances which attended the separation of Lord and Lady Byron, remarks on his domestic conduct, and* a *complete refutation of the calumnies circulated by public writers* (1816), a title which pretty much says it all.[39] Such reconciliation could also be figured by the public's ongoing attempts to keep the imaginary dialogue between the couple alive. The composer George Kiallmark published musical settings for both *Fare Thee Well!* and a reply poem (*Now Each Tie of Love is Broken* [1817?]), reversing Byron's words in Annabella's voice: "Now thy strong appeal too late is, / Vain the words the die is cast, / All I'm now allow'd by fate, is / To forgive and mourn the past."[40] The dual musical settings suggest at least the possibility of a musical evening's entertainment with singers role-playing the disunited couple, or perhaps taking each part in turn.

If Byron's experience of the separation scandal must have resembled Robinson's experience in the wake of her scandalous affair with the Prince of Wales in the 1770s—she recalls being "assailed by pamphlets, by paragraphs, and caricatures, and all the artillery of slander," in an "hourly augmenting torrent of abuse that was poured upon me from all quarters"[41]—in other ways, the separation scandal worked much like the royal family dramas that called forth rapid-fire publication and debate in the Regency years, such as the mourning for Princess Charlotte, or Caroline's adultery trial at the end of the decade. These sensational events provoked at once an outpouring of public sentiment, an eager fascination with the private feelings of the actors involved, and suspicions about the politically motivated theatrics of feeling.[42] As Adela Pinch has described in her analysis of the public emotion around Princess Charlotte's death, displays of sympathy for Charlotte often involved a confusion between Charlotte's feeling and feeling for Charlotte.[43] Similarly, imagining itself into the feelings of Lord and Lady Byron, the public could imagine itself as a public by imagining itself as a feeling body, making itself a party to the domestic feelings involved in the couple's separation.

Particularly resonant in this context is the intertextual connection of "Fare Thee Well!" with Byron's writing on Napoleon, that other world-famous figure whose triumphs and defeats absorbed the public's attention, and Byron's own. Erdman makes the suggestive observation that Byron's last newspaper poem before "Fare Thee Well!" had been "Napoleon's Farewell," in Leigh Hunt's *Examiner* on 30 July 1815, so that the earlier farewell poem may have been on his mind as he crafted his poem to Annabella.[44] The tropes of "Napoleon's Farewell" anticipate Byron's language in "Fare Thee Well!," poising separation against enduring connection, evoking tears and hearts, and representing Napoleon's bond with France as a bond between lovers forged against a hostile world:

Farewell to the Land, where the gloom of my Glory
Arose and o'ershadowed the earth with her name—
She abandons me now,—but the page of her story,
The brightest or blackest, is filled with my fame.

[...]

Farewell to thee, France!—but when Liberty rallies
Once more in thy regions, remember me then—
The violet still grows in the depth of thy valleys;

Though withered, thy tears will unfold it again—
Yet, yet, I may baffle the hosts that surround us,
And yet may thy heart leap awake to my voice—
There are links which must break in the chain that has bound us,
Then turn thee and call on the Chief of thy choice![45]

Byron's 1814 *Ode to Napoleon Buonaparte* had already played off the public's association of himself with Napoleon, even as the poem revised hero-worship into shocked disappointment at an ignominiously fallen idol.[46] In the spring of 1816, Byron publicly returned to the Napoleonic theme with two more poems published in the newspapers under disguised authorship: "Ode from the French" in *The Morning Chronicle* of 15 March and "On the Star of 'The Legion of Honour'," written probably the year before but published in *The Examiner* on 7 April.[47] Both poems purport to present through French eyes a view of liberty temporarily defeated by Waterloo but returning as an unstoppable revolutionary force to triumph over its adversaries; the disguise in each case was quickly penetrated, as Byron of course knew it would be.

Byron's identification with the emperor he called his "little pagod" is notorious.[48] If through the spring of 1816 Byron psychologically merges into his identification with Napoleon his own sense of himself as embattled hero and potential exile, the public connects the poet's domestic circumstances with the lightning rod figure of Napoleon as well. Before the unauthorized publication of "Fare Thee Well!" and "A Sketch," *The Champion* all spring had been conducting a campaign of sensational allusions both to Byron's love life and to the dangerously un-British sympathies of some of Byron's associates, especially Hobhouse and Lord Kinnaird, warning of the threat to "public sentiment" from the "French morals" of the "*Anglo-gallic* school" and at the same time publicizing its knowledge of "certain gross violations of domestic decencies and duties, the news of which has startled the town, and called up a general sense of indignation,—nay, we may say of horror."[49] Once in the public domain, "Fare Thee Well!" and the Napoleonic poems frequently circulated together. William Hone's pirated edition of Byron's *Poems on his Domestic Circumstances,* which went through 15 editions in 1816, featured "Fare Thee Well!" and "A Sketch" but also prominently advertised its inclusion of the equally sensational political poems.[50]

Byron himself continued to act out a connection between the separation drama and reminders of Napoleon, leaving for Europe in a replica of Napoleon's carriage, and shifting in the opening passages of *Childe Harold* Canto III between the pain of separation and the arrival at Waterloo.[51]

As John Clubbe observes, when "Napoleon's Farewell" was republished in 1816, Byron's readers cannot have failed to substitute Byron's own "Farewell to thee, England!" for Napoleon's "Farewell to thee, France!," interpreting the poem through the lens of Byron's own exile.[52] In "Napoleon's Farewell," "Ode (from the French)," and "On the Star of the 'Legion of Honour'," Byron portrays the deeply emotional bond between an entire nation and a single larger-than-life figure, mimicking the mutual preoccupation of the self-mythologizing poet and the British public that alternately assails him and needs him. The separation scandal can be understood as the cultural processing of a mode of celebrity both Byron and Napoleon embodied as highly seductive, provocative figures, icons who inspired both love and horror, and who took on national meaning for the fascinated public. Ghislaine McDayter has shown how such a connection was already implicit in the phenomenon of Byromania, where "the violent energy of past political dissidence seemed to be reformulating itself into the hysteria of fandom."[53]

In *Don Juan* Canto XI, Byron revives the Napoleonic self-comparison, but attributes it to his readers before reclaiming it for himself:

> Even I, albeit I'm sure I did not know it
> Nor sought of foolscap subjects to be king,
> Was reckoned a considerable time
> The grand Napoleon of the realms of rhyme.
>
> But Juan was my Moscow, and Faliero
> My Leipsic, and my Mont Saint Jean seems Cain.
> 'La Belle Alliance' of dunces down at zero,
> Now that the lion's fallen, may rise again.
> But I will fall at least as fell my hero,
> Nor reign at all, or as a monarch reign,
> Or to some lonely isle of jailors go
> With turncoat Southey for my turnkey Lowe
>
> (11.55–6)

"I was rather famous in my time," the narrator of *Don Juan* later insouciantly declares, "until I fairly knocked it up with rhyme" (14.9). By the time he issued this declaration in Canto XIV, the poem's earlier cantos had dismayed many in Byron's original aristocratic fan base and won for him a much wider and increasingly working-class audience.[54] Because new cantos of the poem were written and issued over a period of years, the poem was in the odd position of being able to reflect retrospectively on its own reception and the demolition act it had performed on its author's fame. Thus, the basis of the comparison in the passage above is Napoleonic *celebrity*, a story of meteoric rise and spectacular fall that reinforces a cyclical view of authorial fame as faddishness (authors can at best hope to be on top of the literary world "a considerable time" before they fall off). The shadow figure in the passage is Napoleonic *authority*, the ability to command belief that had made Napoleon Byron's "hero" (as the casualness of his aside suggests he knows his readers all know). The basis for the equation between Byron's career and Napoleon's is that both Byron's literary celebrity and Napoleon's political and military authority depend on their ability to capture popular adulation as they "author" their own careers—the military career looks parodic of the literary, just as the literary looks parodic of the military. Even as, under the sign of parody, he seems to abdicate authority by casting his audience as the original "authors" of the Napoleonic comparison, Byron performs his authority in his extravagant gesture of reappropriating the Napoleonic comparison from the readers he implies (in an act of poetic legerdemain) made it first. Behind the metaphors of combat and conquest, though, is a recognition that Byron's own identity also depends on the public with whom he does battle. The Napoleonic comparison gives Byron, then, both a way to consolidate identity and a figure for a more fundamental and unstable self-difference. Insisting on the hollowness of fame, he elevates fame into a category of ironic understanding, through which the self is understood at once as a meaningful historical actor and as a public construction, authored by the reception it seems to authorize.

Where many commentators on Byron's celebrity saw the poet as imposing a mythic version of himself on the public, an 1825 essay in *Blackwood's* takes the opposite tack, arguing that Byron's career is inseparable from the public's response to him—indeed, that Byron is a creation of his audience.[55] Looking back over Byron's career in the wake of his death, J.G. Lockhart holds off on "any final striking of a balance, in regard to the good and the evil which were blended in Lord Byron's character:" without access to Byron's letters and memoirs, the critic argues, too much is speculation. But, acknowledging Byron's intense "sensitivity" to the public, he argues that the public's treatment of Byron is responsible for the very aspects of his character it deplores:

> From the beginning of his true career—it began with Childe Harold—we, in spite of all manner of disclamations and protestations, insisted upon saddling Byron, himself personally, with every attribute, however dark and repulsive, with which he had chosen to invent a certain fictitious personage, the hero of a romance. [...] How do we know how much our obstinate blending of Harold with Byron, stimulated the proud and indignant Byron to blend himself with Harold? How do we know, that we did not ourselves, by our method of criticizing his work, tempt the poet's haughty mind to brood exclusively on those very trains of dark and misanthropic thought, which, had we done otherwise, might have given way to everything that was happy and genial? [...] We encourage him in every possible way to dissect his own heart for our entertainment—we tempt him, by every bribe most likely to act powerfully on a young and imaginative man, to plunge into the darkest depths of self-knowledge, to madden his brain with eternal self-scrutinies, to find his pride and his pleasure in what others shrunk from as torture—we tempt him to indulge in these dangerous exercises, until they obviously acquire the power of leading him to the very brink of phrenzy—we tempt him to find, and to see in this perilous vocation, the staple of his existence, the food of his ambition, the very essence of his glory—and the moment that, by habits of our own creating, at least of our own encouraging and confirming, he is carried one single step beyond what we happen to approve of, we turn round with all the bitterness of spleen, and reproach him with the unmanliness of entertaining the public with his feelings in regard to his separation from his wife. This was truly the conduct of a fair and liberal public![56]

The writer's figures, of course, are recognizably Byronic, and recognizably Napoleonic as well. Really it is difficult to tell who is creating whom in this account: this is the story of Byron as the creation of a Byronized public. In this characterization, the emotional investment of Byron's readers not only gives rise to the uncontrollable ambition of the poet but also constitutes that readership itself as a "we" that comes to know itself, and its power, through Byron.

Blackwood's had a long, particularly close and particularly complicated relationship to Byron, and the reflections here can be seen in part as an attempt to come to terms with the magazine's own very ambivalent fascination with Byron. But the "we" here also goes beyond the particular magazine or the critical establishment; this is a commentary on how celebrity works in modern culture. Jacqueline Rose attributes the power of modern celebrity in part to the way as a form it "simultaneously evokes and annuls mystery."[57] This is an apt characterization of the separation scandal, which thrives and angers the public because it simultaneously exaggerates and deflates the mystery of Byron. In the *Blackwood's* writer's analysis, the public is driven by an intense, even sadistic, need to expose the truth of Byron's heart, to have him "dissect his heart for our entertainment [...] to plunge into the darkest depths of self-knowledge," and this very need creates the fear, loathing, and shame that celebrity fascination can arouse. The *Blackwood's* essay makes the forceful case that what the public saw in the separation scandal was its own desire mirrored back to it. But if Byron fascinates as a figure for the exposure of a buried emotional truth, the truth of Byron is located here in the systems through which he and his public interact: Byron and his public are both system-effects, and Byron fascinates precisely as an effect of the system built around him.

The opening canto of *Don Juan* replays the separation scandal in a satirical mode, first in Donna Inez's falling-out with Don José and then in the "pleasant scandal" of Juan's affair with Julia and Alfonso's suit for divorce, which was "in the English newspapers, of course" (1.188). Like Annabella, Inez calls "druggists and physicians" to try to prove "her loving lord was mad":

> But as he had some lucid intermissions
> She next decided he was only bad.
> Yet when they asked her for her depositions,
> No sort of explanation could be had,

Save that her duty both to man and God
Required this conduct—which seemed very odd.

(1.27)

By recalling the reader immediately to the story of the separation and to the curiosity that story provoked, Byron frames the poem's thematics of seduction from the outset in terms of his own relationship to his (once-) seduced readership, for whom Lady Byron becomes the exemplar. Donna Inez's treatment of Don José recalls Byron's accusations about Lady Byron's, and the public's, conduct toward him:

She kept a journal, where his faults were noted,
And opened certain of his trunks and letters,
All which might, if occasion served, be quoted,
And then she had all Seville for abettors,
Besides her good old grandmother (who doted).
The hearers of her case became repeaters,
Then advocates, inquisitors, and judges,
Some for amusement, others for old grudges.

(1.28)

The representation of Donna Inez casts Lady Byron as the curious reader par excellence, but also allows her to stand for the thereby feminized, and aggressive, curiosity of the entire reading public, a curiosity about the "truth" of Byron the poet both deplores and incites.

In *Don Juan*, Byron ruminates on his own life and his experience of celebrity, on the relationship between himself and his readers, and on the culture he inhabits. These topics endlessly intertwine because it is the poem's argument that they are inseparable, and because they form the actual situation of the poet writing and of his first readers reading. The poem abandons the lyric intimacy between reader and writer "Fare Thee Well!" aimed for (and at), but takes for granted a bond between reader and writer constructed not through the exchange of passionate feeling but through a shared location within print culture, a mutually mediated existence. As Manning notes, the manifestly oral presence conjured by the narrator's "conversational facility" (*Don Juan* 15.20) creates a sense of intimacy with the reader that depends on Byron and his reader "meeting" in the print marketplace, on their being immersed in the "common things" and "commonplaces" of a shared print culture (*Don Juan* 14.7), and on their sharing the history of Byron's career.[58] In the final pages of this chapter, I follow the dynamics of the separation scandal into *Don Juan*, tracing the connections between Byronic performance, Byron's scandalized readers, and the performative women who populate the poem.

The attack on Lady Byron (and her defenders) through the portrayal of Donna Inez ensured that the rhetoric of the separation would carry over into the critical response to *Don Juan*. Though *Blackwood's* writers, as we've seen, would later take a much more sympathetic view of the poet's role in the separation, the magazine at first reacted with possibly feigned hysteria to the poem's "mockery" of Lady Byron:

> To offend the love of such a woman was wrong—but it might be forgiven; to desert her was unmanly—but he might have returned and wiped for ever from her eyes the tears of her desertion;—but to injure, and to desert, and then to turn back and wound her widowed privacy with unhallowed strains of cold-blooded mockery—was brutally, fiendishly, inexpiably mean.[59]

The reviewer not only takes Lady Byron's side but casts Byron's readers, the reviewer included, as Lady Byrons themselves, as the poet's jilted and deceived lovers:

> We look back with a mixture of wrath and scorn to the delight with which we suffered ourselves to be filled by one who, all the while he was furnishing us with delight, must, we cannot doubt it, have been mocking us with a cruel mockery [...]. The consciousness of the insulting deceit which has been practised upon us, mingles with the nobler pain arising from the contemplation of perverted and degraded genius—to make us wish that no such being as Byron ever had existed.[60]

Such commentary confirms the terms in which *Don Juan* itself frames readerly seduction, in which an always unstable analogy is implicit between, on the one hand, the poet's relationships to individual female readers and, on the other hand, the poet's relationship to his readership at large, the readers for whom *Blackwood's* presumes to speak.

Passionate attachment to Byron was the province of multitudes of readers both male and female, of course, but, like *Don Juan*, cultural representations of such attachment often figured it as particularly feminine or feminizing. The author of "John Bull"'s *Letter to Lord Byron* (probably John Gibson Lockhart) described love for Byron as an adolescent girl's crush, contending that "in spite of all your pranks (Beppo, &c. Don Juan included,) every boarding school in the empire still contains many devout believers in the amazing misery of the black-haired, high-browed, blue-eyed, bare-throated Lord Byron."[61] Claiming to debunk the "humbug" of Byron's performative identity—Byron is not really so melancholy, but thought it would be an "interesting" pose to adopt—the writer demonstrates the effect of such performance through an extraordinary mock-blazon of Byron's commodified body, ventriloquized through the voices of Jane Austen's characters:

> How melancholy you look in the prints! Oh! yes, this is the true cast of face. Now, tell me, Mrs. Goddard, now tell me, Miss Price, now tell me, dear Harriet Smith, and dear, dear, Mrs. Elton, do tell me, is not this just the very look, that one would have fancied for Childe Harold? Oh— what eyes and eyebrows!—Oh! what a chin!—well, after all, who knows what may have happened. One can never know the truth of such stories. Perhaps her *Ladyship* was in the wrong after all.—I am sure if I had married such a man, I would have borne with all his little eccentricities— a man so evidently unhappy.[62]

The joke depends on the way the erotic appeal of Byron's image, and the fascination with such a dangerously sexual figure, supplants any direct response to his poetry.[63] But the joke is also on "John Bull" himself, since the letter just displaces onto the girl readers who supposedly wish themselves into Lady Byron's abandoned place the eagerness of both male and female readers, the *Letter*'s author included, to insist they know the real Byron. Like the girl readers he conjures through Austen's novel, "John Bull" proves in any case an attentive reader of Byron's body as it is commodified and purveyed in the prints.

Don Juan is Byron's reply to the dual charges widely made by cultural commentators and picked up in this passage from the *Letter*: that Byron's popularity depends in large part on his erotic appeal to female readers, and that Byron's own behavior as a husband and father, if uncensured, threatened to corrupt public virtue. Linking the poem with the image of Byron as libertine that emerged from the separation scandal, Caroline Franklin argues that as "Byron himself was already being excoriated by the Tory reviewers as the corrupter of female morals in his poetry, and the epic poem which he now writes should be seen as his considered and devastating attack on—not women themselves—but the notion of reforming society through propagating an ideal of chaste femininity."[64] As Franklin observes, the poem focuses less on Juan himself as anti-hero than on a "gallery of *female* characters, in a variety of nations."[65] *Don Juan* explores the links between the seductive power the poem assigns to women and Byron's own literary and personal powers of seduction, between the forms of public and private authority performative women obtain in the poem and the cultural authority of Byronic performance. If *Don Juan* seems, on the one hand, to play up the popular link between the power of Byron's poetry over the reading public and the poet's own magnetism, then, on the other hand, the power the poem repeatedly ascribes *to* women complicates this scenario of seduction.[66]

At the end of Canto I, Byron famously jokes that "the end of fame" is "but to fill / A certain portion of uncertain paper [...] To have, when the original is dust, / A name, a wretched picture, and worse bust" (1. 218)—and, he might have added, to have bequeathed some widely quoted lines such as these. In Canto IV, he returns to the idea of fame, but this time at once more pensively, more optimistically and more chillingly, contemplating the monuments to individuals that remain once "generations of the dead / Are swept away and tomb inherits tomb," the few epitaphs preserved for later readers among the "universal death" that swallows the "nameless" "once-named myriads" (4.102). Naming Achilles, de Foix, and Dante, whose tombs he has actually visited, Byron signals that if he can be skeptical about the worth of fame he also measures himself against a heroic ideal: observing that whatever happens "there will still be bards," Byron connects "the unquiet feelings" that produce poetry, his or anyone's, with ambition. From these reflections on the worth or possibility of lasting fame the narrator modulates into a meditation on the celebrity of his own "years of fame," a celebrity he asserts was both created and then dashed by fashionable women readers:

> Oh ye, who make the fortunes of all books,
> Benign ceruleans of the second sex!
> Who advertise new poems by your looks,
> Your imprimatur will ye not annex?
> What, must I go to the oblivious cooks,
> Those Cornish plunderers of the Parnassian wrecks?
> Ah, must I then the only minstrel be
> Proscribed from tasting your Castalian tea?
>
> What, can I prove a lion then no more?
> A ballroom bard, a foolscap, hot-press darling?
>
> (4.108–9)

These stanzas betray anxieties both about the poet's subjection to the marketplace forces Byron represents through the exaggerated power of female consumers, and about the relationship between the celebrity he has experienced and a more lasting form of fame. Byron represents celebrity as locating him within a world of women, where the audience for lasting fame is represented as firmly male ("Where are the epitaphs our fathers read?" [4.102]). But if the poem anxiously negotiates its relationship to a female audience, at once defiantly severing ties and noting that Byron's women readers have abandoned him, the poem also draws implicit parallels between the performances of Byron and his narrator and those of many of the female characters to whom the poem gives prominence.

As Susan Wolfson and Nicola Watson have in different ways suggested, the sentimental Julia, the coldly self-masking Adeline, and the cross-dressing Fitz-Fulke each echo different aspects of Byronic performance.[67] Julia's passionate farewell letter revives what this chapter has already shown to be a crucial Byronic genre, the emotional goodbye, and she signs the letter with Byron's own seal. Watson points out that Fitz-Fulke's ghostly friar costume recalls Byron's own masked-ball costume of 1814 and the Gothic costuming of these late cantos, which itself recalls Caroline Lamb's sensationally Gothic rendering of the Byron legend in *Glenarvon* (1816). In Byron's description of Adeline "occupied by fame" and "playing her grand role" as society hostess, we can detect, along with Byron's critique of what he describes as female hypocrisy, a sensitivity to the cost such performance exacts, and—especially when Juan experiences "some doubt how much of Adeline was real"—an allusion to the way Byronic performance was received. As many commentators have observed, Adeline's "mobility" names the characteristic quality of *Don Juan*'s narrator and its title character (16.96). These performative women are both figures for the performative subjectivity *Don Juan* develops and figures against which that subjectivity is measured.

The identifications at work between Byron and his female characters indicate Byron's debt to models of performance associated with the women readers he castigates: Julia's letter borrows, though its itinerary ironically undercuts, the tropes of novelistic sentimentality; the Norman Abbey cantos, revisiting both Newstead Abbey and Regency high society, feature female characters reminiscent of the powerful women who not only championed Byron in his "years of fame" but taught him how to operate in society.[68] Byron's celebrity crosses the gender codes he elsewhere tries to keep emphatically separate. Wolfson and Hofkosh have both shown how *Don Juan*'s sometimes vitriolic misogyny is connected at once to anxieties about the social power of women and to anxieties about the limits of a fantasized masculine autonomy and authority. At work in *Don Juan* is a recognition not only of Byronic identity as a manifestly collaborative product but more specifically of the special role of female readers and female writers in shaping that identity. As I suggested above, however, part of the magic of Byronic authority that is—a "magic" enabled by the gendered and classed discursive codes structuring Byron's reception—is that Byron's identifications with and borrowings from widely divergent authorizing figures, from imperialistic military heroes to sentimental women, and from sentimental men to imperialistic women, only add to the appearance of his singularity.

Authority is precisely in question in the Norman Abbey cantos, where the reader is confronted with a cast of characters—Aurora, Adeline, Henry, Fitz-Fulke—who all look up to something. As in a mystery novel the reader is left unsure who exactly is in control and who is in the know about what. The tale of the ghost who haunts the Amundeville line is, on the surface, a story about patrilineal authority and the threats to it. Adeline and Fitz-Fulke both seem to act independently of their strangely marginalized husbands, and the women seem more in control of the action here than the men; the issue of patriarchal authority is likewise highlighted and complicated by the "double figure" of the pregnant girl who is called to appear before Lord Henry "to name a thing in nomenclature rather / Perplexing for most virgins—a child's father" (16.67). The appearance of the ghost transposes these questions of authority in the household into questions of narrative authority: who knows the truth of this "ghost story"? Are they all in on it, or is someone in particular its "author"? These issues are framed in miniature in the exchange between husband and wife leading up to Adeline's performance of her ballad narrating this inherited story of inheritance, when Adeline proposes to set Henry's story of the Friar "to a tune" and Henry insists that she add the words she has composed (16.38–39). Adeline's sung performance of the story echoes the narrator's story-telling performance—in the previous canto the narrator calls himself an "*improvisatore*" (15.20)—but the relationship of Adeline's poem to the ghost story the narrator tells is uncertain (we never know if there's a real black friar). When the apparent Friar is unmasked in the "double figure" of Fitz-Fulke, these questions of authority are not resolved but rather given a further twist. Fitz-Fulke then appears to be at least the leading candidate for the "author" of this story.[69] The generic play with the Gothic more generally metonymically links Byronic performance, the fantastic power of the ghost story, and the promiscuous female sexuality embodied by Fitz-Fulke.

These final cantos discover, however, neither an assertion of univocal authority *nor* a crisis of authority. Throughout *Don Juan*, but especially in these final cantos, authority shifts through voices to which the narrator and the author lay only partial claim: Byron alternates between portraying himself as scripting his own life and public debate, and portraying both his name and his poem as products of a larger literary and cultural system. Byron makes his authority coextensive with the text's ability to function as a medium for representing, without necessarily resolving, the complex, shifting, intensely gendered and always compromised conditions of identity in Byron's world, the conditions of Byronic celebrity. As Manning notes, "Byron never forgets, or lets us forget, that *Don Juan* is a text shaped within the literary market, subject to the pressures of opinion and the means of distribution."[70] Read this way, *Don Juan* constitutes a running argument against the reification of the performance it enacts, an argument all the more persuasive in that it acknowledges the inevitability of such reification.

At the end of the opening canto, Byron promises the reader they will meet again if they "understand" one another; if not, he will not trouble the reader further. As the poem goes on, however, one gets the sense the narrator is going to keep talking no matter what the reader thinks. Though *Don Juan* gains for Byron a wider audience, the tone of Byron's reflections on fame lead one to imagine he's lost all his readers.[71] Byron's claims on this score might seem disingenuous—he declares his poetry "a bubble" "just to play with, as an infant plays" (14.8) and continues:

> I think that were I certain of success,
> I hardly could compose another line.
> So long I've battled either more or less
> That no defeat can drive me from the Nine.
> This feeling 'tis not easy to express
> And yet 'tis not affected, I opine.
> In play there are two pleasures for your choosing:
> The one is winning and the other losing.
>
> (14.12)

What does Byron mean here by "success"—the goal whose certainty, if it ever came, would end writing—and what does this say about the value, to Byron, of writing itself? William Hazlitt was incensed by the lordly arrogance he detected in lines like these, complaining that Byron is always "ungraciously throwing the offerings of incense heaped on his shrine back in the faces of his admirers."[72] Hazlitt fumes that "he says he will write on, whether he is read or not [but] would never write another page, if it were not to court popular applause, or to affect a superiority over it."[73] But the rhetoric of competition reminds us how fully oppositional Byron's writing in *Don Juan* is: he intends it to make sense only in relation to what he is writing against, the hypocrisy of the "cant" governing morality, politics, and sexuality in Regency culture—a hypocrisy for which the supposedly outraged response to Byron himself becomes exhibit A: "Why do they call me misanthrope? Because / They hate me, not I them" (9.21). Byron's difficulty in giving up the field speaks, I think, to the (self-)exiled poet's continued desire for connection with the nation and the readership from which he is geographically and emotionally distanced: writing is an address he does not want to let drop. Byron's contemporaries Keats and Shelley often imagine fame through a rhetorical appeal to a future audience, though as I argue in my next chapters they are also very much obsessed with the possibilities of a more immediate celebrity. In contrast to these poets, Byron in *Don Juan* looks back on his fame as something already past, a marketplace phenomenon governed by the cyclicality of fashion. But like the speaker of Byron's "Napoleon's Farewell," he addresses an audience from whom his estrangement does not mean final separation. Byron's self-identity is tied to the figure of his public just as in early nineteenth-century Britain the public's self-identity is tied to the figure of Byron.

The poets I discuss in the chapters that follow all must deal with the example of Byron as they negotiate the relationship between poetic identity and celebrity. At times, as we will see, these poets respond directly to this example: Keats with an anxious and skeptical eye on Byronic charisma; Shelley through an intense poetic dialogue with Byron, who becomes both his close friend and rival; Landon and Barrett Browning through explicit gestures of Byronic fandom and of identification with Byron. But these poets also work out their own models of celebrity in a literary culture where the phenomenon of Byron has had a signal impact. The phenomenon of Byron is not the sole engine transforming literary culture, of course, and this phenomenon itself is, as I have argued, the product of a literary and market system involving many individuals, not just the poet himself. But post-Byron, writers must come to grips with a literary field in which celebrity matters in new ways. On the one hand, reader-writer relationships are sensationalized and more powerfully and perhaps more dangerously eroticized, and Byron makes clear what kind of popularity it is possible for a poet to achieve. On the other hand, the phenomenon of Byron makes evident the commercialization not only of poetry but also of poetic identity itself. Byronic performance quickly becomes a cliché, as Byron himself saw, and Byron's celebrity a figure for the efficiency and power of the "systems of literary lionism" (Martineau) writers and readers must now navigate.

2
Keats, Lyric and Personality

Obituaries for Keats staked their claim for attention on that paradoxical but pervasive trope of Romantic celebrity, the narrative of neglected genius. Take, for example, this version from the *London Magazine* notice signed "L.," written by "Barry Cornwall" (Bryan Waller Procter), subsequently picked up by the *Imperial Magazine* (December 1821), *Time's Telescope for 1822*, and American journals, and quoted liberally elsewhere:

> Mr. Keats was, in the truest sense of the word, A POET. [...] He had a fine ear, a tender heart, and at times great force and originality of expression; and notwithstanding all this, he has been suffered to rise and pass away almost without a notice: the laurel has been awarded (for the present) to other brows: the bolder aspirants have been allowed to take their station on the slippery steps of the temple of fame, while he has been nearly hidden among the crowd during his life, and has at last died, solitary and in sorrow, in a foreign land.[1]

Keats's distinction arises because of the very lapse of public attention he inhabits; his distance from celebrity culture ensures his charisma. If he is obscured by the "bolder aspirants" who monopolize public attention—think Byron—that obscurity ("hidden among the crowd") can be transformed with striking ease into a spotlight glow, isolating the poet's figure against an exotic and romantic backdrop ("solitary and in sorrow, in a foreign land"). Poignant, this narrative also has a doubly revisionary potential. On the one hand, the obituary's story that Keats has largely been ignored by the critical establishment downplays the famously bad press Keats did in fact receive: most notoriously, the attacks on *Endymion* that Keats himself argued at least brought him "more into notice."[2] On the other hand, by insisting on Keats's virtual anonymity, the obituary sets up the counter-narrative of Keats's rise to the fame forecasted by the poet himself—"I think I shall be among the English poets after my death" (*KL* I, 161)—and the obituary grants itself a central role in that elevation. The emphasis on the ephemerality of celebrity enables this move. As the obituary-writer slyly notes, the laurel has only been awarded "for the present" to others; the steps of the temple of fame are slippery, and the turning of the wheels of fashion will leave the field clear for the true "POET" to get his due, starting, of course, with this notice.

The *London* notice observes, with what may be an echo of Milton's sonnet on Shakespeare, that the "painfully affecting" story of Keats's death is "well calculated to make a deep impression" on readers (*KCH* 241, 242).[3] The obituary makes evident Keats's own now legendary quotability by quoting his words to Severn on his deathbed as well as chunks of the *Ode to a Nightingale*:

> His sad and beautiful wish is at last accomplished: it was that he might drink "of the warm south," and "leave the world unseen,"—and— (he is addressing the nightingale)—
>
> And with thee fade away ...
>
> Fade far away, dissolve, and quite forget
> What thou among the leaves hast never known,
> The weariness, the fever, and the fret
> Here, where men sit and hear each other groan;
> Where palsy shakes a few, sad, last gray hairs,
> *Where youth grows pale, and spectre-thin, and dies;*
> Where but to think is to be full of sorrow
> And leaden-eyed despairs,
> Where Beauty cannot keep her lustrous eyes,
> Or new Love pine at them beyond to-morrow.
>
> A few weeks before he died, a gentleman who was sitting by his bed-side, spoke of an inscription to his memory, but he declined this altogether,—desiring that there should be no mention of his

> name or country; 'or if any,' said he, 'let it be—*Here lies the body of one whose name was writ in water!*'
>
> (*KCH* 242)

By reading Keats's poetry as the literal expression of the poet's desire to fade away from wearying life, the obituary seems to allow Keats himself to stage-manage the scene of his own death ("his sad wish is now accomplished;" "'let it be'") even as Keats appears to insist on an ultimate anonymity, an exemption from the marketplace of the name. The narrative of the poet's death breaks down the corpus of the poet into discrete pieces of text—choice lines—that can be reproduced and put into cultural circulation. With its romantic Italian backdrop, this scene is itself perfectly packaged for reproduction, and it would in fact be visually reproduced in Severn's drawings of Keats on his deathbed.[4] Part of its appeal is the way the public is allowed access to the most intimate of moments between the dying Keats and his caretaker; we are admitted as privileged guests within a protected circle. The star treatment the figure of the dead or dying poet receives in the obituaries, in Shelley's *Adonais*, in Severn's visual and verbal reproductions of the deathbed scene, and in subsequent biographies and recollections of the poet makes an intimate relation to the body of the poet central to the experience of reading Keats after his death: the 1829 Galignani edition of *Poems by Coleridge, Shelley and Keats*, for example, gives directions to the Protestant Cemetery in Rome, suggesting the imagined connection between the act of reading and the pilgrimage to the body's place of rest.[5]

The narrative advanced by the sympathetic obituaries turns on the disposition of "feeling." Keats is a poet by virtue of his capacity for feeling ("tender heart," "solitary and in sorrow"); the public fails to notice him because it fails to feel. "It is at all times difficult, if not impossible, to argue others into a love of poets and poetry," the notice continues, since "it is altogether a matter of feeling." The phrasing is ambiguous: is it a matter of the different feelings different readers may have, or a matter of whether one feels at all? According to the obituary, in the case of Keats the distinction might be moot: "there was no other Author whatsoever, whose writings would form so good a test by which to try the love one professed to bear towards poetry." Or as the *New Monthly Review* insists: "the mind insensible to the sweetness of his productions must indeed be a miserable one—the very climax of heartlessness" (*KCH* 243–4).[6] Keats becomes, in these terms, not just a Chatterton but a Clarissa, a character in a novelistic plot of sensibility. Instead of a model of the aesthetic based on a marketplace that accounts for differences in taste, the sentimental narrative of the poet's death accounts only for difference in the capacity to feel: if one doesn't fall in love with Keats and his tragic story, it means one can't really love, or (at least) love poetry, at all.

Insisting on the "heartlessness" of those readers immune to Keats's charm clearly counters the class-inflected ridicule of Keats as a "a foolish young man, who, after writing some volumes of very weak, and, in the greater part, of very indecent poetry, died some time since of a consumption: the breaking down of an infirm constitution having, in all probability, been accelerated by the discarding his neckcloth, a practice of the cockney poets, who look upon it as essential to genius," as the *Literary Gazette and Journal of Belles Lettres* described the subject of *Adonais* (*KCH* 245). But, unlike Shelley's deliberately provocative elegy, the sympathetic obituaries keep the politics and the controversy muted. By shifting the terms of evaluation to the feeling of the individual "lover" of poetry, the language of the obituaries collapses aesthetic response and consumer demand in the construction of a desiring relation to the story of Keats the poet as well as to Keats's poetry. By framing Keats's appeal in terms of the capacity of a limited circle of elite readers to catch the writer's intimate address—to recognize their own capability as feeling readers in their emotional response to the "painfully affecting" story and the "sweetness" of the poetry—the obituaries produce the loveliness of Keats as a commodity that looks like a necessarily limited edition but which they open to endless reproduction and consumption.

The spellbinding effects of Keatsian evanescence have been much explored in recent criticism, perhaps most powerfully by Karen Swann, who observes that Keats's "piercing loveliness is always connected to his being elsewhere—lost in a book or a line of poetry, caught up in a drama, arrested by a sudden thought, raptly attentive to some other call." She continues:

> Like Shelley, who is often depicted hanging over the water, Keats has in life the perilous, fragile poise of Narcissus; he seems, retrospectively, to have possessed the sharp beauty of one who is about to leave us.[7]

For Swann, Keats's turning away from contact in the deathbed scene provokes the love we all feel for the narcissist "who won't return our calls." In her reading, the deathbed scene is exemplary of a Romantic configuration of the inaccessible, self-enclosed, self-absorbed and so hopelessly absorbing aesthetic object, tied both to a sense of loss and to the "other scene" of dream or futurity.[8] The glamour Keats wins as famously dead poet reflects and underwrites what Andrew Bennett has described as the "culture of posterity" promoted by Romantic poetry. For Bennett, Romantic poets respond to the increasing commercialization of literature by rejecting the appeal to a contemporary audience, addressing instead a reader who follows the poet's death. Reading within the culture of posterity thus always operates from a horizon of loss.[9]

The very success of such gestures in Keats's posthumous reception, however, may work to occlude the actual relations obtaining between the living poet and the culture of celebrity. My contention in this chapter is that if Keats's poetry anticipates the kind of "celebrity effects" the obituaries will exploit, it does so primarily not by looking to posterity but rather through its sophisticated negotiation of the mass-market structures of the *contemporary* culture of celebrity. In his thinking about fame, Keats's attention focuses much more on the possibility of immediate celebrity, and much less on the scene of posthumous reading, than critics have tended to imagine. What difference does it make to look again at Keats's relationship to fame, not from the perspective of the lasting judgment of futurity, but from a perspective located in the literary scene of the late teens, in the shadow of such figures as Byron, Scott, and Leigh Hunt? Savvy about the ways an emerging, mass-mediated celebrity system can produce a kind of erasure of self or even ghostliness for the writer it retails as a figure of desire, Keats, I argue, learns how to use such erasure strategically to create seductive effects of lyric presence. To read Keats in this fashion acknowledges the impersonality for which he has often been celebrated as the source of potent personality effects.

I focus on early and late poems to demonstrate Keats's growing sophistication, over the course of his career, in coordinating effects of lyric intimacy with aspirations for literary celebrity. In *Sleep and Poetry*, the finale to Keats's 1817 volume, Keats finds his attempt to articulate a poetic personality for himself constantly undone, as the speaker is repeatedly absorbed by the very series of captivating literary, cultural and market systems the poem calls on to authorize that personality. But by 1819, in the dream-vision fragment *The Fall of Hyperion*, Keats experiments more successfully with the kind of self-effacement *Sleep and Poetry* seems to discover inadvertently.[10]

We can turn to *Sleep and Poetry* itself to begin to sketch its place within Keats's developing sense of the figure he might cut as a participant in the contemporary literary scene, for that context is foregrounded by the poem itself. The poem records the speaker's thoughts as he lies awake on the couch in Leigh Hunt's library ("a poet's house who keeps the keys / of pleasure's temple"), the rest of the house having gone to bed (354–5). In his multiple roles as famous writer, as celebrated and daring proponent of liberty, as aesthete and as impresario and host, Hunt represents a crucial entrée to the literary scene for Keats at this point in his career. The 1817 *Poems* is dedicated to Hunt, and he and other members of his circle are the subjects of many of the volume's sonnets and epistles.[11] Not surprisingly, then, given the poem's location in Hunt's library, such a privileged and problematic space in Keats's imagination of literary culture, this is a poem about literary and market systems and composed explicitly from those overlapping systems.

Sleep and Poetry poses as a poetic problem, and a source of poetic capital, the question of the relationship of life and text, the poem and the poet's body. The poem moves through several overlaid plots: a narrative of English poetry from its early, heroic days to its recent period of "schism;" a projected narrative of Keats's career, in which he will one day pass on from the realm of "Flora, and old Pan" to "a nobler life / Where I may find the agonies, the strife / Of human hearts;" and the narrative of the writing of the poem itself, which is characterized by the shift back and forth between two modes, one of sublime inspiration and one of gentle musing. The wavering between these modes is aligned with the poem's wavering between two models of literary production: on the one hand, a concept of literary production animated by a notion of authorial "personality" as the projection of some essential and unique inner imaginative force, a personality construed in terms of sublime, heroic literary ambition; on the other hand, a version of literary production tied to the coterie, in an economy of literary exchange in which individuality is subordinated to sociality.

As Jeffrey Cox has stressed, the poem, like Keats's entire first volume, is characteristic of the values of the Hunt circle in taking its origin "not from lonely inspiration but from shared daily rituals and pleasures":[12]

> The hearty grasp that sends a pleasant sonnet
> Into the brain ere one can think upon it;
> The silence when some rhymes are coming out;
> And when they're come, the very pleasant rout:
> The message certain to be done to-morrow—
> 'Tis perhaps as well that it should be to borrow
> Some precious book from out its snug retreat,
> To cluster round it when we next shall meet.
>
> (319–26)

Throughout the poem, though, this sunny vision of Huntian coterie authorship is darkened by the shadow of Byronic celebrity, a version of authorial charisma hard to ignore for a writer launching his career in 1816, when the poem was written. Keats conjures the celebrity poet most directly in the oft-remarked lines on the dangers of the death-dealing yet fascinating Gothic/Satanic "strength" Byron models: "strength alone though of the Muses born, / Is like a fallen angel: trees uptorn, / Darkness, and worms, and shrouds, and sepulchres / Delight it; for it feeds upon the burrs, / And thorns of life; forgetting the great end / Of poesy, that it should be a friend / To sooth the cares, and lift the thoughts of man" (241–7). The exorcism of Byron here is surely consistent with the programmatic aims of the poem, as Cox persuasively outlines them: "The function of poetry is [...] to transform a culture of despondency into one devoted to the hopes of a world reformed."[13] But we might also see Byronic celebrity as a more significant lure, as a crucial determinant of the poem's imagination of the possibilities for the kind of fame Keats himself might achieve. He already senses he does not want to be a Hunt—that this way lies not just recirculating cliché, but becoming a cliché. Yet he cannot be a Byron, for reasons both philosophical (having to do with Keats's conception of the ends of poetry and poetic character) and practical (having to do with Keats's class and financial position).[14] Still, writing in the wake of Byronic celebrity meant writing with the idea in mind of the kind of unprecedented, commanding fame a Byron could achieve, and also with the knowledge that such a stance was already (by 1816) looking exhausted. At the same time, writing in the wake of Byron meant writing within a literary system whose very systematic character Byronic celebrity had both encouraged and exposed, as we have seen. *Sleep and Poetry* can be read as a provisional negotiation of various models of celebrity operating in the literary culture of the late teens, each enticing but ultimately either unworkable or unavailable to the poet just launching his career.[15]

The burden of the poem is the effort to move from the level of the literal to the level of the figurative—to organize the contingency of the daily life of the writer (expressed in the passages of gentle musing) into the meaningful "shape" of a poetic career (gestured toward in the passages of sublime inspiration). But because the poem is a declaration of the immaturity of the poet's *present* shaping power, its own shapelessness reflects rather the contingency it describes. The poem seems not to have an internal logic that dictates its contours, but rather to bear in a sense the imprint of Keats's shape, the poet lying on the couch in the library, and of the contours of daily life in the Hunt household.

What afflicts the speaker of the poem is the Romantic "phrenzy" diagnosed (viciously) in Keats's case by John Gibson Lockhart as "*Metromanie*." For Lockhart, the contagion of the "just celebrity of Robert Burns and Miss Baillie" means that people who should never imagine themselves poets, given their social origins or identity, suddenly do so: "our very footmen compose tragedies, and there is scarcely a superannuated governess in the island that does not leave a roll of lyrics behind in her band-box."[16] But such contemporary philosophers as Philippe Lacoue-Labarthe and Jean-Luc Nancy diagnose a similar disease in the case of Friedrich Schlegel, whom they describe as subject to "attacks of versification," or "a *mania* for poetizing that cannot fail, at least momentarily, to suggest itself to anyone who sets out to write, in any genre, in the age of literature."[17] According to Lacoue-Labarthe and Nancy, such a mania means "nothing other, in the end, than being briefly fascinated by the Work, by the presentation of the absent and absolute Work." In *Sleep and Poetry*, everything the speaker sees, recalls or imagines can be productive of endless writing, a kind of lyricizing without end, a generativity so extreme that it also interrupts writing, as the writing

"I" is constantly nearly pulled under by the metonymic flow of the images it presents:

> O Poesy! for thee I hold my pen
> That am not yet a glorious denizen
> Of thy wide heaven—Should I rather kneel
> Upon some mountain-top until I feel
> A glowing splendour round about me hung,
> And echo back the voice of thine own tongue?
> O Poesy! for thee I grasp my pen
> That am not yet a glorious denizen
> Of thy wide heaven; yet, to my ardent prayer,
> Yield from thy sanctuary some clear air
>
> [...] 'twill bring to me the fair
> Visions of all places: a bowery nook
> Will be elysium—an eternal book
> Whence I may copy many a lovely saying
> About the leaves, and flowers [...]
>
> (47–56; 62–6)

> Scarce can I scribble on; for lovely airs
> Are fluttering round the room like doves in pairs;
> Many delights of that glad day recalling,
> When first my senses caught their tender falling.
> And with these airs come forms of elegance
> Stooping their shoulders o'er a horse's prance,
> Careless, and grand—fingers soft and round
> Parting luxuriant curls,—and the swift bound
> Of Bacchus from his chariot, when his eye
> Made Ariadne's cheek look blushingly.
> Thus I remember all the pleasant flow
> Of words at opening a portfolio.
>
> Things such as these are ever harbingers
> To trains of peaceful images [...]
>
> (327–39)

Instead of the presentation of the absent Work, the speaker presents a series of systems he draws on to authorize his versions of poetic personality, systems of poetic production and exchange emblematized in the space of Leigh Hunt's library—a place set up for specific practices of reading and writing (for example, looking at and writing in portfolios), and a room whose very decorations—paintings of classical mythology, busts of "bards who sung / In other ages"—embody the reproduction of culture as something precisely reproducible (356–7). The risk the poem seems self-consciously to court is that it is just an element in such systems of recirculation, that the "bubblings" and "pipings" it is thrilled to discover only name its own lyricizing as meaningless noise.

Sleep and Poetry makes use of the liminal state it describes to discover a kind of rhetorical flexibility in which it can write itself into and out of commitments, and this rhetorical mobility is paralleled in the way it commits its speaker to the grave and then writes its speaker out of the grave. It oscillates between the sublime and the pastoral in imagining different versions of the speaker's failure and burial:

> Will not some say that I presumptuously
> Have spoken? that from hastening disgrace
> 'Twere better far to hide my foolish face?
>   [...] How!
> If I do hide myself, it sure shall be
> In the very fane, the light of Poesy:
> If I do fall, at least I will be laid
> Beneath the silence of a poplar shade;
> And over me the grass shall be smooth shaven;
> And there shall be a kind memorial graven
>
> (270–80)

And a few lines later:

>   Therefore should I
> Be but the essence of deformity,
> A coward, did my very eye-lids wink
> At speaking what I have dared to think.
> Ah! rather let me like a madman run
> Over some precipice; let the hot sun

> Melt my Dedalian wings, and drive me down
> Convuls'd and headlong!
>
> (297–304)

In these passages, the speaker's projected death turns out to be either already written—a cliché, as in the Icarus narrative—or to be the excuse for more writing, a "memorial graven." It is hard not to read the speaker's repeated self-interruptions and imaginations of spectacular death as on some level knowing self-parody, a recognition of the speaker's inability to extricate himself from the captivating poetic machineries he calls up. The notion of systematicity is especially underscored in the image of the "kind memorial graven," balanced equivocally between the endpoints of fame and anonymity. The subject-position of the memorialist mirrors the subject-position of the speaker/writer of the poem: each position is at once occupied by a real person in real space and time (Keats in Leigh Hunt's house after everyone else has gone to bed; an unnamed friend or fellow poet, perhaps from Keats's coterie) and at the same time appears essentially empty or mechanical, a writing effect. It is as if one effect of the writing of the poem is to project this memorial *out of itself*, writing the anticipated memorial as itself an effect of writing.[18] Instead of surviving in living memory, the fantasized recognition of originality fades into the cliché of just one more (minor) poet's grave: the idea of the "kind memorial graven" is reassuring in that it assumes what is not necessarily true (that *someone* will read this). Naturalizing absorption by system by figuring poetic failure as absorption into the pastoral, the cliché of the "kind memorial graven" inadvertently makes visible (to us and to Keats) the kind of erasure of the name Keats plays on for more dramatic effect in his reported response to Severn's deathbed inquiry about a memorial inscription: "Here lies the body of one whose name was writ in water."

The Romantic culture of celebrity, known for its outsized personalities, might also be considered a culture of *minor* celebrity: as I discussed in my Introduction, to its participants, the galaxy of stars often looked like a blur of names talked about then forgotten. "Who would wish to be among the commonplace crowd of the little-famous—who are each individually lost in a throng made up of themselves?," Keats wrote to his publisher John Taylor on 23 August 1819, explaining his ambition for a fame beyond the momentary attention of the "literary world" (*KL* II, 144). *Sleep and Poetry* does not succeed in giving Keats a way to project himself out of this crowd, but the forms of self-erasure Keats inadvertently discovers as he composes perhaps help him toward those more strategically manageable versions of self-loss and self-effacement for which the "camelion poet" will later be celebrated. To suggest how this might be so, I turn now to the uncompleted *Fall of Hyperion*, which Keats worked on starting likely in the spring of 1819 and then finally abandoned some time in the autumn of that year. In juxtaposing these poems, my aim is not to construct a teleological narrative of straightforward development or maturation—the fact that Keats abandoned *The Fall* and that it sat unpublished until 1857 makes it unclear what lesson Keats himself drew from this experiment, and means the poem obviously plays no direct role in Keats's early reception. But the juxtaposition of these early and late poems does elucidate the different ways Keats experiments, over the course of his career, with how he casts the reader's role in relation to the articulation of poetic "personality." Keats's experiments with self-effacement in the dream-vision frame he adds in 1819 to his epic *Hyperion* conjure seductive effects of intimacy calculated for success within conditions of market abstraction, but they do so by capitalizing on the very forms of erasure that characterize authorial identity within a mass-mediated celebrity system.

Through much of the *annus mirabilis* 1819, Keats keeps coming back, in his letters, to the question of fame. As a younger poet he had written wonderingly to Hunt in 1817, "what a thing to be in the Mouth of Fame" (*KL* I, 139). Now, he struggles with a set of conflicts probably familiar to any aspiring writer, as artistic ambition knocks up against financial pressure. In the attitudes he projects to his friends, Keats hopes to show that he sees through the reading public and worries that the reading public will claim to see through him. Often, as Sonia Hofkosh has explored in especially fine detail, Keats's resistance to the appearance of dependence on the public's taste takes on an explicitly gendered dimension.[19] "I equally dislike the favour of the public with the love of a woman—they are both a cloying treacle to the wings of independence," he writes in August 1819 to his publisher Taylor, rejecting the idea of selling out as just "a popular writer;" in two sonnets on fame written in the spring of 1819, he casts fame as a seductress whose charms are better resisted.[20]

Hofkosh comments that "the issue for Keats is writing independent of others and of other, worldly concerns, being free to create for himself, privately."[21] Yet, despite his occasional claims to the contrary, Keats constantly thinks about the potential reception of his writing, and consistently imagines sensational possibilities for it. Rather than dismissing or deferring fame, what he is looking for is a celebrity that places him above the mediocre "commonplace crowd of the little-famous," as he writes Taylor (*KL* II, 144). Rather than "beg suffrages for a seat on the benches of a myriad aristocracy in Letters," he has his eye on the kind of apparent autonomy demonstrated by what he calls at the start of 1819 the "three literary kings in our time—Scott—Byron—and then the Scotch novels."[22] He writes to Benjamin Bailey on 14 August 1819: "One of my Ambitions is to make as great a revolution in modern dramatic writing as Kean has done in acting—another to upset the drawling of the blue stocking literary world—if in the course of a few years I do these two things I ought to die content" (*KL* II, 139). After watching "Orator" Henry Hunt's triumphal procession into London in September 1819, the mood electric in the wake of the Peterloo Massacre, Keats wrote excitedly to his brother and sister-in-law, "It would take me a whole day and a quire of paper to give you any thing like detail—I will merely mention that it is calculated that 30.000 people were in the streets waiting for him—The whole distance from the Angel Islington to the Crown and anchor was lined with Multitudes" (*KL* II, 194). In a letter to B.R. Haydon a few days later (3 October 1819), we can catch Keats imagining for himself what this kind of sensational reception might feel like: "I have no cause to complain," he writes, "because I am certain any thing really fine will in these days be felt. I have no doubt that if I had written Othello I should have been cheered by as good a Mob as Hunt" (*KL* II, 219).

Keats's revisions to his epic *Hyperion* over the summer and into the fall of 1819 have often been read in terms of his quest for poetic identity, and Jonathan Bate and Michael O'Neill, among others, have offered compelling accounts of these revisions in terms of Keats's engagement with contemporary political developments.[23] How might we read Keats's work on *The Fall of Hyperion* in terms of his thinking about celebrity and about reader–writer relationships within celebrity culture? As he adds a dream-narrative frame to *Hyperion*, Keats refashions poetic personality by opening up a space for the reader in the poem. In this later poem about poetic vocation, the immediate backdrop of Keats's specific literary community so prominent in *Sleep and Poetry* falls away, so that the poet seems to speak not from an identifiable place within the literary scene but from a barely localized modernity. Where *Sleep and Poetry* makes allusions to specific personalities in Keats's literary world—Hunt, the Lake Poets, Byron—the *Fall* speaks in terms of historically inclusive categories—"dreamers" or "poets" or "all mock lyrists, large self worshippers, / And careless hectorers in proud bad verse" (1:207–8). But while the trappings of the literary system of the early nineteenth century have no obvious presence in the poem, the poem works aggressively to take advantage of the kind of celebrity effects the literary system generates. Moments of impersonality or self-effacement are put to work to produce a form of charisma for the poet (and, I'll argue, for the reader as well). In a pattern the obituaries capitalize on, the persona's move toward self-effacement generates a sense of the poet's auratic and seductive presence. The poet's experiments in this later poem with forms of self-loss or self-effacement grow out of a difficult and complex philosophical struggle around notions of self and empathy for which our convenient shorthand expressions are "negative capability" and "camelion poetics," and I would not want to argue that Keats experiments with these forms only strategically. But I do want to emphasize the way these experiments in self-effacement make use of the kind of absorption of the poetic "I" that bedevils *Sleep and Poetry*.

Ross Chambers shows how the nineteenth-century "art story" produces authority through a tactic of seduction, through the manipulation of the reader's desire.[24] As nineteenth-century fiction feels itself less assured of "some sort of 'natural' thirst for information" that earlier forms of storytelling could take for granted, fiction writers shift the object of the reader's curiosity or fascination from the information being communicated to the narrating instance itself: what Chambers calls "narratorial" authority, or the "art" of seduction, which can then be seen as both the product of the alienated conditions of modern literature and literature's self-aware attempt "to realize the potential for value that that alienation confers on it."[25] Keats's later poetry similarly shifts readerly fascination from personality itself onto the devices through which personality seduces.

This strategy works because of the way the reader is called in to occupy the place of the poetic persona, so that we put ourselves in the posture of Keats as a reader. (This reader-writer relationship is exactly the opposite of *Sleep and Poetry*, in which we are called in to witness Keats's vocational election but excluded from identification by the relentlessly personalizing voice of the poem). This exchange is most marked in the most famous passage where, watching the frozen shapes of Saturn, Thea, and Moneta, the poet takes on the suffering he witnesses as his own burden. Keats here combines the two modes of personality I identified in *Sleep and Poetry*, heroic autonomy and absorptive anonymity:

> A long awful time
> I look'd upon them; still they were the same;
> The frozen God still bending to the earth,
> And the sad Goddess weeping at his feet;
> Moneta silent. Without stay or prop
> But my own weak mortality, I bore
> The load of this eternal quietude,
> The unchanging gloom, and the three fixed shapes
> Ponderous upon my senses a whole moon.
> For by my burning brain I measured sure
> Her silver seasons shedded on the night,
> And every day by day methought I grew
> More gaunt and ghostly. Oftentimes I pray'd
> Intense, that death would take me from the vale
> And all its burthens. Gasping with despair
> Of change, hour after hour I curs'd myself
>
> (1.384–99)

The poet's somatic responses to the scene before him become the object of his own self-fascinated gaze. His "weak mortality" is framed as a spectacle—his feverishly "burning brain," his "gaunt and ghostly" body "gasping." Growing "gaunt" *and* "ghostly" at once, the poet becomes simultaneously *more* and *less* embodied, his ghostliness emphasizing his growing power and his gauntness emphasizing, as the obituaries will, the captivating power of the wasted but self-disciplining body. Encouraged by our knowledge of

Keats's own pathos-laden story, we are drawn to the intensity of the poet's fevered experience even as we feel that experience is beyond us, the poet's burden or privilege.

But if this scene bears the pressure of Keats's personality, it produces its intense affective charge in part because of the way the "I" in the scene is emptied of its proper significance—becomes a kind of surrogate for the reader, or more precisely, becomes identified with a reading consciousness that is both ours and Keats's at once. The "burning brain," at the same time that it is charged with the affective response the reader is asked to share, is emptied out as the stage or screen of the reader's experience of the passage (it is what we look *through* to see this, and where all this, in the dream-vision, happens). The figure of the "burning brain" thus moves in seemingly opposite directions: on the one hand toward the imagined reality of the fevered Keats writing—and as Geoffrey Hartman has shown, to the figurality of "fever" in Keats's writing—and on the other hand toward the flat surface of the page itself, from which we reanimate this scene.[26] The "burning brain" is like a cipher in which we recognize our otherness as readers in this scene. In the "burning brain" passage, Keats redeploys the ghostliness—the impersonality, abstraction and unrealness—of mass-market subjectivity to serve his own ends, making palpable the harrowing experience that is to certify his distinction as a poet. The effacement of self-identity in Keats's absorption in the Titans' tragedy generates powerful personality effects.

The alternation of day and night that marks the experience of time in the passage is paralleled by the movement of the reader's eye across the words and spaces on the page (this effect is particularly prominent in "day by day," "hour after hour"). It is the temporality of reading—our forward movement through the lines—that gives us our experience both of duration and change here, the tropism across the lines that helps us experience the change the passage acts out: the poet's difficult growth in power and sympathetic reach through this exercise of mental concentration, at once disciplined and indulgent. "Measured sure" reminds us that the dramatic effects of this passage are achieved by the technically adept contrast of the suspension of movement (leaving the reader also "gasping with despair of change") against the forward movement of the measures of the poem, a tension of movement and stasis reinforced by the passage's parallel phrasing and intense assonance and alliteration.

As we fixate on his figure, we are here encouraged to stand in Keats's place, drawn emotionally into the scene of his reading, of his authority, insofar as his ghostliness makes room for us, as it were. Our involvement in the poem, like the poet's involvement in Moneta's drama, is encouraged by the way the poem seems to draw no firm boundaries between events and the memory of events, or events and their imaginative re-enactment, so that reading and experience are drawn together. The scenes Moneta remembers are "still swooning" in her brain: historical knowledge itself unfolds in an open-ended time, a temporality that connects the dreamer's experience and the scenes he will see (1.245). When Moneta grants him entry into the scenes of the tragedy, the poet tells us, "there grew / A power within me of enormous ken, / To see as a God sees, and take the depth / Of things as nimbly as the outward eye / Can size and shape pervade. The lofty theme / At those few words hung vast before my mind, / With half unravel'd web" (1.302–8). These lines move dizzyingly across divisions between inside and outside, repeating the way, throughout the poem, mental "space" takes on a topography and external topographies are seen as aspects of mind. (Thus, the "lofty theme" hangs not before the speaker's eyes, but his mind). The half-unravel'd web suggests a parallel reversibility: does the dreamer need to re-weave the web or further unravel it, as one would a mystery? Does the unraveling obscure the full meaning of the "theme," or is the unraveling itself a point of entry—for the poet and for the reader—into the process of meaning-making?

Keats's fragment "This living hand, now warm and capable" sensationalizes the kind of exchange between reader and writer I am suggesting *The Fall*'s dream-vision frame puts into motion. The fragment paradoxically and unnervingly appears to use the spatial or temporal distance between the moment of writing and the moment of reading to register the felt presence of the reader to the writer and the writer to the reader:

> This living hand, now warm and capable
> Of earnest grasping, would, if it were cold
> And in the icy silence of the tomb,
> So haunt thy days and chill thy dreaming nights
> That thou would wish thine own heart dry of blood,

So in my veins red life might stream again,
And thou be conscience-calm'd. See, here it is—
I hold it towards you.

The fragment's affective claims on the reader are intensified by the impossibility of deciding its referential context. The historical accident that deprives these lines of an authorially imposed frame means that we are confronted with the knowledge the lines allegorize: the knowledge, that is, that no voice, intent or consciousness (but our own) animates the lines whose address finds us and which have the power to disturb us with their aggressive insistence on their living presence. As the readers of this "hand," however, we stand accused by it insofar as the mere possibility of a reader refers all writing to a future in which the writer is dead, in which the "now warm and capable" body is no longer.[27]

One of the possible intended contexts for these lines—the uncompleted drama *King Stephen*—suggests the term "usurpation" as a name for the process of reading this poem: the poem dramatizes the reader's usurpation of the authorial voice, the transference of animating power to the reader. Our experience of self-recognition in the "thou" of the poem, though probably inevitable, is still doubly fictitious, since to recognize ourselves as the poem's addressee requires both freezing the lines as lyric address and ignoring the rhetoricity of the address, which renders the reader—the "thou"—as a trope. The dramatic turn in the last lines—"See, here it is— / I hold it towards you"—is so troubling because it confronts us with exactly this knowledge, since the "it" sounds no longer like a "living hand" that is part of a living body, but rather like a hand cut off from the speaker who holds it toward the addressee. The hand held toward us is no longer a synecdoche for a living, speaking, warm and capable totality but a mute object, a sign that hands we take as emblems of our living wholeness are in fact only emblems. Our pretension to self-presence is contradicted by the same deictics that call us so forcefully into the scene of reading.

Given the history of Keats's reception, it is hard to avoid making Keats's own death in some way part of the content of this fragment. But we might also see this fragment as responding not to intimations of mortality, but to the pressure of readerly demand. In almost a parody of Byronic procedure, the fragment gives readers exactly what they desire—the thrill of contact ("I hold it towards you") —and then lampoons them for wishing for it, even while it holds them in thrall. But of course, as I have already noted, neither this fragment nor *The Fall of Hyperion* were published until long after Keats's death, and it is not clear that Keats would have sought publication for these texts, at least as they stand. Given the privileging of the posthumous in our reading of Keats, the delayed itinerary of these texts enhances their value and authority for many lovers of the poet: they have a message-in-a-bottle effect that seems to speak with greater intimacy to us, to accord us greater privilege than Keats's original unknowing public. What looks like Keatsian prescience is an effect of our own hindsight.[28]

It is good to keep in mind, then, that if these poems seem to resonate so powerfully with our own attachments to Keats they may not have finally been seen in the same terms by Keats himself. After all, he gave up on *The Fall*, and we do not know what he planned for "This living hand." Bate sees the shift in political climate prompting Keats's abandonment of *The Fall* in the days just after Henry Hunt's entry into London: in Bate's argument, the "tragic vision" developed in Keats's revisions clashed with the spirit of post-Peterloo progressive politics, an enthusiasm Keats's letters reveal him to have caught.[29] We might speculate as well that after watching the crowds attendant on Hunt's entry Keats thinks anew about possibilities for public address, public influence and public acclaim (a month later, as we have seen, he is still thinking about how a "really fine" writer might be "cheered by a mob as good as Hunt").[30] Keats is at this point under financial strain, and on the verge of deciding, reluctantly, to "traffic" in periodical writing, "on the liberal side of the question, for whoever will pay me" (*KL* II, 178, 176). His hopes for commercial literary success are pinned at the time on his new romance, *Lamia*, and on the play he is finishing, *Otho the Great*, the success of which he hopes will lift him "out of the mire of a bad reputation which is continually rising against me," as he tells the George Keatses in a letter of 17–27 September (*KL* II, 185–6). In a letter to Richard Woodhouse begun the same day (21 September) that he announces to Reynolds his intention to give up *Hyperion* (and transcribing both *To Autumn* and the "induction" to *The Fall*), Keats declines publishing the too "smokeable" romance *Isabella*, declaring "I intend to use more finesse with the public" (*KL* II, 174). *The Fall* may have been dropped as poor strategy, lacking what he asserts *Lamia* does have, "that sort of fire in it which must take hold of people in some way, give them either a pleasant or unpleasant sensation" since "what they want is a sensation of some sort" (*KL* II, 189; *Lamia* would lead the title of the 1820 volume).[31]

My claims for *The Fall* are thus limited: I treat it not as an end-point in Keats's development but as an experiment, one that reflects his sophisticated and ambitious thinking about the forging of writer-reader relationships in a literary marketplace structured by new forms of celebrity. In its ability to charge the scene of reading with affect, his experimentation with novel personality effects in fragments like *The Fall* and "This living hand" looks like a success from our perspective, but our perspective is one shaped by a reception history that has operated out of Keats's control. Neither publication history, reception history nor authorial intention stands fully determinative of meaning or value, of course. While living, Keats inspired fierce devotion among a close circle of friends, but wider fame had to await the efforts of memorialists writing after his death. Like Shelley's, Keats's posthumous celebrity has been characterized by the passionate attachments of readers to the poet as well as to his poetry: the poet becomes an object of intense and complicated feeling.[32] The readings in this chapter have aimed to show Keats actively negotiating the terms of such celebrity, not through an investment in a culture of posterity, but rather through the tactical management of his relationship to a contemporary culture of fame.

3
The Cenci's Celebrity

The image of Shelley as a poet unconcerned with contemporary fame maintains a remarkable tenacity, such that his popular image might still be summed up by the description of him in Edward Trelawny's 1878 *Records of Shelley, Byron and the Author*: "Whilst he lived, his works fell still-born from the press; he never complained of the world's neglect, or expressed any other feeling than surprise at the rancorous abuse wasted on an author who had no readers." Trelawny's description in essence, of course, describes a claim *to* celebrity—a celebrity Shelley maintains despite, or even because of, his lack of readers, and a celebrity Trelawny hoped would sell copies of his memoir. Trelawny indeed continues his account of Shelley's indifference to fame by quoting a telling conversation with the poet: "'But for the reviewers,' he said, laughing, 'I should be entirely unknown.' 'But for them,' I observed, 'Williams and I would never have crossed the Alps in chase of you. Our curiosity as sportsmen was excited to see and have a shot at so strange a monster as they represented you to be.'"[1]

Couched in the leisured language of genteel sportsmanship, Trelawny's account of Shelley's notoriety nicely captures the fraught interdependence of the relationships among the expatriate poet, the reviewing system in Britain, and the public of curious readers (readers of reviews, at least, if not of poems). Thanks to several excellent recent accounts of the way Shelley addresses a range of potential reading publics, we now have a strong sense of the urgency of Shelley's attempted negotiations among both real and imagined audiences, and of the complexity of these audiences themselves.[2]

In this chapter, I offer an account of Shelley's *The Cenci* (1819) that builds on this scholarship through a consideration of the problem of authorial charisma and its cognate, readerly fascination.

Shelley wrote *The Cenci* in the summer of 1819, between work on the third and fourth acts of *Prometheus Unbound*, whose "beautiful idealisms" he says are meant for "the highly refined imaginations of the more select classes of poetical readers."[3] While *Prometheus* would help secure Shelley's posthumous fame as a poet of sensation, Shelley imagined his sensational revenge tragedy garnering more immediate popular acclaim. The preface to the printed version of the play makes it clear that Shelley is banking on the appeal the sensational story has already demonstrated in Italy, where, the preface tells us, "the story of the Cenci was a subject not to be mentioned [...] without awakening a deep and breathless interest. [...] All ranks of people knew the outlines of this history, and participated in the overwhelming interest which it seems to have had the magic of exciting in the human heart."[4] The celebrity of the Cenci story is tied to the fame of Guido Reni's portrait of *la bella parricida*, already one of the most renowned pictures in the city when Shelley arrived in Rome. Like so many nineteenth-century literati, Shelley found himself absorbed by the painting and the story behind it: Trelawny reports Shelley telling him "the image of Beatrice haunted me after seeing her portrait."[5] Shelley's interest in the story is primarily political and ethical: the horror of Beatrice's experience, the example of her resistance to tyrannical authority, and the moral issues raised by her actions clearly drive Shelley's writing. But Shelley's play reflects at the same time a fascination with the way in which readers can be "haunted" by stories, a deep concern with the ethics and structure of readerly fascination itself.[6] As it draws on and refashions the celebrity of its heroine, *The Cenci* also examines the structure of the mass-market celebrity with which it works: the celebrity of cultural objects, such as the captivating portrait and the absorbing tale, as well as the celebrity (or notoriety) of persons, such as the iconic Beatrice and the romantic poet himself.

In a letter to Thomas Love Peacock, Shelley described *The Cenci* as a teaser to engage the attention of a broad audience. Writing from Italy to direct his literary affairs in England, he tells Peacock he has "taken some pains to make [the] play fit for representation," asserting that "as a composition, it is certainly not inferior to any of the modern plays that have been acted, with the exception of [Coleridge's] *Remorse*; that the interest of the plot is incredibly greater and more real; and that there is nothing beyond what the multitude are contented to believe that they can understand, either in imagery, opinion, or sentiment."[7] He outfits the play with the requisite Gothic elements—a dark old castle, a beautiful maiden—and he hopes to recruit the famous actress Eliza O'Neill to play Beatrice's part. Though the question of the incest gives him some anxiety, Shelley claims to have treated the subject with "peculiar delicacy." He asks that the play be submitted anonymously to the Covent Garden theater, and—not committing himself too far—he tells Peacock that "after it had been acted, and successfully (could I hope for such a thing), I would own it if I pleased, & use the celebrity it might acquire to my own purposes."[8] It is a commonplace about celebrity that it can be experienced as a dispossession of self; here, Shelley anticipates that dispossession by describing it as a strategy of dispossessing his work. He disowns his play in advance and scripts "the celebrity it might acquire" as something *out there*, not as an attribute of self but as an alienable possession belonging to the work. Shelley's remark signals a curiously conflicted attitude. Even as he marks out celebrity as his object, he tries to pull off a stance of indifference: the celebrity of the play is after all not Shelley's ultimate object but really a way to further his "own purposes." Shelley doesn't spell out what these purposes are; presumably, he wants to secure demand for poems like *Prometheus* as well as an audience for his political and philosophical writing. But the vagueness that characterizes his bravado in the letter to Peacock also suggests a degree of uncertainty as to what his purposes might or should be.

On one level, this uncertainty points to a historically specific instability in the category of authorship at the moment of a rapidly expanding, radically fragmented literary market. But it also reflects the fact that Shelley writes at a moment in the unfolding of his own literary career when his notoriety far outstrips the actual readership he has secured. Confronted with the spectacular career of his friend and rival Byron and, even closer to home, the popular success of Mary Shelley's *Frankenstein* (1818), by 1819 Percy Shelley was famous mostly as a democrat, an atheist and an associate of Leigh Hunt.[9] Shelley's *Alastor, or the Spirit of Solitude, and Other Poems* (1816) had received a smattering of mixed, mostly baffled reviews, and Hunt's politically oriented

Examiner was printing and promoting Shelley's poetry. Personality attacks on Shelley in the reviews were only just heating up, but Shelley figured as a secondary target to Hunt in *Blackwood's* "Cockney School" assault in full swing in 1818–19.[10] Gossip swirled around his connection to Byron—when the Shelley party met up with Byron at the Villa Diodati in Switzerland curious tourists rented telescopes to watch the goings-on—and the scandal attaching to his elopement with Mary, the subsequent suicide of his first wife, Harriet, and the 1817 Chancery trial which granted custody of his children to Harriet's relatives.[11] In some British circles, at least, Shelley's atheism and his free-love theories (and supposed practices) were notorious.[12] James Chandler comments of Shelley, "one of the most celebrated atheists of the day," that "readers probably knew more about his atheism than his poetry," and Shelley of course played up this role, from getting expelled from Oxford for *The Necessity of Atheism* in 1811 to inscribing himself in hotel registers on his trip across the Alps in 1816, "Democrat, Philanthropist, Atheist" (in Greek)—scandal dutifully reported back to England.[13] At this point in his career, Shelley's "purposes" are difficult for him to formulate with certainty because the term masks the way he writes in tactical response to changing and unpredictable situations within the literary field and the (counter)public sphere.[14] Seeking an effective oppositional public voice that can organize and move a national will, Shelley has no easy map to follow. He must negotiate a social terrain in which public visibility is at once necessary to and at odds with his "purposes."[15]

Stuck in Italy and frustrated with Regency politics and his own prospects, Shelley, I hypothesize, may have found in his vengeful heroine and the revenge tragedy form she acts out both a liberating fantasy of consequential action in England—if only action on the stage—and the fantasy of trying on Beatrice's charisma. In the end, the play would go more than half a century before making it to the stage in a Shelley Society production in 1886. Published by Ollier in 1820, the play's initial print run of 250 sold out, prompting a second edition, an unusually good showing for Shelley but hardly electrifying.[16] The play however frames the question that confronts Shelley in 1819 as he considers the relationship between his writing and its social effects: how to mount an effective public voice against tyranny. As Georgia Strand and Sarah Zimmerman have suggested, what Beatrice has that Shelley wants might be not just a valuable political allegory but also the ability to hold an audience spellbound. What gives the Beatrice of the play this spellbinding capability goes beyond the melodramatic shock value of her "story" and Shelley's imagination of the psychological complexity of her character, impressive as both these are. Rather, I will argue, it is what—in the play as in the portrait—she can't or won't tell us about her own desire that drives the readerly curiosity of her audiences.

Following Earl Wasserman's landmark discussion of the play, Beatrice is often read from the perspective of Shelley's Preface, which etherealizes Beatrice as a transcendently pure "spirit," so that the problem for criticism becomes how to reconcile Beatrice's innocent "essential nature" with the "moral error" she commits in giving way to what Wasserman calls a "subliminal impulse" toward revenge.[17] This line of criticism crucially overlooks the link between Beatrice's desire and readerly desire that I think is very much at issue in Shelley's representation of Beatrice, and it misses the force and the danger, for Shelley, of Beatrice's charisma. I begin by discussing the play's representation of the female subject's relation to language, desire and the law, demonstrating the connection between these issues and the questions of moral authority, public visibility, and charismatic seduction I have begun to raise. The chapter then moves outward to examine the way the play and its preface function within some of the cultural contexts of the play's production and publication, contexts through which the "celebrity" of the play, its heroine and its author are constituted: the trade in print reproductions through which Beatrice's portrait is circulated; the reviewing system that exercises profound influence over the capital of names in the literary market; and the culture of Shakespearean quotation that emerges around Shakespeare's celebrity.

The Cenci is remarkable in its effort to emphasize the historical specificity of Beatrice's situation. The complicated construction of Beatrice as a public figure *within* the play cannot be separated from Shelley's attempt to demonstrate that, as Steven Goldsmith puts it, "all language is embedded in specific social circumstance, or more accurately, in the historical relations of power."[18] The salient quality of his historical setting is the Baroque excess that is practically fetishized in Shelley's description of his subjects' Catholicism:

> To a Protestant apprehension there will appear something unnatural in the earnest and perpetual sentiment of the relations

> between God and men which pervade the tragedy of the Cenci. It will especially be startled at the combination of an undoubting persuasion of the truth of the popular religion with a cool and determined perseverance in enormous guilt. [...] The most atrocious villain may be rigidly devout, and without any shock to established faith, confess himself to be so. Religion pervades intensely the whole frame of society, and is according to the temper of the mind which it inhabits, a passion, a persuasion, an excuse, a refuge; never a check.
>
> (p. 241)

To the apprehension of Shelley's contemporaries, the play's portrayal of Catholic belief will look like superstition; to our eyes, its evocation of the Baroque may sound curiously wondrous; Baroque Italy, juxtaposed against the disenchanted world of Protestant England, seems to hold not just aesthetic interest but the appeal of aesthetic, if not logical, coherence. The Baroque setting is formally resonant, and by focusing for the moment on its connection to the Baroque, I hope to tease out some of the connections the play makes among the father's law, the daughter's sexuality, power, language and silence—the curious combination of powerlessness and power, including power over her readers, embodied in the figure of Beatrice.[19] Beatrice might be usefully compared to a number of predecessors on the Baroque stage (Beatrice-Joanna in *The Changeling*, for example), but perhaps the most striking comparison is to the heroines of Calderón's plays. In Mary Shelley's "Note on The Cenci" in her edition of her late husband's works, she reports that Shelley was "making a study of Calderon at the time" he wrote *The Cenci*, "reading his best tragedies with an accomplished lady living near us, to whom his letter from Leghorn was addressed during the following year."[20] Though she and Percy Shelley both go out of their way to deny any influence of Calderón on the play except for one "plagiarism" of a few lines, such denials suggest there's more to the relationship than meets the eye, just as Mary seems to think there's more to Percy's Calderón study sessions than she'd like.

Two plays of Calderón seem to me to have been particularly relevant to Percy Shelley's thinking about *The Cenci*: *La Vida es Sueño* (*Life's a Dream*) and *La Devoción de la Cruz* (*Devotion to the Cross*).[21] Both plays center on the witting or unwitting cruelty of fathers. In each of these plays, which mix romance and revenge forms, a female heroine steps into a characteristically male role to set the revenge plot in motion. Though Calderón's irony seems very distant from Shelley's intense seriousness, that tonal difference can in fact help open up our reading of Shelley's play. In *Life's a Dream,* Rosaura comes stumbling (literally) onto the stage in the opening scene disguised as a man; she has come to revenge herself on the lover who abandoned her. In the intricate plot of *Devotion to the Cross,* Julia's brother challenges her lover, Eusebio, and Eusebio kills him; after Eusebio flees, Julia enters a convent, but then takes off, like her lover, to become a bandit and, in language Cenci echoes, the "terror of the world, the cutting shears of Fate."[22] Each play ends with the revelation of genealogical narratives that had been kept both from the younger characters and, for the most part, from the audience: Julia and Eusebio turn out to be brother and sister (they have matching birthmarks in the shape of the cross), and Rosaura discovers that Clotaldo, by whom she has been arrested, is her father. The incestuous tension between Clotaldo and Rosaura, like what turns out to have been an incestuous relationship between Julia and Eusebio, underscores the structure of repetition in the plays: incest figures the oppressive pressure of history on the present. The concealment of these genealogical or dynastic narratives means that action in the play is entrapped by structures of repetition that only become clear after (and indeed because) the characters act. A neat emblem for the connection of blindness and agency is the sword Rosaura carries, which was left behind by her father when he deserted her mother. As Rosaura relates the story, when she sets off for Poland to pursue her errant lover, her mother tells her to carry the sword, assuring her that in Poland it would be recognized by someone who can help her; Rosaura does not know who or why. Unable to interpret her situation herself, she depends on Clotaldo to recognize the sword (and so to recognize his daughter and thus his own relation to events). Rosaura's sword is an emblem for the fatality of repetition itself, repetition which both marks and enacts the restoration of the law of the father.

In each play, the revenge tragedy plot is driven by the daughter's desire. The daughter breaks with the father's law by temporarily taking on the role of the vengeful *son* who replaces the father: in Mary Jacobus's phrase, the daughter breaks with the desire of the father by "choosing to be 'like himself' instead of what he likes."[23] In so doing, the daughter, acting out the force of repetition, becomes the agent through whose actions the father's law is ultimately restored. Silhouetted against the background of the Baroque revenge tragedy, it is easier to see Beatrice's desire for revenge—or for a revenge tragedy—not as the sudden impingement of an impulse from outside, as Wasserman would have it, but as consistent with structures of desire produced through the textual (and generic) structures of which her character is an effect (indeed, it is paradoxically the consciousness of being a writing effect that seems at times to inspire Beatrice's despair: "What are the words which you would have me speak?," she cries out bitterly to her stepmother after the rape [3.1.107]). From this perspective, then, it is easier to read her as the subject of desire, and to see that it is the possibility of her desire, even desire for the father, that the play finds it impossible to speak until what she wants is the revenge tragedy plot. Like Rosaura and Julia, Beatrice moves to take control of the plot she finds herself in, casting herself in the role of revenge tragedy heroine, only to discover that she has an impossible relation to her own story. The play makes Beatrice's desire the figure that might answer for a whole series of pressing, but in the end unanswerable, questions of causality: the question of causality in Count Cenci's actions (is she in some way seduced?); the question of how and in what sense the trauma "transforms" Beatrice; the relationship between Cenci's actions and Beatrice's parricidal plot. The ultimate opacity of Beatrice's desire (and its impossible relation to her father's desire) figures the fundamental opacity of the processes of repetition that drive the play's plots of incest and parricide, and, more broadly, the processes of repetition that structure history itself.[24]

The problem of causal relation is one the play underlines through its rhetoric of superstition and through allusion to the Shakespearean supernatural, the *locus classicus* of uncanny causality: "strange thoughts beget strange deeds," the Papal legate comments wryly when Cenci's murder is discovered (4.4.138–9). Superstition pervades the play, and expressions of horror within the play tend to take on a strangely supernatural cast; throughout the play, what's thought or imagined acts forcefully on reality. Cenci's assertions of power themselves trouble the boundary between the natural and the supernatural, between the immateriality of thought and the materiality of the world of things: Cenci (like Macbeth before him) talks as if his words could almost animate the inanimate. Cenci says of the Castle of Petrella that "its thick towers never told tales; though they have heard and seen what might make dumb things speak" and warns Lucretia that he will take her "where you may persuade / The stones you tread on to deliver you" (2.1.170–3, 163–4), but his sarcasm here only seems to reinforce the idea that his "deformity" is so enormous that it might in fact make dumb things speak: "thou most silent air, that shalt not hear / What now I think! Thou, pavement, which I tread / towards her chamber—let your echoes talk / Of my imperious step scorning surprise, / But not of my intent!" (1.2.140–4). Beatrice later experiences Cenci's imposition of his will as just such a warping of the concrete world around her: "The pavement sinks under my feet! The walls / Spin round!" (3.1.8–9). Cenci's conjuring of the inanimate only increases in ambition over the course of the play, culminating in his Lear-like father's curses. The intense pressure that seems to push the spirit world into embodiment corresponds to the pressure on the gap between desire and action, a gap that insists rhetorically through the frequency of the conditional and of the subjunctive. (The emblematic instance is Cenci's echo of Macbeth—"Would that it were done!" [2.1.193]—itself echoed within the play by Lucretia as she waits for word of Cenci's death [4.3.40]). The play is dominated by the language of wishes and wish-fulfillment and by the language of dreams (most notably in Beatrice's nightmares and visions). In perhaps the most eerie intimation of what seems to be Cenci's supernatural agency, he wishes his sons dead and almost immediately receives news that they have perished in freak accidents; though he's delighted, the coincidence seems to unsettle even him.

The rape is the textual site at which relations of cause and effect are rendered most acutely problematic. In the play, the rape itself happens offstage, and like Beatrice, the play never names the crime of which Beatrice is the victim. (The manuscript account from which Shelley worked also names a number of other crimes, most prominently sodomy, that Shelley leaves out.)[25] The occluded relations of cause and effect are intimated in an exchange between Beatrice and her stepmother Lucretia in the "mad scene" following the rape, when Lucretia, realizing that Beatrice is experiencing post-traumatic shock, observes that "her spirit apprehends the sense of pain, / But not its cause; suffering has dried away / The source from which it sprung" (3.1.34–6). Beatrice responds by redirecting Lucretia's genetic figure:

> BEATRICE. Like Parricide ...
> Misery has killed its father, yet its father
> never like mine ...
> Oh, God! What thing am I?
>
> (3.1.37–40)

In Beatrice's simile, which comes before the parricidal plot itself is even articulated, trauma is, strangely, structured like parricide. As William Jewett suggests, it is almost as if the figure sets in motion its own eventual literalization.[26]

Or perhaps the father is already in a sense dead, having broken the very prohibition on which his law is erected. If language is structured by the law of the father, then the rape would be unspeakable precisely because incestuous rape undoes the very conditions of speech. In the seminar on ethics, Lacan in fact describes "the prohibition of incest" as "nothing other than the condition sine qua non of speech."[27] Beatrice herself protests that the crime is literally unspeakable—there is no language for it—and that, if spoken, its effects would be merely sensational:

> If I could find a word that might make known
> The crime of my destroyer; and that done
> My tongue should like a knife tear out the secret
> Which cankers my heart's core; aye, lay all bare
> So that my unpolluted fame should be
> With vilest gossips a stale mouthed story
> A mock, a bye word, an astonishment:
> If this were done, which never shall be done,
> Think of the offender's gold, his dreaded hate,
> And the strange horror of the accuser's tale,
> Baffling belief, and overpowering speech;
> Scarce whispered, unimaginable, wrapt
> In hideous hints ... Oh, most assured redress!
>
> (3.1.154–66)

Lacking the narrative resources of the Romantic poet who can relate the "strange horror" of the tale with Shelley's "peculiar delicacy," Beatrice fears that the secret, if it could be spoken, would be too easy *and* too horrible to retell, or too easy to retell because so horrible to retell, at once a "stale mouthed story" and "scarce whispered." In her initial daze after the rape, she imagines herself precisely as a character in the stories other people tell: "I thought I was that wretched Beatrice / Men speak of" (3.1.42–3). The retelling of her story by others becomes a kind of extended figure for the way she herself is cut off from language, an estrangement echoed in her angry reply to her stepmother's questioning after the rape— "What are the words which you would have me speak?" (3.1.107).

Lucretia, in the mad scene after the rape, asks Beatrice no less than six different times what has happened. The play's elaborate attention to the way characters stop short of telling the full story works to focus our attention on their barely concealed desire for *more*:

> ORSINO. Know that since we met
> Cenci has done an outrage to his daughter.
>
> GIACOMO. What outrage?
>
> ORSINO. That she speaks not, but you may
> Conceive such half conjectures as I do,
> From her fixed paleness, and the lofty grief
> Of her stern brow bent on the idle air,
> And her severe unmodulated voice,
> Drowning both tenderness and dread; and last
> From this: that whilst her step-mother and I,
> Bewildered in our horror, talked together
> With obscure hints; both self-misunderstood
> And darkly guessing, stumbling, in our talk,
> Over the truth, and yet to its revenge,
> She interrupted us, and with a look
> Which told before she spoke it, he must die...
>
> (3.1.349–58)

In Orsino's description, "Beatrice" becomes a signature style of performance—a collection of clichéd attitudes and gestures—that provokes its listeners not just to revenge but to a fever pitch of hermeneutic desire.

What is it that these readers want to know? Contributing to the play's scandal might be the repressed imagination of Beatrice's sexual curiosity, or more accurately, the way that imagination is uncomfortably mirrored in the desire to know that Beatrice's story provokes in its listeners—their intense desire to hear the details of the story, the narrative fascination that the story produces, even the inevitability with which a person (like Shelley himself) "becomes" a story. In Mary Shelley's *Matilda* (1819), a tale of father-daughter incest she writes around the time her husband completes his play, the daughter has a "frantic curiosity" to know her father's secret—a secret that turns out to be his incestuous desire for her.[28] In *The Cenci*, the scandalous curiosity that the play needs to leave unthinkable in Beatrice's case is displaced onto her over-eager, fascinated, star-struck readers.

Beatrice's initial cry for revenge after she's raped uses one of Shelley's favorite tropes for revolutionary action, lightning: "Something must be done; / What, yet I know not … something which shall make / The thing I have suffered but a shadow / In the dread lightning which avenges it; / Brief, rapid, irreversible, destroying / The consequence of what it cannot cure" (3.1.85–90).[29] Lightning figures action both as an absolute interruption of historical sequence and as impersonal, as something that exceeds human agency and intention (even the connection between the "dread lightning" and the "something" that needs to be done is rendered somewhat ambiguous by the tortured syntax of the lines). The ellipses replicate the gap in traumatic experience, structuring the subject's relation to action as itself impossible to represent or know. Later in the same scene, Beatrice, speaking "half to herself," again stresses the need to take action, this time internalizing the language of lightning and shadow into the ghostly representation of thought: "All must be suddenly resolved and done. / What is this undistinguishable mist / Of thoughts, which rise, like shadow after shadow, / Darkening each other?" (3.1.169–72). Retiring "absorbed in thought," Beatrice makes her decision and suddenly re-emerges to declare it as unequivocal: "I have prayed / To God, and I have talked with my own heart, / And have unravelled my entangled will, / And have at length determined what is right" (3.1.218–21).

The fractured language of Beatrice's speech following the rape allows Shelley to experiment with a tense syntactical dynamics—one that proves quotable, and potentially marketable—as well as with the representation of psychic fragmentation under the pressure of traumatic experience. But the scene I've just described, like the play as a whole, gestures conspicuously toward a psychology to which the play's readers and spectators are offered no access. Indeed, what's striking about this scene is that while Beatrice is making the fateful decision, she is off to the side of the stage, silent, while Lucretia and Orsino stand in the foreground bickering about whether they should rely on themselves or on providential intervention to redress their wrong. Beatrice, strangely, almost never speaks in soliloquy, though other characters (Cenci, Orsino, Giacomo) often do.[30] Even though Beatrice, like her whole family, is supposed to suffer from compulsive "self-anatomy," the play seems to resist developing her as a psychological subject. It is not that she becomes a cliché or automaton, but simply that her character remains to an important degree psychologically opaque.[31]

This psychological opacity makes Beatrice a powerful object of what we could call the pathos of failed identification, and at the same time a powerful object of readerly curiosity. Beatrice's character both demands the identificatory gesture of sympathy and refuses to grant it traction. The inquisitorial court's demand that she confess her crime shadows the reader's demand (tell us what you felt, what you thought), and in both cases Beatrice refuses to tell. Because of this simultaneous gesturing toward and hollowing-out of psychological depth, Beatrice's "character" becomes a form— "a mask and a mantle"—that others can step into and embody: the actress Eliza O'Neill in her sublime performance; Claire Clairmont, who in a letter to Byron describes herself as Beatrice and Byron as Cenci; and Shelley himself, who famously takes on the voice of his heroine in a livid letter responding to the news of the Peterloo massacre. When Shelley responds to the news in a letter to Ollier on 6 September 1819, he does so in the voice of Beatrice, who herself echoes hear—"Something must be done [...] I know not yet what"—and he repeats the phrase in a letter to Peacock on 21 September.[32] Shelley inhabits the position of Beatrice in order to discover his relation, or really non-relation, to historical events. The self-quotation (unattributed but in quotation marks) has an oddly proleptic quality to it, since the letter's recipient cannot have read the play yet, and so will only be able to recognize the quotation at some later point. Beatrice will thus seem to echo Shelley's letter, rather than the letter echoing the play.[33]

Indeed, Beatrice, who often speaks on behalf of others, sometimes seems like a figure *for* the displacement of voice: Beatrice's plea to her father's guests—"O, think!" —recalls Isabella's plea in her suit to Angelo in *Measure for Measure*—"O, think on that!" (2.2.77)—and this echo seems to insist that the reader think back to the many ventriloquisms in Shakespeare's play, where Isabella speaks not only on her brother's behalf but with Lucio whispering suggestions in her ear, imploring her in Claudio's voice ("implore her, in my voice" [1.3.170]).[34] Where Isabella, successfully warding off the threat of sexual violence, acts on behalf of self-absenting male authority to repair a broken social order, Beatrice is both the subject and the indirect agent of the kind of violence that is kept away from Isabella's person. Shelley's explicit echoes of *Measure for Measure* underline, however, that as with Isabella we have little sense of what Beatrice is actually thinking, or of whether, and when, she's speaking for herself—and what that would mean.

The opacity I have identified is only exacerbated by Beatrice's refusal, in the final acts of the play, to admit any guilt for the murder of her father. In a cruel irony, a Papal legate arrives with a warrant for Cenci's arrest just after he is murdered, and the family is taken to Rome on strong suspicion of their guilt. Dragged before the inquisitorial court, Beatrice shows no remorse, and in fact consigns the hired murderer Marzio to his death at the rack rather than admit her part in the conspiracy. It is clear that Beatrice inherits her father's penchant for acting a role; what's at issue here for me is not so much whether or not Beatrice is putting on an act but rather what kind of act she is putting on.[35] Beatrice repeatedly rephrases the ethical question of her guilt or innocence as a question of acting, of the correspondence between inside and outside of a character. When Lucretia is overwhelmed by her fear that they will be discovered as criminals, for example, Beatrice tells her mother:

Be bold
As thou art just. 'Tis like a truant child
To fear that others know what thou hast done
Even from thine own strong consciousness, and thus
Write on unsteady eyes and altered cheeks
All thou wouldst hide. Be faithful to thyself ...

> ... we can blind
> Suspicion with such cheap astonishment
> Or overbear it with such guiltless pride
> As murderers cannot feign.
>
> (4.4.35–46)

Beatrice initially describes her role in terms of an opposition between public and private; yet as Beatrice conceives of her role in increasingly public terms, she adopts an increasingly allegorical and public language to describe the plot she finds herself acting. Beatrice could here be speaking "for" the Revolution: it imagines itself acting with "guiltless pride" in remaining "faithful" to itself; its self-faithfulness is never understood as murderous by its actors. When Beatrice and Lucretia are arrested, Savella, the Pope's legate, takes Lucretia's fainting as a sign of her guilt, and Beatrice explains to him, in essence, that Lucretia simply does not understand the allegorical narrative whose plot they are enacting:

> She knows not yet thc uses of the world.
> She fears that power is as a beast which grasps
> And loosens not, a snake whose look transmutes
> All things to guilt which is its nutriment.
> She cannot know how well the supine slaves
> Of blind authority read the truth of things
> When written on a brow of guilelessness.
> She sees not yet triumphant Innocence
> Stand at the judgement-seat of mortal man,
> A judge and an accuser of the wrong
> Which drags it there.
>
> (4.4.181–5)

Beatrice's framing of the story as the tale of "triumphant Innocence" leaves no room for ethical ambiguity and so provokes in the reader the casuistical response—the search for ambiguity—Shelley seeks. Her allegorical language is the public language of the French Revolution and of what Peter Brooks calls the "either/or" logic of republican melodrama, in which there is no position between absolute good (the virtuous republic) and absolute evil (the republic's enemies).[36] Beatrice needs to use this strategy of allegorical self-construction because without it there is no room on a public stage for her: it appears to be a self-conscious strategy to navigate an ethical and political impasse. But in her performance, the impassioned allegorical discourse that seems to speak *through* her voids the distinction between authentic feeling and artifice.

Sensibility prizes the noble performances of suffering women under conditions of extreme duress; though these performances may be represented as highly stylized or self-consciously allegorical, the sublime force with which the viewer is compelled not just to feel for the performer but to participate in the allegory seems to confirm the performance as an incontrovertible truth. In representations of the French Revolution that emerge from a program of sensibility, there is often a special attraction for the sentimental possibilities of the final performances of women with a sensational past, performances in which the woman's power of self-control (in the form of modesty or hauteur) contrasts movingly with the woman's powerlessness to reverse her doom, her subjection to the law.[37] In Helen Maria Williams's eyewitness report of the Revolution, the fascinated narrative of Charlotte Corday, Marat's assassin, ends with the spectacle of Corday's heroic performance of "offended modesty" on the scaffold, and Williams's report zooms in to a fervent description of Corday's blush.[38] Corday's celebrity performance might be said to anticipate Beatrice's. The discrepancy between the knowledge of her guilt and the power of her performance of noble innocence produces, in the spectator, a sublime "truth" of feeling. It might be argued, in fact, that this discrepancy between truth and performance, the ability to rearrange our relation to the truth we thought we knew, is constitutive of the power of the performance. These are performances in which what is affecting is the *dissolution* of the boundary between authentic feeling and artifice. That is what is so affecting, too, about the fantasized performance of the actress Eliza O'Neill, whom Shelley imagines casting as Beatrice. According to Mary Shelley's "Note" to the play, Shelley had seen O'Neill act "several times" "in the zenith of her glory; and [...] was deeply moved by her impersonation of several parts, and by the graceful sweetness, the intense pathos, and sublime vehemence of passion she displayed."[39] In a letter that Mary's "Note" reproduces,

Shelley comments that "the principal character Beatrice is precisely fitted for Miss O'Neil, & it might even seem to have been written for her—(God forbid that I should see her play it—it would tear my nerves to pieces)."[40]

Yet for all its affective power, Beatrice's performance ultimately makes little difference. Nothing she says can change the verdict against her. The potential political effects of Beatrice's performance are possible only because of its survival in the form of the stories about her, both in oral tradition and in the written form of the *relazione* like the manuscript from which Shelley draws the story. The index both of narrative fascination and, in a kind of radical chic, of anti-authoritarian sympathies, Beatrice's fame keeps the story alive so that it can one day have a transformative effect on public opinion, which in turn can transform society. But this effect in turn is only possible if the story finds a reader who can not only find "the poetry which exists in these tempestuous sufferings and crimes," as Shelley puts it in his Preface, but can lend that implicit poetry the form it needs to act on the sympathies and imagination of its audience (*SPP*, p. 239).

Returning to the portrait with which we (and Shelley) began, we might speculate at this point that what makes it so "haunting" is not the glimpse it offers of its subject but rather, like the haunting version of Beatrice in the play, its refusal to confess its "secret"—what it appears to withhold from the viewer rather than what it reveals.[41] After all, as the Preface stresses, "it is in the restless and anatomizing casuistry with which men seek the justification of Beatrice, yet feel that she has done what needs justification; it is in the superstitious horror with which they contemplate alike her wrongs and their revenge; that the dramatic character of what she did and suffered, consists": not Beatrice's psychology but her audience's is Shelley's true object (p. 240). It turns out in fact that the portrait in question was not only not painted by Guido Reni; it is not (though of course Shelley did not know this) a portrait of Beatrice Cenci at all. But this misattribution only emphasizes the way the portrait functions as a screen for the desires of its viewers. With no subject there to claim the feeling it represents, the face of the girl in the portrait has the uncanny ability to become purely a signifier for feeling, feeling that can then be perfectly appropriated by the viewer.

In a market hungry for narrative sensation and for sentimental feeling, a portrait that offers both in spades sells. The fame of the Reni portrait supports a brisk trade in prints: according to Barbara Groseclose, "numberless engravings and canvasses" of Beatrice were "almost omnipresent in the Roman art market ... all hyperbolically treated as duplicates taken directly from the original."[42] This trade in reproductions of Beatrice is indirectly acknowledged in Shelley's Preface with a brief anecdote: "I had a copy of Guido's picture of Beatrice which is preserved in the Colonna Palace, and my servant instantly recognized it as the portrait of *La Cenci*" (p. 239). The classed transaction Shelley narrates maintains a careful distinction between the servant's gaze and Shelley's supervising, almost ethnographic gaze, but the absence of quotation marks in the recounting of the servant's speech allows the servant's enthusiastic response and Shelley's authorial voice to merge in the frisson-producing Italian of *La Cenci*. The exchange between Shelley and his servant occurs at the intersection of the mass-cultural discourses of sensation and celebrity, on the one hand, and the high-cultural practices of cultural tourism and art appreciation, on the other. Indeed, in the scene Shelley recounts, the image of Beatrice Cenci already possesses the quality of a commodity: it can be reproduced (Shelley has a copy) and yet it is mysteriously unique (always *La Cenci*); Shelley's handling of it trades on the kind of instant recognition that characterizes celebrity in mass culture.

Shelley's ekphrastic commentary on the portrait in the Preface, however, produces the image of Beatrice not as a metonymy for the sensational charge of the Cenci story but rather as proof positive of what he claims is "ideal" in Beatrice's nature (though, strikingly, his description repeats some of the language of Orsino's description of Beatrice noted above):

> There is a fixed and pale composure upon the features: she seems sad and stricken down in sprit, yet the despair thus expressed is lightened by the patience of gentleness. Her head is bound with folds of white drapery from which the yellow strings of her golden hair escape, and fall about her neck. The moulding of her face is exquisitely delicate; the eyebrows are distinct and arched: the lips have that permanent meaning of imagination and sensibility which suffering has not repressed and which it seems as if death

> could scarcely extinguish. Her forehead is large and clear; her eyes, which we are told were remarkable for their vivacity, are swollen with weeping and lustreless, but beautifully tender and serene. In the whole mien there is a simplicity and dignity which united with her exquisite loveliness and deep sorrow are inexpressibly pathetic. Beatrice Cenci appears to have been one of those rare persons in whom energy and gentleness dwell together without destroying one another: her nature was simple and profound.
>
> (p. 242)

The portrait is dissolved into abstract emotive terms: a countenance "sad and stricken down," filled with "despair," "gentleness," "sensibility," "tenderness," "serenity," "deep sorrow," words that all add up to a pathos ultimately "inexpressible" in its depth. Describing the portrait as "a just representation of one of the loveliest specimens of the workmanship of Nature," Shelley takes advantage of the way sentimentality's moral lexicon equates its ideal with nature, so that the act of reading or interpreting that produces a figure as sentimental is elided by that very act (p. 242). Compare Mary Shelley's comment that "the character of Beatrice [...] is touched with hues so vivid and so beautiful that the poet seems to have read intimately the secrets of the noble heart imaged in the lovely countenance of the unfortunate girl": the scene of the intimate reading of a heart's secrets is the essential trope of sentimentality, where reading becomes a figure that tries to dissolve the very mediation it names.[43] Shelley's verbal rendering of the image of Beatrice Cenci thus seems to allow the image to perform its own interpretation, on its own authority, while at the same time downplaying the exchange of her image among a series of men (Guido, Shelley, the servant) and between visual and verbal forms of representation.

The servant's instant recognition of "*La Cenci*" is an acknowledgement of the print market in which reproduced images of Beatrice continue to circulate with a promiscuity all too easily connected, for Romantic readers, to the sexuality of Beatrice herself. The trade in images of Beatrice, while it confirms for Shelley the play's marketability, is also a reminder not just of the commodity status of cultural objects but of the way personality can be converted into commodity form, the way the public visibility of objects or persons can entail promiscuous public circulation. Where the commodification of the image threatens to become too visible, or the profit motive for the producer of plays (or prints) too evident, the language of sentimental feeling works to obscure and refigure these material relations, replacing the abstraction of the commercial relationship between producer and consumer—the cash paid for the play or the print—with a relationship imagined in purely affective terms: the "inexpressibly pathetic" power of the portrait over its viewers.[44] The set of material relations among Shelley, these texts and images, and their potential audiences is thus displaced by the Preface onto the relation between the portrait and its many admirers, where Shelley is just one viewer among many. The concrete, embodied experience of seduction by the "magnetic" personality becomes a figure through which to understand the perhaps more disturbing abstraction inherent in the economic exchange between authors and readers of texts.

Sending the play out into the marketplace armed with its sentimentalizing apparatus, Shelley negotiates not just for moral but also literary authority. Making the argument that his play should be read as "serious" literature, he claims in his Preface that his high-cultural product differs from the popular stories about the Cenci family as the sublime works of Shakespeare and Sophocles differ from their own sources, "stories which already existed in tradition, as matters of popular belief and interest." In translating the story into English and into dramatic form, Shelley says he simply needs "to clothe it to the apprehensions of my countrymen in such language and action as would bring it home to their hearts" (p. 239). As many of the play's reviewers noticed, the material with which Shelley "clothes" the story is distinctly Elizabethan; the play's characters speak through what sounds like a patchwork of quotations from Shakespeare and other Elizabethan and Jacobean dramatists. In places, the density of quotation even approaches (surely unintentional) parody. Shakespeare's authority clearly haunts Shelley's play, as an object of desire but also as an intimidating, if ghostly, presence: Shakespeare's sway over the Romantic stage might seem as unbearable as Cenci's over his own household.[45]

The citational feel of the play's style apparently still provokes enough anxiety that the play needs to be defended against charges that it is merely derivative. Citing Stuart Curran, the editors of the Norton edition of *Shelley's Poetry and Prose* insist that "most of Shelley's supposed verbal and situational 'plagiarisms' from Shakespeare, Webster and other Elizabethan dramatists derive from the Italian manuscript *Relation of the Death of the Family of the Cenci* that was Shelley's chief source" (*SPP*, p. 241, n. 9). The "pastiche" quality of the play on the one hand contributes to its extraordinary sense of claustrophobia: the way bits of language are repeated within the play reinforces the connection between language and power by making it feel as if one aspect of the play's historical situation is that there are only so many ways in which one *can* speak, as if there is only so much language to draw on. At the same time, *The Cenci*'s "Shakespeare effect" makes it clear that Shakespeare's celebrity is vital to the play as well as Beatrice's. Nineteenth-century Britain represents "Englishness" to itself not just through the name of Shakespeare but also through his language, extracted and disseminated in bits and pieces through a culture of quotation.[46] Shelley's "antiquing" of the play's diction might offer a way for him to escape his situation of belatedness (in relation to Shakespeare and to the popular oral narratives of the Cenci story) by at once relinquishing the attempt to *follow* Shakespeare in inventing an original voice for the stage, and at the same time wishing himself back in time as the author of a revenge tragedy, the genre Shakespeare, in *Hamlet*, himself leaves behind. The haunting presence of Shakespeare thus marks both Shelley's ambitions and their limit: a father's law that is not so much challenged as side-stepped.

The conservative press, already hostile to Shelley on political grounds, reacted to the play with disdain if not outright horror. With a few exceptions (principally and unsurprisingly Leigh Hunt's) most reviews saw *The Cenci* as primarily a disgusting exercise in sensationalism: the reviewer for the *Literary Gazette* is pithier than most, but not atypical, when he calls the play "the production of a fiend, and calculated for the entertainment of devils in hell."[47] Shelley loved to flirt with diabolism, but the punch here is the accusation that Shelley writes by *calculating* on a taste for horror. Though Shelley would later be identified frequently with Beatrice, in the early reviews he is cast much more often as the willfully perverse Count. Shelley's style, and perhaps implicitly the revenge tragedy form, is identified by some reviews as derivative, at once trendy and out-moded: the *Literary Gazette* bemoans what it calls the play's "multitude of direct plagiarisms;" the *Monthly Review* comments snidely that Shelley is "among the most devoted adherents to the style and manner of the antient English drama" and a participant in what it calls the "old-play insanity" of the day.[48]

Yet in separately addressing what they see as the play's stylistic faults and its moral bad faith, these reviewers actually create an argument for the play's modernity. They detach ethics from aesthetics and identify the play's supposedly bad and perhaps simply imitative style as Shelley's unique style (or at least as a bad style unique to the Cockney School).[49] In repeatedly describing the play *and* its author as "unnatural" (a repeated complaint of the reviewers is that the incest described could not have "really" happened because it is against nature), they articulate the terms of the decadent aestheticism that will later take Shelley as a model. This underlying separation of ethics and aesthetics is apparent as well in reviews that find *The Cenci*'s style representative of a capricious "genius" not bound to nature or rational morality. For these reviewers, Shelley's style is beautiful and *therefore* dangerously seductive. Using Shelley's own figure of lightning, the reviewer for the *Edinburgh Monthly* warns in lines charged with political anxiety:

> The lightnings of genius are, indeed, always beautiful, but it should be remembered, that although their business is to purify the air, they may easily, unless reason lift her conducting rod, be converted into the swiftest and surest instruments of death and desolation. In that case, the measure of the peril answers to the brightness of the flash.[50]

The "lightnings of genius," according to this review, are ontologically prior to their instrumentalization as purifying or destructive forces.[51] John Scott, in *The London Magazine*, finds "the very genius of poesy ... closely connected with the signs of a depraved, nay mawkish, or rather emasculated moral taste, craving after trash, filth and poison, and sickening not wholesome nutriment," and adds, "whatever 'is not to be named amongst men,' Shelley seems to think has a peculiar claim to celebration in poetry."[52] The double operation of Scott's review, typical of the reviews more generally, separates the beauty of Shelley's language from the depravity of his "moral taste," and then grounds the peculiarities of Shelley's "genius" not just in the author's personality but in the author's (diseased) body:

> Mr. Shelley likes to carry about with him the consciousness of his own peculiarities; and a tinge of disease, probably existing in a

> certain part of his constitution, gives to these peculiarities a very offensive cast. This unlucky tendency of his, is at once his pride and his shame: he is tormented by more than suspicions that the general sentiment of society is against him—and, at the same time, he is induced by irritation to keep harping on the same subjects [...] [Shelley] turns from war, rapine, murder, seduction, and infidelity—the vices and calamities with the description of which our common nature and common experience permit the generality of persons to sympathize, —to cull some morbid or maniac sin of rare and doubtful occurrence, and sometimes to found a *system* of practical purity and peace on violations which it is disgraceful even to contemplate.[53]

In the reviews, most of which assume the reader has heard rumors of Shelley's "peculiarities," the taint of "perversion" moves from the play's content to the play's style to the character and the body of the play's author. Shelley's "delicate" refusal to name the crime in the play becomes an opening for the reviews implicitly to associate Shelley himself with all manner of "violations," not just incest but also, perhaps especially, sodomy, which in the manuscript version of the story is among Cenci's chief sins—but they do so by imitating Shelley's refusal to name the crime. The language of the reviews collaborates with the production of the poet they discuss to imagine a sensationalist aesthetic, and to create the "strange [...] monster" that draws the curious Trelawny to Italy.

4
Shelley's Glamour

John Addington Symonds's 1878 life of Shelley closes with a line of argument typical of Victorian appreciations of the poet, making the case that Shelley's "life and work are indissolubly connected," and indeed that the poet's life rivals the poet's work for the critic's interest:

> He acted what he thought and felt, with a directness rare among his brethren of the poet's craft; while his verse, with the exception of *The Cenci*, expressed little but the animating thoughts and aspirations of his life. That life, moreover, was "a miracle of thirty years," so crowded with striking incident and varied experience that, as he said himself, he had already lived longer than his father, and ought to be reckoned with the men of ninety. Through all vicissitudes he preserved his youth inviolate, and died, like one whom the gods love, or like a hero of Hellenic story, young, despite grey hairs and suffering. His life has, therefore, to be told, in order that his life-work may be rightly valued: for, great as that was, he, the man, was somehow greater; and noble as it truly is, the memory of himself is nobler.[1]

While Shelley's notoriety during his lifetime far exceeded in scope the limited audience for his works, readers in the later nineteenth century invested the figure of the poet with a different kind of glamour. In the second half of the century, Shelley became famous as a lyric poet whose widely anthologized verse proved capable of surprisingly intimate effects.[2] Readers like Symonds found themselves moved and entranced not only by Shelley's poetry but also by the spectacle of the lovely, care-worn youth, "sweet, generous, tender, beautiful, and born a bard; from his birth aglow with the transcendental rapture," in the breathless words of a contemporary literary history.[3]

Shelley's afterlife in nineteenth-century culture exemplifies the affective dynamics this study has been tracing around literary celebrity. The poet's renown, influence and staying power in culture were closely bound up not just with the power of his poetry but with the fascination exerted by the figure of the poet and the emotional response elicited by the poet's life story.[4] Fraught with the scandalous innuendo Symonds mutes as "extraordinary incident," the story of Shelley's life and early death carried sensational allure for a widening public, while for some readers, traces of the poet's presence became charged with a more personal feeling that speaks to the poet's importance in the reader's own emotional and imaginative life. Readers fixated on the poet's body as a correlate to the seductive force of the poetry and, as in Symonds's account of Shelley dying "like a hero of Hellenic story, young, despite grey hairs and suffering," they wove the body into the story of what the poet had uniquely felt and suffered. Because Victorian readers like Symonds identified Shelley with an ideal of lyric expressivity, Shelley's poetry was understood as revealing the poet's most intimate feelings. Conversely, many readers saw the most intimate details of the poet's life (not least, the exact nature of his relationships with the women in his life) as elemental to their understanding of his poetry.[5]

Such a model of reading generated sensations of unusual closeness to the poet. One of the poet's most ardent admirers, Richard Garnett, testifies to this experience of intimacy in the Introduction to his 1862 *Relics of Shelley* (quoting Shelley's lyric "Wedded Souls"):[6]

> Few have borne so severe a scrutiny. Almost every verse he ever pencilled down, has now become the property of the public, and any reader [...] may say in his own words:—
>
> "I am as a spirit who has dwelt
> Within his heart of hearts, and I have felt
> His feelings, and have thought his thoughts, and
> known
> The inmost converse of his soul."[7]

The thrill associated with Shelley's physical presence is similarly palpable in the first stanza of Robert Browning's short poem

"Memorabilia" (1855), sparked by the wonder the younger poet feels at overhearing a stranger's casual reference to having met Shelley, the idol of Browning's youth:

> Ah, did you once see Shelley plain?
> And did he turn and speak to you?
> And did you speak to him again?
> How strange it seems, and new![8]

The stanza renders in tense lyric terms the potency of what we might call Shelley's celebrity effects: the way the celebrity's body becomes (like lyric) the locus of both collective and private memory, and the point of exchange between public and private; the way the celebrity encounter has the potential to interrupt ordinary time, becoming an event both more and less real than the everyday; the dynamics of desire and distancing, wonder and embarrassment provoked in those who encounter a celebrity by the profoundly personal meanings they attach to a celebrity body that remains both fantastic and, in truth, fantastically ordinary.[9]

While in each of my other chapters I focus on the interactions between poets and their contemporary audiences of passionate readers, in this chapter I examine the way Shelley's feeling readers in the later nineteenth century, long after his death, negotiated these celebrity effects surrounding the poet. In the first part of this chapter, I take as a kind of case-study two essays on Shelley by Matthew Arnold, each of which deals explicitly with Arnold's very mixed feelings about Shelley's glamour and his celebrity. Shelley's brief but striking appearance in "The Study of Poetry" (1880) allows Arnold to examine the relationship between the poet's seductive but fleeting forms and what he describes as the overinvested response of the poet's "votaries."[10] In his 1888 review of Edward Dowden's important *Life* of Shelley, Arnold extends these reflections to include a more sustained meditation on Shelley's life, his work, and the conditions of publicity they inhabit.[11] Taken together, these two essays on Shelley provide us both with Arnold's analysis of the practices and institutions of reading through which Shelley's celebrity is constituted, and with a compelling view of the way one reader grapples with his own complicated affective relationship to the poet. In the second part of the chapter, I connect Arnold's response to Shelley with Shelley's own poetics as articulated in the *Defence of Poetry* (c. 1821) and with a broader pattern of response that extends from the poet's nineteenth-century readers to our own critical moment, in which the staging of Shelley's celebrity creates a kind of sensational drama around the reading and transmission of Romanticism.

My reading of Arnold's reaction to Shelley revises the conventional literary-historical understanding of Shelley's late nineteenth-century glamour. Arnold was by no means Shelley's most unreservedly enthusiastic fan, but he was certainly one of the most influential and most conflicted readers of the poet he memorably, perhaps indelibly, tagged a "beautiful but ineffectual angel, beating in the void his luminous wings in vain."[12] Critics have frequently seen in Arnold's ambivalence about Shelley an index of the Victorians' self-conflicted working through of their own youthful Romanticism, a Romanticism charged with the excesses Arnold's image of the "beautiful angel" evokes: a flight away from objective reality and social connection into a purely subjective world of imagination and ideality.[13] In what follows, I argue, by contrast, that Arnold's anxiety about Shelley concerns not so much relationships of influence as technologies of reception: the ways in which "Shelley" is mediated by literary and market systems and by institutions of reading. Arnold is both fascinated and troubled by his inability to shake the sense of an intimate connection to Shelley's alternately seductive and maddening personality, a personality that makes strong emotional claims on the responsive reader. That Shelley's verse seems to render his feelings almost obtrusively palpable to the responsive reader contributes to Shelley's Victorian prestige as well as to the discomfort of later modernist and New Critical readers.[14] Yet if Arnold finds it difficult to separate Shelley's poetry from his personality, he consistently links such personality effects to the impersonality of the literary and market systems in which poetic subjectivity finally seems to inhere. What feels initially like access to an essential interiority turns into the paradox of an intimate connection with a radically public subjectivity, a subjectivity fully proper to no individual.

When the University of Dublin professor and Shelley "votary" Edward Dowden's *Life of Shelley* appeared in 1886, it came at the crest of a wave of publication about Shelley's life spanning three decades. In the late 1850s, Shelley's friends Peacock, Trelawny and Thomas Jefferson Hogg had all published memoirs of the poet, following earlier ventures in anecdotal biography by Hogg (in the *New Monthly Magazine* in 1832–3) and Medwin (in the *Athenaeum* in 1832–3, and in his *Life of Percy Bysshe Shelley* in 1847), and Mary Shelley's own very influential biographical notes to her 1839 edition of her husband's poetry. Moxon, the publisher of Hogg's memoir, added Lady Shelley's *Shelley Memorials* and Richard Garnett's *Relics of Shelley* to his growing list of "Shelleyana" in 1859 and 1862, respectively. The 1870s alone saw W.M. Rossetti's memoir of Shelley attached to his edition of Shelley's *Poetical Works* (1870), D.F. MacCarthy's *Shelley's Early Life, from original sources, with curious incidents, letters and writings* (1872), the Symonds biography quoted above (1878), R.H. Stoddard's *Anecdote Biography* of Shelley in the *Sans Souci* series (1877), George Barnett Smith's critical biography (1877), and Trelawny's expanded *Records of Shelley, Byron and the Author* (1878), not to mention a slew of reminiscences by nearly everyone who had encountered Shelley and, it seems, nearly everyone who had encountered someone who had encountered Shelley, many of these in the perennially popular "conversations with " genre. As this flood of biographical writing attests, Shelley was a figure whose reputation was steadily growing but also undecided. Since evaluation of his poetry was so dependent on opinion of his character, these biographers sought especially to intervene in disputes over the more troubling passages in the poet's life, especially the tragic denouement of his marriage to Harriet Westbrook. Though the materials for writing Shelley's life were "almost overwhelmingly copious and strangely discordant," Symonds comments, Shelley's character remained difficult to fix: "Those who ought to meet in love over his grave, have spent their time quarrelling over him, and baffling the most eager seeker for the truth. Through the turbid atmosphere of their recriminations it is impossible to discern the whole personality of the man."[15]

The distinction of Dowden's work was that he had been granted unfettered access to the vast trove of Shelley documents that Lady Shelley had literally enshrined at Boscombe, along with other relics of the poet. Promising a more complete, more truthful picture of Shelley than had yet emerged, Dowden's two volumes trained new light on the more scandalous and provocative episodes in Shelley's life, including the marriage with Harriet, the elopement with Mary, the relations with Claire Clairmont, Emilia Viviani, and others, though Dowden offers sentimentalizing defenses of the poet at each turn. To exasperated readers like Arnold, the effect of these revelations was to produce an unfamiliar and unwelcome view of a Shelley of unchecked passions and dangerous seductiveness. "I have read those volumes with the deepest interest," says Arnold in his response to Dowden's work,

> but I regret their publication, and am surprised, I confess, that Shelley's family should have desired or assisted it. For my own part, at any rate, I would gladly have been left with the impression, the ineffaceable impression, made upon me by Mrs. Shelley's first edition of her husband's collected poems. The charm of the poems flowed in upon us from that, and the charm of the character.
>
> (XI, 305–6)[16]

It is the split personality of the poet of personality that troubles Arnold here, prompting a searching discussion of Shelley's psychology and of the limits of public curiosity, of Arnold's own mixed feelings of love and distrust for the poet, and of the difficulty of locating a "real" Shelley among all the representations of the poet in circulation. But the riddle that Shelley's life poses only further increases the fascination with his figure, since Arnold's disgust at the biography's revelations is evidently matched by his desire to puzzle out the incoherence. Shelley's life, that is, becomes more obviously textualized.

"Nowadays all things appear in print sooner or later," Arnold acknowledges with some resignation at the start of the review, signaling that the essay's topic is not just the character of the poet but the character of that print culture in which Shelley's "character" is constructed and circulated. Paradoxically, though, the more that appears in print, the more elusive the "truth" of Shelley appears. Wading through Dowden's *Life*, Arnold complains,

> one feels sickened for ever of the subject of irregular relations; God forbid that I should go into the scandals about Shelley's "Neapolitan charge," about Shelley and Emilia Viviani, about Shelley and Miss Clairmont, and the rest of it! I will only say that it is visible enough that when the passion of love was aroused in Shelley (and it was aroused easily) one could not be sure of him, his friends could not trust him.
>
> (XI, 308–9)

Arnold's "sickened" feeling registers the queasiness of an emotional overload—so much loss, so much sadness in the Shelley circle—but also a narrative surfeit: there is just too much Shelley to take in. When Arnold comments on Shelley's self-isolating unreliability, the concern is epistemological as well as ethical: "one could not be sure of him." The vagueness of the pronoun "one" allows Arnold to place himself and his reader in the position of Shelley's friends, loving, frustrated, unable to trust.

Arnold's concern here is overdetermined. On one level, he is reacting as a reader and as a public figure himself to the distressing invasiveness of celebrity culture: the way in which matters that should remain private inevitably become part of an endless series of "scandals" drawn before the public with mortifying repetition. Implicit in his essay are a set of important questions about authorial biography: What do readers need to know about the lives of writers? What kind of knowledge is possible, or desirable, of writer's lives or of the relationship of life and work? On another level, Arnold responds as a baffled and perhaps self-protective critic. Browning's famous 1852 description of Shelley as the type of the "subjective" poet had considered Shelley's poetry as less a concrete work than an "effluence" representing "the very radiance and aroma of his personality, projected from it but not separated."[17] Reading Shelley's poetry, therefore, "we necessarily approach the personality of the poet, in apprehending it we apprehend him, and certainly we cannot love it without loving him."[18] Browning's concept of "personality" here suggests that a poet might possess an unchanging, essential selfhood, a deep interiority that abides beneath the momentary poses a poet might strike (or mistakes a poet might make) and that rests immune to the variety of fluctuating public characterizations of the poet; such a personality is knowable but securely the poet's.[19] Dowden's detailing of Shelley's "irregular relations" replaces a knowable (and lovable) "personality" with an erratic impulsiveness.[20] Shelley's over-susceptibility to love, as portrayed by Arnold, exaggerates to fatal effect the emotional responsiveness that is precisely what is valued about the poet by his mainstream readers in the nineteenth century. If Shelley's poetry and personality are identified with one another, losing one's confidence in Shelley renders aesthetic judgments about the poetry uncertain.

Arnold writes at a moment when Shelley's "votaries" have themselves become famous for their displays of excessive feeling for the poet, expressing their idolatry through critical superlatives, through tribute poems, through imitation, or through more macabre practices.[21] As Judith Pascoe recounts, fanatic collectors avidly sought out any object associated with the poet—miniatures of the poet, the poet's notebooks and letters, but also his guitar, his sofa, even pieces of his body.[22] Throughout the century, Shelley's friend Trelawny, who had supervised the cremation of the poet's body, kept distributing to the poet's family, friends and admirers pieces of the body he claimed had been left unconsumed: Shelley's heart and bits of bone. The enthusiast, editor and collector William Michael Rossetti proudly displayed to visitors a "piece of [Shelley's] blackened skull, given me by Trelawny," commenting that "the regard in which I hold this relic makes me understand the feelings of a Roman Catholic in parallel cases."[23] (The last sofa Shelley slept on [supposedly], another piece in William Rossetti's possession, was the subject of a sonnet by Dante Gabriel Rossetti.) The lengths to which the American Shelley-lover Edward Silsbee was willing to go in his pursuit of Shelleyana gave Henry James the basis for the obsessive narrator of *The Aspern Papers* (1888).[24] From the Cambridge Apostles on, falling for Shelley was frequently described as an experience like religious conversion, idolizing the poet eventually a faddish Victorian stance. As Eric O. Clarke has shown, "Shelley-love" itself became a suspect, if widespread, condition: both Shelley's admirers and his detractors in the nineteenth century frequently associate Shelley with heterodox forms of desire, especially homoerotic desire, an association mapped onto the sexuality of the poet's seduced readers as well.[25] "While Shelley's scorched organ provided a material symbol of the poet's own depth of feeling," Clarke notes, "his figurative heart became the object of the 'abnormal feeling' towards him that others felt: the passionate identification between Shelley's body and corpus, the loving union of aesthetic and affective value."[26] Though clearly wary of such excessive devotion, Arnold nonetheless casts an overinvested relationship to Shelley in terms that emphasize the shared, social ground of such desire. As he tracks the very personal meanings of Shelley to his admiring readers, Arnold emphasizes the role of the institutions of reading that condition personal response.

Animated by feelings of real anger and betrayal directed both at Dowden and at Shelley himself, Arnold's essay ultimately seeks less epistemological certainty than ethical consolation: he wants to find his way back to loving Shelley. The essay mourns the loss of a collectively admired Shelley: "our ideal Shelley," "the true Shelley after all:" "our original Shelley [...] the Shelley of the lovely and well-known picture, [...] the Shelley with 'flushed, feminine, artless face,' the Shelley 'blushing like a girl,' of Trelawny" (XI, 326). Notice how Arnold both emphasizes possession—"our" Shelley—and then displaces possession through quotation. "Our original" Shelley, a figure of sweetness and light, is in fact a conspicuously mediated figure, comfortably possessed, comfortably private because comfortably shared, "well-known," public. The avowed project of Arnold's essay is to circumscribe "what is ridiculous and odious in the Shelley brought to our knowledge by the new materials, and then to show that our beautiful and lovable Shelley nevertheless persists" (XI, 309).

Neil Fraistat has described Shelley's stardom in the second half of the century as achieved through "various reductive readings of Shelley and his poetry: reductions to sensation, to the lyric moment, to spirituality, and to beauty."[27] Fraistat writes,

> The master trope of these reductions was "purity," and its product was "pure poetry." Shelley thus became at once a signifier of "pure poetry" and a means by which pure poetry could be argued for as a cultural standard of England's national literature. Behind the argument for purity lay the general anxiety that the increasingly empowered middle classes felt about the potentially transgressive power of poetry and the specific transgressions of Shelley's poetry and life, which can be classified as political, sexual, and religious.[28]

Though Dowden adheres to such a view of Shelley, his biography complicates this etherealizing project. Dowden's picture of Shelley as frequently overmastered by impulse ties the nature of poetic identity uncomfortably to the passions of the body; it unintentionally rewrites Shelley's emotional responsiveness, part of the poet's claim to fame, as a dangerous form of transport. Dowden's biography so disturbs Arnold in part because, whatever its intent, it corporealizes Shelley in such a way as to pull the reader's passion for the poet into the decidedly impure, unstable zone of the poet's own passions. Thus the horror with which Arnold responds when confronted with such a picture of Shelley's world as insistently and surprisingly material, embodied and for the body: "Godwin's house of sordid horror, and Godwin preaching and holding the hat, and the green-spectacled Mrs. Godwin, and Hogg the faithful friend, and Hunt the Horace of this precious world, and [...] Lord Byron with his deep grain of coarseness and commonness, his affectation, his brutal selfishness—what a set!" (XI, 320).

Against such a depressingly bodily version of Romanticism, Arnold at the close of his essay attempts to recuperate the "beautiful and lovable" Shelley by reenchanting the poet's body, remaking it as a glamorous and otherworldly object. He cites to that end two testimonials recounted by Dowden. First, a Miss Rose tells us that Shelley "was the most interesting figure I ever saw; his eyes like a deer's, bright but rather wild; his white throat unfettered; his slender but to me almost faultless shape" (XI, 326). "This feminine enthusiasm may be deemed suspicious," Arnold comments, "but a Captain Kennedy must surely be able to keep his head."[29] However, the military man, who met the young Shelley at Field Place, practically swoons:

> I fancy I see him now as he sate by the window, and hear his voice, the tones of which impressed me with his sincerity and simplicity. His resemblance to his sister Elizabeth was as striking as if they had been twins. His eyes were most expressive; his complexion beautifully fair, his features exquisitely fine; his hair was dark, and no peculiar attention to its arrangement was manifest. [...] One would at once pronounce of him that he was different from other men. [...] I never met a man who so immediately won upon me.
>
> (XI, 326–7)

Through the voice of Captain Kennedy, Arnold here lingers on Shelley's exquisite body, through which the poet's character is ideally visible. This visual apprehension downplays the sexualized agency of the poet, and renders his difference "from other men" an attribute of feminized poetic sensitivity rather than an explanation for the "irregular" passion that troubles Arnold earlier in the essay. The way Arnold's impatience with Shelley's perverse body nonetheless breaks out again at the close of the essay—"The man Shelley, in very truth, is not entirely sane, and Shelley's poetry is not entirely sane either," he warns us after all this (XI, 327)—suggests that the real stakes in this essay involve Arnold's vulnerability to the emotional claims Shelley seems peculiarly to make on his readers. Yet Arnold locates the history of his own sensitivity to Shelley consistently within a public context of response and within a collective system of representations of the poet. In part a distancing mechanism, this also hints at a recognition: instead of casting lyric intimacy as the relationship of the individual reader to the individual poet, Arnold seems to understand lyric intimacy in terms of the structuring relationship of both reader and poet to the institutions of reading they mutually inhabit. Though deeply involved with the individual histories of feeling, lyric intimacy on this view is irreducibly social and performative.

Such a recognition likewise seems to animate Arnold's earlier remarks on Shelley's glamour in his 1880 essay "The Study of Poetry," originally the Introduction to Thomas Humphry Ward's anthology *The English Poets*.[30] In "The Study of Poetry," Arnold premises the construction of a national canon on a critical approach that would preserve, amid an anaesthetizing flood of "multitudes of a common sort of readers, and masses of a common sort of literature," the capacity for deeply felt aesthetic experience (IX, 188). Through a series of exercises in discrimination, he attempts to model the necessary "sense for the best," a sense that cannot be swayed by merely personal likings or affinities, or by the importance of a poet to one's personal history. Arnold's ultimate example of taste in need of correction (as it happens, by wholesome "contact" with the "soundness" of Burns), is the errant lover of Shelley,

> the votary misled by a personal estimate of Shelley, as so many of us have been, are, and will be,—of that beautiful spirit building his many-coloured haze of words and images
>
> Pinnacled dim in the intense inane—
>
> (IX, 187)

"Haze," Arnold's figure for Shelley's poetry, tellingly straddles what Steven Connor describes as "two traditions or sets of associations with regard to haze" active at the end of the nineteenth century: on the one hand, "Romantic haze," "the haze of glamour or diffused radiance;" on the other hand, the "tradition of the vaporous" associated with "will o' the wisps, and other such atmospheric mirages," according to which "perception is endangered by the exhalations from the ground, just as bodily health is."[31] Arnold's wording charts a complicated course of identification and disidentification, locating delusive passion for the glamorous Shelley in the distanced "votary," then avowing that passion as a past, present and future condition of a community of readers to which "many of us" belong, then finally (across a light allusion to *Mont Blanc*'s "many-colour'd, many-voiced vale") merging his own voice with Shelley's in the quotation from *Prometheus Unbound*—a quotation that graphically trails off into the empty space it describes. Though Arnold steps back at the end of this passage to fold the specific example of Shelley's "votaries" into a problem the Romantics more generally pose for the Victorians (passions about Byron and Wordsworth are also too intense for Arnold's liking), it is clear that Shelley is more than a mere instance of a general condition.

Why does Arnold single Shelley out like this? The crux of the issue, in my reading, lies in the way the discussion slides between the "misleading" charm of Shelley's personality and the non-referentiality of Shelley's language—"his many-coloured haze of words and images." David Riede has argued that problems of reference plague Arnold's critical prose: Arnold's attempts to account for acts of critical judgment tend to rely on essentially circular definitions, so that Arnold frequently relies on a critical language that "has nothing to refer to but itself."[32] Certainly, Shelley functions for Arnold as a figure for imagination's potential to soar away from reality, to lose contact with anything but subjective feeling. Insofar as Shelley also functions as an exemplary figure for language's more general capacity to operate without reference, however, Shelley gets placed into a kind of critical quarantine as a way to block off the idea that Arnold's own critical prose cannot escape a circular grounding in its own "words and images."

Arnold's characterization of Shelley's poetry as a "many-coloured haze" echoes a broader tradition of writing on the poet, however—for example, William Hazlitt's comment that "the colours of his style, for their gaudy, changeful, startling effect, resemble the display of fire-works in the dark, and, like them, have neither durability, nor keeping, nor discriminate form."[33] For these readers, the essence of Shelley's poetry is its non-essentiality—Hazlitt's review of Shelley's *Posthumous Poems* argues, "Mr. Shelley is the maker of his own poetry—out of nothing."[34] Elsewhere, comparing Shelley to Byron,

Arnold asserts, "All the personal charm of Shelley cannot hinder us from at last discovering in his poetry the incurable want, in general, of a sound subject-matter, and incurable fault, in consequence, of insubstantiality" (IX, 218). The problem of reading Shelley, for Arnold as for Hazlitt, is the problem of apprehending the ephemerality of sensation without being possessed by its seductive, illusory effects. One paradox of the poetry is that such immateriality produces such a powerful sense for readers of Shelley's seductive physical presence, as if the seeming formlessness of Shelley's poetry compelled a greater fascination with the form of the poet himself. Indeed, readers often transferred the qualities of the one to the other: in Thomas Jefferson Hogg's recollection, for example, "Shelley was fugitive, volatile; he evaporated like ether, his nature being ethereal; he suddenly escaped, like some fragrant essence; evanescent as a quintessence. He was a lovely, a graceful image, vanishing speedily from our sight, being portrayed in flying colours."[35] At the turn of the century, Edmund Gosse still picks up and refines the atmospheric figures for Shelley: "His intellectual ardour threw out, not puffs of smoke, like Byron's did, but a white vapour."[36]

Shelley's nineteenth-century readers feel in his evanescent forms the hazy "radiance" of his "personality," the lyrical expression of a unique subjectivity. But what if—as Arnold's lines seem to suggest—the "beautiful spirit" with whom readers fall in love is itself essentially indistinct from the "many-coloured haze of words and images" it is building? From this perspective, the glamorous subjectivity that seems to inhere in Shelley's poetry is not a prior origin for the poetry but rather the vaporous, evanescent effect of the turnings of the verse. Indeed, the effect of Arnold's quotation from *Prometheus Unbound* is to locate Shelley's act of composition itself within the infinite space of Shelley's language. We would expect Shelley's language to be the medium for the expression of subjectivity, but the "haze of words and images" seems to communicate nothing but its own radiant presence. The problem with Shelley for Arnold, then, is not that his poetry is too personal but that, as purely a "haze of words and images," it cannot really be personal at all. Shelley's person as well as his poetry looks like a set of "arresting surface effects" subject to sensuous apprehension but productive of no determinate knowledge.[37] Arnold operates along lines developed by Arthur Henry Hallam's description of Keats and Shelley as poets of sensation rather than reflection, whose acute, immediate emotional responsiveness to "colors, and sounds, and movements" "tended to involve their whole being into the energy of sense," so that they "lived in a world of images."[38] But where the poetry of sensation is usually associated with a retreat into a private world of imagination and feeling, Shelley's poetry is here conceived as in a sense radically public.

In "The Study of Poetry," Arnold connects the waywardness of Shelley's forms to the wayward desire of the poet and his passionate readers. The intertwining of issues of sexuality and aesthetics raised by Shelley's glamour becomes clear in the examples Arnold offers to compare Shelley with Burns. Side by side with these lines from *Prometheus Unbound*:

> On the brink of the night and the morning
> My coursers are wont to respire,
> But the Earth has just whispered a warning
> That their flight must be swifter than fire[39]

—"how very salutary," Arnold says, to read these from *Tam Glen*:

> My minnie does constantly deave me
> And bids me beware o' young men;
> They flatter, she says, to deceive me;
> But wha can think sae o' Tam Glen?
>
> (IX, 187)

The juxtaposition, at first glance, looks fairly arbitrary—though the meters match nicely enough—but Arnold seems to consider its significance self-evident. Burns's lines are earthy where Shelley's describe an impulse for transcendent flight; Burns's speaker is a real being where Shelley's is a spirit (the Spirit of the Hour); Burns's lines emphasize their grounding in the continuity of a localized oral tradition, where Shelley's lines voice (in the context of the poem) an impatient anticipation of universal apocalyptic renovation. But this context plays in the background. Upfront, Arnold's choice of lines from Burns reframes the problem of reading Shelley more explicitly in terms of sexual seduction. Burns's lines place desire within a network of human relationships; in citing them, Arnold seems to emphasize precisely the kind of human relation he argues in his later essay that Shelley, desiring only abstractions, cannot see. In this excerpted version at least, Shelley's lines appear to refer to no "real thing" outside of Shelley's poetry of desire itself—they become self-parodic, consequently, too imitable, where Burns can take on the role of the female speaker and still be inimitably himself. Aligning himself with *Tam Glen*'s female speaker—or with her minnie—Arnold implicitly warns that the reader of Shelley's poems had best beware the deceptive charms of "young men;" at the same time, he implicitly aligns the lack of fidelity to real things in Shelley's poetry with the unreliability of Shelley's seductive person itself.

Insofar as it connects powerful "personality effects" with the impersonality of figural systems and with structures of reception, Arnold's discussion of Shelley's celebrity accords in provocative ways with Shelley's own account of poetic subjectivity. Implicit in Arnold is the recognition Shelley's poetics asserts in more explicit terms: that the subjectivity expressed by Shelley's poetry is inextricable from structures exterior to any individual. In the *Defence of Poetry*, for example, Shelley makes the argument that what the lyric poet experiences as an "inmost self," the origin of its poetry, is in fact a radically impersonal set of transient effects. The penultimate sentence of the *Defence* revolves around just this paradox: "Poets," Shelley there declares, "are the hierophants of an unapprehended inspiration, the mirrors of the gigantic shadows which futurity casts upon the present, the words which express what they understand not; the trumpets which sing in battle, and feel not what they inspire; the influence which is moved not, but moves."[40] This remarkable sentence begins by instrumentalizing poets as an effect of the "futurity" they mirror, but by the end of the sentence, poets are imagined as the influence that makes futurity itself possible: poets are mirrors of the shadows of the unapprehendable futurity opened up as an effect of poetry.[41] Poets, in this account, are properly nothing in themselves, but are rather an element in a circuit of effects.[42] The sentence displaces poetic "inspiration" into a futurity outside the poet, as the effect of the trumpet singing in battle, rather than the breath that makes the trumpet sing. In earlier passages of the *Defence*, however, poetry arises unconsciously from within the poet: "the mind in creation is as a fading coal which some invisible influence, like an inconstant wind, awakens to transitory brightness; this power arises from within, like the colour of a flower which fades and changes as it is developed, and the conscious portions of our natures are unprophetic either of its approach or its departure."[43] The similes here work not to naturalize inspiration but rather to hold it apart from the natural: it is a process of effects whose cause will always remain unapprehended, and indeed cannot be conceived in terms of an originary cause. Poetic power, like all power, has no essence but is rather, like movement or change itself, a relation only visible in its effects or traces: "It is as it were the interpenetration of a diviner nature though our own; but its footsteps are like those of a wind over a sea, which the coming calm erases, and whose traces remain only as on the wrinkled sand which paves it."[44] Poetic creation is the expression of an interiority so fundamental that it lies beyond the poet's conscious grasp, and, at the same time, poetic power is something not proper to any subject, a paradoxically anticipatory "influence" that looks forward to the futurity, by definition other to the poet, whose very possibility it calls into being.

Surprisingly, such a non-essential subjectivity proved highly adaptable to the needs of a market system that purports to privilege an essential interiority. The paradoxical logic of this description of poetic subjectivity offers one way to account for the fascination Shelley's body (living or dead) holds for readers across the nineteenth century and into our own critical moment. Signifying both the uniqueness of poetic identity and a self-difference fundamental to that identity, Shelley's body plays out for his readers the instabilities of his poetics. Shelley's seductive body can appear as a figure for interiority and intentionality—Hazlitt recalled Shelley's person as "a type and shadow of his genius. His complexion, fair, golden, freckled, seemed transparent with an inward light, and his spirit within him

> 'so divinely wrought,
> That you might almost say his body thought.'[45]

Or the body can appear as the location of an impulse exterior to consciousness that exceeds and undoes intention. Similarly, relics of the poet can seem expressive of poetic intentionality, and so meaningful in their own right, or merely material, non-intentional objects, whose meaning is projected onto them by the literary and market economies through which they travel. Shelley's successful afterlife might be due in part to the way this oscillation between personality and impersonality turns out to be in itself so strangely seductive.

In the remainder of this chapter, I want to show first how the issues raised in my reading of Arnold might connect with the staging of Shelley's celebrity in another key nineteenth-century text—Trelawny's narrative of Shelley's cremation—then how these issues track across two more recent theoretical texts that replay the drama Trelawny creates. The story itself has proved perennially gripping. When Shelley's drowned body washed up on the shore near Via Reggio in 1822, Trelawny, quickly on the scene, had the theatrical instincts to make the most of the moment. In his account of the cremation of the bodies, Trelawny gives special attention to the details of his elaborate preparations: "I got a furnace made at Leghorn, of iron bars and strong sheet-iron, supported on a stand, and laid in a stock of fuel, and such things as were said to be used by Shelley's much loved Hellenes on their funeral pyres."[46] With Byron, Hunt, and a complement of Italian officials, soldiers and workmen in attendance, Trelawny supervised the disinterment and cremation of the corpses of Shelley and his sailing companion Edward Williams. On the funeral pyres, the bodies are lavished with frankincense, wine, oil and salt. In what looks retrospectively like the ur-moment of intimacy between writer and reader, Trelawny famously reaches into the pyre holding Shelley's burning corpse for a gory souvenir: "The only portions that were not consumed were some fragments of bones, the jaw, and the skull," he reports, "but what surprised us all, was that the heart remained entire. In snatching this relic from the fiery furnace, my hand was severely burnt; and had anyone seen me do the act I should have been put into quarantine" (pp. 134–5).

Trelawny's heart-snatching expresses the contradictory nature of fandom, a gesture at once of fierce attachment and of violation, of loyalty and desperate possessiveness. Deeply intimate and wildly theatrical, Trelawny's act sets the stage for a later generation's fetishization of Shelley's relics, their appropriation of Shelley's physical remains and the objects the poet leaves behind as vehicles for a metaphorical contact with the author's spirit. The scene's framing emphasizes the authorizing presence of Shelley's spirit in the proceedings but also their transgressive quality.

The sensational appeal of this scene is so obvious that Leigh Hunt's account of the episode included a disclaimer that the scene was *not* made for the market: "The friends of the deceased, though they took no pains to publish the proceeding, were accused of wishing to make a sensation, of doing a horrible and unfeeling thing, etc."[47] Unsurprisingly, given its sensational qualities, the scene quickly became a staple in popular representations of Romanticism.[48] When Trelawny finally publishes his account of the proceedings in 1858, then, he is revisiting what is already a familiar scene, but his language gives the narrative new energy. Trelawny's description moves quickly from painting the picturesque backdrop—"The lonely and grand scenery that surrounded us so exactly harmonized with Shelley's genius, that I could imagine his spirit soaring over us" (*Recollections*, p. 132)—to a morbid focus on the body itself:

> As I thought of the delight Shelley felt in such scenes of loneliness and grandeur whilst living, I felt we were no better than a herd of wolves or a pack of wild dogs, in tearing out his battered and naked body from the pure yellow sand that lay so lightly over it, to drag him back to the light of day; but the dead have no voice, nor had I power to check the sacrilege.
>
> (pp. 132–3)

A few lines later:

> We were startled and drawn together by a dull hollow sound that followed the blow of a mattock; the iron had struck a skull, and the body was soon uncovered.
>
> (p. 133)

And then, Trelawny rushes forward into a description of the cremation that spares no gruesome detail:

> The heat from the sun and fire was so intense that the atmosphere was tremulous and wavy. The corpse fell open and the heart was laid bare. The frontal bone of the skull, where it had been struck with the mattock, fell off; and, as the back of the head rested on the red-hot bottom bars of the furnace, the brains literally seethed, bubbled and boiled as in a cauldron, for a very long time.
>
> (p. 134)

Echoing the oscillation between personality and impersonality that characterizes both Arnold and Shelley's accounts of poetic subjectivity, Trelawny's narrative exploits to sensational effect the indeterminacy of the body that is at once fully charged with human meaning and perfectly material, inhuman. As many readers have noticed, the scene's pathos lies in the distance between Shelley's soaring "spirit" and the shocking materiality of the body (another of Shelley's mourners, Marianne Hunt, who received a piece of the jaw-bone, wrote in an 1822 diary entry, "I look at my little box and think of the lip that covers what it contains until I can bear it no longer. A lip from whence every pure and generous feeling issued daily, hourly, and momentarily").[49] Karen Swann describes Trelawny's narrative as granting the poet's corpse an almost magical charisma: "The fire consumes the elaborate machinery Trelawny has mobilized to produce this spectacle on a recalcitrant, modern landscape: in the end, all that stays with us is the boiling, fabulous body, with its unorchestrated energies, utterly transfigured into something rich and strange—into the elusive, ungraspable figure of poetic genius."[50] The scene also, however, enacts a transference of charisma from the dead poet to the narrative itself, whose pyrotechnics are after all as much on display as the burning corpse. Through his privileged proximity to the poet, as if he has himself moved between worlds, Trelawny's seared hand becomes as much a fantastic object as the relic it seizes. That the corpse becomes at once the object of passionate attachment and the excuse for the literary machinery around it is precisely the logic of Trelawny's account.

Trelawny's staging of the cremation scene acts out a peculiarly Romantic form of transmission. As in De Quincey's narrative of his initial encounter with the living Wordsworth, the survival of poetic charisma is constructed by Romanticism's feeling readers as dependent on those readers' transformative and privileged experience of contact with a spectacular but absented authorial body. Substituting corpse for corpus, this logic of transmission is forecasted by the fundamentally anticipatory nature of Shelley's poetics. The title-page epigraph to *Recollections* is Shelley's pronouncement in *Defence of Poetry* that "No living poet ever arrived at the fullness of his fame." The quotation points on the one hand to what Samantha Matthews has called the "shame of historical neglect" exploited by Shelley's Victorian champions, and on the other hand to the role Shelley's theory of poetry opens up for the agency of the reader.[51] Both Shelley's poetry and his theory of poetry make the value or life of poems dependent on the activity of the reader who inhabits the futurity the poetry itself makes possible.[52] In the *Defence*, Shelley describes the relationship between Dante's poetry and successive generations of readers as fundamentally generative, using figures that parallel those of *Ode to the West Wind*:

> His very words are instinct with spirit; each is as a spark, a burning atom of inextinguishable thought; and many yet lie covered in the ashes of their birth, and pregnant with a lightning which has yet found no conductor. All high poetry is infinite; it is as the first acorn, which contained all oaks potentially. Veil after veil may be withdrawn, and the inmost naked beauty of the meaning never exposed. A great Poem is a fountain for ever overflowing with the waters of wisdom and delight; and after one person and one age has exhausted all its divine effluence which their peculiar relations enable them to share, another and yet another succeeds, and new relations are ever developed, the source of an unforeseen and an unconceived delight.[53]

Shelley claims not only that the meaning of poetry is produced by the particular historically contingent "relations" inhabited by readers, but that the activity of those readers is necessary to realize poetic ends "unforeseen and unconceived" by the writer. Weirdly anticipating in its figures of ashes and sparks the imagery of the cremation scene, Shelley's language locates meaning in the historical temporality that separates and connects the act of composition and the act of responsive reading: many words "*yet* lie covered in the ashes of their birth, and pregnant with a lightning which *has yet* found no conductor." Trelawny implicitly allies his communication of Shelley's personality to a future generation with such a structure of poetic transmission. Just as De Quincey asserts he would not be De Quincey without Wordsworth, but also that Wordsworth (in ways he cannot realize) requires De Quincey to be Wordsworth, Trelawny makes his own staging of the celebrity body essential to Shelley's futurity.

Though the possession of Shelley's heart promises continuity, as does the ability to renarrate the scene, the drowned body of the poet is also, obviously, terminal, the end of a certain living Romanticism.

Trelawny makes this clear in his harrowing description of Shelley's disfigured body:

> The face and hands, and parts of the body not protected by the dress, were fleshless. The tall slight figure, the jacket, the volume of Sophocles in one pocket, and Keats's poems in the other, doubled back, as if the reader, in the act of reading, had hastily thrust it away, were all too familiar to me to leave a doubt in my mind that this mutilated corpse was any other than Shelley's.
>
> (*Recollections*, p. 120)

The poignancy of the image Trelawny conjures of Shelley familiarly lost in his book, reading Keats as the storm rushes in, affirms the possibility of the survival of something of the poet: others will give to Shelley the loving attention he gave to Keats. But the ravaged body also reminds us that this scene marks a discontinuity, a gap that cannot be overcome.

Smoothly translating liminal ritual into vendable scene, Trelawny's narrative participates in disseminating a charismatic image of the Romantic poet, and at the same time demonstrates how the reception of authorial charisma can generate a kind of charisma for the reader. Though Trelawny claimed he made no money from his *Recollections*, the volume helped bring him back into the public eye (as did the expanded 1878 edition, *Records of Shelley, Byron, and the Author*, in the title of which, as Anne Barton notes, Trelawny claims equal billing with the poets), and Trelawny's memoirs helped make the cremation scene a popular subject for painters in the latter years of the century (see, for example, Louis-Edouard Fournier's *The Funeral of Shelley*).[54] The transferential effects exploited by Trelawny, moreover, become an important part of the legacy of Romanticism, on display in striking ways in two of the most ambitious and self-consciously influential theoretical statements in contemporary Romantic criticism, virtually contemporary though not in any obvious dialogue: Jerome McGann's 1983 *Romantic Ideology* and Paul de Man's essay "Shelley Disfigured," first published in 1979 and reprinted in *The Rhetoric of Romanticism* in 1984.[55]

McGann's polemic *Romantic Ideology*, which became a key text for New Historicist work in Romanticism, takes as its epigraph Trelawny's lines about snatching Shelley's heart. In his Introduction, McGann cites this most extraordinary moment of literary fetishism as a sort of parable for the kind of reading that, in so far as it historicizes the forms of thought present in the literary object, resists seduction by the ideologies encoded in that object. This kind of critical reading, McGann argues, exposes the way ideologies both of the past and of the present operate to disguise or abstract material realities. As a result of such a reading, McGann claims, "the abstractions and ideologies of the present are laid open to critique from another human world, and one which—by the privilege of its historical backwardness, as it were—can know nothing of our current historical illusions."[56] He goes on to compare the historicizing reader to Trelawny himself: "Like Trelawney at the cremation of Shelley, we shall reach for the unconsumed heart of the poem only if we are prepared to suffer a genuine change through its possession. Poetry is not to be had in the easy forms of our current ideologies."[57]

Paul de Man's roughly contemporary essay "Shelley Disfigured," described by Orrin Wang as de Man's "most violent statement on the unreadability of history," also uses Shelley's corpse as a figure against which to articulate critical difficulty.[58] De Man contends that the thematization and performance throughout Shelley's *The Triumph of Life* of a process of "disfiguration"— "the repetitive erasures by which language performs the erasure of its own positions"—demonstrates the text's warning that "nothing, whether deed, word, thought, or text, ever happens in relation, positive or negative, to anything that precedes, follows, or exists elsewhere, but only as a random event whose power, like the power of death, is due to the randomness of its occurrence."[59] This performance is, however, arrested by an event "outside" the poem, the text's "reduction to the status of a fragment brought about by the actual death and subsequent disfigurement of Shelley's body, burned after his boat capsized and he drowned off the coast of Lerici."[60] Shelley's actual death in fact leaves the poem incomplete, but by the same token freezes the poem as an aesthetic object, its contours marked by the interruption, in both senses, of the life.

De Man's rhetoric climaxes in a remarkable series of sentences, oratorical in tone, that gesture toward the hortatory conclusion he deliberately withholds: "For what we have done with the dead Shelley, and with all the other dead bodies that appear in Romantic literature [...] is simply to bury them, to bury them in their own texts made into epitaphs and monumental graves. They have been made into statues for the benefit of future archaeologists 'digging in the grounds for the new foundations' of their own monuments. They have been transformed into historical and aesthetic objects." In de Man's view, our critical and historical narratives grant a coherence or meaningfulness to lives, texts and histories, but this apparent meaningfulness or shape is really a fiction imposed on the actual randomness of events. To make the dead Shelley into a monument is thus to remove Shelley's life and texts from the historicity of their condition, isolating them from the real effects of temporality in the same gesture that we inscribe them within a meaningful history (for example, one which makes sense of Shelley's death by reading it as predicted by his poetry). But "such monumentalization is by no means necessarily a naive or evasive gesture, and it certainly is not a gesture that anyone can pretend to avoid making."[61] As we have seen, Symonds, Trelawny and Arnold each in his own way obviously seeks to effect such a transformation, but, absorbing the sensational effect of the dead poet's body into the movement of his own rhetoric, de Man himself uses the dramatic effect of "producing" Shelley's captivating corpse to amplify the persuasive power of his claims. (Evidence of this rhetorical investment comes in various linguistic strategies de Man uses to increase a sense of pathos: for instance, the actually extraneous detail of his mildly alliterative reference to "the actual death and subsequent disfigurement of Shelley's body, burned after his boat capsized and he drowned off the coast of Lerici," and the repetition of the contrasting pronouns "we" and "them"—"what we have done [...] is to bury them, to bury them.")

Though de Man and McGann approach Shelley from very different critical positions—with de Man insisting on a kind of historicity that would undermine the very possibility of the historical referentiality McGann would restore—Trelawny's staging of the cremation scene echoes through the work of both critics as each, like Trelawny, draws attention to the potency of his own act of transmission. As a scene of transmission, Trelawny's narrative holds out the promise of continuity (legible in the seared hand, tangible in the heart or bone) and at the same time marks its own failure, the brutal fact that Shelley is now forever devastatingly unreachable. As with Keats, the pathos of the poet's early death often underwrites a transfer of meaning between the poetry and the body whose accidental itinerary seems so eerily predicted by the poetry. De Man shows that our desire to grant the poet's death a literary significance stems from the difficulty of recognizing the true randomness of the event, and our need (like that we see in Arnold) to fix the writer's life and the writer's texts within a stabilizing, reassuring web of meaning. De Man's essay demonstrates as well how the felt impersonality or meaninglessness of the writer's body can also be an element of its affective charge.

The cremation scene remains a focal point for Romantic criticism because it encodes unsettled and unsettling relationships between authorial body and authorial intention, and between the body of the author and the feeling reader, just those that Arnold explores in his meditation on Shelley's celebrity. We keep returning to this scene because we find in it the expression of a powerfully charismatic image of the Romantic poet and of Romanticism, but also because it offers a renewable source of charisma for the reader who transmits such an image. Whether as a passionate truth-seeker, politically daring rebel, acolyte of beauty and sensation, angelic dreamer, or angel of deconstruction, charismatic versions of Shelley's character have been so vital to the history of the poet's reception that, no matter how we expose the processes through which these images are constructed, the affective pull of such images may remain. Though we operate now within different institutions of reading, in negotiating our own relationship to Romanticism's glamour we still work through the affective dynamics Arnold, Trelawny and other nineteenth-century readers of Shelley set in motion.

5
"The Atmosphere of Authorship": Landon, Byron and Literary Culture

In my previous chapters, I focused on a group of male poets—Byron, Keats and Shelley—whose lives and afterlives in literary culture helped to define distinctively Romantic modes of fame. In this and the following chapter, I turn to the work of two female poets, Letitia Landon and Elizabeth Barrett Browning, who brought Romantic tropes of literary celebrity forward into the more industrialized literary market of the early Victorian period. Byron-worshippers in their youth, both Landon and Barrett wrote in a moment after the initial revolutionary energies of Romanticism had been absorbed into cliché. These final two chapters make a case for reading the celebrity of these poets in terms of a "long Romanticism" that crosses period and gender divides. But they will also demonstrate the crucial difference gender makes in the ways poetic celebrity could be constructed and experienced.

A transatlantic sensation in the 1820s and 1830s, Landon is now back on the critical radar screen after going missing for most of the twentieth century, but her rediscovery by critics has often been accompanied by an element of suspicion.[1] Under the initials "L.E.L.," Landon came to public notice contributing poems to the *Literary Gazette* and other periodicals in the early 1820s, then burst into international celebrity with her romance *The Improvisatrice, and Other Poems* (1824), going on to become a prolific reviewer and critic, a relatively successful novelist, and a prominent figure in the efflorescence of one of the era's most significant literary commercial innovations, the annual or gift book.[2] Many modern critics portray Landon as writing in disturbing conformity to the "poetess" ideal, endlessly repeating stories of lovelorn, abandoned, suicidal heroines. Her poetry, they point out, is suffused with an eroticized language of feeling—pulses, throbs, thrills, chills, burning hearts, the "touching voice."[3] In Angela Leighton's view, such writing plays off a traditional equation of women with their bodies, "assert[ing] an easy equivalence of body and text, as the one provides a visible motive for the other."[4] Emphasizing Landon's work for the annuals, Anne Mellor charges that Landon "commodified herself as a purchasable icon of female beauty," and finds her entrapped within a cultural fantasy of femininity.[5] Richard Cronin similarly contends that "L.E.L. was a device that from the first invited the reader to decode the poem and reveal the poet, to pry beneath the text, which is conceived as a somewhat diaphanous material scarcely obscuring the warm and palpitating body of the woman who wrote it."[6] Though willing to see Landon's aesthetic in more rewardingly complicated terms, Jerome McGann also sees her poetry as exemplifying a kind of bad faith, knowingly rehearsing Byronic language and poses to produce a jaded "Art of Disillusion" that merely "recycles popularity."[7] To a number of modern critics, even Landon's death in West Africa in 1838, soon after her marriage to the colonial governor George MacLean, itself reflects the logic of her poetry: according to these accounts, her poetry, like Sappho's, announces its author's dark fate, not in the mode of the supposed prescience of a Keats or Shelley, but as a sensational cliché.[8]

Such critical assessments indeed parallel constructions of L.E.L.'s celebrity by some of her own contemporaries. Reviewers did in fact frequently describe Landon's verse in the terms Mellor and Cronin propose, drawing the faintest of lines between admiration for Landon's talent and admiration for her beauty. William Maginn's 1824 review of *The Improvisatrice* in *Blackwood's*, for example, links these forms of admiration with a disingenuous protest that "it is not because she is a very pretty girl, and a very good girl, that we are going to praise her poems, but because we like them."[9] Landon herself, her promoters, and her readers frequently identify her persona with poetess archetypes such as Sappho and Corinne, and describe her poetry in terms that signal, within the gender ideology of the period, a distinctly "feminine" poetics characterized by emotional expressiveness and an almost exclusive focus on love. When the *Literary Gazette*'s editor William Jerdan reviewed his star author's *Improvisatrice, and Other*

Poems in those pages—incurring well-deserved charges of "puffery"—the terms he uses are like a lexicon of the poetess idea: in Landon's poems, he writes, "simplicity, gracefulness, fancy and pathos seem to gush forth in spontaneous and sweet union," earning L.E.L. the title "the English Sappho."[10] Landon herself sometimes acknowledges her poetry as programmatically sentimental, as in her Preface to the *Venetian Bracelet* (1829): "Aware that to elevate I must first soften, and that if I wished to purify I must first touch, I have ever endeavored to bring forward grief, disappointment, the fallen leaf, the faded flower, the broken heart, and the early grave."[11] That such characterizations of her poetry operate within the systematically developed ethos of periodicals like Jerdan's *Gazette* can be seen at once from a glimpse at a typical page: in one issue, for example, a series of L.E.L.'s poems, "Medallion Wafers," depicting scenes of intense passion, shares the page with two different representations of female artists dying for love.[12] The "Sketches of Society" department contains a sensational account of "the Sappho-like death" of the German poet Louisa Brachmann, whose demise is attributed to "unhappy love," while a report on recent art exhibitions in Paris describes M. Ducis's portrait of the "unhappy Properzia Rossi, a celebrated female sculptor at Bologna in the sixteenth century, who died the victim of despised love" (the inspiration for Hemans's poem of the same name).

But even within contemporary responses these constructions of L.E.L., and sometimes her own self-constructions, jostle against understandings of her writing that challenge such clichés. As Tricia Lootens has argued powerfully, the poetess mythology obscures both the generic range and the topical reach of Landon's writing, replicating one version of the writer at the expense of all the ways in which she plays against type.[13] Through the pioneering work of Lootens, Isobel Armstrong, Adriana Craciun and others, we have recently seen Landon reemerging as a savvy, multifaceted writer with sharp critical purchase on the cultural contradictions she inhabits and examines.[14] This chapter corroborates and builds on these revisionary accounts, demonstrating that the "thrills" and "chills" of Landon's poetry bear a more complex relation to the marketplace and to the conditions of public visibility than they have often been granted.

I focus in particular on the multiple ways Landon, in her writing and in her public personae, reworks and redeploys the tropes of Byronic celebrity. I argue that she mobilizes the resources of Byronic fandom—an eroticized gaze at Byron and an ambivalent identification with Byron—in order to examine and reconfigure the gendered relations of spectator and spectacle in which she works both as a cultural producer and as a reader of culture. I read her ambivalent appropriation of Byronic gestures as key to her attempt to forge an identity as a literary professional in the 1820s and 1830s, decades when the professional woman writer lacks a secure model through which to occupy the public stage as a professional. But though Landon's writing obviously parallels the affective strategies of Byron and of her contemporary Hemans, I argue that her rhetoric of feeling also at times breaks significantly with the model of sympathetic response invoked by these poets, instead opening up alternatives to the circuit of readerly feeling with which L.E.L. is so often conflated.

In the nineteenth-century cultural imagination Byronic celebrity is a dominant model through which the careers of women poets might be understood. When Frederic Rowton's mid-century anthology *The Female Poets of Great Britain* (1848) identifies Landon as the "Byron of our poetesses," for example, it's a sobriquet he has to take back from Caroline Norton.[15] But the title "Byron of our poetesses" is tellingly ambivalent.[16] Rowton's comparison of Landon to Byron aims to mark the power of her writing and of her legend, but also registers caution about both. In Rowton's take, not only Landon's poetry but her celebrity bears Byronic strains. She is Byronic not only because "Passion and Sadness are the idols of her pen," but because, as in Byron's case, the melancholy of the poetry and the tragic spectacle of the poet's life hauntingly shadow each other: Landon and Byron "both acquired a world-wide fame in youth; both were shamefully maligned and misrepresented; both became gloomy and misanthropical under the falsehoods asserted of them; both died young, and abroad."[17] Like Byron's, Landon's poetry is dangerous to the reader, Rowton warns, because it exposes so affectingly the naked truth of a heart that feels in error. "We must suppose that she *felt* what she wrote: and if so, her written sadness was a real sadness," Rowton argues, but Landon's view of life is so melancholy as to "libel Providence and dishearten man."[18] Echoing the language of Byron's reception, Rowton proposes that Landon exerts a fascination that needs to be treated warily: "There is an evil spirit in such sentiments which should be bidden behind us."[19] But if, to readers like Rowton, Landon rivals Byron in both poetic power and power to disturb, she is still also described as a "female Byron," stuck in a secondary status being compared to the male celebrity.

Rowton's discussion of Landon is in some ways the flip side of the iconography of L.E.L. in conservative venues like *Fraser's*. In direct contrast to Rowton, *Fraser's* writers insist on assimilating L.E.L. to the magazine's own version of a feminine ideal: beautiful, unthreatening, and essentially domestic in her writing. In the commentary accompanying Landon's portrait in the "Gallery of Literary Figures," for example, Francis Mahony rebukes an imaginary, ungallant critic who complains that L.E.L. writes only about love. "How, Squaretoes, can there be too much of love in a young lady's writings?," Mahony asks rhetorically, continuing, "Is she to write of politics, of political economy, or pugilism, or punch?"[20] (The viciously unflattering portrait of Harriet Martineau in the next month's installment of the "Gallery" demonstrates what the *Fraser's* crew thinks of women who do write about such topics.) Mahony's image of L.E.L. is the antithesis of Rowton's "female Byron": "a very nice, unbluestockingish, well-dressed, and trim-looking young lady, fond of sitting pretty much as Croquis [the illustrator] has depicted her, in neat and carefully-arrayed costume, at her table, chatting, in pleasant and cheering style, with all and sundry who approach her."[21] But while domesticating L.E.L.'s poetry, the review publicizes her as a sexually available figure in a manner that ultimately aligns her with the trope of the "female Byron," with its overtones of scandalous sexual exposure. Mahony's essay begins by riffing on Landon's own play with Edmund Burke's rhetoric of chivalry (Burke provides the title page motto for Landon's volume *The Troubadour*):[22]

> LETITIA ELIZABETH LANDON! Burke said, that ten thousand swords ought to have leaped out of their scabbards at the mention of the name of Marie Antoinette; and in like manner we maintain, that ten thousand pens should leap out of their inkbottles to pay homage to L.E.L. In Burke's time, Jacobinism had banished chivalry—at least, out of France—and the swords remained unbared for the queen; we shall prove, that our pens shall be uninked for the poetess.[23]

The uncomfortable joke here is the way the sexually aggressive language plays against the professions of chivalry, a subtext reinforced by the allusions to Burke's notorious rendition of the crowd entering Marie Antoinette's chamber as a scene of sexual assault, and by the cultural history of representations of Marie Antoinette's body, with its pornographic associations. Similarly, Maginn's commentary on Landon's image in a *Fraser's* illustration of prominent women writers ("Regina's Maids of Honor" [1836]) merges Landon's desirable body with her affecting writing: "the swan-like neck we trace, and the figure full of grace, and the mignon hand whose pen wrote the *Golden Violet,* and the *Lit'rary Gazette,* and *Francesca*'s mournful story. (Isn't she painted *con amore*?)"[24] As David Higgins notes, the parenthetical comment, connecting Landon's habit of writing about love and her status as love object for the reader, would have particular resonance for Landon's contemporaries given the circulation of rumors linking her romantically with Maginn and with the *Fraser's* illustrator Maclise, as well as with Jerdan and with Edward Bulwer-Lytton.[25] The close of Mahony's essay likewise communicates the idea of Landon's availability, positioning her readers as potential suitors: "But why is she Miss Landon? 'A fault like this should be corrected,' as Whistlecraft says."[26] An American newspaper of the same year goes even further, arguing in a review of *The Three Histories* by Maria Jane Jewsbury (now "Mrs. Fletcher") that "literary ladies, like the Amazons, should never marry" to preserve their availability as fantasy objects for the male reader:

> Above all, who would not be sorry to see the peerless Letitia Emilia Landon—the cynosure of a thousand minds, the delight of every heart—whose magic initials call up such varied, such instant emotions, coldly *married,* and changing the deathless wreath that flashes, sanctis ignis, round her virgin name, into the unpoetic *"Mrs."* of a city money-changer or office underling. Oh no, the charm would be broken, the talisman destroyed.[27]

The differing constructions of Landon by Rowton's anthology and the *Fraser's* writers indicate that L.E.L.'s public identity is neither uniform nor stable but contradictory and contested, like the "poetess" ideal itself. Yet where Rowton reads Landon's verse as powerfully autobiographical and *Fraser's* sees it as highly conventional, in both constructions Landon herself becomes spectacle: the object of the curious reader's gaze, an object of desire, fascination or pity. Rather than allowing these critical constructions to determine my own reading of L.E.L., however, I propose to show how her writing in fact unsettles these conditions of display through its manipulation of the dynamics of fandom. That is, while on one level Landon's romances obviously cater to the discourse that takes L.E.L. herself as the object of the reader's desire, her romances also reproduce and interrogate an already available fandom that takes the male body as romantic object. In these dynamics, the male poet is himself the spectacle, and Landon appears as a consumer and as a producer of culture who negotiates in both roles the erotic and cultural power of the Byronic signifier. Emphasizing Landon's critical replaying of Byronic tropes and plots, Craciun points out both Landon's attention to "Byronic heroines as victims of a misogynist ethos" and her parallel "fascination with the possibilities of the Byronic hero for the woman poet."[28] As Craciun suggests, Landon's romances encode a response to Byron and his texts that is at once desiring, identificatory and resistant. Reading Landon in these terms shifts our focus from the way L.E.L. is put on display as the object of desire (and especially the male reader's desire) to the way the female reader emerges as the subject rather than the object of the desiring gaze. In proposing *The Improvisatrice* and subsequent productions like *The Troubadour* as texts that represent the fan's desire, I do not mean to describe them as confessional, however. Rather, the central cultural position of Byron makes the kind of response Landon represents in her poems less personal than public; she registers a cultural phenomenon. It is possible to speculate then that while male critics labored to identify Landon's rhetoric of feeling with the poet herself, male and female readers of her poems may have also identified with her feeling, seeing their own Byronic fandom reflected and heightened in hers.[29]

Byron's presence in Landon's verse is prominently marked through borrowings within the tales—characters, plots, settings and language that are clearly modeled on *Childe Harold* and the Oriental Tales. Lorenzo, the love-object of *The Improvisatrice*, is almost egregiously Byronic, with his "dark and flashing eye" that "mingled gloom and flame," "raven curls," "high and haughty brow" and a lip that would pour "lava floods of eloquence" were it not for his reserve; Raymond, the hero of Landon's follow-up *The Troubadour* (1825), follows in the same tradition.[30] Likewise, the marketing of Landon's volumes plays up such Byronic affiliations: *The Troubadour,* for example, bore a frontispiece depicting a scene from a *Giaour*-like inset tale of "a Moorish maiden's flight / In secret with a Christian knight."[31] Jerdan's review of *The Improvisatrice* underscores these identifications by positioning Landon as the explicit heir to Scott and Byron, the poet who will carry forward the torch of romance now that "the minstrel of the Border is hushed and the light of *Childe Harold* is extinguished."[32] In *Blackwood's*, the fictional Christopher North countered by arguing that he "could see nothing of the originality, vigour, and so forth, they all chatter about. Very elegant, flowing verses they are, but all made up of Moore and Byron."[33]

More is going on here than mere imitation, which might indeed create the threat that Christopher North acts to defuse. Landon's writing at once affirms and interrogates the charismatic power of Byron and Byronic romance for the female reader and the female artist. Take, for example, the scene early in *The Improvisatrice* in which the heroine first encounters the Byron-figure Lorenzo. Sinking beneath Lorenzo's thrilling, "burning gaze," the Improvisatrice is overcome:

> My hand kept wandering on my lute,
> In music, but unconsciously
> My pulses throbbed, my heart beat high,
> A flush of dizzy ecstasy
> Crimsoned my cheek; I felt warm tears
> Dimming my sight, yet was it sweet,
> My wild heart's most bewildering beat,
> Consciousness, without hopes or fears,
> Of a new power within me waking [...]
>
> I left the boat—the crowd: my mood
> Made my soul pant for solitude.
>
> (459–472, 474–5)

If this scenario seems quite obviously to play into the discourse that takes L.E.L.'s poetry and her body as the object of male voyeurism, it also asserts the usefulness of the Byronic signifier for the pleasure of the female gazer, or fantasist. Read as a scene of reading rather than just quotation, the scene asserts the female reader's ability to incorporate the Byronic signifier into an autoerotic economy: to appropriate the male celebrity body solely as a signifier *for* the female reader. Incorporating Byron's style, Landon sets up a desiring, not a simply derivative, relationship to the poet, manifested in the kind of affect reading Byron reportedly did produce: throbbing pulses, high heart beats, a flush of "dizzy ecstasy," and for many emboldened readers perhaps a "consciousness of new powers waking."[34]

Dorothy Mermin has shown how Byron occupied a powerful place in the imagination of many young women in the nineteenth century, including Elizabeth Barrett and Charlotte Brontë, both of whom when quite young wrote erotically charged fantasy experimenting with looking *at* and writing *as* Byron. In the case of many successful women writers in the nineteenth century, Mermin argues, "Byron was a model on many levels—stylistic, political, moral, erotic—for the rebellion implicit in the fact of female ambition," so that for these writers, "Byronism was not just a stage to be outgrown: it was a psychological impulsion to be cherished and an artistic problem they had to resolve."[35] If de Staël's *Corinne* offers one major figure through which women writers can probe the possibilities and perils of female celebrity—and *The Improvisatrice* is obviously modeled in part on that novel—Byron gives writers like Landon an imaginative model for fame with greater mobility across gender lines. Such an identification with Byron is, however, deeply complicated by the gender relations inscribed in and around Byronic romance, as I suggested above. The female writers who follow in Byron's wake exploit the way his romances put the male body on display; at the same time, these writers question the limitation of female agency in the world of the romances and implicitly defy Byron's denigration of female activity in the world of writing.

If love stories in Landon's romances almost always end in loneliness and desperation if not death, at least the female characters are allowed a pleasure in desire—a star turn in their performance of longing, grief, or disappointment—from which the male characters are fully disbarred. Where the Improvisatrice gives a final performance of spectacular theatricality—"LORENZO! be this kiss a spell! / My first!—my last! FAREWELL!—FAREWELL!" (l. 1529–30)—Lorenzo is immured in a voiceless grief, "his sole employ to brood / Silently over his sick heart / In sorrow and in solitude" (l. 1542–4). This is no Heathcliff, uttering growls or depredations or cries of longing for his lost love; when the unnamed tourist who narrates the final section arrives at this odd shrine, all Lorenzo can do is stand mutely by the portrait and inscription on the wall, "LORENZO TO HIS MINSTREL LOVE," which must speak for him. Yes, the female artist dies for want of love, but the Improvisatrice gets to go out with a dazzling final number, while Lorenzo is sentenced to a lifetime of silent, obsessive worship of her image; and the unnamed final narrator allows Landon to slip into the voice of expert authority to close her poem. Jonah Siegel identifies this final narrator as a male "connoisseur" figure typical of the "art romance."[36] But the voice of connoisseurship is one Landon skillfully develops in her poems on images, in her editorial activities, and in her reviews. Landon's own voice might as easily be identified with this final narrator as with the Improvisatrice herself. Inscribed in the poem's putatively tragic close is the female artist's mastery.

Landon's later poem "The Portrait of Lord Byron, at Newstead Abbey," published with a reproduction of the 1813 Westall portrait in *Fisher's Drawing Room Scrapbook* (1840), suggestively recalls and reverses the visual iconography that closes *The Improvisatrice.*[37] Focusing more on the Abbey and its grounds than on the portrait in particular, the poem is written from the perspective of an unnamed visitor, or visitors, to Byron's former home—an inclusive "we" that at once calls to mind a party of tourists and links the reader to Landon in its proposition of a shared experience of Byronic personality:

His name is on the haunted shade,
His name is in the air,
We walk the forest's twilight glade,
And only he is there.
The ivy wandering o'er the wall,
The fountain falling musical
Proclaim him everywhere,
The heart is full of him, and flings
Itself on all surrounding things.[38]

Dwelling on the talismanic power of Byron's glamorous name, Landon spectralizes his haunting and pervasive presence. The poem registers both the viewer's emotional investment in Byron's history—"the heart is full of him"—and the viewer's adoption of a form of subjectivity Byron popularized, the heart that "flings / Itself on all surrounding things" (the dedication of the poem to Byron's sister

Augusta further locates the writer within the emotional ambit of the actual Byron and within the social world in which his personal relationships still figure). Asking how Newstead's Gothic gloom might have shaped Byron's boyhood fantasies and his adult personality, the poem reviews Byron's life story with an eye at once affectionate and critical, distancing the viewer from Byron and bringing her closer. At the poem's close, Landon underlines the poem's equivocal view of Byron and the attachment Byron inspires. Noting "the deep enchantment we have felt, / When every thought and feeling dwelt / Beneath his spirit's thrall," Landon concludes by placing both Byron and this enchantment firmly in the viewer's, and the public's, past, so that Newstead represents not only Byron's younger self but the reader's: "Sad, softened are the hearts that come / To gaze around his boyish home."[39] The Byron of the poem is not the poetic precursor to the visiting poet but the aspiring youth—ever more about to be—on whom the sadder and wiser adult visitor gazes.

As she does in these lines on Byron, Landon frequently scripts the scene of reception in terms of the reader's heightened emotional responsiveness to the feeling the writer is imagined as expressing or wishing to communicate, in conformity with popular theories of the lyric, especially poetry by women, as ideally expressive. Armstrong has noticed, however, that the relationship between nineteenth-century women poets and expressive theory is "ambiguous" in practice.[40] Landon both idealizes and pulls away from a model of poetic expression that construes the reader–writer relationship in terms of a desire for sympathetic understanding. In her essay "On the Character of Mrs. Hemans's Writings," published after Hemans's death, for example, Landon argues that "fame, which the Greeks idealized so nobly, is but the fulfillment of that desire for sympathy which can never be brought home to the individual."[41] Quoting a line from de Staël's *Corinne* also quoted by Hemans—"Oh! mes amis, rapellez-vous quelquefois mes vers; mon âme y est empreinte"—Landon contends that poetry works through an "intimate" exchange of feeling between the poet who seeks to confide and the properly receptive reader, who finds in the poem an echo of his or her own experience, so that the poem's "haunted words will be to us even as our own."[42] It is no accident then that the essay on Hemans begins with a quotation of a quotation, since this model of reading poetry is in essence a model of quotation: those words seem haunted by my feeling—they are even as my own words. In the model Landon articulates here, poets provide the language through which we realize our responses to our own emotional history and to our own surroundings; those responses are thus imprinted with the identity of the poet whose language teaches us to feel. What endorses the lyric feeling for which Landon celebrates Hemans and Byron and Corinne, and implicitly her own poetry, is its ability not only to be quoted but to feel like a quotation. The language of genuine interiority on this model is necessarily one that has already been in public circulation.

If Byron is one primary authorizing figure for L.E.L., so too is Corinne, and behind Corinne, Sappho. Exploring the rich variety of Victorian appropriations of Sappho, Yopie Prins sees in the "self-replicating performance of Sappho's suicide in Victorian women's verse [...] a gesture of de-personification, demonstrating how 'woman' is personified to produce a pathos that is curiously impersonal, or 'sentimental' precisely because it poses a question about how to read such personifications."[43] While the thrills and chills of Landon's verse obviously recall what Marlon Ross calls the "affectional poetics" of Hemans—for whom Byron, Corinne, and Sappho are also central—Landon's figures of feeling sometimes break with the sympathetic compact underscoring this poetics in ways that Prins's observation helps us to read.[44] Landon herself emphasizes that the sentimental economies of Hemans's poetry aim at sympathy: they are designed to include the reader in the circulation of feeling mapped by the poem, as thrills of horror, grief, longing or joy pass from character to character, from speaker to song, and implicitly between reader and poem as well. This circulation of feeling is frequently underlined explicitly—the "deep horror chilling every vein" at the close of *The Last Banquet of Antony and Cleopatra,* the "deep thrill" lingering on the lyre at the close of "Properzia Rossi"—and is often sped along by the poem's imagery—the kindling and leaping of burning feeling imaged in the wreathing fires in "Casabianca" and "The Bride of the Greek Isle," for example—or by the poem's final couplets, which often provide an epigrammatic summary that might voice the reader's concluding feeling (see "Woman and Fame" and "Corinne at the Capitol," for example).[45] Landon's poetry by contrast contains oddly affecting moments in which strongly registered feeling resists such circulation to become concretized in a different way—moments where what holds the reader is neither sympathetic excitement nor sympathetic sorrow, but a sense of the strangeness of the feeling rendered, its exteriority or impersonality. The chills and thrills that afflict Landon's verse have a habit of spinning loose of subjectivity, interrupting the circuit of sympathetic feeling that supposedly links reader, poem and poet.

Consider this passage, from the inset narrative "The Charmed Cup" in *The Improvisatrice*:

> And she whom JULIAN left—she stood
> A cold white statue: as the blood
> Had, when in vain her last wild prayer,
> Flown to her heart, and frozen there,
> Upon her temple, each dark vein
> Swelled in its agony of pain.
> Chill, heavy damps were on her brow:
> Her arms were stretched at length, though now
> Their clasp was on the empty air:
> A funeral pall—her long black hair
> Fell over her; herself the tomb
> Of her own youth, and breath, and bloom.
>
> (588–99)

The image draws on theatrical convention, the stock poses in the tradition of Siddons discussed by Judith Pascoe as a primary source for Landon's portrayal of her deathbound heroines, and the lines on one level constitute a conventional invitation for the audience's sympathy.[46] But isolated moments of bodily distortion in this passage are really striking in their physicality—"each dark vein / Swelled in its agony of pain;" "chill, heavy damps [...] on her brow;" the "blood [...] flown to her heart, and frozen there;" a few lines later, "Her hair is wet with rain and sleet / And blood is on her small snow feet" (612–13). The emphasis in passages such as this one shifts noticeably from, on the one hand, the body as what gives communicable voice to emotion, to, on the other hand, the sensation or numbness of the body as body, the physical fact of the head or the heart or the feet being cold or wet or swollen or bloody. Or compare the description the Improvisatrice gives of her painting of

Ariadne: "Her naked feet the pebbles prest; / The tempest-wind sang in her vest: / A wild stare in her glassy eyes; / White lips, as parched by their hot sighs; / And cheek more pallid than the spray, / Which, cold and colourless, on it lay" (1329–34). The painting is offered as an image of the Improvisatrice's despair, but it seems to me Landon's interest in these lines lies not with the history of feeling that leads to this moment, but with the body itself and its sensations: the lines privilege tactility, sensory experience, over the communication of emotion. This is true even of the detailing of physical sensation, the "wild heart's most bewildering beat," in the lines I quoted above from the Improvisatrice's initial response to Lorenzo's gaze: the body's responses take over attention from the feeling they are meant to signify. Indeed, read in these terms, the "wild heart's most bewildering beat" seems not really a response to an emotion, but rather an insistence of the physical that provokes a psychic disorientation registered at the level of the metrical line.

If the body in distress signifies within the poem's narratives of desire and heartbreak, it also has the tendency to become an autonomous object of analysis, its sensations strangely impersonal and inaccessible, in ways that loosen the connection of the body's distress to the referential ground of feeling metaphorically represented by the longing, bewildered or broken heart. Landon's poetry takes the body to extremes that rival, and sometimes surpass or simply break free from, the emotional extremes for which her poetry became famous. Landon's fascination with such extremes is evident in such poems as "The Frozen Ship," in which the pathos of the shipwreck is centered on a remarkably rendered loss of *physical* sensation: as the sailors freeze to death, "Each look'd upon his comrade's face, / Pale as funereal stone; / Yet none could touch the other's hand / For none could feel his own."[47] What's especially chilling about these lines is the turn from the possibility of emotional interchange (the exchange of gaze and touch) to the devastating and paradoxically shared isolation of the body *in extremis* ("none could feel his own").

These distressed, frozen or overheated, swollen, bloodied, and fragmented bodies direct our attention both to the alienating force of social machineries—the distortive gender ideologies encoded in the romance logics that produce Landon's suffering heroines, for example—and to the power of Landon's poetry as a machinery for generating affect. Landon's figures of feeling often contest, rather than endorse, the grounds for the kind of reading that sees L.E.L. as inviting the reader to treat the poem (in Cronin's words) simply "as a somewhat diaphanous material scarcely obscuring the warm and palpitating body of the woman who wrote it."[48] As Prins argues, rather, her sentimental personifications raise questions precisely about the process of personification and its implications. The bodily extremes of Landon's poetry experiment with new possibilities for poetic subjectivity, exploring the ability of textually rendered sensation to become detached from the emotional history we call personality, and the ability of poetry to analyze, as well as express, the way bodies feel.

So far in this chapter I have discussed Landon's language of feeling first in terms of Byron-inspired fandom and then as an investigation of states of sensation that departs from the romances of Byron or Hemans. In the final section of the chapter, I turn to consider Landon's language of feeling in one more light: as a rhetoric of professionalization. Like many of her contemporary women writers, Landon repeatedly represents female celebrity as pathos; borrowing the title of a Hemans poem, we might call this the topos of "woman and fame." In the reiterated scenario, a spectacularly talented woman is torn between vociferous public acclaim and the claims of romantic love or familial devotion; the convention sets up an irresolvable conflict between identity as an artist and identity as a woman, so that brilliant artistic success turns out always to be hollow for the female celebrity. "What is fame to a woman but a dazzling degradation?," asks Jewsbury's 1830 novella *The History of an Enthusiast*, echoing Hemans's artist-figure Properzia Rossi—"Worthless fame! / That in *his* bosom wins not for my name / Th'abiding-place it ask'd!" (l. 81–3)—and Landon's anagrammatic surrogate Eulalie, in *History of a Lyre* (1829): "I am a woman:—tell me not of fame."[49] This reiterated complaint reflects the collision of cultural assumptions about the woman artist: while on the one hand nineteenth-century culture tends to construe the woman artist entirely in terms of public performance and self-display, on the other hand, the culture idealizes an essentially private "womanhood," constituted in terms of the intimate bonds of romantic or familial affection. (In her fascinating novel *Ethel Churchill*, Landon splits the analysis of celebrity through two characters, the aspiring writer Walter Maynard and the performative, admiration-craving Lady Marchmont; neither character finds emotional fulfillment, and both meet disastrous ends.)[50] If Landon's exploration of Byronic fandom connects her to the position of many of her readers, Landon's relationship to Byron also has to do with Landon's self-positioning as a writer and literary personality within the terms of this dilemma. The language of Byronism serves Landon's effort to forge an identity for herself as a literary *professional*, in decades in which—as *Fraser's* awkward treatment of female authorship suggests—no easy model for such an identity exists for women poets. Thomas Pfau notes that "professionalization pivots on the emergence of an entirely new *aesthetics* of social appearance, one that identifies some individuals as professionals and, by the same token, confers on them the social credit of a dedicated professional community."[51] For Landon, as we have seen, Byron is a figure against whom she can test her own ambition and her own experience of visibility. With Scott's, however, his romances are also the resource for a professionalizing aesthetics in Pfau's sense, which she deploys through the "themes of chivalry and romance, feudal pageants and Eastern splendour" Mary Howitt identified as her characteristic province.[52]

Jerdan's review of *The Improvisatrice*, the reader will recall, has Landon filling in the gap left in the world of (bestselling) romance now that "the minstrel of the Border is hushed and the light of *Childe Harold* is extinguished." Byron and Scott are particularly appealing models for Landon because their celebrity sutures the romance of originary authorship and the new-found glamour of the publishing scene: their success points at once to a residual notion of authorial power and to the power of the literary system as a system. As the heroic ideal of authorship morphed by fits and starts into the idea of the literary professional, the publishing "scene" began in the 1820s and 1830s to acquire a glamour in its own right. Publishers and editors were recognized as key literary players, and the behind-the-scenes action of publishing became sensationalized as an object of public fascination. In Moore's 1830 *Life* of Byron, for example, Byron's correspondence with his publisher Murray is reproduced as a central piece of the drama of the poet's career, and the action in Murray's establishment is restaged as a prime object of the reader's fascination.[53] Even as it foregrounds the grubby mechanics of the industrialized world of publishing, the highly self-reflexive commentary on the literary scene in the periodicals seems to trade on the reader's desire to go behind the scenes, somewhat in the manner of a Hollywood confidential.[54] In the 1830s, *Fraser's* "Gallery" gives prominence to editors and publishers as well as writers (it begins in fact with a portrait of William Jerdan) and, like the "Noctes Ambrosianae" series in *Blackwood's* in the 1820s, trades in literary gossip that satirizes its objects, writers or editors, but also flaunts its knowingness in a way that seems to anticipate (or to call for) public curiosity about the literary scene *as* scene.[55] If the glamour that attaches not only to authors themselves but also to the apparatus of authorship reflects the mythic power accorded individual "genius" in these decades, the growing recognition of the power of the publishing apparatus also calls such myths of individual genius into question.

Male writers in these decades have access to an emergent ideal of what Patrick Leary terms the "author-businessman as respectable literary professional" that at least partially reconciles genius and the marketplace by subduing a heroic ideal of Romantic authorship to Victorian ideas of productivity and propriety.[56] But while women writers of these decades proved themselves extremely adept and successful professionals, it was riskier for them to appear in this character in public, especially without the cover of an aristocratic title; indeed, a model for women comparable to the "author-business*man*" did not yet exist. For women, as we have seen already in the cases of Landon and Martineau, fame as a working writer could often spell association either with sexual scandal or with aggressive masculinity; in the early nineteenth century, the scandalizing example of Mary Wollstonecraft still resonated loudly. Hemans responded to this dilemma by publicly distancing herself from the publishing scene: though a tough and acute negotiator of contracts (she demanded, and got, a higher fee for her contributions to *Blackwood's* than any of the magazine's male contributors), she never visited London, staying in Wales with her brood of children (and so, in fact, devoting herself to writing).[57] Landon, by contrast, identified herself closely with the London literary scene, moving in fashionable society circles (including Caroline Lamb's), forging friendships with writers and editors, attaining prominence as an editor and reviewer herself, and writing about the literary scene in her fiction. Contemporary discourse about L.E.L. consistently locates her within this world as well: *Blackwood's* review of *The Improvisatrice*, for example, does so literally in its introduction to the writer by taking the reader on a meandering stroll through London, passing "the new house Mr. Murray of Albemarle Street has just taken in that corner of the world" before finally arriving at Landon's home at 131 Sloane Street.[58] A letter Landon wrote congratulating a friend on an upcoming publication gives a good flavor of Landon's self-awareness about celebrity in these terms and her sense of the imperative of professionalization. Here is Landon in late 1825, writing to Katherine Thomson, whose *Memoirs of the Court of Henry VIII* was about to appear:

> My dearest Mrs. Thomson, your appearance in the atmosphere of authorship is a consummation devoutly to be wished by all who have the good name of their profession at heart. I shall think of my calling, "my shame in crowds," with somewhat of complacency, when I can call up your image, instead of visions of longitude in blue, and latitude in yellow. Already I see you a regular lioness. "Have you got Mrs. Thomson's autograph? I am sure you will be at my party when I tell you Mrs. Thomson is to be there—she is the great historianess, a most charming, delightful woman." "Good gracious! can that be an authoress?" "Why, dear me, ma'am, she has such a fine family!"[59]

The pun on "atmosphere" as elevated region and as milieu or ambience suggests the conjunction Landon negotiates between the thrill of recognition as a writer and a somewhat embarrassed, practical embrace of the performative identity expected of the writer. Getting published is not so much a mark of distinction as the ticket to a group identity: one joins the club, for better or for worse, and it helps to have colleagues one likes. The "atmosphere of authorship" is the path to a professional identity, and the romances of Byron and Scott provide Landon with its code.

We can see the ambivalent relationship of women writers of the period to such professionalizing aesthetics inscribed in their attacks on male versions of such performative identity. In Jewsbury's sketch "The Young Author," the hero, an aspiring writer, makes up for his lack of talent with a carefully cultivated display of attitude—his to-do list includes, for example, "to appear at Monday's ball without a neckcloth; to order an amethyst-coloured waistcoat; wear my arm in a sling, and sport bad spirits during the next week."[60] His strategy for professional advancement involves both cultivating female fans—becoming the "oracle of the tea table"—and outright misogyny: congratulating himself on giving *The Improvisatrice* "a regular cutting up" in a review, he comments that it is "perfectly infamous for a woman to write, and write well."[61] The thrust of the satire here is aimed, I would argue, not primarily at the pretentiousness of the feminized, foppish literary character the "young author" seeks to display, but rather at the male privilege that underwrites it. The absurd cliché the young author inhabits also underscores the different set of possibilities, and the more dangerous potential consequences, confronted by women who, like the young author Jewsbury herself, likewise seek to launch literary careers.

The History of an Enthusiast tracks the story of a talented young woman who, unlike the pathetic male young author of her earlier sketch, does achieve wealth and fame. The novella subjects the "woman and fame" topos to careful critical analysis by mapping it onto the contemporary literary scene. The heroine Julia Osborne's intelligence, energy and ambition recall Jewsbury's own, and her own frustrations.[62] But (unlike Jewsbury's own story) Julia's idealistic vision of literary fame—keyed for the reader through Shelleyan chapter epigraphs—is washed away by a more bitter reality only because she really does triumph, making a brilliant living as an independent and celebrated writer in London. With Julia overworked and burdened by the demands of celebrity, the narrator reflects on the gap between the aspiring writer's dreams and the harsh facts of the life of even the successful literary professional:

> Then fame (using the word in the mere popular sense) was become tangible, something to be seen, and felt, and understood; its ethereal aspect was gone, it was no longer a bright mystery like the stars; or like the wind freighted with melody and fragrance, a celestial and impalpable element, but by comparison a common thing, the birth of common life. It might be calculated, weighed, measured, and debated upon; it consisted in being looked at with curiosity, in being talked about, and the materials that went to its composition, were the notice of superiors, the homage of equals, the envy of inferiors, and the hatred of rivals.[63]

The potential antidote to Julia's melancholy appears when Cecil, the man she's loved, shows up in London, but he has already chosen a perfectly ordinary, untalented, unchallenging woman for a wife, and Julia—after a brief descent into madness—decides to leave for the Continent. What the novella diagnoses through this story, however, is not an essential contradiction between womanhood and fame—not a failure of womanhood in Julia's ambition. Rather, as Wolfson points out, the novella is a critique of the structural conditions of authorship generally, and the particular challenges faced by women writers in nineteenth-century Britain, including the anxiety with which men like Cecil (a "passionless twit," in Wolfson's nice summation) respond to female intelligence and ambition.[64] Jewsbury's novella isolates the specific costs to women writers of a culturally and institutionally embedded misogyny, but it also protests against the ways in which the unevenly professionalizing literary culture of the 1830s turns the author's labor against the author's creativity.

Making her literary début, Julia is adopted by one Mrs. Lawrence Hervey, "a *lion-hunter* [who] during the season is seldom without some world's wonder of an author, artist, or preacher, whom she burns incense to, and persecutes with an apotheosis."[65] Mrs. Hervey eventually tires of each new acquisition, and then "the matchless favorite is marched off into Bluebeard's blue room, and another and another still succeeds."[66] The lion-hunter figures the complex overlap between an older system of patronage and a newer market economy, in which authors feel themselves dependent on the caprices of *both* predatory institutions. The author is subjected to a market system whose institutional longevity, predicated on the author's novelty, in fact requires the author's essential disposability. Lions come and go—in fact, because they are lions by virtue of their novelty, they *have* to come and go—but the market "system" they support remains in place. Fame can be a "dazzling degradation" to any author in this system; Mrs. Hervey is institutional. In *Ethel Churchill*, similarly, Landon explores the exploitative conditions faced by the professional writer through a male character, Walter Maynard, who descends into illness and poverty while working feverishly on the play he hopes will make his reputation. To survive, he becomes personal secretary to the malicious politician Sir George Kingston. Sir George uses the love letters he commissions from Walter to seduce Walter's childhood friend Henrietta, now the glamorous society figure Lady Marchmont; she goes mad after poisoning her unfeeling husband and her faithless lover, who still has time to fatally wound Walter in a duel. The novel details both the cold ruthlessness of life in fashionable society circles, and the grueling conditions of the writer's work—the humiliating meetings with publishers, the exhausting labor of writing, the economic uncertainty, the dependence on an indifferent public. Lootens observes incisively that through the depiction of Maynard's writing as "alienated labor" Landon herself "claims her place as a writer among writers, a profession whose struggles are inflected and intensified, not fully created, by her gender."[67]

Jewsbury's novella ends just where the Byronic romance starts, with a saddened, world-weary Julia about to depart for the Continent. In her stimulating recent reading of the *History*, however, Wolfson points out that the author refuses to foreclose her heroine's story, leaving open the possibility that she finds fame and happiness, even, or even without, love.[68] As we will see in the next chapter, Barrett Browning's *Aurora Leigh* picks up this possibility. *Aurora Leigh* also tracks the gap between literary celebrity and literary vocation; like Julia, Aurora departs for the Continent a successful but unsatisfied young poet, disappointed in love; in the end, however, Aurora gets both artistic success and her man. Yet, placing *Aurora Leigh* against these earlier, more mournful stories of women and fame, I am not trying to make a case for Barrett Browning's superior vision, or Landon or Jewsbury's comparative limitation (Linda Peterson does make such a comparison between Landon's *History of a Lyre* and *Aurora Leigh*).[69] The metropolitan poet Aurora Leigh in some ways recalls Barrett Browning's fellow city poet L.E.L. (and, insofar as she presents a version of L.E.L., the portrait of Aurora cleans up the scandalous side of Landon's story). All three writers—Landon, Jewsbury, and Barrett Browning—use tropes of Romantic celebrity to test the contradictions and the possibilities for the woman writer inherent in the growing professionalization of writing and in the growing commercialization of literary culture.[70] They discover severe costs, but also mark out real opportunities, and in different ways they use these opportunities to craft public and influential careers.

6

Elizabeth Barrett Browning and the Energies of Fandom

In letters written just after the publication of her remarkable "novel-poem" *Aurora Leigh* (1856), Elizabeth Barrett Browning tracked what these days we would call the poem's buzz. The letters reflect her excitement and apparent mystification about the poem's reception. In a letter to her sister Arabella dated 10–18 December 1856, she wrote that the poem is "taken up with favour with certain persons, to the amount of a mania;" in a letter to Anna Jameson dated 2 February 1857, she reported on the "extravagant" fan mail she received, and jokingly marveled at the spectacle of "quite decent women taking the part of the book in a sort of *effervescence* which I hear of with astonishment."[1] Some of these women indeed wrote directly to Barrett Browning to thank her for "'help'—for new views of 'love, truth, and purity,'" as she informed Julia Martin in a letter dated 10 March 1857.[2] Influential readers were vocal in their enthusiasm: John Ruskin wrote to Robert Browning assuring him "all the best people shout with me, rapturously" in praise of the poem.[3] While reviews in the major periodicals were mixed, the passionate response the poem aroused in many individual readers is striking—as is Barrett Browning's surprised, delighted and sometimes bemused fascination with the "extravagances" of her readers.[4]

A poem about a literary celebrity and her adoring fans, *Aurora Leigh* critically refashions tropes of Romantic poetic celebrity and lyric intimacy for a mid-Victorian market dominated by the realist novel and structured by the mass audience the novel's success had helped produce. The poem engages Victorian practices of admiration and consumption that grow out of an earlier Romantic culture of fame, but that are now (in the 1840s and 1850s) more securely institutionalized and more explicitly "popular," as we began to see in the previous chapter. The poem's emphases reflect its participation in a shift in the center of cultural gravity from the market institutions discussed in Chapter 5—the institutions of the publishing industry—to the imagined community of admiring readers themselves, as establishers of new institutions of reading. This chapter considers *Aurora Leigh* in the context of Barrett Browning's own history of fandom. As I will argue, Barrett Browning's relationship to the fan's desire was crucially reflexive. Understanding Barrett Browning as a participant in an emerging culture of fandom can productively revise our sense of Barrett Browning as an author, putting into new perspective the formal mechanisms through which *Aurora Leigh* engages and resists the kinds of passionate, idealizing reading it describes and in fact produced.

Literary criticism has had an ambivalent and until recently largely unexamined relationship to the culture of literary fandom.[5] As critics, we set our disciplined habits of reading apart from the fan's supposedly naive, possibly obsessive, often transferential forms of desire. The relationship between the critic and the fan is especially vexed, however, in the case of Barrett Browning. As Tricia Lootens has shown, the idealizing extravagances of Barrett Browning's early defenders contributed (alongside more hostile critical judgments) to what became a near-total eclipse of her poetry by the legend of her life before the 1970s' revival of interest in her as a poet. Those engaged in the work of critical recovery have been forced to be acutely self-conscious about their own investments in the poet in order to intervene in these mechanisms of legend and canon-formation without becoming enmeshed by them.[6] Yet, as I will argue below, if the figure of the fan retains a double-edged potency in the critical imaginary, academic discussion of Barrett Browning still needs to come to terms with the way her authorial self-positioning is inextricable from the mid-Victorian culture of literary celebrity in which she read, wrote, and was admired.

Barrett Browning may have seen in the enthusiastic response to *Aurora Leigh* a reflection of what she herself, a confessed "hero-worshipper," felt for some contemporaries, most famously for George Sand.[7] Behind the public stance of her sonnets to Sand are her wonderful, almost hungry, private comments, such as the remark to her friend Mary Russell Mitford, in a letter dated 28 September 1844: "I would give anything to have a letter from her, though it smelt of cigar. And it would, of course!"[8] William Wordsworth provoked a similar response: when he wrote in 1842 to commend the younger poet on her sonnet "Wordsworth on Helvellyn," she confided to Mitford, "A letter from Wordsworth! Don't tell anybody, but I *kissed* it" (*EBB–MRM* II, 60). She displayed her fandom, too, when so often in her letters she obsessively ranked authors in literary hierarchies, as if she were a character in a Nick Hornby novel. Appropriating the masculine language of the sublime to describe her power of recognizing genius, she told Mitford that her "organ of veneration" was "as large as a Welsh mountain," "overtopping as a pyramid" (*EBB–MRM* I, 145: I, 300). Irresistibly drawn to "lionizing," she once trekked across London "just to look at [Thomas] Campbell's house" (*EBB–MRM* I, 145). Always curious about people and personalities, an inveterate reader of letters and biographies, she soaked up literary gossip and followed her contemporaries' careers with a fascination that combines an anxious jockeying for position with savvy professionalism, but that also goes beyond these forms of self-interest to a more general fascination with celebrity and fan culture.

Indeed, as she admitted to Mitford in a letter of 4 February 1842, she was "capable of all sorts of foolishnesses (which Mr. Kenyon thinks so degrading that he does me the honor of not believing a word of them—at least he *says* so) about autographs & such like *niaiseries*." She elaborates: "I might, if I were tempted, be caught in the overt act of gathering a thistle because Wordsworth had trodden it down ... of gathering it eagerly like his own ass [in *Peter Bell*]!" (*EBB–MRM* I, 344).[9] The playful exhibitionism of these comments—especially visible in her relaying John Kenyon's disapproval—typifies the letters' exchanges about celebrity. In this last, for example, we are hard-pressed to tell which is the greater temptation: the idea of gathering the thistle brushed by fame or the idea of being caught in this (overt) act. Meanwhile, the passionate hero-worship is undercut by the ironic image of the Nature Poet treading down thistles in the first place.

What I want to stress is that the poet's "foolishnesses [...] about autographs & such like *niaiseries*," her "impulses to lionizing," and her "strong heart for making pilgrimages to certain shrines" (*EBB–MRM* I, 145) are intentionally clichéd attitudes, elements of contemporary institutions of reading.[10] I grant that by characterizing these institutions as aspects of "fan culture," I risk obscuring their particularity. The forms of feeling linking nineteenth-century writers with developing communities of readers are more various and more historically specific than the general label "fan" suggests—we might take for example here the Christian sentimentality of those readers who write to thank Barrett Browning for "new views of 'love, truth, and purity'." Yet where one might reach for more Victorian (and more explicitly religious) terms such as "enthusiast" or "votary" to describe the readers I have in mind, I like the anachronistic term "fan" because it identifies something specific and important for us.[11] The delirious partisanship of fandom is a mass-cultural phenomenon; it belongs to the space of leisure, consumption and spectacle; it is ritualized and participatory; it is both highly individual and stereotypical; it involves complex fantasy dynamics of exhibition and shame, desire and sublimation, identification and objectification. Fandom often seeks out an aura of the transgressive and liminal, though it is also routinized, and types of fandom can range from the extremely passionate to the very casual. This is all familiar to us from twenty-first-century media culture—but hence its usefulness.[12] It is partly because we know this concept so well that "fandom" allows us to think about Barrett Browning's sense of herself as a writer and reader in psychologically suggestive ways. Indeed, rather than merely offering "presentist" assumptions, the identification of writer and fan suggests more historically specific ways in which we might think about forms of literary transmission and authorial self-construction.[13]

When Elizabeth Barrett, in these letters of the early 1840s, kisses Wordsworth's letter, fantasizes about correspondence with Sand, or indulges in *niaiseries* about autographs or thistles, she is adopting routinized practices of literary fandom to play with the roles of insider and outsider in relation to authorial genius.[14] She fantasizes about authorial power she might take on (the cigar!), drawing it close to her, indeed magnifying (through her display of abasement) the power she might assume, but also about opening up a space for her own authorial celebrity.[15] The playfulness of her remarks makes clear that such displays of fandom are both deeply felt attitudes and stances she can manipulate to craft her own authorial image.[16] Her fascination with celebrity reflects and dissimulates the aspiring poet's anxieties and desires: she is ambitious but also self-conscious about the propriety of ambition; she is wary of publicity but eager for recognition and canny about how she might achieve it.[17] Like Robert Browning, she strategically uses displays of hero-worship to create a mythology of self. Both writers surround themselves with portraits and other artifacts of literary genius, a collection that becomes part of their own joint legend, documented in reminiscences, catalogs, and photographs, dispersed by sale at auction, and gathered in literary shrines like Baylor's Armstrong Browning Library.

Confessing to Mitford that she is an "adorer" of Thomas Carlyle, Barrett asks, "Do you recognize the estate of mind when it waxes impatient of admiration & longs to throw it off at the feet of the admired? I have felt it often!" (*EBB–MRM* I, 378). This pressing admiration does not sublimate creative ambition or rivalry but seems to represent, for the poet, a complementary dynamic of impatient desire. The mass-mediated discourse of fandom provides her with a grammar through which to amplify reading's thrilling sense of intimacy and indeed to extend this thrill beyond the moment of reading. When she first read Sand, she tells Mitford, she "had a romantic scheme of writing my whole mind to her of her works [...] and I lay awake all night in a vision of letters anonymous & onymous" (*EBB–MRM* II, 460). Books make intimate claims on us; Barrett's fandom here provides a way of fantasizing about returning a response and being recognized in responding. That she dreams, in her lovely phrase, of letters "anonymous & onymous" suggests something central to the fantasy: while wanting to reach out to Sand, she at the same time wants to hold onto the pleasurable anonymity of reading.[18] Literary fandom, in my account, thus describes how the reader's private experience of the text expands to include a risky, passionate and sustained transferential exchange with an authorial subjectivity imagined as a body one can see, touch and hear, but also invested with a fascinating otherness. The material practices around fandom—autograph collecting, cultural tourism, the writing of fan mail—help to shape and sustain such a mode of reading, and testify to its ordinariness.

Compared with Barrett Browning's exchanges with Mitford in the 1840s, *Aurora Leigh*—written when Barrett Browning was already widely recognized as a writer of moment—reflects more ambivalence about the readerly desire associated with literary celebrity.[19] The energies of fandom appear in *Aurora Leigh* predominantly as a check on Aurora's creative energies.[20] Aurora's foregrounding of literary labor de-idealizes the bardic singer as a hard-working "printing woman," a kind of anti-*improvisatrice* (but also echoes accounts of Landon's fatiguing labor and the descriptions of the writer's working life in her *Ethel Churchill* and in Jewsbury's *History of an Enthusiast*). Aurora's initiation into poetry—her experience of poetry's "divine first finger-touch"—suggests the passionate love we associate with fandom, but is so unmediated as to seem antithetical to the material culture of fame (1.851). In contrast, the trappings of celebrity—answering fan mail, fending off lion-hunters—are represented as chores, curbs on Aurora's cherished autonomy. Aurora desires the public's admiration but easily waxes impatient of it: in the first flush of her success as a writer, she is deluged with fan letters but complains, "the very love they lavished so / Proved me inferior" (3.231–2).

Still, while the poem charts poetic authority in opposition to the public visibility of "frivolous fame" (3.235), it is as a *celebrity* poet that Aurora can work her magic on the world: she flees her merely curious readers, but she needs to have readers who fall in love with her own passion for the ideal. She gets these when she publishes the long poem that sounds so much like *Aurora Leigh* itself in that everyone in England is talking about it. Aurora's exemplary admirer Kate Ward not only has her books "by heart" but has herself painted in a cloak like Aurora's, holding Aurora's "last book folded in her dimpled hands" (7.603, 607). (Barrett Browning's real-life fan of fans, Kate Field, would similarly have herself painted as Aurora.) Most strikingly, Romney's reunion with Aurora is mediated by his transformative experience of reading her book, which (he tells her) "[l]ives in me, wakes in me, and dreams in me" (8.265–6).[21]

Later in the same conversation, Romney describes the experience of reading Aurora's poetry through sexualized, interiorizing language:

> You have written poems, sweet,
> Which moved me in secret, as the sap is moved
> In still March-branches, signless as a stone:
> But this last book o'ercame me like soft rain
> Which falls at midnight, when the tightened bark
> Breaks out into unhesitating buds
> And sudden protestations of the spring.
>
> (8.592–8)

This is the language of a lover, but in the peculiarly intimate, affective power it assigns to reading, the passage parallels many in the novel-poem, from Aurora's own experience of "poetry's divine first finger-touch" to her imagining "[a]ffianced lovers, leaning face to face" reading her poetry (1.851; 5.449). Even scenes of reading structured by hostility are charged with a kind of intimate violence—consider Aurora's reading of Lady Waldemar's letter ("I tore the meaning out with passionate haste / Much rather than I read it" [8.1252–3]); her comparison of opening her mail to the opening of the seals of the apocalypse (3.98–9); or her description of Lady Waldemar's reading of her own character ("[S]he takes me up / As if she had fingered me and dog-eared me / And spelled me by the fireside half a life!" [5.1053–5]). Whatever bardic poses Aurora adopts, the poem imagines a private scene of reading and the reader's intimate, emotional response to its language, an affective response that charges the material page itself.[22] The poem, that is, projects as its imagined response not the public scene of admirers enraptured by the poet's oral performance (as in de Staël's *Corinne*) but the very contemporary mode of readerly disturbance and enchantment represented by Barrett Browning's own experience of fandom. What is exemplary about *Aurora Leigh* is the sophistication with which its formal strategies call up such a readerly response, especially through the interplay of idealism and realism.

Readers of *Aurora Leigh* are invited to identify their desires with the poem's passionate desire for the ideal, a desire manifested not just in the extravagance of Aurora's figures for poetic aspiration but in the energy of her writing itself. It is easy to see how the poem's amalgam of spiritual idealism and novelistic realism—calculated to sell in the mid-Victorian literary market—might promote such readerly identification. A *Künstlerroman* in nine books of blank verse, the poem blends genres to capture both the prestige of the epic and the currency of the novel.[23] Drawn into Aurora's story by the immediacy of her narration and thrilled by her outsized figures for poetic aspiration—"catch / Upon the burning lava of a song / The full-veined, heaving, double-breasted Age"—the passionate reader finds the narrative interest and the sheer exhilaration of the poem's formal ambition linked to the urgency of its social vision (5.214–16).[24]

So much we know. What I contend, however, is that the poem conjures its effects of passionate intensity not so much by fusing realism and idealism but by running the formal codes of realism and idealism *against one another*. This is admittedly an abstract way of putting things; fortunately the poem, self-conscious about these effects, provides me with a concrete emblem for the process I want to describe. It does so just at a point of intense readerly involvement: Romney's long-deferred declaration of love, a scene whose affective power is at once heightened and muted by the way Aurora filters Romney's words for us through her tear-swept retrospective narration. As Romney confesses his love, Aurora tells us, his breath against her face "confused his words, yet made them more intense / (As when the sudden finger of the wind / Will wipe a row of single city-lamps / To a pure white line of flame, more luminous / Because of obliteration)" (9.744–7). This image of luminous erasure echoes a host of figures of obliteration in the poem, from the grandly apocalyptic (in Book 3, Aurora describes the fog obscuring the city "as if a spunge / Had wiped out London" [3.182–3]) to the banal (Lady Waldemar's letter to Aurora uses a similar figure to describe her break with Romney, saying she "wiped [him] wholly out [...] from heart and slate" ([9.122–23]). Here, the parenthetical figure of obliteration encapsulates a local mechanism of readerly desire, a mechanism that aligns our feeling with Aurora's in the rush of transcendence she experiences. But in producing a "pure white line of flame" through the obliterative blurring of particulars ("single city-lamps"), the figure of obliteration also reflects in miniature what I will argue is the poem's more general narrative strategy: an erasure of the narrative concreteness associated with realism in a deliberate turn to the rival aesthetic mode of novelistic idealism. This turn away from the concrete shapes the kind of reading the poem solicits—surprisingly so, because in recent critical appraisals the poem's effectiveness has been more often associated with Aurora's refusal to idealize a distressing reality.[25]

Barrett Browning's image of luminous obliteration calls to mind Naomi Schor's description of how nineteenth-century literary idealism was practiced by its key exemplar, George Sand.[26] In Schor's account, Sand's novelistic idealism constitutes "an art of deliberate erasure," a passing over of the details whose plenitude, by contrast, is so crucial to the art of mainstream realism.[27] Sand's idealism, Schor argues, represents both a politics and an aesthetic: its refusal of mimetic realism links it to utopian idealism. Reading psychoanalytically, Schor in turn connects aesthetic and political idealism to intersubjective idealization.[28] Idealism in these particular intersecting senses is, as I will show, a narrative problem in *Aurora Leigh.*

In one sense, it is unsurprising to link *Aurora Leigh* to Sand: Aurora's name echoes Sand's given name (Aurore), and many of the poem's first readers saw in it the "taint" of Sand.[29] But to connect the poem with Sandian idealism in opposition to the codes of mimetic realism might seem counterintuitive. After all, *Aurora Leigh* trumpets its attempt to grapple with the "live, throbbing age" (5.203), and its speaker consistently advocates attention to unsightly human particulars. This realist ethos is cast explicitly against the abstract or anti-realist tendencies of various idealisms, including Romney's Fourierist social theory as well as poetry that dreams too exclusively of other times or other worlds.[30] Whatever their verdict on the success or advisability of such gestures, readers have thus seen the poem as seeking in some degree to adapt to poetry the techniques and subject matter of the contemporary realist novel. Frequently taking the poem's interest in realism as the measure of its commitment to political or social ideals, readers have had little trouble reconciling such realist gestures with the poem's spiritual idealism, since Barrett Browning conceives the poem's function as keeping open the lines of communication between everyday reality and higher spiritual truth. According to this reading, then, the poem rejects both materialism and an empty idealism by demonstrating the immanence of the ideal in the real.

We see the poem in a new way, however, when we notice its strategic affiliation with a discourse of idealism such as that Schor identifies with Sand—that is, an anti-realist practice distinct from the spiritual idealism (influenced by Carlyle and Swedenborg) with which Barrett Browning is more obviously identified. From this perspective, the poem is neither wholly "realist" nor "anti-realist" but rather brings a formally anti-realist impulse to challenge from within its own impulse to mimetic realism. Locating such a tension between realism and idealism in the poem's form, we can also re-evaluate the poem's structures of political idealism and psychological idealization. As Schor proposes, the literary-historical triumph of realism has left us a powerful "aesthetic legacy linking referential illusion and political efficacy with the detailed representation of a blemished reality."[31] From this perspective, idealism looks like escapism, naïveté or a failure of nerve.[32] But Schor argues that idealism in fact offers an alternative mode "open to those who do not enjoy the privileges of subjecthood in the real."[33] This perspective allows us to see *Aurora Leigh*'s idealism—the controversial idealization of Marian, for example, or the utopian vision of a new dawn at the close of the poem—not as a falling-off from realism but rather as the outcome of a logic central to the poem's unconventional politics. The poem's strength and its difficulty lie in the way it stakes out ideality itself as a site of contradiction, marking the violence or blindness of idealization in interpersonal as well as political structures (as when Aurora and Romney admit they had seen each other in a mistaken light, or when Romney's idealistic schemes repeatedly fail) while at the same time identifying idealization with the transformative recognition of alterity.

Such scenes of idealized and satiating intersubjectivity—where the intimacy of the "face-to-face" encounter momentarily dissolves the boundaries between self and other—are bathed in sentimental feeling. Consider the image of Marian bending over her infant, "Self-forgot, cast out of self, / And drowning in the transport of the sight" (6.603–4), or the description of Aurora's collapse before Marian, "weeping in a tender rage" as she "clung about her waist / And kissed her hair and eyes" (6.780–3), or the account of how Romney and Aurora's "[c]omplete communication" is interrupted by the "passionate rain" of tears (9.749–50, 727). Like Aurora's use of epistolary and diaristic forms, the language of feeling connects such scenes to a sentimental tradition that imagines the scene of reading as the site of intimate emotional bonds. Indeed, reading provides the poem's primary model for the emotional transport that can bridge the "gulph" that isolates the self, as when in Aurora's words we "gloriously forget ourselves and plunge / Soul-forward, headlong, into a book's profound, / Impassioned for its beauty and salt of truth" (1.705–8). Locating truth in what is most intensely felt rather than in what is seen, *Aurora Leigh*'s idealist mode models and invites reading as a form of emotional transport: reading as love.

In an interesting discussion of *Aurora Leigh* in relation to the novel, Virginia Woolf comments:

> [I]f Mrs. Browning meant by a novel-poem a book in which character is closely and subtly revealed, the relations of many hearts laid bare, and a story unfalteringly unfolded, she failed completely.

> But if she meant rather to give a sense of life in general, of people who are unmistakably Victorian, wrestling with the problems of their own time, all brightened, intensified, and compacted by the fire of poetry, she succeeded [...] The broader aspects of what it felt like to be a Victorian are seized as surely and stamped as vividly upon us as in any novel by Trollope or Mrs. Gaskell.[34]

My reading reframes Woolf's dichotomy diachronically: the novel-poem deliberately works its idealist mode (life "brightened, intensified, and compacted by the fire of poetry") against the realist density of incident and psychological characterization that is to my mind also, *pace* Woolf, emphatically present in the poem.

The poem's representation of the working-class Marian Erle serves as a useful index of this contradictory dynamic. In so far as she is metonymically linked to all the terrors she endures, from the poverty of the London slums to her kidnapping and rape, Marian stands as a limit-figure for the poem's affiliation with a strenuous realism. Yet Marian also emerges toward the poem's close as a figure so dramatically idealized as to stand outside the protocols of realist character representation. Sidelined in the final books, she seems more symbol than realistic character. When she descends like an apparition in the final scene between Romney and Aurora, it is as a transparent figure for ideal feeling: "She stood there, still and pallid as a saint, / Dilated, like a saint in ecstasy, / As if the floating moonshine interposed / Betwixt her foot and the earth, and raised her up / To float upon it" (9.187–90). Cora Kaplan plausibly argues that such idealization indicates the poem's inability fully to accommodate working-class subjectivity, while Deirdre David sees Marian's idealized portrayal as one instance of a general failure: "the characters are not only idealised in *Aurora Leigh*, they are hardly characters at all; they possess no finely nuanced and registered shades of consciousness."[35] Indeed, David's analysis echoes some early reviewers—the *Saturday Review*, for example, complained, "[T]he characters are few and unreal—the incidents, though scanty, are almost inconceivable."[36] Like this review, David's argument confirms Schor's contention that, read with expectations shaped by the realist novel, an idealist mode of representation produces what looks like not just awkwardness but lack.

Reading outside a realist tradition, however, we might see the apotheosized Marian as a type of character that functions as ideal sign. Whether as defense or victory over vicissitude, Marian achieves a distillation to an idealized essence. We might compare this distillation of character to Aurora's marvelously sentimental image of Keats, that "strong excepted soul" who "ensphered himself in twenty perfect years / And died, not young (the life of a long life / Distilled to a mere drop, falling like a tear / Upon the world's cold cheek to make it burn / For ever)" (1.1006–10).[37] If the shift from heavily realistic to heavily idealized description in Marian's representation can thus be understood as psychologically meaningful, it still need not be assimilated to the scheme of consistent development demanded by realistic characterization. Such a break from realism may suggest instead a cut within the structure of *Bildung* (a form in any case always split by its simultaneous orientation to an individual process in time and an exemplary perfection out of time) that might compel us to look anew at Aurora's own fiction of development.[38]

The complications of the relationship between Aurora's narrative procedures and the protocols of realism are not merely formal but involve Aurora's conflicted relationship to the real. Consider the eerie realism of the portrait of Aurora's mother, painted "after she was dead," less an emblem of the "de-animating power of representation" than an element of a deadly reality, at once vitiated and preternaturally kinetic.[39] (In childhood, Aurora is transfixed by the image, "that swan-like supernatural white life / Just sailing upward from the red stiff silk / Which seemed to have no part in it nor power / To keep it from quite breaking out of bounds" [1.128, 139–42].) Images marked as particularly realistic acquire in the poem an intense psychic charge linked to a disturbing hyper-reality, as in that portrait or the uncannily ordinary image of Marian's face that haunts Aurora in Paris:

> That face persists,
> It floats up, it turns over in my mind,
> As like to Marian, as one dead is like
> The same alive. In very deed a face
> And not a fancy, though it vanished so;
> The small fair face between the darks of hair,
> I used to liken, when I saw her first,
> To a point of moonlit water down a well:
> The low brow, the frank space between the eyes,
> Which always had the brown pathetic look

> Of a dumb creature who had been beaten once
> And never since was easy with the world.
>
> (6.308–19)

Such a hallucinatory intensity recurs in the passage describing Aurora's train ride to Italy, where the disorienting experience of rail travel functions (like Aurora's venture into London's slums) as a point of contact between the epic poem and realism as a *generic* discourse of modernity.

Thus, while the poem enthusiastically embraces the call to represent the reality of its own "live, throbbing age" and seems at many points to make realism an ethical goal, realism also haunts the poem as the sign of separation, isolation, and disorientation. (The poem's most straightforwardly realist section is Book 7, where, in Italian exile and excluded from the mother-child dyad of Marian and her infant, Aurora stops writing, reading, or even speaking, and describes herself as ghost-like [7.1272; 7.1306]). Against the force of the real, the poem offers the passionate transport of reading as a redemptive form of self-oblivion, as when, in the lines I cited above, "We gloriously forget ourselves, and plunge / Soul-forward, headlong, into a book's profound" (1.706–7). In her childhood, reading inducts Aurora into the quest romance, as she ventures forth into the world of books like an errant knight, a "young wayfaring soul [...] unconscious of the perilous road" (1.740–1). The imagery Aurora uses for the absorbing transport of reading recurs at a moment when the poem veers explicitly into romance, as Aurora sits half-reading and gazing out from her terrace near Florence:

> The purple and transparent shadows slow
> Had filled up the whole valley to the brim,
> And flooded all the city, which you saw
> As some drowned city in some enchanted sea,
> Cut off from nature, - drawing you who gaze,
> With passionate desire, to leap and plunge
> And find a sea-king with a voice of waves,
> And treacherous soft eyes, and slippery locks
> You cannot kiss but you shall bring away
> Their salt upon your lips.
> . . . .

Methinks I have plunged, I see it all so clear ...
And, O my heart, ... the sea-king!

In my ears
The sound of waters. There he stood, my king!

I felt him, rather than beheld him.

(8.35–45; 58–62)

Aurora's plunge, with its Sapphic echoes, is a narrative fulcrum. In a love story dominated by blocks and missed communications, this fantasy ending now swings into view as an inevitability: whatever potential hazards come up hereafter, we know the poem has such closure in its sights.[40] Letting herself go, Aurora is brought up short not by the gap between reality and romance but by the instantaneous granting of her wish: Romney reappears as a dream come true, and in the poem's final books Aurora's task is not to give up on romance, as in a conventionally realist plot, but to stop denying romance—a denial that may have fostered her autonomy, but to which she has become over-attached. Since Aurora, Romney, and the poem's reader are now all headed for the same goal—an idealized ending in which erotic desire, readerly desire, and the desire for the political ideal are all mutually sanctified by marriage—Aurora's story really does become a romance of the author.

The passage recounting Aurora's "plunge" interestingly flags for us the poem's drawing-together of the temporalities of reading and writing, past, present and future. The shift from the realist description of landscape to the psychic terrain of enchantment is marked syntactically by the shift to "you" ("which you saw") and then by the shift in tenses across present to future—"drawing you who gaze [...] to leap and plunge," "you cannot kiss but you shall bring away their salt upon your lips"—while the blurring between the moment of writing and the narrated moment ("Methinks I have plunged") precipitates a momentary interruption of our clear reception of Aurora's narrative voice, as the signal drops out in the ellipses (an effect which itself brings close the experience of reading and the narrated "leap"). For Aurora the writer, and for the reader, the passage bridges the seductiveness of lyric absorption and the narrative drive of Aurora's romance, pulling us into that romance as the poem pulls toward the utopian conclusion that suddenly becomes an inevitability.

In staging this kind of absorption in her own story, Aurora solicits the reader's involvement along the lines of the intimate reading-as-love we have seen associated with Barrett Browning's own literary fandom. The poem asks us to identify our desire with Aurora's, and this identification is most intense at moments in which the poem is momentarily unmoored from narrative concreteness:

> But oh, the night! oh, bitter-sweet! oh, sweet!
> O dark, O moon and stars, O ecstasy
> Of darkness! O great mystery of love,
> In which absorbed, loss, anguish, treason's self
> Enlarges rapture, - as a pebble dropt
> In some full wine-cup over-brims the wine!
>
> (9.814–19)

The dilating "rapture" of these lines might be keyed back to Marian's transport at the sight of her infant or, more tensely, to the "mother's rapture" that Aurora says killed her own mother, but the "ecstasy / Of darkness" is staged here through the temporary suppression of all narrative context, even personal pronouns, a suppression that opens the lines out to any reader.

Spilling over with feeling, the poem is also subject to a necessary temporal overflow. The poem's final lines translate Romney's closing thought of "perfect noon" into Aurora's vision, quoted from Revelation, of the gem-like building blocks of a New Jerusalem: a utopian horizon along which, Herbert F. Tucker suggests, "the transparent stones of revelation, like the many books or building blocks of the poem, are the gradual structures of Aurora's processive identity."[41] As Tucker emphasizes, though, this ending is softened by Aurora's reminders that her writing follows and exceeds these final words, so that this terminal image is not the end. Just as Romney's words are blurred by his breath as he declares his love, Aurora's writing is blurred by emotion as she writes about his declaration, her tears streaking the page:

> But what he said .. I have written day by day,
> With somewhat even writing. Did I think

That such a passionate rain would intercept
And dash this last page?

(9.725–8)

In a basic sense, these reminders that Aurora writes what we read provide evidence that Aurora survives the marriage plot and goes on writing. In another sense, the prosaic and reader-friendly voice of the diarist holds the narrative open to the reader, identifying our feelings with her own. Refusing a total absorption in the lyric time to which it seductively gestures, Aurora's idealizing vision is grounded in the everyday reality of writing ("I have written day by day").

Aurora's writing thus pulls in two directions. The accretive, metonymic, and passionate movement of the activity of writing sustains a lyric impulse that, working along a metaphoric axis and through a process of subtraction and erasure, aims to realize a realm of feeling unmoored from narrative time. These alternate pressures—extensive and intensive, as it were—create in its audience those absorbing, transferential effects modeled in the gripped readers it describes—Kate Ward, Romney, and Aurora herself (her own closest [re-]reader).

Aurora Leigh makes the emotive force of its idealism materially available to the reader through this formal tension between inscription and erasure. This tension parallels contemporary critical discourse around Barrett Browning, where a central element of the poet's developing legend, her "extraordinary vitality of spirit," imaginative aspiration, and capacity for sympathy, is taken to be registered in the unruly "vehemence" of her language.[42] Especially where the energy of her imaginative aspiration appears as a distension of form—William Stigand's 1861 *Edinburgh Review* article cites (for starters) *Aurora Leigh*'s "many deformities and faults of construction, the prosaic baldness of much of the narrative, its distorted ingenuity, the harsh discordances, transitions, elaborate conceits and grotesqueness of much of the dialogue, the utter impossibility of the story, and the unreality of all its actors"—the vitality that distinguishes her writing is visible in the poem's very distance from decorum.[43] It is not *Aurora Leigh*'s excessive realism but its unreality that Stigand identifies with the passionate labour of Barrett Browning's writing. Stigand claims to be able to resist *Aurora Leigh*'s strategies for seducing the reader, at least on a second reading (he confesses to total absorption the first time through), but in linking the energetic activity of the writing that gives rise to the poem to the obtrusive *failure* of its realist effects, Stigand's censure paradoxically illuminates the dynamic of (prosaic) writing and idealist erasure that is key to the poem's success.[44]

That the poem in fact produced, indeed institutionalized, powerfully identificatory reading is attested by many of its real-life readers: Susan B. Anthony's inscription on a copy of *Aurora Leigh* given to the Library of Congress states, "This book was carried in my satchel for years and read and reread— … I have always cherished it above all other books—I now present it to the Congressional Library, Washington, D.C., with the hope that women may more and more be like 'Aurora Leigh'"[45] Yet even *within* the poem not all of Aurora's readers read her so lovingly, of course. Against the adulation of a Kate Ward the poem sets Lady Waldemar's hostility: Aurora complains she "takes me up / As if she had fingered me and dog-eared me / And spelled me by the fireside half a life! / She knows my turns, my feeble points" (5.1053–61). The letter from Lady Waldemar transcribed at the start of Book 9 similarly recounts her ungenerous reading of Aurora's book: Lady Waldemar makes her heart cold to the poem's seductions. But Lady Waldemar's "ungenerous" reading of Aurora also reflects an understanding that Aurora herself lacks ("she knows my turns, my feeble points"). In the poem's final book, it is Lady Waldemar's letter to Aurora, delivered by Romney, that becomes the text of Aurora's self-knowledge. Reading Lady Waldemar's profession of hate, Aurora finally understands the nature of her own love. Lady Waldemar's role in Aurora's story reminds us that Aurora's vulnerability to her readers is real but also, paradoxically, a source of power. Both Lady Waldemar and Kate Ward are, in their own way, idealizing readers (Lady Waldemar's first words to Aurora are "Is this the Muse?" [3.363]). But in her antagonism, Lady Waldemar strangely ends up being more useful to Aurora than her fan Kate Ward is in her love—and Aurora must learn to negotiate both models of reading in rereading her own story.

If falling in love with Barrett Browning has inspired work of serious scholarship and serious political import, the romanticization of the poet has also inspired some delightful and some almost frightening kitsch.[46] However we evaluate it, though, such fandom is an aspect of the high-cultural project of Barrett Browning's poetry, not, or not only, a perversion of it. Indeed, the cultural fascination with the romance between the Brownings might itself have to do in part with the way the love between the two artists can stand as an idealized reflection of the reader's own transferential relation to admirable or seductive literary texts. In its cultural reverberation, the Brownings' romance becomes a kind of second-order reflection on fandom, both codifying and mystifying readerly desire. The letters, poems, journals, observations, and artifacts that give us access to this romance are so tantalizing to readers in part because, in their intimacy and their very quotidian nature, they promise a privileged contact with that which they help create: the "mystery" of art and the magic of its hold on us. Like the "autographs & such like *niaiseries*" Barrett Browning finds seductive, such records of personal presence tempt us because they suggest they might have an answer to the question the fan seeks to resolve: that of the ambiguous relation between the seductive work of art and the person of the artist who created it.

Part of the legacy of Romanticism, the dynamics of fandom and celebrity remain at once at the heart and at the limit of modern literary culture, as novels from James's *The Aspern Papers* to Nicholson Baker's *U and I* (1991) and Julian Barnes's *Flaubert's Parrot* (1984) suggest. If idiosyncratic obsessives like the narrators of these novels illustrate the extremes to which readers can go in a transferential relationship to the celebrity author, the narrators' fandom also points to an entanglement of authorial charisma and absorptive identification still vital to the pleasures of reading, pleasures at once deeply personal and importantly shared. This book does not, of course, call for an uncritical celebration of the kinds of fandom it has described, nor (even less) does it aim to recuperate for criticism a mode of reading that takes the figure of the author as the site for the reader's identifications. Indeed, my emphasis throughout has been on the array of textual and market systems and strategies through which readerly desire and authorial personality were mutually produced by and around nineteenth-century poetry. The point I make now is rather simply that as readers of this poetry (and inhabitants of modern literary culture) we necessarily negotiate these forms of celebrity and fandom ourselves. Our thinking about literary form, meaning and value will be sharpened by acknowledging and examining what I noted at the start of this chapter teachers and critics of literature too routinely disavow: the dynamics of fandom in our own critical practice, in our pedagogy, and in our own motivations and resistances as readers.

Notes

Introduction

1. Collections of portraits of contemporary authors were popular both as luxury books and as staples in the periodicals. See, for example, Henry F. Chorley's *The Authors of England: A Series of Medallion Portraits of Modern Literary Characters, Engraved from the Works of British Artists* (London: Charles Tilt, 1838). For a historical survey of images of poets and their cultural uses, see David Piper, *The Image of the Poet: British Poets and Their Portraits* (Oxford: Clarendon Press, 1982). On the paraphernalia of Bardolatry, see John Brewer, *The Pleasures of the Imagination* (London: HarperCollins, 1997). John Clare reports on a Chatterton memorial handkerchief his mother once brought him as a gift from a country fair, commenting, "she little thought I should be a poet then as she should have felt fearful if she had for Chattertons name was clouded in mellancholy [*sic*] memory which [for while?] his extraordinary Genius was scarcely know[n]" (*By Himself*, ed. Eric Robinson and David Powell [Ashington and Manchester: Mid-Northumberland Arts Group and Carcanet, 1996], p. 99). "An exemplary sentimental text [...] designed to absorb the very tears it caused to flow," as David Fairer comments, the handkerchief seems to literalize the conversion of authorial personality into the ephemeral stuff of market exchange ("Chatterton's Poetic Afterlife, 1770–1794: A Context for Coleridge's *Monody*," in *Thomas Chatterton and Romantic Culture*, ed. Nick Groom [New York: St. Martin's, 1999], pp. 228–49 [p. 245]).
2. Prominent recent critical discussions emphasizing the defensive posture of Romantic poets with regard to contemporary celebrity include Andrew Bennett's *Romantic Poets and the Culture of Posterity* (Cambridge: Cambridge UP, 1999) and Lucy Newlyn's *Reading, Writing and Romanticism: The Anxiety of Reception* (Oxford: Oxford UP, 2000). A number of recent studies have drawn revelatory connections between Romantic authorship and celebrity cultures. Groundbreaking in this regard are Peter Manning's "*Childe Harold* in the Marketplace: From *Romaunt* to Handbook," *MLQ* 52 (1991) 170–90, and his "*Don Juan* and the Revisionary Self," in *Romantic Revisions*, ed. Robert Brinkley and Keith Hanley (Cambridge: Cambridge UP, 1992), pp. 210–26. Judith Pascoe's *Romantic Theatricality: Gender, Poetry and Spectatorship* (Ithaca, NY: Cornell UP, 1997) makes the case for the public dimension of Romantic authorship, discussing the performance of authorship by poets, including Mary Robinson, William Wordsworth and Landon in relation to the celebrity of figures like Sarah Siddons. Karen Swann traces the "star power" of Keats and Shelley to

figures of the aesthetic in her "The Strange Time of Reading," *European Romantic Review* 9 (1998) 275–82, and her "Shelley's Pod People," *Romanticism and the Insistence of the Aesthetic*, ed. Forest Pyle (February 2005), Romantic Circles, accessed 7 March 2006, http://www.rc.umd.edu/praxis/aesthetic/swann/swann.html. Susan J. Wolfson carefully teases out the difference gender makes in Romantic fame in a number of books and articles: see, for example, "The Mouth of Fame: Celebrity, Transgression and the Romantic Poet" in *Essays on Transgressive Readings: Reading over the Lines*, ed. Georgia Johnston (Lewiston: E. Mellen Press, 1997), pp. 3–34; "Keats Enters History: Autopsy, Adonais, and the Fame of Keats" in *Keats and History*, ed. Nicholas Roe (Cambridge: Cambridge UP, 1995), pp.17–45; and her recent *Borderlines: The Shiftings of Gender in British Romanticism* (Stanford: Stanford UP, 2006). Sarah M. Zimmerman's discussion of Charlotte Smith's relationship to her audience shows how the development of new kinds of lyric interiority, as in Smith's poetry, took advantage of the fascination with other selves that also motivated the popularity of "literary lives," from Rousseau's *Confessions* to Johnson's *Lives of the Poets* to Boswell's *Life of Johnson*. See Sarah M. Zimmerman, *Romanticism, Lyricism, and History* (New York: SUNY Press, 1999), especially pp. 34–6. See also Jason Goldsmith's recent analysis of John Clare's relationship to fame and fandom, "The Promiscuity of Print: John Clare's *Don Juan* and the Culture of Romantic Celebrity," *SEL* 46: 4 (Autumn 2006) 803–32. Despite these excellent studies, the default critical position remains the notion that (with the possible exception of Byron) Romantic poets focused on "posterity" and simply distanced themselves from, or ignored, or were hapless about, modes of contemporary celebrity.

3. For an entertaining and eye-opening survey of such practices, see Richard Altick, *Lives and Letters: A History of Literary Biography in England* (New York: Knopf, 1965), pp. 112–45. See also, on nineteenth-century collectors, Pascoe's *The Hummingbird Cabinet: A Rare and Curious History of Romantic Collectors* (Ithaca, NY: Cornell UP, 2005) and, on cultural tourism, Nicola J. Watson's *The Literary Tourist: Readers and Places in Romantic and Victorian Britain* (Basingstoke: Palgrave Macmillan, 2006). On the phenomenon of "author-love" in the eighteenth and nineteenth centuries, see Helen Deutsch, *Loving Dr. Johnson* (Chicago: University of Chicago Press, 2005), as well as the essays collected in Frances Wilson, ed., *Byromania: Portraits of the Artist in Nineteenth- and Twentieth-Century Culture* (New York: St. Martin's, 1999) and Deidre Lynch, ed., *Janeites: Austen's Disciples and Devotees* (Princeton: Princeton UP, 2000).
4. For this understanding of the lyric, see Helen Vendler, *Invisible Listeners: Lyric Intimacy in Herbert, Whitman and Ashbery* (Princeton: Princeton UP, 2005) and my discussion below. On "lyric reading" as a category, see Virginia Jackson and Yopie Prins, "Lyrical Studies" (*Victorian Literature and Culture* 27: 2 [1999] 521–30). Compare Jonathan Arac's suggestive idea of the lyric as a mode of "mass transport" in his "Afterword: Lyric Poetry and the Bounds of New Criticism," in *Lyric Poetry: Beyond New*

Criticism, ed. Chaviva Hosek and Patricia Parker (Ithaca, NY: Cornell UP, 1985), pp. 345–56.

5. See Lynch, *Janeites*.
6. Tom Mole, *Byron's Romantic Celebrity: Industrial Culture and the Hermeneutic of Intimacy* (Basingstoke: Palgrave Macmillan, 2007), xii. See Mole's Chapter 1 for an excellent survey of Romantic celebrity and an argument that modern celebrity begins with Byron (pp. 1–27). The *OED*'s first record for celebrity as a type of person is 1849, but the term is in use (often with quotation marks that indicate its novelty) by the 1830s; an unsigned 1834 article about the follies of literary stardom, "The Duchess D'Abrantès and the Countess of Blessington," mentions "literary celebrities" (*Tait's Edinburgh Magazine* [1834] 204–6, p. 205). The most comprehensive history of celebrity is Leo Braudy's *Frenzy of Renown: Fame and Its History* (New York: Vintage, 1997). Other useful introductions to the topic include Joshua Gamson's *Claims to Fame: Celebrity in Contemporary America* (Berkeley: University of California Press, 1994) and Graeme Turner's *Understanding Celebrity* (London: Sage, 2004). Richard Schickel's *Intimate Strangers: The Culture of Celebrity* (Garden City, NY: Doubleday, 1986) is the most prominent of many discussions of fame and intimacy in modern culture; Virginia L. Blum's treatment of celebrity and identification in *Flesh Wounds: The Culture of Cosmetic Surgery* (Berkeley: University of California Press, 2003) is among the most subtle and provocative. Frank Donoghue's *The Fame Machine: Book Reviewing and Eighteenth-Century Literary Careers* (Stanford: Stanford UP, 1996) is excellent on the lead-up to the Romantic period, while Claire Brock's *The Feminization of Fame, 1750–1830* (Basingstoke: Palgrave Macmillan, 2006) covers the late eighteenth and early nineteenth-century developments. Clara Tuite's "Tainted Love and Romantic Literary Celebrity" explores the Lamb-Byron affair as an episode in scandalous celebrity poised between older aristocratic codes and a modern public sphere (*ELH* 74: 1 [Spring 2007] 59–88). On celebrity as a point of contact between public and private in the nineteenth century, see Nicholas Dames's "Brushes with Fame: Thackeray and the Work of Celebrity" (*Nineteenth-Century Literature* 56: 1 [2001] 23–51). For poetic celebrity in nineteenth-century American context, see David Haven Blake, *Walt Whitman and the Culture of American Celebrity* (New Haven: Yale UP, 2006) and Eliza Richards, *Gender and the Poetics of Reception in Poe's Circle* (New York: Cambridge UP, 2004).
7. On the expansion of the reading public, see Richard Altick, *The English Common Reader: A Social History of the Mass Reading Public, 1800–1900* (Chicago: University of Chicago Press, 1957), pp. 30–77. New data on this expansion is cataloged and analyzed by William St. Clair in *The Reading Nation in the Romantic Period* (Cambridge: Cambridge UP, 2004). For examples of very different kinds of arguments emphasizing the growing distance between writers and readers, see Jon P. Klancher, *The Making of English Reading Audiences, 1790–1832* (Madison: University of Wisconsin, 1987) and Andrew Franta, *Romanticism and the Rise of the*

Mass Public (Cambridge: Cambridge UP, 2007). On the advent of a mass public, see Susan Stewart's *Crimes of Writing: Problems in the Containment of Representation* (New York: Oxford UP, 1991). See also Tilottama Rajan's *The Supplement of Reading: Figures of Understanding in Romantic Theory and Practice* (Ithaca, NY: Cornell UP, 1990) on self and audience seen through theories of hermeneutics.

8. "The Writer" (1968), quoted in Stewart, *Crimes*, p. 4.
9. To John Lodge, 20 July 1830, in Felicia Hemans, *Poems, Letters, Reception Materials*, ed. Susan J. Wolfson (Princeton: Princeton UP, 2000), pp. 510–11. Quoting from Hemans's letters, Norma Clarke describes Hemans's vexed relationship to her overwhelming celebrity: "Readers, American readers in particular, were relentless in pursuit of her. Demand for her lyrics was insatiable. Feeling 'conspicuous,' 'unprotected,' and in 'constant want of protection and domestic support,' she lived and worked in a 'constant excitement, homage' which made her profoundly uneasy" (*Ambitious Heights: Writing, Friendship, Love—The Jewsbury Sisters, Felicia Hemans and Jane Welsh Carlyle* [New York: Routledge: 1990], p. 50).
10. Thomas Medwin, "Memoir of Shelley," *The Athenaeum* (1832) 472–4, 488–9, 502–4, 522–4, 535–7, 554–5 (p. 522). According to Medwin, the stranger immediately disappeared but was soon identified as "an Englishman, and an officer in the Portuguese service" (p. 522).
11. "The Young Author," in "M.J.J." [Maria Jane Jewsbury], *Phantasmagoria, or, Sketches of Life and Literature*, 2 vols (London: Hurst, Robinson, 1825), I, 189–98 (pp. 190, 193). First published in *Literary Souvenir* (1825) 85–93.
12. Lamb addressed her anonymous letter of 9 March 1812 to "Childe Harold:" "I have read your Book & cannot refrain from telling you that I think it & that all those whom I live with & whose opinions are far more worth having—think it beautiful [...] As this is the first letter I ever wrote without my name & could not well put it, will you promise to burn it immediately & never to mention it? If you take the trouble you may very easily find out who it is, but I shall think less well of Child[e] Harold if he tries—though the greatest wish I have is one day to see him & be acquainted with him" (Paul Douglass, ed., *The Whole Disgraceful Truth: Selected Letters of Lady Caroline Lamb* [Basingstoke: Palgrave Macmillan, 2006], p. 77). Barrett Browning's letter is quoted in Patricia Thomson, *George Sand and the Victorians: Her Influence and Reputation in Nineteenth-Century England* (New York: Columbia UP, 1977), pp. 50–1. I discuss Trelawny's relationship to Shelley in Chapters 3 and 4 and Barrett Browning's fandom in Chapter 6.
13. Quoted in Leslie Marchand, *Byron: A Biography* (New York: Knopf, 1957), p. 608.
14. Stephen Gill, *Wordsworth and the Victorians* (Oxford: Clarendon Press, 1998), p. 15, and Pascoe, *Hummingbird* p. 3. On the development of literary tourism generally, see Watson, *Literary Tourist* and James Buzard, *The Beaten Track: European Tourism, Literature, and the Ways to Culture, 1800–1918* (Oxford: Oxford UP, 1993). In eighteenth-century France, so

many curious readers came to see their beloved Jean-Jacques in person that Rousseau was forced to build a trap door in his home to escape them (Robert Darnton, "Readers Respond to Rousseau: The Fabrication of Romantic Sensitivity" in *The Great Cat Massacre and Other Episodes in French Cultural History* [New York: Vintage Books, 1985], pp. 215–56 [p. 234]).

15. In "The Periodical Press" (1823), for example, William Hazlitt sums up the situation by observing that fame has become ephemeral: "A modern author may (without much imputation of his wisdom) declare for a short life and a merry one. Literary immortality is now let on short leases, and he must be contented to succeed by rotation" (*Edinburgh Review* 71 [May 1823] 349–78, [p. 358]).
16. Annette Wheeler Cafarelli, *Prose in the Age of Poets: Romanticism and Biographical Narrative from Johnson to De Quincey* (Philadelphia: University of Pennsylvania Press, 1990), p. 70. Writing in 1810 in *The Friend,* Coleridge bemoans a pathological curiosity on the part of readers, a "mania for busying ourselves with the names of others," that appeals to the same vulgar feelings of curiosity as does the village gossip:

    > For to what do these [anecdote-mongering] Publications appeal, whether they present themselves as Biography or as anonymous Criticism, but to the same feelings which the scandal-bearers and time-killers of ordinary life seek to gratify in themselves and their listeners? And both the authors and admirers of such publications, in what respect are they less truants and deserters from their own hearts, and from their appointed task of understanding and amending them, than the most garrulous female Chronicler, of the goings-on of yesterday in the families of her neighbours and townsfolk!
    >
    > (II, 286)

    In Coleridge's hysterical account, the endless prying into the private lives of individuals erases the very boundaries between public and private, not just for the *objects* of such curiosity but for the reader as well: "For a crime it is [...] thus to introduce the spirit of vulgar scandal, and personal inquietude into the Closet and the Library, environing with evil passions the very Sanctuaries, to which we should flee for refuge from them!" (Coleridge, *The Friend*, ed. Barbara Rooke [1818] 2 vols [Princeton: Princeton UP, 1969], II, 286).
17. The works of Adela Pinch, Julie Ellison and Claudia Johnson have helped shape my understanding of the interpersonal circulation of feeling and the importance of the ways feeling can go public in the nineteenth century (and in our own cultural moment). See Pinch, *Strange Fits of Passion: Epistemologies of Emotion, Hume to Austen* (Stanford: Stanford UP, 1996); Ellison, *Cato's Tears and the Making of Anglo-American Emotion* (Chicago: University of Chicago Press, 1999); and Johnson, *Equivocal Beings: Politics, Gender, and Sentimentality in the 1790's: Wollstonecraft, Radcliffe, Burney,*

Austen (Chicago: University of Chicago Press, 1995). For an astute analysis of the affective complexity of celebrity-audience relations, see Jacqueline Rose's psychoanalytic essay "The Cult of Celebrity" (*New Formations* 36 [1999] 9–20). Rose asks, "How far is pleasure—the pleasure we take in celebrity, for example—bound up with perversion, or with something we experience as perverse?" (10).

18. Barrett Browning's phrase is from a letter to Mary Russell Mitford (*Women of Letters: Selected Letters of Elizabeth Barrett Browning and Mary Russell Mitford*, ed. Meredith B. Raymond and Mary Rose Sullivan [Boston: Twayne, 1987], p. 145). Braudy makes the point that Byron "was a fan before he was a star [...] All sorts of fame intrigued him" (p. 406). See my individual chapters for fuller developments of these poets' relationships to fan practices.
19. Thomas De Quincey, *Reminiscences of the English Lake Poets*, ed. John E. Jordan (New York: Dutton, 1961). Hereafter cited parenthetically in the text.
20. The marked quotation is from *The White Doe of Rylstone* (l. 1829–30), describing Emily's companionship with the Doe: "How happy in its turn to meet / The recognition! the mild glance / Beamed from that gracious countenance; / Communication, like the ray / of a new morning, to the nature / And prospects of the inferior Creature!" De Quincey's language also recalls the Lucy poem "She dwelt among th'untrodden ways."
21. De Quincey, p. 87. I slightly adjust the force of De Quincey's phrase here: in context, he is speaking of his desired connection not with Wordsworth himself but with the Lake District, whose landscape fascinates him "under the anticipation that very probably I might here form personal ties which would for ever connect me with their sweet solitudes by powers deep as life and awful as death" (p. 87).
22. See for a fuller discussion of De Quincey's figurations of sublime textual power, to which I am indebted, Charles J. Rzepka, *Sacramental Commodities: Gift, Text and the Sublime in De Quincey* (Amherst: University of Massachusetts Press, 1995). In her *De Quincey's Romanticism: Canonical Minority and the Forms of Transmission* (Cambridge: Cambridge UP, 1997), Margaret Russett also discusses the connections between "physical proximity to the poet's body" and the "doublets of autobiography" in De Quincey's *Reminiscences* (p. 178).
23. Rzepka, *Sacramental Commodities*, p. 191.
24. James Boswell, *The Life of Samuel Johnson* (1791), Oxford Standard Edition (New York: Oxford UP, 1948). In the hopes of meeting the great man, Boswell frequented the bookshop run by the actor Thomas Davies ("one of the best of the many imitators of [Johnson's] voice and manner"), who had assured the impatient acolyte Johnson might visit. Boswell's description of the encounter is worth quoting in full:

> At last, on Monday the 16th of May, when I was sitting in Mr. Davies's back-parlour, after having drunk tea with him and Mrs. Davies,

> Johnson unexpectedly came into the shop; and Mr. Davies having perceived him through the glass-door in the room in which we were sitting, advancing towards us,—he announced his aweful approach to me, somewhat in the manner of an actor in the part of Horatio, when he addresses Hamlet on the appearance of his father's ghost, "Look, my Lord, it comes."
>
> (pp. 261–2)

25. Boswell, *Life*, pp. 261–2.
26. See David Higgins, *Romantic Genius and the Literary Magazine: Biography, Celebrity, Politics* (New York: Routledge, 2005), pp. 85–9.
27. See John Brewer, *The Pleasures of the Imagination* (London: HarperCollins, 1997), pp. 125–66; Raymond Williams, *Culture and Society 1780–1950* (New York: Columbia UP, 1958, 1983), pp. 30–48; and Martha Woodmansee, *The Author, Art and the Market: Rereading the History of Aesthetics* (New York: Columbia UP, 1994), pp. 53–5. The connection of writing to the unique self of the author is closely related to developments in copyright law (Brewer, *Pleasures*, p. 150). On authorship and the history of copyright, see also Woodmansee, *The Author, Art and the Market*, pp. 35–57.
28. Harriet Martineau, "Literary Lionism," *London and Westminster Review* 32 (1839) 263–80 (p. 271).
29. Ibid. Martineau herself was the object of vicious commentary in the press, and her body the object of intrusive curiosity. Strikingly, in her essay on literary lionism, her own experiences as the subject of publicity are never explicitly mentioned (and the "lion" in her picture is a man parading before female admirers). For Martineau, the lion may stand in opposition to the working journalist; she erases the productive work of the writer on display, whose mere objecthood stands in contrast to her own journalistic activity. Richard Salmon's *James and the Culture of Publicity* (New York: Cambridge UP, 1997) describes, from a later vantage point, the nineteenth-century "emergence of new practices of biographical and journalistic representation in which both the 'personality' of the author and the material site of artistic labour were systematically exhibited as objects of public consumption" (p. 79).
30. Unless otherwise noted all Byron poems are quoted from *The Complete Poetical Works*, ed. Jerome J. McGann, 7 vols (Oxford: Clarendon Press, 1980–93), hereafter abbreviated *CPW*. References to *Don Juan* will be given parenthetically in the text by canto and stanza number.
31. Martineau, "Literary Lionism," p. 271.
32. Altick provides the following figures: Scott's "*The Lay of the Last Minstrel* (1805), published, like his other volumes of poetry, in sumptuous format, sold 15,050 copies in three years at 25*s*.; *Marmion* (1808) went through four editions, totaling 11,000 copies, in the first year at 31*s*.6*d*.; and *The Lady of the Lake* (1810) sold 20,300 copies in its first year at the even steeper price of 42*s*." (*English Common Reader* pp. 262–3). The first two cantos of *Childe Harold* (1812) sold 4500 copies in less than two months; *The Corsair* (1814) sold 10,000 copies in a day.

33. Byron's *The Corsair* could sell like it did, Manning explains, because of a particular confluence of technological and cultural conditions: "presses could produce ten thousand copies, booksellers' dinners crystallized the market, the inclusion of such scandalous tidbits as Byron's 'Lines to a Lady Weeping' [on Princess Charlotte] could be made known by judicious advance leaks to the newspapers, and the great quarterly reviews formed and perpetuated taste" (Manning, "Marketplace" p. 184).
34. For a discussion of Hemans's profits from her poetry, see Paula Feldman, "The Poet and the Profits: Felicia Hemans," *Women's Poetry: Late Romantic to Late Victorian: Gender and Genre, 1830–1900*, ed. Isobel Armstrong and Virginia Blain (Basingstoke: Macmillan, 1999), pp. 71–101.
35. For discussion of the business of authorship amid changes in the publishing industry, see Lee Erickson, *The Economy of Literary Form: English Literature and the Industrialization of Publishing, 1800–1850* (Baltimore: Johns Hopkins UP, 1996).
36. Print runs for editions of new poetry generally did not exceed 750 copies, and usually far fewer sold. By contrast, the circulation for the most prestigious reviews—the *Edinburgh* (founded 1802), the *Quarterly* (founded 1809), *Blackwood's* (1817), and the *London Magazine* (1820), for example—could range over 10,000 copies, with multiple readers for each copy. For detailed figures and discussion of typical print runs and periodical circulation, see St. Clair. On the periodical context for Romanticism, see Mark Parker, *Literary Magazines and British Romanticism* (Cambridge: Cambridge UP, 2000).
37. The inaugural shot appears in "On the Cockney School of Poetry. No. I.," *Blackwood's Edinburgh Magazine* 2 (October 1817) 38–41; installments continue through the next two years. The essays have just been usefully reprinted in volume 5 (*Selected Criticism, 1817–19*, ed. Tom Mole) of Nicholas Mason, ed., *Blackwood's Magazine, 1817–25: Selections from Maga's Infancy*, 6 vols (London: Pickering and Chatto, 2006). "Z." is generally identified as John Gibson Lockhart.
38. "Noctes Ambrosianae, No. I," *Blackwood's Edinburgh Magazine* 11 (1822) 369–71 (p. 362).
39. On magazine writers and the construction of personality, see Parker, *Literary Magazines*; Russet, *De Quincey's Romanticism*; and Peter Murphy, "Impersonation and Authorship in Romantic Britain," *ELH* 59 (1992) 625–49.
40. Pierre Bourdieu, "The Field of Cultural Production, or: The Economic World Reversed," in *The Field of Cultural Production: Essays on Art and Literature*, ed. Randal Johnson (New York: Columbia UP, 1993), pp. 29–74.
41. The *Fraser's* gallery thus contrasts with earlier collections of notable figures in which literary celebrity was just one form of eccentricity or singularity among others. A representative example is the 1803 *Eccentric Biography; or, Memoirs of Remarkable Female Characters, Ancient and Modern. Including Actresses, Adventurers, Authoresses, Fortune-Tellers, Gipsies, Dwarfs, Swindlers, Vagrants and others who have distinguished*

themselves by their Chastity, Desperation, Intrepidity, Learning, Abstinence, Credulity, &c, &c, Alphabetically Arranged, Forming a mirror of reflection to the FEMALE MIND. *Ornamented with portraits of the most singular characters in the Work* (London: printed by J. Cundee, 1803). Higgins discusses the *Fraser's* "Gallery" in the context of other galleries of living authors of the period, such as John Scott's "Living Authors" series (in the *Champion*, 1814), Hunt's "Sketches of the Living Poets" (in the *Examiner*, 1821), or Gilfillan's *Gallery of Literary Portraits* (first published in the *Dumfries Herald* 1842–4) (Higgins, *Romantic Genius*, p. 163, n. 7). On *Fraser's*, see also Judith L. Fisher, "'In the Present Famine of Anything Substantial': *Fraser's* 'Portraits' and the Construction of Literary Celebrity; or, 'Personality, Personality Is the Appetite of the Age'," *Victorian Periodicals Review* 39 (2006) 97–135.

42. For Bourdieu, the literary field or field of cultural production emerges in the Romantic period as a network or system of writers, texts and institutions, "a structured space with its own laws of functioning and its own relations of force independent of those of politics and the economy" (Randal Johnson, "Introduction," *The Field of Cultural Production: Essays on Art and Literature*, p. 6). The field is defined by the relationship among the various positions taken by agents within it, and the structure of the whole is altered by each new act of self-positioning.
43. Bourdieu, "Field," p. 37.
44. My study seeks to respond, but in different methodological terms than Bourdieu's, to the challenge he proposes: "The work of art is an object which exists as such only by virtue of the (collective) belief which knows and acknowledges it as a work of art. Consequently, in order to escape from the usual choice between celebratory effusions and the reductive analysis which, failing to take account of the fact of belief in the work of art and of the social conditions which produce that belief, destroys the work of art as such, a rigorous science of art must, *pace* both the unbelievers and iconoclasts and also the believers, assert the possibility and necessity of understanding the work in its reality as fetish; it has to take into account everything which helps to constitute the work as such, not least the discourses of direct or disguised celebration which are the social conditions of production of the work of art *qua* object of belief" ("Field," p. 35). I understand the celebrity of writers, in the terms I have laid out, as a crucial element of such production of belief.
45. I derive this verdict on lyric poetry from Jonathan Culler's chapter "Apostrophe" in *The Pursuit of Signs: Semiotics, Literature, Deconstruction* (Ithaca, NY: Cornell UP, 1981), pp. 135–54. Culler's case-study here is Keats's fragment "This living hand, now warm and capable," which I discuss in Chapter 2. My own reading suggests that the lyric effects Culler observes in the fragment are historically as well as structurally determined. In his *Poetry's Touch: On Lyric Address* (Ithaca, NY: Cornell UP, 2003), William Waters manages the impressive feat of analyzing constructions of lyric intimacy from antiquity to the late twentieth century, persuasively historicizing his discussion throughout.

46. For an example of such symptomatic reading, see Marilyn Butler's *Romantics, Rebels and Reactionaries, English Literature and Its Background 1760–1830* (New York: Oxford UP, 1982): "The first three decades of the nineteenth century saw the emergence of a heightened interest in the personality of the artist, evidenced in the phenomenal spate of biography. The rage for these literary *Lives*, copiously illustrated by letters, was part of a passion for documenting the natural world, including the human and social world; it was a manifestation of a scientific curiosity that extended equally to the animal kingdom, to plants and to fossils. But where the poet was the subject, something more than curiosity was conveyed: a taste was beginning to emerge to see the artist *as a hero*, and this perhaps is the symptom of a special need" (p. 2).
47. For discussions of the various approaches listed, see Stephen Colclough, "Readers: Books and Biography," *A Companion to the History of the Book*, ed. Simon Eliot and Jonathan Rose (Oxford: Blackwell, 2007), and the essays collected in Jane P. Tompkins, ed., *Reader-Response Criticism: From Formalism to Post-Structuralism* (Baltimore: Johns Hopkins UP, 1980), especially the overview in Tompkins's own essay on "The Reader in History: The Changing Shape of Literary Response" (pp. 201–32). Another good sampling of approaches is on offer in the collection edited by James Raven, Helen Small and Naomi Tedmor, *The Practice and Representation of Reading in England* (Cambridge: Cambridge UP, 1996).
48. See John Brewer, "Reconstructing the Reader: Prescriptions, Texts and Strategies in Anna Larpent's Reading," in Raven, Small and Tedmor, pp. 226–45. Brewer reconstructs the reading practices of one individual (Anna Larpent), and provides a useful discussion of the methodological questions this approach raises.
49. See, for example, John Rodden, *The Politics of Literary Reputation: The Making and Claiming of 'St. George' Orwell* (New York: Oxford UP, 1989).
50. Garrett Stewart, *Dear Reader: The Conscripted Audience in Nineteenth-Century British Fiction* (Baltimore: Johns Hopkins UP, 1996), p. 8. Compare Waters's characterization of his own approach in *Poetry's Touch*. Waters is interested in reading's "*phenomenology:* namely, *what it is like to be someone reading* (here, now)," differentiating this mode of analysis from a focus on "the reader" of reader-response theory ("the abstract or faceless functionary of the cognitive operations of interpretation") or "the reader in history as a culturally constructed participant in a given era's system of social codes and concerns" (p. 15, n. 26). In the late stages of preparing this book for the press I discovered Rita Felski's *The Uses of Literature* (Oxford: Blackwell, 2008), which explores what a new phenomenology of reading might look like, following the insights of cultural studies and the historicist criticism of the past few decades.
51. Kate Flint, *The Woman Reader, 1837–1914* (Oxford: Oxford UP, 1993), p. 187.
52. In describing such readerly "practices" my terminology indicates the influence of Roger Chartier and Michel de Certeau. See Chartier, *The Order*

of Books: Authors, Readers and Libraries in Europe between the Fourteenth and the Eighteenth Centuries (Stanford: Stanford UP, 1994), p. 23.

53. Leah Price, *The Anthology and the Rise of the Novel: From Richardson to George Eliot* (Cambridge: Cambridge UP, 2000), p. 12.
54. See Wolfson's *Borderlines*, Dorothy Mermin's *Godiva's Ride: Women of Letters in England, 1830–1880* (Bloomington and Indianapolis: Indiana UP, 1993), and Sonia Hofkosh, "The Writer's Ravishment: Women and the Romantic Author—The Example of Byron," in *Romanticism and Feminism*, ed. Anne K. Mellor (Bloomington: Indiana UP, 1988), pp. 93–114.
55. To George and Georgiana Keats, 1819, in *Letters of John Keats*, ed. Hyder Edward Rollins, 2 vols (Cambridge: Harvard UP, 1958), II, 16. Hereafter abbreviated *KL* and cited parenthetically in the text.
56. Andrew Elfenbein, *Byron and the Victorians* (Cambridge: Cambridge UP, 1995), p. 49.
57. Vendler, *Invisible Listeners*, p. 3.
58. The Introduction to a recent special issue of *Critical Inquiry* on forms of transmission proposes "a new program of study" focusing on the way knowledge is shaped by "the transmissive means through which it is developed, organized and passed on." See James Chandler, Arnold I. Davidson and Adrian Johns, "Arts of Transmission, an Introduction," *Critical Inquiry* 31: 1 (Autumn 2004) 1–6 (p. 2). "Rather than approaching the arts of transmission atomistically, as if one could write separately a history of material culture, a history of practices and skills, and a history of forms of thought," the volume emphasizes "the interconnectedness of what are too often conceived of as independent realms" (p. 3). Celebrity should be understood in this way as an element of literary culture and its transmission.
59. For Keats's comment, see the letter to J. H. Reynolds of 11–13 July 1818 (KL I, 324). Online, one can purchase Burns ties, Burns CDs and Burns chess sets. The Burns National Heritage Park website promises one can enjoy the "humor and excitement" of Burns's "best-loved tale" in the multimedia "'Tam O'Shanter' experience" ("Robert Burns National Heritage Park—Welcome," Burns National Heritage Park, accessed 13 April 2003, http://www.burnsheritagepark.com).
60. I had the privilege of presenting an earlier version of material from Chapter 6 of this book at the Elizabeth Barrett Browning bicentenary celebration and conference at the Armstrong Library. I thank the library for hosting the conference and Alison Chapman for organizing the panel on which I presented.

1 Systems of Literary Lionism

1. For an account of *Childe Harold*'s initial publication and reception, see Manning, "Marketplace." In Manning's compelling analysis, Byron points at once "to the aristocratic world that his heroes inhabit and from which he came, and to the world of commerce that contested it," and so

"Byron became mythic because, like all myths, he appeared to resolve a contradiction by vividly embodying it" (p. 182).

2. Thomas Moore, *Letters and Journals of Lord Byron: With Notices of His Life* (1830), 2 vols (New York: Harper & Brothers, 1868), I, 158–9. Nicholas Mason cautions against Moore's hyperbole, observing that "the real story of *Childe Harold* I and II is not so much one of a text speaking to its age as one of a marketing-savvy publisher and a poet with a flair for self-promotion converging at an ideal moment in literary and advertising history" ("Building Brand Byron: Early-Nineteenth-Century Advertising and the Marketing of Childe Harold's Pilgrimage," *MLQ* 63: 4 [December 2002] 411–40 [p. 425]).
3. Quoted in Leslie A. Marchand, *Byron: A Biography*, 3 Vols (New York: Knopf, 1957), p. 335.
4. Stephen Behrendt makes this point about Byron's debt to female predecessors in "The Gap That Is Not a Gap" in *Romanticism and Women Poets: Opening the Doors of Reception*, ed. Harriet Kramer Linkin and Stephen Behrendt (Lexington: University Press of Kentucky), p. 27.
5. Mary Darby Robinson, *Memoirs of the Late Mrs. Robinson* (London: R. Phillips, 1801), pp. 178–9.
6. See Pascoe, *Romantic Theatricality* and Pascoe's Introduction to her edition of Robinson's *Selected Poems* (Toronto: Broadview, 1985), pp. 19–62. See also Adriana Craciun, *Fatal Women of Romanticism* (Cambridge: Cambridge UP, 2003), pp. 76–109; Jacqueline M. Labbe, "Selling One's Sorrows: Charlotte Smith, Mary Robinson, and the Marketing of Poetry," *Wordsworth Circle* 25 (1994) 68–71; Elizabeth Fay, "Framing Romantic Dress: Mary Robinson, Princess Caroline and the Sex/Text," *Historicizing Romantic Sexuality*, ed. Richard Sha (January 2006) Romantic Circles, accessed 15 March 2007, http://www.rc.umd.edu/praxis/sexuality/fay/fay.html; and Anne Mellor, "Mary Robinson and the Scripts of Female Sexuality," in *Representations of the Self from the Renaissance to Romanticism*, ed. Patrick Coleman, Jayne Lewis and Jill Kowalik (Cambridge: Cambridge UP, 2000), pp. 230–59.
7. Gillray's 1782 "Monuments lately discovered in Salisbury Plain" shows Robinson complaining while the Prince of Wales professes his love for Mary Amelia, the Marchioness of Salisbury; the Marquess of Salisbury, looking on, insists he leave his wife alone. "Paridise Regain'd" (1783), likely also by Gillray, links Robinson with the Prince of Wales and the Whig politician Charles James Fox. Mellor ("Mary Robinson") and Fay both provide close analyses of public images of Robinson. Pornographic fictionalizations such as *Memoirs of Perdita* (1784) imagined Robinson's trysts with various public figures.
8. Fay, par. 1.
9. Labbe, p. 70.
10. Mary Darby Robinson, *Letter to the Women of England on the Injustice of Mental Subordination* (1799), ed. Adriana Craciun, Anne Irmen Close, Megan Musgrave and Orianne Smith, Romantic Circles, accessed 10 November 2008, http://www.rc.umd.edu/editions/robinson/, p. 64.
11. Robinson, *Memoirs*, pp. 64–5.

12. On Robinson's *Letter* and ideas of female celebrity and genius, see Craciun, *Fatal Women*, pp. 76–110.
13. Mellor, "Mary Robinson," p. 253.
14. Unsigned review, *Poems* (1791), by Mary Robinson, *Critical Review* n.s. 2 (July 1791) 309–14, p. 314.
15. For a typical instance, see the fan letter from a young girl, Isabella Harvey, who wrote to Byron in 1823 under the assumed name Zorina Handley (Byron wrote back): Peter Quennell and George Paston, *To Lord Byron: Feminine Profiles Based on Unpublished Letters 1807–1824* (London: John Murray, 1937), pp. 261–2.
16. Jerome Christensen, *Lord Byron's Strength: Romantic Writing and Commercial Society* (Baltimore: Johns Hopkins UP, 1993), p. xvi.
17. Various aspects of this system have been examined in expert detail by McGann, in his "Byron and 'The Truth in Masquerade'" in *Romantic Revisions*, pp. 191–209; by Manning in a number of essays, especially "*Childe Harold* in the Marketplace" and "*Don Juan* and the Revisionary Self;" and by Tom Mole, in *Byron's Romantic Celebrity*. On images of Byron, see the excellent essays in Christine Kenyon Jones, ed., *Byron: The Image of the Poet* (Newark, DE: University of Delaware Press, 2007), especially those by Mole, Annette Peach, Kenyon Jones and Bernard Beatty. See also Ghislaine McDayter, "Conjuring Byron: Byromania, Literary Commodification, and the Birth of Celebrity," in Frances Wilson, ed. *Byromania: Portraits of the Artist in Nineteenth- and Twentieth-Century Culture* (New York: St. Martin's, 1999), pp. 43–62. Nicholas Mason connects the promotion of Byron and early nineteenth-century advertising strategies in his "Building Brand Byron."
18. On Byron and serial publication, see Christensen and Manning, "Revisionary."
19. As I explain below my argument engages directly with McGann's discussion of "Fare Thee Well!" in "Byron and 'The Truth in Masquerade.'"
20. Jürgen Habermas notes that in modernity intimacy is always oriented toward an audience, and he differentiates between this inherent "publicity" of the private and scandalous "indiscretion." Where the former links private subjectivity to public life in a way that underwrites both categories, the latter threatens not only privacy but the rational organization of the public sphere: "Subjectivity, as the innermost core of the private, was always already oriented to an audience (*Publikum*). The opposite of the intimateness whose vehicle was the written word was indiscretion and not publicity as such" (*The Structural Transformation of the Public Sphere: An Inquiry into a Category of Bourgeois Society*, trans. Thomas Burger [Cambridge, MA: MIT Press, 1991], p. 49). Yet celebrity's public is organized through embodied and affective, if highly mediated, exchanges that challenge and exceed such conceptions of the public sphere.
21. *Byron's Letters and Journals*, ed. Leslie A. Marchand, 13 vols (London: John Murray, 1973–94), V, 30. Hereafter abbreviated *BLJ*.
22. These are precisely the questions addressed by Paul Elledge's subtle reading of the poem; Elledge concludes that the poem reveals a Byron

equivocating between a desire for separation and a desire for connection. See "Talented Equivocation: Byron's 'Fare Thee Well!'" *Keats-Shelley Journal* 35 (1986) 42–61.

23. David Erdman, "'Fare Thee Well!'—Byron's Last Days in England," in *Shelley and His Circle, 1773–1822*, ed. Kenneth Neil Cameron (Cambridge, MA: Harvard UP, 1961–), IV, 638–55 (p. 642).
24. Ibid., p. 642.
25. John Murray, *Letters of John Murray to Lord Byron*, ed. Andrew Nicholson (Liverpool: Liverpool UP, 2007), p. 162.
26. Though *The Champion*'s move is often described as motivated by Tory politics, Erdman notes that "Scott's *Champion* and Hunt's *Examiner* were both independent Opposition papers" (p. 647). Tory papers rallied to the attack, however.
27. A summary of the immediate periodical response, which did break largely along political lines, can be found in Erdman, "Fare Thee Well!," pp. 645–7 and p. 663, n. 4.
28. McGann, "Truth in Masquerade," pp. 199–200.
29. Ibid., pp. 198–9.
30. Elledge, "Talented Equivocation," pp. 42–61.
31. Quoted in Malcolm Elwin, *Lord Byron's Wife* (New York: Harcourt Brace, 1962), p. 394. The quotation comes from a 4 February 1816 letter from Lady Byron to Dr. Lushington, her adviser. For letters between the various concerned parties throughout the spring, see Elwin, pp. 339–471. Lady Byron did compose her own reply verses to "Fare Thee Well!," entitled "By thee forsaken" (Elwin, p. 470).
32. "C." [Mary Cockle], *Reply to Lord Byron's "Fare Thee Well"*(Newcastle: Printed by S. Hodgson, 1817).
33. [R. Exton], *Lady Byron's Responsive "Fare Thee Well!," with Other Poems, by the Same Author* (London: Richard Edwards, 1816), p. 13. For a partial discussion of this and other pamphlets, see Samuel C. Chew, "The Pamphlets of the Byron Separation," *Modern Language Notes* 34: 3 (March 1919) 155–62.
34. [Mary Cockle], *Lines Addressed to Lady Byron* (Newcastle: Printed by S. Hodgson, 1817), p. 1; Cockle, *Reply*, p. 1.
35. Cockle, *Reply*, p. 1.
36. Compare Cockle's "Address to the Subscribers" to a volume published by her friend Mrs. E.-G. Bayfield, cited and discussed in the headnote to the section on Bayfield in Paula Feldman's anthology *British Women Poets of the Romantic Era* (Baltimore: Johns Hopkins UP, 2001), p. 84. Cockle also wrote an elegy on the death of Princess Charlotte.
37. Cockle, *Lines*, pp. 3–4.
38. Tom Mole, "Ways of Seeing Byron," in Kenyon Jones, ed., *Images*, pp. 68–78 (p. 73).
39. *A Narrative ...* (London: Printed for the author and sold by R. Edwards, 1816).
40. G. Kiallmark, *Now Each Tie of Love Is Broken: Answer to Lord Byron's Fare Thee Well!* (London: Goulding D'Almaine, [ca. 1817]), p. 1.

41. Robinson, *Memoirs*, pp. 178 and 185–6.
42. Manning discusses the impact of Byron's own poem on Princess Charlotte, "Lines to a Lady Weeping," in "Tales and Politics: *Lara, the Corsair* and *the White Doe of Rylstone*," in his *Reading Romantics: Texts and Contexts* (New York: Oxford UP, 1990), pp. 195–215.
43. Pinch, *Strange Fits of Passion*, p. 184. On the recirculation of Byron's separation scandal in the Queen Caroline affair of 1820–1, see Kristin Flieger Samuelian, *Royal Romances, 1778–1821* (Basingstoke: Palgrave Macmillan, forthcoming).
44. Erdman, "Fare Thee Well!," p. 639.
45. *CPW* III, 312–13.
46. Byron, *Ode to Napoleon Buonaparte* (London: John Murray, 1814).
47. McGann dates the composition of "On the Star of the 'Legion of Honour'" to September 1815, the month Lady Caroline Lamb sent Byron "a cross of the 'Legion of Honour'" (*CPW* III, 474–5; *BLJ* IV, 312).
48. *BLJ* IV, 256.
49. Cited in Erdman, "Fare Thee Well!," p. 651.
50. Hone's volume went through 15 editions in 1816. The title page to the fourteenth edition reads: "*Poems on His Domestic Circumstances, &c, &c.* By Lord Byron. With his memoirs and portrait. Containing NINE POEMS. FARE THEE WELL! A SKETCH FROM PRIVATE LIFE. ON THE STAR OF 'THE LEGION OF HONOUR.' ADIEU TO MALTA. THE CURSE OF MINERVA. WATERLOO. AND THREE OTHERS. LONDON: W. HONE, 1816." "The Curse of Minerva" was only added to later editions of the piracy.
51. See John Clubbe's "Between Emperor and Exile: Byron and Napoleon, 1814–1816," *Napoleonic Scholarship* 1: 1 (April 1997), accessed 10 November 2008, http://www.napoleon-series.org/ins/scholarship97/c_byron.html.
52. Clubbe, "Between Emperor and Exile" par. 68.
53. McDayter, "Conjuring Byron," p. 49.
54. Byron had broken off with his long-time publisher Murray and published Cantos 6–8 with the radical John Hunt. The first cantos of the poem had been immediately pirated and circulated widely in cheap unauthorized editions. Murray, who had been left with unsold copies of his expensive initial edition of the poem, began with subsequent volumes issuing the poem in both luxury and cheaper formats. Hunt published Cantos 6–8 in 1823 in three formats: an 8vo copy priced at 9.5 shillings, with a print run of 1500 copies; a "small paper" edition priced at 7 shillings with a print run of 3000 copies; and a "common edition" at 1 shilling with a print run of 16,000 copies (St. Clair, p. 686).
55. "Lord Byron," *Blackwood's Edinburgh Magazine* (February 1825) 131–51.
56. Ibid., p. 136.
57. Rose, "Cult," p. 18.
58. See Manning, "Revisionary," pp. 213–17.
59. [John Gibson Lockhart?], "Remarks on *Don Juan*," *Blackwood's Magazine* 5 (August 1819) 512–18, reprinted in Andrew Rutherford, ed., *Byron: The Critical Heritage* (New York: Barnes and Noble, 1970), pp. 166–73.
60. Ibid., pp. 170–1.

61. "John Bull," *Letter to the Right Hon. Lord Byron* (London: William Wright, 1821), reprinted as *John Bull's Letter to Lord Byron*, ed. Alan Lang Strout (Norman: University of Oklahoma Press, 1947), p. 80.
62. Ibid.
63. I am indebted here to Kristin Samuelian's conference paper "Looking at/in the Prints: Byron, Queen Caroline, and Embodying the Ephemeral" (International Conference on Romanticism, Towson University and Loyola College, Baltimore, MD, October 2007).
64. Caroline Franklin, *Byron's Heroines* (Oxford: Clarendon Press, 1992), p. 101.
65. Ibid., emphasis in original.
66. I am indebted here and in what follows to Hofkosh, as well as to Wolfson, "'Their She Condition': Cross-Dressing and the Politics of Gender in *Don Juan*" *ELH* 54 (1987) 586–617. Wolfson's essay, expanded in *Borderlines*, pp. 164–204, explores how gender oppositions are both activated and destabilized by Byronic performance. Hofkosh's starting point is the way Lady Byron's circulation of her own version of Byron contests the control Byron might claim over his own identity. Nicola J. Watson explores a similar problem in Byron's personal and literary relationship with Caroline Lamb in her essay "Transfiguring Byronic Identity," in *At the Limits of Romanticism: Essays in Cultural, Feminist, and Materialist Criticism*, ed. Mary Favret and Nicola J. Watson (Bloomington: Indiana UP, 1994), pp. 185–206.
67. See Wolfson, "'Their She Condition'" and Watson, "Transfiguring."
68. See Peter W. Graham, *Don Juan and Regency England* (Charlottesville: UP Virginia, 1990), p. 163.
69. Watson makes the point that Fitz-Fulke is linked to generic plots that challenge the legitimacy of paternal authority. Fitz-Fulke "combines in a debased register a number of revolutionary/sentimental features: she is in the habit of conducting adulterous flirtations that turn young men into suicidal Werthers [14.64]; her name indicates that, like so many jacobinical villains, she is not only Irish but from an illegitimate branch of the family; and she refigures Glenarvon's female counterpart, the cross-dressing Irish revolutionary Elinor, herself a figure [...] for Caroline Lamb" ("Transfiguring," p. 196). Similarly, "the debased sentimental heroine is throughout [*Don Juan*] closely identified with Byron's own writerly identity, however extravagantly Juan-ish: Julia uses his own "seal," *Elle vous suit partout*; furthermore, resurfacing as the disguised Fitz-Fulke, the sentimental heroine is translated into his own masquerade likeness as Black Friar, only to be revealed as an even more thoroughly promiscuous woman" (p. 196).
70. Manning, "Revisionary," p. 221.
71. For sales figures see n. 20 above.
72. William Hazlitt, "Lord Byron," *The Spirit of the Age*, 1825, reprinted in Rutherford, pp. 268–78 (p. 276).
73. Ibid., p. 275. Hazlitt's scorn has its basis in Byron's manipulation of class privilege: "Perhaps the chief cause of most of Lord Byron's errors is, that he is that anomaly in letters and in society, a Noble Poet. It is a double privilege, almost too much for humanity" (p. 277).

2 Keats, Lyric and Personality

1. "Town Conversation. No. IV," Baldwin's *London Magazine* (April 1821) 426–7, reprinted in G.M. Matthews, ed., *Keats: The Critical Heritage* (New York: Barnes and Noble, 1971), pp. 241–2 (p. 241). Subsequent references to Matthews will be cited parenthetically as *KCH*.
2. The attacks on Keats in the *Quarterly* and *Blackwood's* figure centrally in other massively influential accounts of the poet's death, of course: Shelley's *Adonais* spins Keats as a martyr felled by the poison pen of the reviews—Shelley claims in his preface to that poem that "the savage criticism on his *Endymion*, which appeared in the *Quarterly Review*, produced the most violent effect on his susceptible mind: the agitation thus originated ended in the rupture of a blood-vessel in the lungs" (Donald Reiman and Sharon Powers, ed., *Shelley's Poetry and Prose* [New York: Norton, 1977], p. 391). Meanwhile, Byron famously mocks such myth making in *Don Juan*, faux-memorializing "John Keats, who was killed off by one critique, / Just as he promised something great, / If not intelligible:" "'Tis strange the mind, that very fiery particle, / Should let itself be snuffed out by an article" (11.60). On the "cultural processing" of Keats's death, and particularly the conflicting cultural motives for feminizing Keats, see Wolfson's "Keats Enters History," as well as her essay "Feminizing Keats" in *Critical Essays on John Keats*, ed. Hermione de Almeida (Boston: G.K. Hall, 1990), pp. 317–57.
3. Compare Milton's claim about Shakespeare "that each heart / hath from the leaves of thy unvalued book / Those Delphic lines with deep impression took."
4. On Severn's role in the construction and dissemination of representations of Keats's death, see Grant Scott, "Writing Keats's Last Days: Severn, Sharp, and Romantic Autobiography," *Studies in Romanticism* 42 (Spring 2003) 3–26. On Keats's afterlife in the visual arts, see Sarah Wooton, *Consuming Keats: Nineteenth-Century Re-Presentations in Art and Literature* (Basingstoke: Palgrave Macmillan, 2005).
5. Tourists need not have read Keats, of course, to wax thoughtful about his story. Visiting the Protestant Cemetery in 1833, N.P. Willis, the American literary celebrity, wrote of Keats that "every reader knows his history and the cause of his death," but he doesn't say whether every reader knows his poetry (*KCH* 28). James Najarian gives an impressive account of the centrality of Keats's death, and his body, to the poet's posthumous reception, with particularly strong attention to the way later writers use the figure of Keats. See his *Victorian Keats: Manliness, Sexuality and Desire* (Basingstoke: Palgrave Macmillan, 2002), especially Chapter 1.
6. Obituary for John Keats in *New Monthly Magazine and Literary Journal* 3 (1 May 1821) 256–7, reprinted in *KCH* 243–4.
7. "The Strange Time of Reading," *European Romantic Review* 9 (1998): 275–82 (p. 277).
8. Swann notes that Keats appears to anticipate "the loving, mournful work of his circle. If he refuses all glances of the 'hand,' it is only the better

to keep alive the cultic power of relics, to sustain by a certain self-denial an inexhaustible, charged, poetic world. Like a true mourner, he refuses to do the work of mourning, insofar as that suggests a working through to the end of mourning [...] [T]he mourner refuses to let loss dissipate" ("Strange Time of Reading," p. 280). See also her "*Endymion's* Beautiful Dreamers," in *The Cambridge Companion to Keats*, ed. Susan J. Wolfson (Cambridge: Cambridge UP, 2001), pp. 20–36.

9. Bennett, especially Chapters 1 and 2. See also Jeffrey C. Robinson's ambitious and original *Reception and Poetics in Keats: 'My Ended Poet'* (New York: St. Martin's Press, 1998).
10. All citations of Keats's poetry are from Jack Stillinger, ed., *The Complete Poems of John Keats* (Cambridge, UP: Harvard, 1978). Karen Swann's comments on an early version of this chapter helped me sharpen the terms of my argument here and below.
11. John Keats, *Poems* (London: C. and J. Ollier, 1817).
12. Jeffrey Cox, *Poetry and Politics in the Cockney School: Keats, Shelley, Hunt and Their Circle* (Cambridge: Cambridge UP, 1998), p. 104.
13. Ibid.
14. See Wolfson's discussion of Keats's "camelion poetics" and Byronic character in *Borderlines*, pp. 207–9. On Byron's response to Keats, see William Keach, "Byron Reads Keats," in *Cambridge Companion to John Keats*, pp. 203–13.
15. For a discussion of the evidence for Keats's attitudes toward Byron, see Beth Lau, *Keats's Reading of the Romantic Poets* (Ann Arbor: University of Michigan Press, 1991), pp. 115–46, especially pp. 128–37. Lau argues that "Keats felt alternately challenged, threatened, and defeated by Byron's commercial and critical success" but also at times adopted Byron as a model (p. 132). Byron's nobility (and height) added sting to the rivalry; witness Keats's famous aside, "You see what it is to be under six foot and not a lord" (*KL* II, 61). Byron recurs as a point of comparison in Keats's letters with significant but by no means obsessive frequency. Keats tracks his publications and sales figures, writing, for example, to George and Georgiana Keats on February 14, 1819: "I was surprised to hear from Taylor the amount of Murray the Booksellers last sale—what think you of £25000? He sold 4000 coppies of Lord Byron" (*KL* II, 62).
16. "Z.," "Cockney School of Poetry, No. IV," *Blackwood's* 3 (August 1818) 519–24, reprinted in Tom Mole, ed., *Blackwood's Magazine, 1817–1825: Selections from Maga's Infancy, Volume 5: Selected Criticism, 1817–19* (London: Pickering & Chatto, 2006), pp. 191–202.
17. *The Literary Absolute: The Theory of Literature in German Romanticism*, trans. Philip Barnard and Cheryl Lester (Albany: State University of New York Press, 1988), p. 126.
18. Note, however, that, unlike, say, Shakespeare's sonnets, Keats's poem does not imagine itself as its writer's own monument.
19. Hofkosh, "The Writer's Ravishment."
20. To John Taylor, August 23, 1819, *KL* II, 144; for the sonnets, see Stillinger, ed., *Complete Poems*, pp. 277–8.
21. Hofkosh, "The Writer's Ravishment," p. 106.

22. To John Taylor, August 23, 1819, *KL* II, 144; To George and Georgiana Keats, *KL* II, 16.
23. Michael O'Neill, "'When this warm scribe my hand': Writing and History in *Hyperion* and *The Fall of Hyperion*," in *Keats and History*, pp. 143–64, and Jonathan Bate, "Keats's Two *Hyperions* and the Problem of Milton," in *Romantic Revisions*, pp. 321–38.
24. Ross Chambers, *Story and Situation: Narrative Seduction and the Power of Fiction* (Minneapolis: University of Minnesota Press, 1984).
25. Ibid., pp. 11, 13.
26. See Geoffrey Hartman, "Spectral Symbolism and Authorial Self in Keats's 'Hyperion,'" in *The Fate of Reading and Other Essays* (Chicago: University of Chicago Press, 1975), pp. 57–73.
27. For helpful accounts of this poem to which I am here indebted, see Culler, "Apostrophe;" Timothy Bahti, *The Ends of the Lyric: Direction and Consequence in Western Poetry* (Baltimore: Johns Hopkins UP, 1996); Swann, "The Strange Time of Reading;" and Waters, *Poetry's Touch*.
28. Bennett's chapter "Keats's prescience" (pp. 139–57) describes the successive acts through which Keats's reception history invests the figure of the poet with such prescience, from early to recent biographies. But Bennett's chapter also participates in the tradition it describes: for example, Keats's lines on Burns "presciently inscribe the living poet into a posthumous life, into after-fame" (p. 155).
29. Bate surmises that the epic *Hyperion*, which Keats did publish, might have seemed more in tune with the times with its more explicitly progressive narrative (p. 336).
30. James Chandler floats this possibility in *England in 1819: The Politics of Literary Culture and the Case of Romantic Historicism* (Chicago: University of Chicago Press, 1998), p. 432.
31. Keats, *Lamia, Isabella, the Eve of St. Agnes, and Other Poems* (London: Taylor and Hessey, 1820).
32. See Najarian, Chapter 1.

3 *The Cenci*'s Celebrity

1. Edward Trelawny, *Records of Shelley, Byron and the Author* (1878) (New York: New York Review of Books, 2000), p. 164.
2. See, for example, Stephen Behrendt, *Shelley and His Audiences* (Lincoln: University of Nebraska Press, 1989); Susan Wolfson, *Formal Charges: The Shaping of Poetic Form in British Romanticism* (Stanford: Stanford UP, 1997), pp. 193–226; and Kim Wheatley, *Shelley and His Readers: Beyond Paranoid Politics* (Columbia: University of Missouri Press, 1999). In "Finding an Audience: Beatrice Cenci, Percy Shelley, and the Stage," Georgia Strand and Sarah Zimmerman read *The Cenci* specifically in terms of Shelley's search for an effective public voice (*European Romantic Review* 6: 2 [Winter 1996] 246–68).

3. P.B. Shelley, Preface to *Prometheus Unbound*, in Reiman and Powers, ed., *Shelley's Poetry and Prose*, p. 135. Readers often see *The Cenci* as one step in a dialectic of ideas about morality and tyranny that extends over Shelley's career; in this sense, it is often read as a response to or modification of *Prometheus Unbound*. A dialectical schema underlies the discussions of the play by Earl Wasserman and Jerrold Hogle. See Wasserman's *Shelley: A Critical Reading* (Baltimore: Johns Hopkins UP, 1971), pp. 84–130; and Hogle's *Shelley's Process: Radical Transference and the Development of His Major Works* (New York: Oxford UP, 1988), pp.147–62. Alan Richardson's insightful discussion of the play as an example of "mental theater" continues this trend, emphasizing the way *The Cenci* and *Prometheus Unbound* "complement and illuminate one another" over the difference between the play meant for Covent Garden and the lyrical drama meant for the library of the elite reader. See *A Mental Theater: Poetic Drama and Consciousness in the Romantic Age* (University Park: Pennsylvania State UP, 1988), p. 103. For other important discussions of the play, see Stuart Curran, *Shelley's* Cenci: *Scorpions Ringed with Fire* (Princeton: Princeton UP, 1970); Julie Carlson, *In the Theater of Romanticism: Coleridge, Nationalism, Women* (Cambridge: Cambridge UP, 1994); Stuart Sperry, *Shelley's Major Verse: The Narrative and Dramatic Poetry* (Cambridge: Harvard UP, 1988); and Chandler, *England in 1819*. Steven Goldsmith sees the play as charting a path from Shelley's writing practice of early 1819, "with its disregard of a wide readership in favor of a coterie of like-minded intellectuals," toward a more emphatically "social" practice which culminates in *The Mask of Anarchy*. For Goldsmith, where *Prometheus Unbound* sought to "remove aesthetic experience from the complex social context in which it functions," *The Cenci* represents Shelley's growing concern with the way "all language is embedded in specific social circumstance, or more accurately, in the historical relations of power" (*Unbuilding Jerusalem: Apocalypse and Romantic Representation* [Ithaca, NY: Cornell UP, 1993], pp. 236–7). I wish to underline Goldsmith's identification of the social dimensions of Shelley's writing practice, but I do not agree that *Prometheus* so radically removes aesthetic experience from its social context—in any case, a coterie is still a social context. Shelley continues to use both "popular" and "elite" modes of address throughout his career.
4. P.B. Shelley, Preface to *The Cenci*, in *Shelley's Poetry and Prose*, p. 238. All references to *The Cenci* and its Preface are to the Reiman and Powers edition of *Shelley's Poetry and Prose*, hereafter abbreviated *SPP*. References to the Preface are given parenthetically with page numbers; references to the play are given parenthetically by act, scene and line number.
5. Trelawny, *Records*, p. 86. Curran notes that in the nineteenth century the portrait "held a place of honor in the great gallery of the Palazzo Barbarini, and the grand tour sidled by in dutiful homage. Beatrice Cenci was one of the most famous attractions of Rome; reproduced ubiquitously, the portrait was hardly less compelling to visitors than the Bernini fountains or the Sistine frescoes" (*Shelley's* Cenci, p. xi).

6. Shelley's Preface presents the play's dramatization of ethical ambiguity as its central object: "It is in the restless and anatomizing casuistry with which men seek the justification of Beatrice, yet feel that she has done what needs justification; it is in the superstitious horror with which they contemplate alike her wrongs and their revenge; that the dramatic character of what she did and suffered, consists" (p. 240). In *England in 1819*, Chandler connects Shelley's treatment of Beatrice as a moral "case" with the centrality of the "case form" to Romantic historical thinking (pp. 498–515).
7. To Thomas Love Peacock, 20? July 1819, in *The Letters of Percy Bysshe Shelley*, ed. Frederick Jones, 2 vols (Oxford: Clarendon Press, 1964), II, 103. The letter is partially reproduced by Mary Shelley in her "Note to *The Cenci*," reprinted in *The Complete Poems of Percy Bysshe Shelley* (New York: Random House, 1994).
8. Ibid.
9. See Behrendt, *Shelley and His Audiences*, pp. 171–4 on Shelley's jealousy of Byron's fame (and of his money—as Behrendt points out, Shelley recognized that capital investment would be instrumental in securing the recognition he coveted). On the association with Hunt, see Cox.
10. John Taylor Coleridge's unsigned 1818 review of Hunt's *Foliage* in *The Quarterly* takes swipes at Shelley without mentioning him by name (*Quarterly Review* 18: 36 [January 1818] 324–55; attribution from Jonathan Cutmore, ed., *Quarterly Review Archive*, Romantic Circles, accessed 20 December 2008, http://www.rc.umd.edu/reference/qr/index/36.html). Wheatley notes that "before it even reviews his work, the *Quarterly* blasts Shelley's reputation" but argues that "these personal attacks teach the poet [...] the potential benefit to be gained from the reviewers' efforts at character assassination" (*Shelley and His Readers*, p. 45). *The Revolt of Islam* (1818) attracted relatively mild notice from *Blackwood's*; see the unsigned review of the poem in *Blackwood's* 4 (January 1819) 475–86. The reviewer, probably Lockhart, praises Shelley as "a scholar, a gentleman, and a poet" but goes on to comment witheringly, "he must therefore despise from his soul the only eulogies to which he has hitherto been accustomed—paragraphs from the Examiner and sonnets from Jonny Keats" (p. 486); see the helpful editorial commentary on attribution and context that accompanies the reprint in Mole, ed., *Blackwood's Magazine, 1817–25*, V, 243–5. The *Revolt* occasioned a scathing attack from the *Quarterly Review* in its April 1819 issue, but this was not published until September ([John Taylor Coleridge], unsigned review of *Laon and Cythna/Revolt of Islam* by Percy Shelley, *Quarterly Review*, 21:42 [April 1819] 460–71). St. Clair observes that, despite Byron's comment that the *Quarterly Review* inadvertently boosted Shelley's sales, "quantification destroys a good story—the record shows that Shelley's sales remained minuscule" (*Reading Nation*, pp. 188–9; cf. *BLJ* VI, 83).
11. *Queen Mab* was put into evidence at the Chancery trial to demonstrate Shelley's unfitness as a father. On *Queen Mab* and Shelley's reputation, see Wheatley, *Shelley and His Readers*, pp. 82–5. Michael Kohler argues that

the Chancery trial experience informs the representation of the legal system in *The Cenci* in his interesting "Shelley in Chancery: The Paternalist State in *The Cenci*" (*Studies in Romanticism* 37 [1998] 589–90). For the Diodati incident, see Marchand, *Byron: A Biography*, II, 627.

12. On free love, see Byron's rant about Robert Southey's comment linking the two poets in a "league of incest" at Lake Geneva (*BLJ* VI, 76).
13. Chandler, *England in 1819*, p. 27. A June 1819 review of *Rosalind and Helen* in the *London Chronicle* reports the hotel register inscriptions; see Richard Holmes, *Shelley: The Pursuit* (New York: E.P. Dutton, 1975), p. 342, and George L. Marsh, "The Early Reviews of Shelley," *Modern Philology* 27: 1 (August 1929) 73–95 (p. 78). See also Medwin's account discussed in my Introduction.
14. In "Hallam, Tennyson, and the Poetry of Sensation: Aestheticist Allegories of a Counter-Public Sphere" (*Studies in Romanticism* 33 [1994] 527–37), Chandler usefully summarizes the notion of the counter-public sphere and offers a suggestive application of that theory to our understanding of British Romanticism, especially to the "cockney" sensationalism of Keats and Shelley and its reception and reformulation by Hallam and Tennyson. Negt and Kluge developed the concept of a counter-public sphere to address "the need they saw to theorize domains of publicity that might be appropriated for use in the service of proletarian interests" in contrast to the Habermasian model of the bourgeois public sphere and its "idealization of the rationality of communicative exchange" ("Poetry of Sensation," pp. 527–8). Chandler suggests that the "poetry of sensation," as Hallam and Tennyson describe and practice it, "might indeed be construable as part of an effort to effect a kind of counter-public sphere" and thus "where Habermas sees the bourgeois epoch as defined by the developing power of public opinion to determine political outcomes, so cockney sensationalism would have to be understood in some kind of tension with, and as some kind of alternative to, that regnant bourgeois domain" (p. 534).
15. The example of *Julian and Maddalo* (1818–19, published 1824) shows how much Shelley is concerned at this period not just with the formation of an elite audience but with the problem of romanticism's public and of the nature of its public appeal. The poem figures complex relationships among audiences within and outside the poem, first in the way the sophisticates Julian and Maddalo watch as the Maniac's music entrances the inmates of the insane asylum, then in the way Julian sets up a distinction between a restricted and a mass audience by refusing, at the end of the poem, to retell the Maniac's story to the unfeeling world.
16. Percy B. Shelley, *The Cenci: A Tragedy in Five Acts* (Italy: Printed for C. and J. Ollier, London, 1819). William Benbow printed pirated editions of the play in the 1820s, and both authorized and pirated posthumous collections of Shelley included *The Cenci*.
17. Wasserman, *Shelley*, p. 121. By contrast, see Roger Blood's deconstructive reading of the play in "Allegory and Dramatic Representation in *The Cenci*", *Studies in Romanticism* 33 (1994) 355–89. Kohler's discussion

of the play provides both a good summary of the strands of the play's more recent critical reception and a strong argument for situating the play undecidably between a deconstructive reading—exemplified for Kohler by Blood—and a humanist reading as exemplified by Wasserman ("Shelley in Chancery," p. 588).

18. Goldsmith, *Unbuilding*, p. 236.
19. My sense of the "Baroque" as a formal category is indebted to Walter Benjamin's *The Origin of German Tragic Drama*, trans. John Osborne (London: Verso, 1977).
20. "Note," p. 364. Mary Shelley feminizes the scene of writing, placing it in a network of female influence (she and Percy go over the play together as he writes, and in fact she says Percy had first wanted *her* to write a play on the subject). Conversely, Percy Shelley's dedicatory letter to Hunt describes a scene of male bonding through radical chic: "Had I known a person more highly endowed than yourself with all that it becomes a man to possess, I had solicited for this work the ornament of his name ... In that patient and irreconcilable enmity with domestic and political tyranny and imposture which the tenor of your life has illustrated, and which, had I health and talents, should illustrate mine, let us, comforting each other in our task, live and die" (*SPP*, p. 238).
21. Both in *Calderón de la Barca: Six Plays*, trans. Edwin Honig (New York: Institute for Advanced Studies in the Theatre Arts, 1993). I should make it clear that I am not arguing for (or against) a genetic relationship between the Calderón plays and *The Cenci*. It is very difficult to reconstruct exactly when Shelley was reading what and to correlate this with his writing; it does seem clear that he began work on the play before he began his "study" of Calderón, but that he was reading Calderón while finishing the first draft of the play and then revising it heavily. For my purposes, it is enough that both Percy and Mary are thinking about Calderón and *The Cenci* together, and directing the reader's attention to this relationship.
22. Ibid., p. 119.
23. See Mary Jacobus, *Reading Woman: Essays in Feminist Criticism* (New York: Columbia UP, 1986). This phrase is from Jacobus's description of the "unavoidably hysterical dilemma" she sees as facing "the woman under patriarchy": "She can either submit to the desire of the father, identifying herself with it so completely that she becomes what he desires her to be; that is, all body, the fetish who veils the horror of absence in the male hysterical fantasy which (as Freud admits) afflicts all men in the face of their mothers. This is why, for the hysteric, the death of the father fractures the system of representations in which she has taken up her assigned position. Alternatively, a woman can break with the desire of the father by choosing to be 'like himself' instead of what he likes" (*Reading Woman*, p. 274).
24. The question of Beatrice's desire is raised briefly in her odd, early exchange with Orsino, where she refers fleetingly to her feelings for him in the past but insists that now he has become a priest she can only "swear a cold fidelity" (1.2.26). That exchange strangely displaces Beatrice's confession—the end point the play never reaches—to a time

before the play: "two long years are past / Since, on an April midnight, underneath / The moon-light ruins of mount Palantine / I did confess to you my secret mind" (1.2.4–7). For most of the play, the relationship between Orsino and Beatrice takes a back seat to the homosocial relationship between Orsino and her brother Giacomo.

25. See Curran, *Shelley's* Cenci, pp. 42–3.
26. William Jewett, *Fatal Autonomy: Romantic Drama and the Rhetoric of Agency* (Ithaca, NY: Cornell UP, 1997), p. 151.
27. *The Ethics of Psychoanalysis 1959–1960*, trans. Dennis Porter (New York: Norton, 1992), p. 69.
28. Mary Shelley, *Matilda* in Mary Shelley and Mary Wollstonecraft, *Mary, Maria, Matilda*, ed. Janet Todd (New York: Penguin, 1992), p. 172.
29. Cf., for example, the "Ode to Liberty" (1820).
30. Their soliloquies are uniformly clichéd and unconvincing; they feel almost parodies of the Shakespearean soliloquies (Iago, Macbeth, Lady Macbeth) they echo. As I argue later, this might suggest less Shelley's inexperience, as some suggest, than that Romantic drama is in a transitional moment when Shakespeare simply looms too large.
31. The "dramatic character" of what she does and suffers is located, after all, not in some psychological truth of personality but in the "casuistry" and "superstitious horror" with which "men" respond to the story: not Beatrice's psychology but her audience's is the drama's object. Though her father is given to more explicit "self-anatomy," his character seems rather in crucial ways "unmotivated," as we say today; in his case, "self-anatomy" is however easily assignable to narcissistic obsession—a fatal narcissism that renders the self a cadaver to be dissected—whereas the trouble with Beatrice is that she might be guilty of "self-anatomy" or might not be, might be narcissistically obsessed or might not be, and we can't really know. See Richardson, *Mental Theater* and Hogle, *Shelley's Process* for discussions of "self-anatomy" and the psychology of narcissism in the play.
32. Shelley, *Letters* II, 117; II, 120.
33. Quoting one's own writing both advertises its 'quotability' and treats the quotation as a nugget of received wisdom, but the circuit also indicates Shelley's estrangement from events in England. It might be that Shelley adopts Beatrice's stance of not-knowing: that this position is scripted as a woman's, and so to take it on Shelley slips into momentary drag, as it were.
34. "O, think!" becomes a tic in Beatrice's speech patterns that shows up again, repeatedly, in her plea before the inquisitional court in Act V. Later in the play, Beatrice echoes Claudio directly, as many critics have noted.
35. For discussions of Beatrice as a performer, see Carlson, pp. 181–98 and Andrea Henderson, *Romantic Identities: Varieties of Subjectivity 1774–1830* (Cambridge: Cambridge UP, 1996), pp. 96–129.
36. Peter Brooks, "The Revolutionary Body," in *Fictions of the French Revolution*, ed. Bernadette Fort (Evanston: Northwestern UP, 1991), pp. 35–54 (pp. 36–7).

37. See Claudia Johnson's *Equivocal Beings: Politics, Gender, and Sentimentality in the 1790's: Wollstonecraft, Radcliffe, Burney, Austen* for a discussion of sentimental emotion that takes Burke's use of Marie-Antoinette as one organizing instance.
38. Helen Maria Williams, *Letters Written in France and Letters Containing a Sketch of the Politics of France* (1796), reprinted in *Letters from France*, intro. Janet Todd (Delmar, New York: Scholars' Facsimiles and Reprints, 1975). Williams describes the scene as a performance: "The women who were called furies of the guillotine, and who had assembled to insult her on leaving the prison, were awed into silence by her demeanor, while some of the spectators uncovered their heads before her, and others gave loud tokens of applause. There was such an air of chastened exaltation thrown over her countenance, that she inspired sentiments of love, rather than the sensations of pity ... When [the executioner] took off her handkerchief, the moment before she bent under the fatal stroke, she blushed deeply; and her head, which was held up to the multitude the moment after, exhibited this last impression of offended modesty" (pp. 133–4). Brooks discusses the male hysterical reaction to Corday, arguing that she became, for male writers, the exemplary instance of the danger of women in politics ("The Revolutionary Body," p. 39).
39. Mary Shelley, "Note," p. 364.
40. Ibid., p. 365.
41. Compare the fascinating scene in Hawthorne's *The Marble Faun* (New York: Penguin, 1990) in which Hilda and Miriam confront a drawing of Beatrice Cenci's portrait. The "mysterious force" of the portrait has to do not only with the strength of its emotional grip on the viewer but also with the way it both solicits and evades interpretation (p. 65). The more its enigma is pursued, the more it seems to come alive, and what animates the portrait is precisely its resistance or evasion of the viewer's interpretative or sympathetic gaze: as Hilda complains, "the forlorn creature so longs to elude our eyes, and forever vanish away into nothingness" (p. 66). Transfixed by the portrait, Miriam proclaims desperately: "If I could only get within her consciousness! If I could but clasp Beatrice Cenci's ghost, and draw it into myself! I would give my life to know whether she thought herself innocent, or the one great criminal since time began!" (pp. 66–7).
42. Barbara Groseclose, "The Incest Motif in Shelley's *The Cenci*," *Comparative Drama*. 19 (Fall 1985) 222–39 (p. 223). Groseclose is also my source for the problem of the portrait's attribution. She notes that after Shelley's play is published, "the number and variety of images of Beatrice dramatically increase. The trade in copies of Guido's portrait becomes virtually a mania" (p. 235).
43. Mary Shelley, "Note," p. 366.
44. My argument about commodity relations here runs along lines somewhat parallel to Rzepka's discussion of De Quincey's strategy of the rhetorical substitution of relations of gift exchange for relations of market exchange: "what the reader's reception of the literary commodity as a

gift seems to ratify is the historical writer's apotheosis as an *origin and bestower*, rather than as a *worker or retailer*, of language" (*Sacramental Commodities*, p. 9).

45. Mary's "Note" to the play quotes tellingly from a letter Percy wrote urging her to write a tragedy on Charles I:

> Remember, remember Charles I. I have been already imagining how you would conduct some scenes. The second volume of *St. Leon* begins with this proud and true sentiment: "There is nothing which the human mind can conceive which it may not execute." Shakespeare was only a human being.
>
> (p. 363)

To insist that Shakespeare is after all only human in this context, of course, suggests that he is felt as more than human. The embedded quotation from Godwin, Mary's father, the allusion to Hamlet, the parallel with Cenci's remarks on the mind's power (e.g., 1.1.87), and Percy's paternalistic voice ("Remember, remember") make this, for Mary, a dizzyingly complex injunction to write (or to remember).

46. Jane Austen comments somewhat wryly on this culture of quotation when, in *Mansfield Park*, she has Henry Crawford remark that Shakespeare "is part of an Englishman's constitution. His thoughts and beauties are so spread abroad that one touches them every where, one is intimate with him by instinct." As Edmund comments in response, Shakespearean language is pervasive, despite or perhaps because of the fact his plays are only known "in bits and scraps": "His celebrated passages are quoted by every body; they are in half the books we open, and we all talk Shakespeare, use his similes, and describe with his quotations" ([Oxford: Oxford UP, 1990], p. 306).
47. Review of *The Cenci* (1819), *Literary Gazette* (April 1820) 209–10, reprinted in Donald Reiman, *The Romantics Reviewed: Contemporary Reviews of British Romantic Writers, Part C: Shelley, Keats and London Radical Writers*, 2 vols (New York: Garland, 1972), pp. 517–18 (p. 517). *The Romantics Reviewed, Part C* hereafter abbreviated *RR: C*.
48. Review of *The Cenci* (1819), *Monthly Review* 2nd series 94 (February 1821) 161–8, reprinted in *RR:C*, pp. 720–3 (p. 720).
49. The review of the play in *Gold's London Magazine* explicitly identifies Shelley's style with the "new-fangled style of poetry, facetiously yclept the Cockney School" ([Gold's] *London Magazine* 1 [April 1820] 401–7, reprinted in *RR: C*, pp. 605–612 [p. 605]).
50. Review of *The Cenci* (1819), *Edinburgh Monthly Review* 3 (May 1820) 591–604, reprinted in *RR: C*, pp. 346–52 (p. 347).
51. For a detailed and illuminating reading of the interaction between Shelley's poetic figures and the language of his reviewers, see Wheatley's chapter "*Prometheus Unbound:* Reforming the Reviewers" in *Shelley and His Readers*, pp. 109–50.

52. John Scott, Review of *The Cenci* (1819), [Baldwin's] *London Magazine* 1 (May 1820) 546–55, reprinted in *RR: C*, pp. 566–75.
53. Ibid., p. 568.

4 Shelley's Glamour

1. John Addington Symonds, *Shelley* (1878) (London: Macmillan, 1881), p. 183.
2. General accounts of Shelley's ascendant reputation include Newman Ivey White, *Shelley*, 2 vols (New York: Knopf, 1940) II, 389–418; Sylva Norman, *The Flight of the Skylark: The Development of Shelley's Reputation* (Normal: University of Oklahoma Press, 1954); and Karsten K. Engelberg, *The Making of the Shelley Myth: An Annotated Bibliography of Criticism of Percy Bysshe Shelley, 1822–1860* (London: Mansell, 1988). Miriam Allott provides a concise and thoughtful overview of Shelley's reception with a good discussion of Arnold in particular; see her "Attitudes to Shelley: the Vagaries of a Critical Reputation," in *Essays on Shelley*, ed. Miriam Allott (Liverpool: Liverpool UP, 1982), pp. 1–38. For accounts of significant moments in the cultural absorption and dissemination of the image of Shelley as a lyric poet, see Richard Cronin, "Shelley, Tennyson and the Apostles, 1828–1832," *Keats-Shelley Review* 5 (Autumn 1990) 14–40, and Neil Fraistat, "Illegitimate Shelley: Radical Piracy and the Textual Edition as Cultural Performance." *PMLA* 109: 3 (May 1994) 409–23. Mark Kipperman shows how a "Romantic" Shelley is produced to serve the needs of the teaching of English literature in the late nineteenth century; see his "Absorbing a Revolution: Shelley Becomes a Romantic, 1889–1903," *Nineteenth-Century Literature* 47: 2 (September 1992) 187–211. My focus in this chapter is not on the history of Shelley's reputation but rather on the affective dynamics that structure reader-writer relationships at specific moments in this history.
3. Alfred Hix Welsh, *Development of English Literature and Language*, 2 vols (Chicago: S. C. Griggs, 1885), II, 283.
4. Three studies of Shelley's passionate readers have been especially helpful to me: Swann's "Shelley's Pod People;" Pascoe's *The Hummingbird Cabinet*; and Eric O. Clarke's chapter "Shelley's Heart," in *Virtuous Vice: Homoeroticism and the Public Sphere* (Durham: Duke UP, 2000). Analyzing the persistent eroticization of Shelley by his readers, Clarke shows that "the process by which Shelley came to be valued was irreducibly entangled in nineteenth-century sexual politics: the question of Shelley's cultural value and his erotic value were in many ways one and the same" (pp. 149–50). Swann analyzes the connection between "the exquisite loveliness of Shelley himself as he appears in the accounts of his contemporaries" and the "construction of 'the aesthetic' that descends to us from Kant through Adorno: 'the aesthetic' as autonomous, enigmatic, auratic form" (par. 2–3). Pascoe's discussion of Shelley collectors connects their passion for the poet to the more general way in which "Romantic poetry's acute awareness of passing time and human loss contributed to,

and reflected, a culture's new understanding of the past as an idealized lost world, partly salvageable through the recovery and preservation of old objects and documents" (p. 4).

5. For an analysis of Shelley's "poetics of personality" and Keatsian impersonality as contrasting and overlapping strands in poetics through modernism and beyond, see Robert Kaufman, "Negatively Capable Dialectics: Keats, Vendler, Adorno, and the Theory of the Avant Garde," *Critical Inquiry* 37: 2 (2001) 354–84.
6. Richard Garnett, *Relics of Shelley* (London: Moxon, 1862).
7. Garnett, *Relics of Shelley*, p. x. Garnett cites these lines from the fragment "Wedded Souls," which he prints later in his *Relics*. It is worth giving the fragment in its entirety here, since it makes the eroticization and the power dynamics of such intimate reading more explicit:

   I am as a spirit who has dwelt
   Within his heart of hearts, and I have felt
   His feelings, and have thought his thoughts, and known
   The inmost converse of his soul, the tone
   Unheard but in the silence of his blood,
   When all the pulses in their multitude
   Image the trembling calm of summer seas.
   I have unlocked the golden melodies
   Of his deep soul, as with a master-key,
   And loosened them and bathed myself therein—
   Even as an eagle in a thunder-mist
   Clothing his wings with lightning.

8. Robert Browning, *Men and Women* (1855), (Boston: Ticknor and Fields, 1856), p. 183.
9. Dames's account of the celebrity encounter in Thackeray is particularly suggestive when read against the crossings of public and private, memory and the present in Browning's lyric. "In the 'celebrity,'" Dames argues, "mid-Victorian culture found a social and perceptual category that could [...] root itself more deeply into the heretofore private consciousness of the public and, therefore, could reorient consciousness (particularly memory) toward a newly configured public realm" (p. 25). On Browning's relationship to Shelley and its place in literary lore, see Frederick Pottle, *Shelley and Browning: A Myth and Some Facts* (Chicago: Pembroke Press, 1923).
10. Matthew Arnold, "The Study of Poetry" (1880), in *The Complete Prose Works of Matthew Arnold*, ed. R. H. Super, 11 vols (Ann Arbor: University of Michigan Press, 1977), IX, 161–88.
11. Arnold, "Shelley" (*The Nineteenth Century* 1888; *Essays in Criticism, Second Series*, 1895) in *Complete Prose Works of Matthew Arnold* XI, 305–27.
12. For a useful summary of Arnold's ambivalence, see Allott, "Attitudes to Shelley." Park Honan's biography *Matthew Arnold: A Life* (New York: McGraw-Hill, 1981) gives an account of the psychological role Shelley played in Arnold's "dreamy, emotive early life" (p. 414); for Arnold's own

testimony, see his letters to Clough on Shelley (*Letters of Matthew Arnold to Arthur Hugh Clough*, ed. H.T. Lowry [Oxford: Oxford UP, 1932], pp. 97, 124, 146).

13. Arthur Henry Hallam's "On Some of the Characteristics of Modern Poetry" (1833), which defines Keats and Shelley as "poets of sensation, rather than [Wordsworthian] reflection," marks a key moment in the evolution of such a view of Romantic aestheticism. See "On Some of the Characteristics of Modern Poetry, and on the Lyrical Poems of Alfred Tennyson," *The Writings of Arthur Hallam*, ed. T.H.V. Motter (New York: MLA, 1943), pp. 182–97.
14. See Kaufman on the contrasting and overlapping legacies assigned to "the Keatsian dissolution of selfhood and concomitant building up of form, which in turn serves an intellectual sensorium ultimately capable of dissolving the object-world," on the one hand, and to "the Shelleyan prophetic and disseminative negationalism that pays tribute to realty by beginning in opposition to it," on the other (p. 383). Compare T.S. Eliot's insistence that "Poetry is not a turning loose of emotion, but an escape from emotion; it is not the expression of personality, but an escape from personality. But, of course, only those who have personality and emotions know what it means to want to escape from these things" ("Tradition and the Individual Talent" [1919], in *Selected Essays* [New York: Harcourt, 1964], pp. 3–11 [p. 10]).
15. Symonds, *Shelley*, p. 187.
16. Arnold's essay first appeared in *The Nineteenth Century*, January 1888, and was then reprinted in *Essays in Criticism, Second Series*. Clarke also discusses the sexual politics of the essay, though not its politics of form.
17. Robert Browning,"Essay on Shelley" (1852) in *Collected Works*, ed. Roma King et al. (Athens: Ohio UP; Waco, Texas: Baylor University, 1981) V, 137–51 (p. 139).
18. Ibid.
19. Browning's influential essay on Shelley was originally the Introduction to a set of supposed Shelley letters which proved to be forgeries. It is easy to see Browning's essay on Shelley as defensive in relation to conditions of poetic celebrity: against Shelleyan self-exposure, Browning maps out for himself an alternative form of poetic fame more insulated from publicity, identifying himself with the "objective" poet for whom personality and work are more obliquely related.
20. Such a charge about Shelley would not be new, of course; for a representative earlier opinion on Shelley's impulsiveness, see the *Quarterly Review*'s 1861 discussion of Shelley biographies (Unsigned review of Mary Shelley, ed., *The Works of Percy Bysshe Shelley*; T. J. Hogg, *Life of P. B. Shelley*; Lady Shelley, *Shelley Memorials*; and T. L. Peacock, *Memoir of P. B. Shelley*, *Quarterly Review* 220 [1861] 289–328). In the reviewer's summary, "his emotions found fruit in action without let or struggle; they were generally good and noble" but "when they were vicious, he had neither the nerve nor the will to control them. He acted, in short, professedly from impulse, and not from duty" (pp. 320–1).

21. Norman is still the most entertaining and wide-ranging account of such practices. See also Clarke, Swann "Shelley's Pod People," and Pascoe, *Hummingbird*.
22. Pascoe, *Hummingbird*, pp. 1–2.
23. To James Thomson, April 21, 1873, in *Selected Letters*, ed. Roger W. Peattie (University Park: Penn State UP, 1990), p. 307.
24. Henry James, *The Aspern Papers* in *the Aspern Papers and the Turn of the Screw*, ed. Anthony Curtis (New York: Penguin, 1984), pp. 43–142.
25. Najarian traces the entanglement of Victorian "love for Keats" with ideas of masculinity and same-sex desire; see especially his chapter on Arnold.
26. Clarke, p. 151.
27. Fraistat, "Illegitimate Shelley," p. 410.
28. Ibid.
29. Clarke discusses this passage as well, but argues that Captain Kennedy's masculinity is intended to ward off the feminizing effects of "enthusiasm" for the poet.
30. Arnold also contributed introductions to the selections from Gray and Keats in Ward's anthology. In 1888 the essay was republished as the opening essay to *Essays in Criticism, Second Series*.
31. Steven Connor, "Haze: On Nebular Modernism," paper presented at Trinity College, Oxford, May 12, 2006, on line, accessed 12 April 2007, http://www.stevenconnor.com/haze/, p. 3.
32. David G. Riede, *Matthew Arnold and the Betrayal of Language* (Charlottesville: University Press of Virginia, 1988), p. 4.
33. William Hazlitt, review of *Posthumous Poems*, by Percy Shelley, *Edinburgh Review* 11 (July 1824) 494–514, reprinted in *Shelley: The Critical Heritage*, ed. James Barcus (Boston: Routledge, 1975), pp. 335–45 (p. 336).
34. Ibid., p. 335.
35. Thomas Jefferson Hogg, *The Life of Percy Bysshe Shelley*, 4 vols (London: Moxon, 1858), II, 46. Compare also Hogg's analogy of telling Shelley's life to exhibiting "a phantasmagoria, a magic lantern, a spectrum of prismatic colours" (II, 46).
36. Edmund Gosse, *Modern English Literature: A Short History* (1897) (New York: Frederick A. Stokes, 1906), p. 313.
37. McGann, *The Romantic Ideology: A Critical Investigation* (Chicago: University of Chicago Press, 1983), p. 115.
38. Hallam, "On Some of the Characteristics of Modern Poetry", p. 186.
39. The lines are spoken by the Spirit of the Hour, to Asia and Panthea, at the start of Act II, Scene 5. To make it match the selection from Burns, I assume, Arnold leaves off the final line of the Spirit's speech: "They shall drink the hot speed of desire!" It seems to me that for Arnold's purposes this last line would have been all he really needed to quote.
40. Shelley, *Defence of Poetry* (c. 1821), in *SPP*, p. 508.
41. For a strong analysis of the logic of futurity in the *Defence*, see Deborah Elise White's discussion of this sentence in her *Romantic Returns: Superstition, Imagination, History* (Stanford: Stanford UP, 2000), pp. 121–8.

42. That the poet should be the (instrumentalized) term of accommodation between sets of effects parallels the logic of the Aeolian lyre passage earlier in the *Defence*, which similarly defines "man" in terms of an accommodation of effects to one another (*SPP*, p. 480).
43. Ibid., pp. 503–4.
44. Ibid., p. 504.
45. Hazlitt, Review of *Posthumous Poems*, p. 336.
46. *Recollections of the Last Days of Shelley and Byron* (London: Moxon, 1858), p. 120. Hereafter cited parenthetically. Marchand notes ten different manuscript versions of Trelawny's account of the death and cremation; see his "Trelawny on the Death of Shelley," *Keats-Shelley Memorial Bulletin* 4 (1952) 9–34. On the various representations of the cremation scene over the course of the century, see Kim Wheatley, "'Attracted by the Body': Accounts of Shelley's Cremation," *Keats-Shelley Journal* 49 (2000) 162–82; Timothy Webb, "Religion of the Heart: Leigh Hunt's Unpublished Tribute to Shelley." Keats-Shelley Review 7 (Fall 1992) 1–61; and Samantha Matthews, *Poetical Remains: Poets' Graves, Bodies and Books in the Nineteenth Century* (Oxford: Oxford UP, 2004).
47. Leigh Hunt, *Lord Byron and Some of His Contemporaries, with Recollections of the Author's Life and of His Visit to Italy*, 2 vols (London: Henry Colburn, 1828), I, 338.
48. Though the cremation is not mentioned by obituaries for the poet, something of the episode's reach in the years just following Shelley's death is suggested by *The Curious Book* of 1828, a sort of *Reader's Digest*, which includes alphabetically ordered entries on such topics as "Hair Powder;" "How to Grow Rich;" and, sandwiched between "Sabbath-Day" and "Sublime View," an account of "Shelley the Poet, Death of," lifted from Medwin's version in *Conversations with Lord Byron*. See *The Curious Book* (Edinburgh: John Thomson, and London: Baldwin, Cradock, and Joy, 1828), pp. 381–90.
49. Marianne Hunt, *Unpublished Diary of Mrs. Leigh Hunt, Pisa, Sept. 18, 1822—Genoa, Oct. 24, 1822.* (London: Macmillan, [n.d.]), p. 6.
50. Swann, "Shelley's Pod People" par. 6.
51. S. Matthews, *Poetical Remains*, p. 116.
52. This argument has been made in compelling terms by Andrew Franta, who contends that in late writings like the *Defence* and *Ode to the West Wind* Shelley identifies "poetry's power with its reception" ("Shelley and the Poetics of Political Indirection," *Poetics Today* 22: 4 [2001] 765–93 [p. 791]; see also his *Romanticism and the Rise of the Mass Public*). For related arguments, see also Chandler, *England in 1819* and Rajan.
53. *SPP*, p. 500.
54. Anne Barton, Introduction to Trelawny's *Records of Shelley, Byron and the Author* (1878) (New York: New York Review of Books, 2000), pp. xix–xxiv. For Trelawny's claim, see David Crane, *Lord Byron's Jackal: The Life of Edward John Trelawny* (London: HarperCollins, 1998), p. 332.
55. Paul de Man, "Shelley Disfigured," in *The Rhetoric of Romanticism* (New York: Columbia UP, 1984), pp. 93–124.
56. McGann, *Romantic Ideology*, p. 13.

57. Ibid. McGann's formulation recalls the epigraph on Shelley's tomb, chosen by Hunt and Trelawny: "Nothing of him that doth fade / But doth suffer a sea-change / Into something rich and strange."
58. "Disfiguring Monuments: History in Paul de Man's 'Shelley Disfigured' and Percy Bysshe Shelley's 'The Triumph of Life,'" *ELH* 58: 3 (1991) 633–55 (p. 633).
59. De Man, "Shelley Disfigured," pp. 119, 122.
60. Ibid., p. 120.
61. Ibid., pp. 121–2.

5 "The Atmosphere of Authorship": Landon, Byron and Literary Culture

1. In addition to the studies by Leighton, Mellor, Cronin, McGann, Armstrong, Craciun and Lootens cited below, prominent critical treatments of Landon include Linda H. Peterson, "Rewriting *A History of the Lyre*: Letitia Landon, Elizabeth Barrett Browning, and the (Re)construction of the Nineteenth-Century Woman Poet," in *Women's Poetry, Late Romantic to Late Victorian*, pp. 115–32; Glennis Stephenson, *Letitia Landon: The Woman behind L.E.L.* (Manchester and New York: Manchester UP, 1995); Emma Francis, "Letitia Landon: Public Fantasy and the Private Sphere," *Essays and Studies* 51 (1998) 93–115; and earlier, Germaine Greer, "The Tulsa Center for Women's Literature: What We Are Doing and Why We Are Doing It," *Tulsa Studies in Women's Literature* 1: 1 (Spring 1982) 5–26.
2. For a detailed analysis of the production and marketing of the annuals, the scholarly apparatus for the electronic edition of *The Keepsake* (1829) at the Romantic Circles website is terrific. See Terence Hoagwood, Kathryn Ledbetter, and Martin M. Jacobsen, ed., *L.E.L.'s "Verses" and The Keepsake of 1829*, Romantic Circles, accessed 1 December 2008, http://www.rc.umd.edu/editions/lel/index.html.
3. The quotation is from *The History of a Lyre* (Letitia Landon, *Selected Writings*, ed. Jerome McGann and Daniel Riess [Orchard Park, New York: Broadview, 1997] p. 104). Subsequent references to Landon's writing are to the McGann and Riess edition unless otherwise noted.
4. Angela Leighton, *Victorian Women Poets: Writing against the Heart* (New York: Harvester Wheatshaft, 1992), p. 58.
5. Anne Mellor, *Romanticism and Gender* (London: Routledge, 1993), p. 112.
6. Richard Cronin, *Romantic Victorians: English Literature, 1824–1840* (Basingstoke: Palgrave Macmillan, 2002), p. 86.
7. Jerome McGann, *The Poetics of Sensibility: A Revolution in Literary Style* (New York: Oxford UP, 1996), p. 147.
8. The mysterious circumstances of Landon's death—she was found lying on the floor with an empty bottle of prussic acid in her hand—have provoked speculation ever since the news first arrived back in England. While some Victorian and twentieth-century biographers hypothesized murder and others suicide, McGann and Riess point out a 1942 study

by Anne Ethel Wyly attributing the cause of death not to an overdose of prussic acid but to an epileptic seizure (McGann and Riess, Introduction to Landon's *Selected Writings*, p. 16).

9. "Miss Landon's Poetry," *Blackwood's Edinburgh Magazine* 16 (August 1824) 189–93, p. 190.
10. William Jerdan, Unsigned review of *The Improvisatrice, and Other Poems*, *Literary Gazette* 389 (July 3, 1824), p. 419.
11. Landon, Preface to *The Venetian Bracelet*, in *Selected Writings*, p.163.
12. *Literary Gazette* 316 (8 February 1823), p. 91.
13. Tricia Lootens, "Receiving the Legend, Rethinking the Writer: Letitia Landon and the Poetess Tradition," in *Romanticism and Women Poets*, pp. 242–59.
14. See Craciun's chapter on Landon in her *Fatal Women of Romanticism* (Cambridge: Cambridge University Press, 2003), pp. 195–250, and Armstrong's *Victorian Poetry: Poetry, Poetics, and Politics* (London and New York: Routledge, 1993).
15. Frederic Rowton, *The Female Poets of Great Britain* (1848; Philadelphia: Henry C. Baird, 1853), ed. Marilyn L. Williamson (Detroit: Wayne State UP, 1981).
16. On the instabilities of the "female Byron" label, see the discussions in Yopie Prins, "Personifying the Poetess: Caroline Norton, 'The Picture of Sappho'" in *Women's Poetry: Late Romantic to Late Victorian*, pp. 50–67; Wolfson, *Borderlines*; and Craciun, *Fatal Women*, p. 204.
17. Rowton, *The Female Poets*, p. 424.
18. Ibid., p. 431.
19. Ibid., p. 432.
20. "Gallery of Literary Characters. No. XLI. Miss Landon," *Fraser's Magazine* 8 (October 1833) 433.
21. Ibid.
22. Letitia Landon, *The Troubadour, Catalogue of Pictures, and Historical Sketches* (London: Hurst, Robinson, and Co., 1825). Second edition.
23. "Gallery," *Fraser's Magazine*, p. 433.
24. "Regina's Maids of Honour," *Fraser's Magazine* 13 (January 1836) 80.
25. See David Higgins, "'Isn't She Painted *Con Amore*?"': *Fraser's Magazine* and the Spectacle of Female Genius," *Romanticism on the Net* 46 (May 2007), accessed July 21, 2008, http://www.erudit.org/revue/ron/2007/v/n46/016139ar.html. On the possibility that Landon had three children by William Jerdan, see Cynthia Lawford, "Diary," *London Review of Books* 22: 18 (September 21, 2000) 36–7.
26. Mahoney, "Gallery," p. 433.
27. Unsigned review of *The Three Histories* (1830) by Maria Jane Jewsbury, *Knickerbocker Magazine* 1 (May 1833) 319–20 (p. 319).
28. Craciun, *Fatal Women*, p. 208.
29. Stephen Colclough describes a commonplace book in a private collection that includes a transcription of *The Improvisatrice* ("Recovering the Reader: Commonplace Books and Diaries as Sources of Reading Experience,"

Publishing History 44 [1998] 5–37). The transcript "occupies fifty-two pages of the book, includes a copy of the advertisement, and is followed by two more short poems from the same volume" (p. 17). Noting that such a long extract is atypical, Colclough cites this transcription as evidence of the prohibitive cost of books, or readers' thrifty habits: one could borrow a book and copy it out rather than buy it. But copying over a poem in this way might also be conducive to a particular identificatory effects (and intriguingly, Colclough notes that it looks like a male hand, in a book with entries in different hands).

30. Landon, *Improvisatrice*, lines 422–37; subsequent citations will appear parenthetically by line number. For evidence of *The Troubadour*'s Byronic echoes, consider the opening description of Raymond: "on his cold, pale cheek were caught / The traces of some deeper thought, / A something seen of pride and gloom, / Not like youth's hour of light and bloom: / A brow of pride, a lip of scorn,— / Yet beautiful in scorn and pride [...] He was the last of a proud race / Who left him but his sword and name, / And boyhood past in restless dreams / Of future dreams and future fame" (*The Troubadour*, p. 9).
31. The quotation is from *The Troubadour*, p. 180. The first edition of *The Improvisatrice* (1824) carried a frontispiece illustration emphasizing the volume's Gothic sensationalism, but this is replaced in subsequent editions (1825) by a view of Florence emphasizing the poem's affiliation with a more rarefied discourse of art and culture.
32. Jerdan, Review of the *Improvisatrice*, p. 420.
33. "Noctes Ambrosianae. No. XVI." *Blackwood's Edinburgh Magazine* 16 (August 1824) 231–50 (p. 237).
34. On such physiological language of the heart, see Kirstie Blair, *Victorian Poetry and the Culture of the Heart* (Oxford: Oxford UP, 2006).
35. Mermin, *Godiva's Ride*, pp. 8, 11.
36. Jonah Siegel, *Haunted Museum: Longing, Travel and the Art-Romance Tradition* (Princeton: Princeton University Press, 2005), pp. 50–1.
37. *Fisher's Drawing Room Scrap-Book* (London: Fisher, Son, & Co., 1840), pp. 11–14.
38. Ibid., p. 11.
39. Ibid., p. 14.
40. Armstrong, *Victorian Poetry*, pp. 323–4.
41. "On the Character of Mrs. Hemans's Writings," *New Monthly Magazine* 44 (August 1835) 425–33, reprinted in McGann and Riess, *Selected Writings*, pp. 173–86 (p. 173).
42. Ibid., pp. 173, 175.
43. Yopie Prins, *Victorian Sappho* (Princeton: Princeton UP, 1999), p. 179. Especially relevant here is Prins's discussion of Landon's poem "Sappho" as a "meditation on how a lyric figure is mediated by the recurring moment of its reception" (p. 192).
44. Marlon B. Ross, *The Contours of Masculine Desire: Romanticism and the Rise of Women's Poetry* (New York: Oxford UP, 1989), p. 292.

45. Hemans's poems are quoted from Wolfson's edition. On Hemans's figures of feeling, see Jason R. Rudy, "Hemans's Passion," *Studies in Romanticism* 45: 4 (Winter 2006) 543–62.
46. Pascoe, *Romantic Theatricality*, pp. 245–6.
47. Landon, "The Frozen Ship," in Letitia Landon, *Works*, 2 vols (Boston: Phillips, Sampson, 1853), pp. 231–2. The poem appeared originally in *The Vow of the Peacock and Other Poems* (London: Saunders, Otley, 1835), pp. 256–60.
48. Cronin, *Romantic Victorians*, p. 86.
49. Maria Jane Jewsbury, *The History of an Enthusiast* in *The Three Histories* (1830) (Boston: Perkins and Marvin, 1831).
50. Landon, *Ethel Churchill, or, the Two Brides* (1837) in *Works* (1853) II, pp. 1–163.
51. Thomas Pfau, *Wordsworth's Profession: Form, Class and the Logic of Early Romantic Cultural Production* (Stanford: Stanford UP, 1997), p. 26.
52. Mary Howitt, "L.E.L.," in *Fisher's Drawing-Room Scrapbook* (1840), pp. 5–8 (p. 6).
53. See Moore, *Letters*, Preface to vol. II.
54. For a good discussion of the origins and style of the "Noctes," see Parker, *Literary Magazines*, pp. 106–34.
55. See Patrick Leary, "*Fraser's Magazine* and the Literary Life: 1830–1847," *Victorian Periodicals Review* 27 (Summer 1994) 105–26.
56. Leary, "*Fraser's Magazine* and the Literary Life," p. 106.
57. See Feldman, "The Poet and the Profits."
58. "Miss Landon's Poetry," p. 190.
59. Landon, *Letters*, ed. F.J. Sypher (Ann Arbor: Scholars' Facsimiles and Reprints, 2001) pp. 23–5 (p. 23). The letter was printed in Laman Blanchard's *Life and Literary Remains of L.E.L.*, 2 vols (London: Lea and Blanchard, 1841), pp. 47–51.
60. Jewsbury, "The Young Author," p. 195. The sex of *Phantasmagoria*'s author was masked under the gender-neutral "M.J.J."
61. Ibid. The embedded compliment is an off-echo of Jewsbury's own response to *The Improvisatrice*, which recognizes Landon's power with a more openly admiring but still competitive spirit. Wolfson notes that "the first venue of this rant, *The Literary Souvenir*, thickens Jewsbury's satire with its intertext," as the volume included three of L.E.L.'s poems (*Borderlines*, p. 100).
62. Wolfson, *Borderlines*, pp. 105–22.
63. Jewsbury, *History*, p. 107.
64. Ibid., p. 144.
65. Ibid., p. 79.
66. Ibid., pp. 79–80.
67. Lootens, "Receiving," p. 248.
68. Wolfson, *Borderlines*, pp. 125–6.
69. Peterson, "Rewriting," pp. 115–16.
70. Ellen Peel and Nanora Sweet trace a similar itinerary of images of the woman poet in their "Corinne and the Woman as Poet in England: Hemans, Jewsbury, and Barrett Browning," in *The Novel's Seductions: Staël's*

Corinne *in Critical Inquiry*, ed. Karyna Szmurlo (Lewisburg, PA: Bucknell UP, 1999), pp. 204–20.

6 Elizabeth Barrett Browning and the Energies of Fandom

1. To Arabella Barrett, in *Letters of Elizabeth Barrett Browning to Her Sister Arabella*, ed. Scott Lewis (Waco, TX: Wedgestone Press, 2001), II, 272–7 (p. 273); To Anna Jameson, reprinted in *Aurora Leigh*, ed. Margaret Reynolds (New York: Norton, 1996), p. 342.
2. Letter of March 10 [1857] to Julia Martin, reprinted in Reynolds, pp. 345–6 (p. 346).
3. Quoted in Dorothy Mermin, *Elizabeth Barrett Browning: The Origins of a New Poetry* (Chicago: University of Chicago Press, 1989), p. 220.
4. For a good overview of the reviews and Barrett Browning's responses to them, see Mermin, *Elizabeth Barrett Browning*, pp. 220–4; see also Marjorie Stone, *Elizabeth Barrett Browning* (Basingstoke: Macmillan, 1995), pp. 139–42.
5. For a strong recent essay collection examining such ambivalence, see Lynch, *Janeites*.
6. See, for example, the thoughtful discussion of the dangers of a simple "recanonization" in Tricia Lootens, *Lost Saints: Silence, Gender and Victorian Literary Canonization* (Charlottesville: UP of Virginia, 1996), p. 13.
7. "Hero-worship" becomes a thorny issue, especially in the political contexts of Barrett Browning's later poetry. Here, though, I highlight the term mainly to indicate, as Elizabeth Barrett did herself, the Carlylean tenor of these ideas about creative genius. On Sand's importance to Barrett Browning and to English writers generally, see Thomson.
8. Elizabeth Barrett Browning, *Women of Letters: Selected Letters of Elizabeth Barrett Browning and Mary Russell Mitford*, ed. Meredith B. Raymond and Mary Rose Sullivan (Boston: Twayne, 1987), II, 460. Hereafter abbreviated *EBB—MRM* and cited parenthetically.
9. The discussion of autograph collecting in the letter is prompted by Mitford's offer to show her an autographed letter from Dryden.
10. In another letter to Mitford, Barrett Browning requests that Mitford send her some autographs to pass along to a friend, and she describes herself as having been an autograph collector once herself (*EBB–MRM*, II, 319). One advantage to being a writer in correspondence with other notables of the day, of course, is that through this correspondence one comes into the possession of valuable autographs.
11. In its modern sense as enthusiast, the term "fan" was first used in the context of American professional sports, originally baseball; the *OED*'s first citation of this usage is from 1889 ("fan," def. 2). Braudy calls the audiences that flocked around the eighteenth-century celebrity "fans," arguing that the term is appropriate to "distinguish a new quality of psychic connection between those who watch and those who, willingly or

not, perform on the public stage" (p. 360). I wish to emphasize the relative novelty, in the 1840s and 1850s, of the forms of admiration and consumption I am discussing. My thinking here has been influenced by Ian Duncan's argument for a specifically nineteenth-century "romance of the author" and by period commentary that sees practices such as autograph collecting as leisure activities symptomatic of new, newly widespread and newly routinized attitudes toward authors on the part of the middle and upper class, especially young women. See Duncan's *Modern Romance and the Transformations of the Novel: the Gothic, Scott, Dickens* (Cambridge: Cambridge UP, 1992).

12. A thoughtful and influential discussion of media fandom and its history, focusing on the United States, can be found in Gamson, *Claims to Fame*.
13. See Laura Mandell, "A Forum: Presentism vs. Archivalism in Research and the Classroom" (February 2002) Romantic Circles, accessed 30 March 2006, http://www.rc.umd.edu/praxis/contemporary/mandell/forum_intro.html.
14. Elsewhere (in a letter to Mitford of 16? January 1844) Barrett Browning argues that what Mitford had called "the inconvenience of celebrity"—the curiosity of the public about the writer's private life—is a "noble tax to pay after all," because such interest expresses the public's love for the writer—a love the writer has created through his works (she uses the masculine pronoun) (p. 375). The immediate context for this discussion is Martineau's frustration with an intrusive public curiosity Barrett Browning suggests she has courted; in the background is the experience of other female authors such as Caroline Norton. Especially in this context, however, Barrett Browning's equation of public "curiosity" and "love" is suspiciously shaky.
15. "I cd. kiss the footsteps of a great man—or woman either—& feel higher for the stooping" (*EBB–MRM*, p. 145).
16. My discussion of Barrett Browning's relationship to literary celebrity differs markedly from that of Linda Shires in her "The Author as Spectacle and Commodity: Elizabeth Barrett Browning and Thomas Hardy," *Victorian Literature and the Victorian Visual Imagination*, ed. Carol Christ and John Jordan (Berkeley: University of California Press, 1995), pp. 198–212. Comparing the careers of Barrett Browning and Hardy, Shires concludes that by "attempting to be honest and direct, Barrett Browning earned less literary fame than Hardy, who fairly early in his career grasped both the arbitrariness of fame and the value of controlling all aspects of the performance" (p. 209). Shires's discussion mostly ignores issues of genre and overlooks the ways in which "directness" might itself be a sophisticated strategic posture.
17. Significant to Barrett Browning's self-positioning as a fan are her friendships with various celebrities who themselves not only hunger for public attention but capitalize in different (and sometimes dangerous) ways on their own brushes with fame, including *her* fame—most especially Benjamin Robert Haydon, but also Mitford and Anna Jameson.

18. I borrow the language of enchantment from Emily Dickinson's writing about the experience of reading Barrett Browning; see the thoughtful essay by Ann Swyderski, "Dickinson's Enchantment: The Barrett Browning Fascicles." *Symbiosis* 7: 1 (April 2003) 76–98.
19. All references to *Aurora Leigh* are to the scholarly edition by Margaret Reynolds (Athens, OH: Ohio UP, 1992), hereafter cited parenthetically with book and line numbers.
20. Peterson ("Rewriting") notes that the details of Aurora's struggles as a writer in London—living in a garret, taking in hack work to make ends meet—reflect the real-life experience not of Barrett Browning but of Landon. The move to the garret is also a key element in Sand's mythology.
21. These lines were heavily revised in manuscript: "for the book is <with me still / And beats (i.w.)>with all my pulses in me> [Dreams in me <walks in me, talks out of me>]" (Reynolds, p. 516, n.)
22. Garrett Stewart's account of the novelistic construction of readerly intimacy in the period has been helpful in thinking about *Aurora Leigh*'s address to the reader; on contemporary deployments of novelistic forms of intimate address, see also Carol Bock, *Charlotte Brontë and the Storyteller's Audience* (Iowa City: University of Iowa Press, 1992).
23. See Marjorie Stone, "Genre Subversion and Gender Inversion: *The Princess* and *Aurora Leigh*," *Victorian Poetry* 25: 2 (1987) 101–27.
24. Compare Virginia Woolf's assertion that we are "floated off our feet" by the poem's "speed and energy, forthrightness and complete self-confidence" as "Mrs. Browning pours out in nine volumes of blank verse the story of Aurora Leigh" (Woolf, "*Aurora Leigh*," in *The Second Common Reader*, ed. Andrew McNeillie [New York: Harcourt, Brace, 1986], p. 204). Of course not every reader has this reaction, or has it in full measure, but my point is that the poem self-consciously aims for such a response and often enough finds it.
25. Barrett Browning linked the poem's forcefulness to its unflinching gaze at reality in responding to Julia Martin's complaint about the poem's representation of unpleasant social facts: the urgency of problems like prostitution compel her, she says, to use "plain words—words which look like blots, and which you yourself would put away—words which, if blurred or softened, would imperil the force and righteousness of the moral influence" (quoted in Elizabeth Helsinger, Robin Lauterbach Sheets and William Veeder, ed., *The Woman Question: Society and Literature in Britain and America, 1837–1883* [New York: Garland, 1983], III, 47).
26. Naomi Schor, *George Sand and Idealism* (New York: Columbia UP, 1993).
27. Ibid., p. 46.
28. Ibid., pp. 14–16.
29. William Bell Scott deemed *Aurora Leigh* "only a novel à la Jane Eyre, a little tainted by Sand" (quoted in Thomson, p. 54). For a late nineteenth-century discussion of Barrett Browning and idealism in the French context, see Joseph Texte, "Elisabeth Browning et l'idéalisme contemporaine," in *Etudes de Littérature Européenne* (Paris: A. Collin, 1898), pp. 239–77.

30. Most recent critics of the poem have aligned a realism/idealism divide in the poem with a division between novels and poetry (as opposed to a division between types of novelistic discourse). Amanda Anderson suggests, "Barrett Browning's innovative formal synthesis of epic poetry and realist fiction corresponds to Aurora's attempt to forge thematic links between art and philanthropy, the literary and the social, spirit and utility" (*Tainted Souls and Painted Faces: The Rhetoric of Fallenness in Victorian Culture* [Ithaca, NY: Cornell UP, 1993], p. 170). Anderson cautions, though, that "novelistic form corresponds to the thematic pole of social action or philanthropy only insofar as it attempts to convey 'realistically' the material conditions of the age and to particularize and locate social actors within a 'realistic' setting. [...] Barrett Browning actually makes claims for the socially transformative power of poetry itself, but she can properly do so only within a work of poetry that integrates novelistic technique, a work that dramatizes the spiritualizing effect of poetry on character and the failure of other forms of engagement with the social realm" (p. 171).
31. Schor, *George Sand and Idealism*, p. 35.
32. Ibid.
33. Ibid., p. 54.
34. Woolf, "*Aurora Leigh*," p. 212.
35. Cora Kaplan, Introduction to *Elizabeth Barrett Browning, Aurora Leigh and Other Poems* (London: Women's Press, 1978), p. 25; Deirdre David, *Intellectual Women and Victorian Patriarchy: Harriet Martineau, Elizabeth Barrett Browning, George Eliot* (London: Macmillan, 1987), p. 115.
36. Quoted in Helsinger, Sheets and Veeder, *The Woman Question*, III, 39.
37. Marian's total absorption in herself and her child stands in an intriguing mirror-relation to Keatsian artistic self-absorption; by idealizing Marian as mother, Aurora frees herself to work out her relation to this vocational imperative outside the maternal imaginary.
38. Marc Redfield, *Phantom Formations: Aesthetic Ideology and the Bildungsroman* (Ithaca, NY: Cornell UP, 1996).
39. The quotation is from Anderson, p. 183.
40. I have learned a great deal from Herbert F. Tucker's provocative discussion of the poem's modes of resisting the impetus to closure organized by the marriage plot; see his "*Aurora Leigh*: Epic Solutions to Novel Ends" in *Famous Last Words: Changes in Gender and Narrative Closure*, ed. Alison Booth (Charlottesville: UP of Virginia, 1993), pp. 62–85. Where Tucker allies the closure of the marriage plot with novelistic realism, however, I read the way the poem ultimately scripts that closure in terms of a strong turn-away from realism to idealism, with serious consequences for how we view Aurora's story from the perspective of its (non-)ending.
41. Tucker, "Epic Solutions," p. 80.
42. Kate Field, "Elizabeth Barrett Browning," *Atlantic Monthly* 8 (September 1861) 368–76 (p. 368); Unsigned review by William Stigand, "The Works of Elizabeth Barrett Browning" *Edinburgh Review* 114 (1861) 513–34 (p. 530). Such links between poetic intensity and the bodily experience

of both poet and reader are given wider cultural play by spasmodic poetics generally. For a recent discussion of *Aurora Leigh* in this context that makes some of these same points about the poem's effects from a different angle, see Tucker's "Glandular Omnism and Beyond: The Victorian Spasmodic Epic," *Victorian Poetry* 42: 4 (2004) 429–50.

43. Tucker, "Epic Solutions," p. 80.
44. Beginning with the simultaneously performative and professional gesture of substituting "I write" (1.29) for the conventional epic "I sing," Aurora consistently puts the action of her writing on display. The poem's first nine lines have five instances of the verb *to write*—"writing" (1.1), "written" (1.2), "write" (1.3), "write" (1.4) and "writing" (1.9).
45. Quoted in Lootens, *Lost Saints*, p. 14.
46. Lootens (*Lost Saints*) details the history of Barrett Browning's "unstable cultural presence," with special attention to the way the *Sonnets from the Portuguese* dominated the image of Barrett Browning in the twentieth century. Lootens identifies four primary stages in Barrett Browning's posthumous reception: "After E.B.B.'s death, she emerges first as a Promethean intellectual; then as a still-powerful 'wife, mother, and poet'; then as a great lover whose glory may no longer depend upon her poetry; and finally as an Andromeda (or Peau d'Ane) in Wimpole Street, whose physical and mental frailty adds poignancy to her role as a heroine of nostalgically conceived romance" (p. 128).

Index

Printed in Great Britain
by Amazon

59463035R00126

DEA
SO
PAT

R

AGAIN!
KIM

THE DEVIL IN THE DEAL

Praise for *Work Diva: How to climb the corporate ladder without selling your soul* and *Deal Diva: How to negotiate your way to success without selling your soul*

'[*Work Diva*] should be in the hands of every living, breathing woman' **– Jenna Clifford**

'[*Work Diva*] isn't your run-of-the-mill business book and, even better, it's written by a South African woman in business, making it all the more relevant to local readers' **- all4women.co.za**

Work Diva: listed by Kalahari.net as 'one of the business books you should own'

'*Work Diva* … shows you the way to success with wit and style, and offers some very good practical advice along the way. A must-read if you want to get ahead and stay sane' **– Kate Turkington, Jozi.co.za**

'A must-read for all female SALESGURU fans, *Deal Diva* is an exciting and interesting look at the way in which women negotiate and do business' **– SALESGURU**

THE DEVIL IN THE DEAL

50 SECRETS TO SUCCESSFUL DEALMAKING

KIM MEREDITH

Published by Zebra Press
an imprint of Penguin Random House (Pty) Ltd
Company Reg. No. 1953/000441/07
The Estuaries No. 4, Oxbow Crescent, Century Avenue,
Century City, Cape Town, 7441
www.penguinrandomhouse.co.za

Penguin Random House South Africa

First published 2012
Reprinted in 2012

3 5 7 9 10 8 6 4 2

PUBLISHER: Marlene Fryer
MANAGING EDITOR: Ronel Richter-Herbert
EDITOR: Angela Voges
PROOFREADER: Bronwen Leak
COVER AND TEXT DESIGNER: Sean Robertson
TYPESETTER: Monique van den Berg

Set in 11 pt on 14.25 pt Adobe Caslon

Printed by **novus print**, a division of Novus Holdings

MIX
Paper from responsible sources
FSC® C022948

Penguin Random House is committed to a sustainable future for our business, our readers and our planet. This book is made from Forest Stewardship Council ® certified paper.

ISBN 978 1 77022 179 6 (print)
ISBN 978 177022 270 0 (ePub)
ISBN 978 1 77022 271 7 (PDF)

For my gorgeous girlfriends – Anna, Brenda, Cat, Jules, Karen, Nix.
You keep me sane

CONTENTS

ABOUT THE AUTHOR

Kim Meredith is an internationally acclaimed lecturer, sales strategist, negotiator and dealmaker. Kim is chief executive officer of the globally represented The Dealmaker Programmes Company based in Mauritius. She currently lectures and consults in the USA, Latin America, Europe and Africa. She has been working with and consulting for international companies for nearly 20 years.

Having held executive positions in business since the late 1980s, Kim was one of only 179 women on the boards of the top 300 Johannesburg Stock Exchange–listed companies in 2000. She has held directorships in some form or another since she was 24, thanks to many prescient mentors.

Kim's most recent corporate position was with a listed information technology group, where she spent four years on the main board as Executive Director of Strategy. During this time, she was responsible for global strategy, including actively driving negotiations for key mergers, acquisitions and disposals.

Although Kim holds a BA degree in Clinical Psychology and English, she insists she would be a rubbish psychologist. She is passionate about business but not terribly handy with tissues. Kim's drive in business saw her named runner-up in her local chamber of commerce Businesswoman of the Year awards in 2009, a finalist in the 2010 South African Chamber of Commerce Businesswoman of the Year awards, and winner of the 1st for Women Business Icon and Entrepreneur Feather awards for 2011.

Kim's two other published books, *Work Diva: How to climb the corporate ladder without selling your soul* and *Deal Diva: How to negotiate your way to success without selling your soul*, aimed at women, came about as a result of her tendency to flagrantly tell people what to do with their lives.

ACKNOWLEDGEMENTS

Running two businesses, writing a book a year, having a family life and a social life, and trying to be a good wife, daughter, friend, boss and business-person is an endless juggle – and I seem to drop a lot of balls along the way. If it wasn't for the wonderful people around me, I would have lost my marbles a long time ago. I'm incredibly grateful to have so many people to thank.

My husband, Simon Carpenter. You are a saint, my angel. I am one very lucky woman.

My mom and dad, John and Colleen Meredith. Thank you for forgiving me for being a bad daughter – an especially bad one when I am writing.

My girlfriends, who give me unconditional love, support and ideas. This book is dedicated to you – especially Julie Purkis, Cathrine Moncur, Karen Evans, Nicola Coetzer, Brenda Bensted-Smith, and Anna Breytenbach. Thank you also to Jules and Cat for the flowers and other edibles you sent every week during my self-imposed exile.

My manfriends: Chris v. d. W., George O. and Riaan v. Z. I'm connected to you forever, you unlucky sods.

My team at work and at home. Thank you for shouldering the weight while I was in hiding, notably Suri Moonsamy, Charmaine Nortman and Tembani Matrina Ngcobo.

And where would I be without my wonderful and wily mentors? A special thank you to Wendy Luhabe for having been such an inspiration to me.

Ronel Richter-Herbert and Marlene Fryer at Zebra Press, an imprint of

Random House Struik. Thank you for your belief in me and your delicious sense of the ridiculous. You are the Thelma and Louise of my life.

Angela Voges – the thought of a new editor filled me with horror. Thank you for respecting the way in which I wanted to use the words.

My family, particularly the irrepressibly noisy ones who came to stay from Zambia while I was writing. Judes, Alistair, Dylan – I was an awful host. Thank you for not being fusspot-moanalot-sickup.

My dogs, Daisy and Rufus, for ensuring that I got up from my writing desk to play with them, and escape their toxic fumes, every few hours.

Champagne and chocolate.

Endless novels about witches and psychics to help me sleep, above all those by Juliet Blackwell.

And Simon. Again.

INTRODUCTION

Learning business lessons shouldn't be that difficult – the essentials ought to be passed on from parents to children, in the classroom, at university, and especially through business school. The harsh reality is that in countless families, talking about money and business – especially at the dinner table – is infra dig. Schooling systems don't teach 'real business' as a subject; universities (if one is privileged enough to attend) are no better. And then we get the business schools.

In his iconic book of 1984, *What They Don't Teach You at Harvard Business School*, Mark McCormack (American sports agent and writer, 1930–) was already taking issue with business schools. Not much, unfortunately, has changed. The vast majority of business schools (Harvard may be an exception) seem mired in the mindset of business as it was done decades ago.

Take negotiation, for example. Early research into negotiation was conducted in the first half of the twentieth century, and generally espoused win–lose outcomes – for one party to achieve success, the other party had to be beaten. In the 1970s, negotiating theory started to change. Based largely on the industrial relations events of the time, it was suggested that win–lose was fine for short-term goals, but that win–win was needed to entrench longer-term relationships. In today's business world, negotiation is all about value. In exchanging value for value, both sides automatically achieve win–win. The problem with win–win is that it's fairly intangible – not good enough in business nowadays – which is why value for value is the current dealmaking nirvana.

Now consider selling. The ever sardonic and extremely rude website www.urbandictionary.com (be warned, it is not for the politically correct) describes 'sales' as 'a job or category of jobs where you make lots of money for doing absolutely nothing'. How did the noble art of salesmanship get to be so maligned? Why is selling not recognised as being one of the most – if not *the* most – vital skills for achieving business (and personal) goals?

Firstly, how many business schools teach selling? Not so many. Is this because the subject of sales is beneath them? Or perhaps they were chased off by the writings of Yale's Professor Arthur Allen Leff, who believed that there is a very fine line between swindling and selling?

Secondly, why is selling separated from negotiation in business? Experience has taught me, and all the successful businesspeople I know, that selling and negotiation should not be divorced; that they are seamless, integrated and mutually dependent components of deals.

This brings us to the subject of dealmaking. Dealmaking is not brokering house sales, or trading stocks on the market, or dealing cards in a casino. Dealmaking is not synonymous with negotiation. Dealmaking is the lifeblood of business. The heart. That which makes business tick. Why do businesspeople have to learn about dealmaking by picking up scars on their backs? Why isn't dealmaking the number-one subject in business schools? Maybe because business schools (or is it the academics?) can't let go of their firmly held ideas about negotiation and selling. Time to change? People in business seem to learn about dealmaking more from the rough-and-tumble of experience, from generous mentors, from bespoke development programmes, and even from meditating, than from institutions of higher learning.

The Devil in the Deal: 50 secrets to successful dealmaking gives you exactly what it says – the 50 secrets you should have been taught about business from way back, from when you were a kid selling lemonade on the street corner (or mud pies, in my case), and the 50 little devils that break deals.

Business can be rough and tough and awfully John Wayne. It is closer to the world of *Glengarry Glen Ross* than to the safe environment of the MBA. There are devils and disasters around every corner. *The Devil in the Deal* is essential reading about real deals for the real world.

PART 1

THE BARE BASICS

The naked truth is always better than the best dressed lie.

Ann Landers (American advice columnist, 1918–2002)

SECRET #1
DEALMAKERS USE SPECIFIC SKILLS TO GET WHAT THEY WANT

Here is a basic, undressed truth. I'm a rubbish cook. I may be a skilled dealmaker, but when it comes to cooking, my bull terriers could probably do a better job than me. My long-suffering husband, Simon, accepted early on that he would need to become the cook in our household or eat two-minute noodles for the rest of his life. Simon has become an expert and passionate cook. He has been to cooking schools all over the world and has now got to the point where, in my opinion, he knows more about cooking than the top-class instructors.

For a recent birthday, Simon was given a book by his friend and cooking buddy, Dave Bensted-Smith, called *The Basics* (published by Homarus Cookbooks). Dave was nervous to give the book as he thought it may offend Simon. The book, after all, really is the basics of cooking. But Simon, being the self-effacing man he is, was delighted with the gift. It gave him the opportunity to confirm that he had the essentials right. He continually refers to this book.

Dealmaking in the business world is fraught with obstacles and complications that bedevil the process – inability to close the deal, dodgy business ethics, complex legal requirements and accounting practices, self-serving agendas, ego … Of all the failed deals I have seen, ego has been the biggest stumbling block. We are not superheroes who can turn off the 'ego villain' with a thought, but if a clear strategy and process is followed – if we stick to the basics and remove emotion and greed – most deals are within our reach.

When I first became a strategic 'dealmaker' – buying and selling companies, and handling corporate-finance-type transactions – I thought I knew my oats about negotiation and sales. And I did, but I had no idea what it took to be a world-class dealmaker. I reckoned that being a really good negotiator was enough (much like the current business-school thinking), but did I get my backside kicked! I couldn't understand why I was failing at something I expected to be easy for me, so I started writing down all the lessons I was learning about dealmaking.

The book you are now reading is the dealmaking equivalent of Simon's *The Basics* cookbook. This is, in essence, a book that strips naked all the nonsense around the subject of dealmaking, and looks at what it takes to dodge those pesky devils and be an expert dealmaker.

To make the book read more easily, it has been divided into 50 fundamentals, or secrets, of dealmaking that every business-minded person needs to know. There will be material you know (like how to stir-fry), material that will challenge your current thinking (don't just use the carcass for a chicken stock, use the whole chicken), and new material (did you know that a 'liaison' is not just the French word for a connection – that it involves *eggs*?).

So what, really, is a dealmaker?

Use specific skills to get what you want

Do you know what the devil did in the Charlie Daniels song 'The Devil Went Down to Georgia'? When one looks at the definitions of 'dealmaker' in the dictionaries, Charlie Daniels offers remarkable insight by comparison. He, at least, sang about doing a deal – the devil trades a fiddle of gold for a soul.

The website www.thefreedictionary.com defines a 'dealmaker' as 'one that [*sic*] makes deals, as in business, finance or politics'. *Encarta Concise English Dictionary* is not much better, with 'somebody who arranges deals, especially in business or politics'. These formal definitions are about as much use to a businessperson as a bicycle is to a fish. And www.thesaurus.com has nothing to offer (as in zero results) for 'dealmaker' or 'deal-maker' or 'deal maker'.

While writing down the lessons I was learning about dealmaking (i.e. licking my wounds), I spent a lot of time researching the collective qualities that characterise the world's leading dealmakers. Based on my findings, I boldly posited a new definition for 'dealmaker'. This definition forms the cornerstone of The Dealmaker programmes developed for my company: 'A person skilled in using instinct, processes and expertise in primarily negotiation, selling and communication, and able to leverage or adjust the balance of power to bring closure to transactions that usually benefit all parties' (© The Dealmaker Programmes Company).

There are a few words I would not want to see removed from the definition, as they are critical to mastering dealmaking: instinct; processes; expertise; negotiation; selling; communication; power; closure; benefit all. We will delve into each of these concepts in detail, but for the moment, let's start with *instinct.*

Harvard Business School has spent time and energy disputing the role of instinct (see 'When Not to Trust Your Gut' by Max H. Bazerman and Deepak Malhotra), while Donald Trump (American business entrepreneur, 1946–), on the other hand, has this to say: 'Dealmaking is not about being brilliant – it does take a certain intelligence – but mostly it's about instinct.' Having watched and worked with some exceptional dealmakers, I have seen that these business gurus rely as much on their instinct and intuition as they do on their ability to persuade or negotiate or communicate.

There is a difference between instinct and intuition. 'Instinct' is described by www.thefreedictionary.com as 'an inborn pattern of behaviour or innate capability', whereas 'intuition' is 'knowing or sensing without the use of rational processes'.

Intuition and instinct will be covered in the secrets on communication, but back to instinct in the context of the dealmaker definition. There is an opinion to which I hold firm – everyone is *born* with basic dealmaking skills. The evidence to support this theory is overwhelming, as you will see in Secret #7. Although the huge majority of us lose our dealmaking skills early in our lives, instinct is an innate ability, so it is not that difficult to recapture.

A quick look at *processes* and *expertise*. These two issues are interwoven throughout the book. They apply to so many principles that it would be impossible to separate them from the central tenets of dealmaking.

The other key words – negotiation, selling, communication, power, closure, and benefit all – are discussed individually, as they are elements of such importance that no first-rate dealmaker would want to be without them.

SECRET #1 Dealmakers use specific skills to get what they want
Stripping down the definition of a successful dealmaker into a basic single sentence, this is how it reads: A dealmaker is someone who is able to get what they want by using a finely tuned set of skills.

DEVIL #1
Assuming that a dealmaker is a salesperson or a negotiator will not only inhibit your ability to close world-class deals, it will leave you unprepared and vulnerable when you do meet a proficient dealmaker.

SECRET #2
SELLING IS NOT A SWEAR WORD

In the Introduction to this book, I asked the questions: 'How did the noble art of salesmanship get to be so maligned?' and 'Why is selling not recognised as being one of the most essential skills for being a success in business?' I suggested that this is because sales is not generally taught as an MBA subject, and that selling is seen by many in business as being independent of dealmaking. There is far more to sales than meets the eye.

The definition of a dealmaker in Secret #1 is 'a person skilled in primarily negotiation, selling and communication'. *Encarta Concise English Dictionary* describes 'selling' as 'the activity or process of persuading people to buy a product or service'. Their definition of 'persuade' is 'to successfully urge someone to perform a particular action, especially by reasoning, pleading or coaxing' – which you may recognise as the punchline of a rather rude joke! Ironically, these two definitions aren't as bad as they may seem – at least they don't inextricably tie selling to the sales profession.

Even so, the association with foreplay is too close for comfort, so this description was developed for The Dealmaker programmes: 'Activity or process of persuading another party to accept a specific deal, overcoming differences in objectives and/or viewpoints' (© The Dealmaker Programmes Company).

As you can see, this is not a job description for a salesperson. To be a great dealmaker, to get what you want in business – or in life in general – you *must* be able to sell – to persuade or convince. It is an absolutely vital skill.

If you are thinking to yourself that you don't know how to sell, that you've never had sales training, stop. If you could not sell, you would not have been able to get what you want in terms of jobs, dates, friends, memberships and deals. To be offered employment or a contract or marriage or any deal, you must have convinced someone, somewhere, to say yes. The truth is that we sell ourselves every single day. We convince other people to take whatever it is we are offering. Don't believe me? Argue with Charles M. Schwab (American steel magnate and one of the men who 'broke the bank in Monte Carlo', 1862–1939), who said: 'We are all salesmen every day of our lives. We are selling our ideas, our plans, our enthusiasms to those with whom we come in contact.'

Does this make you suspect that selling is a bit like being a slag? Well, it is. Whether someone is promoting their unique expertise or their company's products or their beautiful mind (or body), they are, in fact, selling. And yes, this is solicitation. Think about it from an employment perspective. If you are looking for a job, do you not try to present your skills, capabilities and knowledge in the most attractive manner possible?

Selling, or persuading, or convincing, is actually easy and fun. Remember what www.urbandictionary.com had to say about sales? When you get it right, it does feel as if you are making 'lots of money for doing absolutely nothing'. Getting what you want – closing deals fruitfully – should not be a continual uphill battle. As Robert 'Bob' Basso (American actor, 1938–) said, 'If it's not fun, you're not doing it right.'

Selling allows you to persuade someone to give you what you want. If you're still not convinced that everyone can sell, think about this – selling is a skill with which we are born, and a process that anyone can learn. There is no excuse for not arming yourself with one of the best dealmaking tools imaginable.

If it's so simple, then why doesn't selling always work? The answer lies in the definition – the part that says 'accept a specific deal, overcoming differences in objectives and/or viewpoints'. The problem is that when a person's viewpoint is driven by strong emotion or personal motives, it is very difficult to convince them to do what you want them to do, regardless of your capability to sell. Emotion, ego and greed in any situation can make people behave irrationally – their inner devil is provoked.

Let's take a complex, real-life situation to illustrate the point: the Mexican drug war. Over 15 000 people lost their lives in 2010 alone. Just for background, here is an adaptation of what www.wikipedia.com has to say about the conflict:

> The Mexican Drug War is an ongoing armed conflict taking place among rival drug cartels who fight each other for regional control, and the Mexican government forces who seek to combat drug trafficking. Although Mexican drug cartels, or drug trafficking organizations, have existed for a few decades, they have become more powerful since the demise of Colombia's cartels in the 1990s. Mexican drug cartels now dominate the wholesale illicit drug market in the United States. Arrests of key cartel leaders, particularly in the Tijuana and Gulf cartels, have led to increasing drug violence as cartels fight for control of the trafficking routes into the United States. The U.S. Department of Justice estimates that the wholesale earnings from illicit drug sales range from $13.6 billion to $48.4 billion annually.

What chance, in your opinion, has the Tijuana drug cartel (also known as the Arellano-Félix Organization) got of convincing the Mexican government to release the 21 hit men the government captured in April 2009? What if the Tijuana cartel promises that the hit men won't 'hit' anyone again? Silly, right? Now throw into the mix the allegations made on US National Public Radio (NPR) in May 2009 that the Mexican federal police and military were working in collusion with the Sinaloa cartel, the Tijuana cartel's arch-rivals.

Persuasion is an incredibly powerful and cheap way to get what you want, but it will not work in every situation. If emotion and/or greed are in the mix, you're going to have to try an alternative form of dealmaking to get what you want.

SECRET #2 Selling is not a swear word
Selling often allows you to get what you want using just the power of persuasion, making it an essential dealmaking process and tool.

DEVIL #2
Believing that you have limited sales capabilities, or that selling is for lesser mortals, completely undermines your potential to be a brilliant dealmaker.

SECRET #3

NEGOTIATION IS THE WORLD'S OLDEST PROFESSION

Alongside selling, another competency vital to the expert dealmaker is negotiation. *Encarta Concise English Dictionary* describes 'negotiation' as 'the resolving of disagreements; the reaching of agreement through discussion and compromise'. Compromise? Seriously? Here is what the same dictionary says 'compromise' means: 'agreement; settlement of a dispute in which two or more sides agree to accept less than they originally wanted'. *No* self-respecting dealmaker goes into a deal intending to accept less than they wanted. Maybe I'm being a bit harsh – only incompetent people go into negotiations with this objective.

On account of the lame definitions offered by the establishment, an alternative definition of negotiation was developed for The Dealmaker programmes: 'Activity or process of reaching a deal acceptable to all parties, accommodating differences in objectives and/or viewpoints, through trading' (© The Dealmaker Programmes Company).

This may, at first glance, seem pretty similar to the definition of selling, but there are important distinctions. Firstly, while selling centres around using *persuasion* to get what you want, negotiation is all about *trading* – quid pro quo, or something for something. Secondly, selling requires the *overcoming* of differences in opinion, whereas negotiation is about *accommodating* differences.

If you initially thought that selling sounded a bit dodgy, negotiation is not much better. Let's use the employment example for a minute. You have sold your skills, expertise and knowledge to a prospective employer and they now want to hire you. Are you going to work for nothing? Of course not. You expect a decent salary and benefits in exchange for your contribution to the company.

You would presumably negotiate the value of your salary package, your working hours, your title, office size, company car, and an almost endless list of other variables. You make a proposal, they counter-offer, you counter their counter, they offer again – this is how negotiation works. You can call it horse-trading if you like, but it is more like a dance; a tango. And how, exactly, does prostitution differ from you negotiating your salary package and contract conditions? Are services not exchanged for cash (or similar) in both transactions? Fair trade!

Negotiation is about giving to get. You get what you want by giving the other party what they want – in other words, you trade. It is easier, believe it or not, to negotiate with someone when you want different outcomes from a deal than if you pursue the same objective. When both parties want, for instance, the best price, you as the seller will want the highest price, while the buying party will chase the lowest price. Deadlock is far more likely to occur than when, say, you want high volumes and they want a low price.

The downside of negotiating is that you have to make concessions, whereas in selling you simply have to convince the other party to give you what you want. With *compromise*, you just give, and give, and give – once you start the giving, the other side will inevitably get greedy.

There is one word in negotiation that crops up all the time – 'if'. *If* you give me more leave, I will accept a lower salary; *if* you want a cheaper price, I need a longer contract; *if* you release the hostages, we will withdraw our snipers from the roof. Horse-trading it may be, but it is this conditional giving to get that characterises negotiation.

A point to note: When I talk about 'the other party' (or team or side or people or guys), I mean a person or group that is not you and/or your team. There are often more than two sides involved in a deal, but for the sake of simplicity, I will refer to transactions as if there is only you (and your team) and another person (or group) involved.

How, practically, would this apply to our Mexican drug-war case?

To get the Mexican government to agree to release the 21 Tijuana hit men, the Tijuana cartel is going to have to make some serious concessions to the Mexican government – concessions attractive to the government, not to the cartel. If the rumours are true, and the government is colluding with the Sinaloa cartel, the Tijuana cartel needs to figure out why. What is the Sinaloa cartel giving the government that they can better? Guns? Information? Money?

In all likelihood, the Mexican government would be supporting the Sinaloa cartel because they are the lesser of two evils, and they will use the Sinaloa cartel to get rid of the Tijuana gang – similar to the way in which the Reagan administration supported the Afghan *mujahideen* to beat off the Soviet occupation of Afghanistan in the 1980s.

What if, in exchange for the release of their hit men, the Tijuana cartel offered to hand over all the weapons they captured from the Sinaloa cartel? Or that they would assist the Mexican authorities in finding and destroying the Sinaloa drug factories? Or what if they went to the US and offered the US government intelligence on the other six cartels involved in the war, in exchange for the US negotiating the release of their men with the Mexican government?

Regardless of the route pursued, the Tijuana cartel would have to give the Mexican authorities something the government values highly to get their hit men released. Negotiation can be expensive. Selling is invariably a cheaper option. Are there other alternatives? Yes – in the next secret.

SECRET #3 Negotiation is the world's oldest profession
Negotiating is about giving to get – you trade something of value to the other party in exchange for getting what you want and value.

DEVIL #3
Prostitution or not, every competent dealmaker is able to negotiate and trade with ease, and without compromising their position.

SECRET #4
THERE IS POWER IN HAVING ALTERNATIVES

Dealmaking is driven largely by persuasion, negotiation and communication. We'll get to communication a little later, but for the moment, we are concentrating on the innate skills and learnt processes that enable a dealmaker to close their deals.

In Secret #3, I mentioned that there are alternatives to selling and negotiating that one can use to drive the deal. You may have heard of BATNA, or 'Best Alternative to a Negotiated Agreement'. This term was coined by Harvard negotiation researchers Roger Fisher and William Ury in their negotiation books (the first being *Getting to Yes: Negotiating Agreement Without Giving In*). Fisher and Ury had, perhaps unwittingly, used the early game-theory studies of Dr John Forbes Nash (American professor and Nobel Laureate, 1928–) as the basis for their BATNA idea. Just for interest's sake, the movie *A Beautiful Mind* was based on the life and times of Dr Nash.

When Fisher and Ury wrote *Getting to Yes* (it was published in 1981), negotiation was moving out of the win–lose era into that of win–win. This meant that, at the time, negotiations often failed. The high preponderance of failed deals would have necessitated the focus on alternatives.

While BATNA was originally intended to describe the options available if (or when) negotiations failed, it has become very popular with negotiators, all of whom add their own spin to the subject. These days, BATNA is more commonly used for leverage or as a means of adjusting power. This interpretation sits comfortably with me, as it suggests negotiation is moving away from the original concept of positional bargaining towards the realm of dealmaking. Assuming BATNA offers alternatives that one can use as options to get a deal, what are these alternatives and how are they used to gain leverage?

By now you have realised that to get what you want, you will most often resort to the options of selling (persuading) or negotiating (trading). Selling can be time-consuming, while trading can be expensive – particularly if you are dealing with high-value or high-cost items – so you need to consider all the options before you rush in like the proverbial fool. Because of the potentially high cost, negotiation is seldom a dealmaker's first choice.

To help avoid the temptation to read ahead to see what the options are, I have put together a list (it is not exhaustive) for quick reference.

1. Negotiate (trade)
2. Bribe or blackmail (not recommended!)
3. Sell (persuade)
4. Argue (wear down)
5. Surrender (roll over)
6. Conquer (dictate)
7. Postpone
8. Compromise or haggle or settle for less
9. Problem-solve
10. Conflict-resolve
11. Gamble (take a bet, flip a coin)
12. Walk away (wash your hands)
13. Deadlock

14. External options (e.g. arbitration, mediation, legal action)
15. Neutral options (e.g. auction, tender)
16. And many more …

The easiest way to exemplify how to choose between the different alternatives is to use an example. We will move away from the Mexican drug war, in case you are starting to get the impression that dealmaking only applies to matters of global importance or disreputable agreements. Let's work with an example that is a little closer to home.

Imagine a close-knit family with one child, a son, who is clever, handsome, popular (like all sons are to their mothers) and about to leave school. He has to choose a career and desperately wants to study Zoology so that he can become a game ranger. He has, without his parents' permission, applied to and been accepted by the University of Johannesburg for a B.Sc. in Zoology.

The problem is that his parents want him to become a lawyer, like his father and his grandfather. Their plan is for him eventually to take over the family's successful law practice. His parents have said to him that they are only prepared to pay for his studies if he chooses law. They know that his grades are not good enough for him to get a bursary or scholarship, and that the banks will want them to sign surety on a student loan. They believe they are helping their son to make a responsible decision.

Now imagine the situation from the son's perspective. What are his options?

1. Negotiate

Firstly, let's look at how the son could negotiate with his parents. Negotiation is about trading – about giving to get – so what could he offer his parents to get them to pay for his degree or stand surety on a loan? He may offer to support them financially once they have retired, or propose to repay double or even triple the amount of the university fees once he starts working, or he could promise to send them on a cruise around the world after he has worked for three years. The list is endless, but the son would need to offer his parents whatever presses their Hot Buttons.

What is the cost of this to the son? He could be mortgaging his financial future. It is because of the costs and risks associated with negotiation that Fisher and Ury originally posited BATNA.

2. Bribe or blackmail

You might be thinking by now that negotiation sounds pretty similar to bribery – and you would be on the money. There is one key difference between negotiation and bribery: the latter is generally seen in a negative light. According to the definitions of bribery, it is not necessarily illegal. The site www.thefreedictionary.com defines 'bribery' as '1. something, such as money or a favour, offered or given to a person in a position of trust to influence that person's views or conduct; or 2. something serving to influence or persuade'. It's all about ethics – one man's bribery is another man's negotiation.

You would never stoop to bribery, right? Well, let me ask you this: What do you offer your kids as a reward for eating their vegetables? Or someone at work to cover for you? Or your partner to take you out for dinner? Or your teenage son to clean his room? 'But that's entirely different,' you may argue. Actually, it's not.

At what point does negotiation become bribery? You need to draw your own line in the sand based on your value system, but I use the following delineation – if offering somebody something, in exchange for getting what I want, is going to land me in trouble with the law, my family or friends, or my customers or colleagues, it is the wrong side of negotiation.

Blackmail is a form of negotiation that contains a threat or disincentive. If someone doesn't do *x* for you, then *y* will happen to them. It is similar to bribery, but the upside is that the other person gets to avoid an unpleasant outcome, rather than receive a concession. For example, if your teenager does not keep his room tidy, he won't get his allowance or be permitted to use the car that week. Don't feel too bad about doing this with an errant teenager: one of the definitions of 'blackmail' suggested by the online dictionary is a 'tribute formerly paid to freebooters along the Scottish border for protection from pillage'.

A proposal containing a disincentive in business, however, is never first prize, as it can seriously harm the relationship. As with the ethical versus moral line regarding the point at which blackmail or bribery becomes illegal, if in doubt, steer clear.

Back to our example to summarise – bribery would be where the father offers his son a Ferrari (or Land Cruiser or whatever the boy desperately wants) if he graduates from law school, while blackmail would be that the son is disinherited if he does not study law. Very fine lines, are they not?

3. Sell or persuade

You know that if you can persuade someone to let you have what you want, you will usually not have to make any sacrifices or give any concessions. First prize would thus be for the son to convince his parents of the merits of becoming a game ranger. His arguments would range from the importance of following a passion, to the expanding tourism industry, to the need for conservation to give future generations an environmental legacy, and so on. Will the parents buy his justifications? They might, so this option is definitely worth a try.

The son could also try to manipulate his parents by telling them that he loves them deeply and respects that they are only trying to do what is best for him, but if they really loved him, they would support his choice. Or he might suggest that if they stop him from pursuing his dreams, he will always feel betrayed or resentful.

Before you get self-righteous and sanctimonious about manipulation because *you* would *never* use emotional persuasion yourself, consider whether the parents are manipulating their son or not. Everyone injects a little emotion into getting what they want, wittingly or not.

Persuasion costs time, so when you do have time constraints, persuasion is not the best option to use to get the deal. Also, if a situation is becoming charged with emotion, it is better to try another option. Persuasion can turn into arguing in one or two dumb moves.

4. Argue

So what is the difference between arguing and persuading? It depends on how you see arguing. Is arguing verbal sparring, or the presenting of a case?

Let's start with sparring. We are all inclined to squabble or bicker, even those of us who are pretty passive. Arguing can take the form of a bit of negotiation, some persuasion, a hint of manipulation, the issuing of threats and insults, using vicious and cold logic (a left-brain favourite), or shouting, stomping and the throwing of crockery. By arguing in this way, we are hoping to wear down the other side. The problem with arguing is that it can damage a relationship – much is said in the heat of an argument that is later cause for regret.

Arguing, in the legal or mathematical sense, is positive in that it gives us (and the other party) the opportunity to present our case, any supporting evidence or suppositions, and so on. The downside to *any* form of arguing is that it can quickly slip into the personal and emotional, ending in tears.

Back to the wannabe game ranger. He could argue with his parents and try to wear them down, but given their strong view on him studying law, it will probably be a waste of time. Argument is a useful tool if you have the patience and inclination, but the potential fallout makes it a risky option.

5. Surrender

Another alternative, of course, would be for the son simply to accept his parents' decision – roll over and play lawyer. But this, too, has a price. What will the cost of this be to his future happiness? Will he ever get his own way with his parents again? Will they respect him for giving in and showing no perseverance? Is this a better option for the son than negotiating with his parents?

While not immediately measurable, the consequences of surrender can be enormous. Apart from not getting what you want in a deal, precedent is difficult to reverse. When you start asserting yourself, you will get labelled a 'hard-ass' or a 'bitch' or 'difficult' – even if you are standing up for yourself for the first time! Surrender is only an option when the outcome or consequences of the deal are of minor importance to you, or when you believe you have limited choice or power.

Mohandas 'Mahatma' Gandhi (Indian political and spiritual leader, 1869–1948) warned that '[a]ny compromise on mere fundamentals is a surrender. For it is all give and no take.'

6. Conquer

The opposite option to surrendering would be for the son to defy his parents and do exactly as he pleases. He may be able to approach another family member, perhaps an uncle or aunt with whom he has a good relationship, to fund his fees or sign surety. Or he could start working in whatever job he can find to pay for a distance-learning degree. Taking the conquer route, like the surrender option, has huge costs. What will the price of this be to the son's relationship with his parents? Will they tell him to leave the house immediately? Will they make his life a misery?

Dealmakers typically only pursue this option if they have no choice, or if they don't care about the outcome, or if they think they hold all the power and believe they will hold it for a long time to come. What if the tide turns against them? What was the end result for Libyan dictator Muammar Gaddafi?

7. Postpone

Another alternative available to the son in this example would be for him to delay the decision to study, or even the timing of when he approaches his parents. He could wait to catch them in a more receptive frame of mind. He could postpone studying and redo his final year of high school so that he can get better grades and qualify for a bursary. He can wait until his parents have passed on and use his inheritance to pay for his studies. Cynical? Maybe, but it is still an option.

Postponing is a preferred tactic of mine. Hoping for the balance of power to shift in my favour, pausing to give myself more time to think, or adjourning to create or reduce tension seldom fails to pay dividends. Postponement, of course, does not work if there is a possibility of the power moving away from you, or when you have strict deadlines to meet. As a BATNA alternative, however, it is one a dealmaker should always consider.

8. Compromise

You already know what Gandhi thinks of compromise. My view is the same – only losers are satisfied with getting less than they want. No self-respecting dealmaker goes into a deal intending to accept less than they deserve. Sure, dealmakers may be flexible in the way their deal is structured, but just agreeing to less is nothing more than surrendering at worst, haggling at best. This is not value for value, and any fool can come away with a bad deal.

If you are not PC, prissy or faint of heart, have a look at what www.urbandictionary.com says about haggling – the sublime definition for me is 'a term used when haggling with a pimp to get a better price on his hoes'. Apparently, and my father insists this is a true story, my maternal grandfather was shot dead in a Glaswegian pub arguing about the price of a prostitute. I say no more.

Compromise is common with people (women in particular) who prefer to avoid conflict, but running away from conflict is usually not the right move – it is akin to surrender.

In terms of our study example, why would the son agree to complete a law degree but vow never to practise law? What is the point? Would this give him or his parents what they want? Of course not – compromise is the death of mutually beneficial deals.

9. Problem-solve

Most of us are quite good at problem-solving, as it helps to avoid or contain conflict. We have become so adept at problem-solving, however, that we tend to use it, with a helping of compromise, to close deals. All you can expect from this particular cocktail is a very weak deal. Flick back quickly to our definition of a dealmaker. Where does it say, pray tell, that to get a deal one must be a wimp and go for the easy options?

Back to the study example. If the son selected the problem-solving alternative, his first step would be to look at where he had common ground with his parents. He wants to study and his parents want him to study. A tick in that box. There is money available. Another tick. He would prefer to study close to home. Tick. And so it goes, until all the boxes in which the son and his parents agree have been ticked. What remains? The huge elephant in the middle of the room.

What the son would effectively have done is remove everything from the table except the main issue – *what* he studies. The problem is that conflict is far more likely when there is only one contentious issue left unresolved than when you can work with, and trade off, several issues. In a situation fraught with tension, choosing the problem-solving option is more likely to intensify the conflict than reduce it.

10. Conflict-resolve

We have already touched briefly on the subject of conflict. In the real world, conflict resolution experts are seldom the same people as dealmakers. These are, in my experience, two extremely different schools of thought following two very different approaches.

As I fall into the camp of dealmakers, there's not much I can offer in the way of input other than to say that in our example, where the son and his parents presumably want a decent relationship going forward, it may be advisable to engage the services of a person external to the family unit to handle conflict resolution.

Whether this is an *arbitrator* (someone who hears both sides of the story and then makes a decision, like a judge) or a *mediator* (a person who attempts to find the common ground for the parties and helps them to *compromise* (eek)), the family would be placing their future in the hands of a third party. The cost of this, especially if the third party is not particularly talented, may ultimately be higher than the negotiating option.

We have only looked at a few of the 15-odd options I mentioned, but these are the most common alternatives. What is critical is that you consider as many alternatives as you can when you're doing a deal. The more time you spend preparing and analysing the pros and cons – or costs and benefits – of each and every option, the stronger your leverage or power as a dealmaker.

The next question, of course, is whether every transaction is open to alternatives, especially when it comes to selling and negotiating a deal.

SECRET #4 There is power in having alternatives
There are lots of alternatives a dealmaker can use to get the deal, but they all have a cost – choose the most appropriate one for each situation, but keep other options in your back pocket for leverage and to adjust power.

DEVIL #4
Going into a deal relying on only one closing strategy is a big mistake – if the other side plays a game for which you have not prepared, you will be outmanoeuvred – even if you can think on your feet.

SECRET #5
EVERYTHING IS OPEN TO A DEAL

In my book *Deal Diva: How to Negotiate Your Way to Success Without Selling Your Soul* I asked the question: 'Is everything open to negotiation?' If negotiation is just one alternative in the dealmaker's arsenal, do the same rules apply when the question is expanded to dealmaking, rather than just relative to negotiation?

What do *you* think? Is everything open to selling or negotiation – or problem-solving or surrendering or conquering for that matter? What about your ethics and morals? Or your beliefs and values? How about attitudes? Either way, yes or no, we are going to test your view.

Did you see the movie *Indecent Proposal* with Demi Moore and Woody Harrelson? Here is a light-hearted synopsis of the movie from www.amazon.com:

> Yuppie melodrama that poses the conundrum of whether the loving husband of an equally loving wife will accept $1 million to allow his wife to spend one night with a billionaire who looks like Robert Redford. Demi Moore and Woody Harrelson play Diana and David Murphy, high-school sweethearts who marry and who are doing very well — Diana is a successful real-estate agent, and David is an idealistic architect who has built a dream house by the ocean — until the recession hits. Suddenly, David loses his job, and they can't make the mortgage payments. Dead broke, they borrow $5,000 from David's father and head

> to Las Vegas to try to win money to pay the mortgage on their house. At first, they get $25,000 ahead — but inevitably the house always wins, and they end up losing it all. While Diana is in the fancy casino boutique trying to lift some candy, she is spotted by billionaire John Gage (Robert Redford), who is immediately attracted to her. John invites Diana and David to an opulent party, and it is there that John offers David $1 million for a night with his wife.

Now be honest. If you were being offered one million dollars for your partner, would you take it? If you are a woman and can't get your mind around Robert Redford making you an offer for your man, pretend it is Demi Moore that's making you the offer.

If you would say ***no*** *to the offer, read here.* You are about to lose your house. Still not? Why not? Is it jealousy? No? Is it because of your morals or values? If so, you have a dirty mind! Nowhere in the movie, nor in the outline above, does anyone mention s.e.x. Can it be that you don't trust your partner to keep their hands to themselves? You think I am missing the point, don't you?

Let me ask you this question – and do not answer 'none': Under what circumstances would you let your partner spend the night with Robert Redford (or Demi Moore)? What if there was no physical contact? What if you chaperoned them? Still not an option? Okay, you clearly have an issue with the ethics.

Now pretend that Robert Redford (or Demi) is holding your partner by the ankles over the edge of a 20-storey building and saying, 'If you don't let him/her spend the night with me, I'll drop them.' 'Ah, but that's a completely different situation,' you reply. Not so. It's just a haggle about the price – a life, or a million bucks? The price differential may be a big one, but the issue – spending the night – remains the same.

If you would say ***yes*** *to the offer, read here.* What if you could have got more than a million dollars? That was, after all, only the opening offer. Would Robert (or Demi) have been prepared to go to two, or five, or 10 million? Or give you his yacht? Maybe you could have introduced a sliding scale, with different prices for different favours?

If you would have wanted ***more money*** *at the outset, read here.* You are a dealmaker after my own heart (given my dubious grandfather, what did you expect?). Good for you.

I am not just being flippant. Even in this 'indecent' situation, you need to look at your choices. Which of the BATNA options would apply? Let's measure the *Indecent Proposal* against the alternatives in Secret #4 (the numbering below relates back to page 20).

1. Negotiate

The definition of negotiation, in a nutshell, is giving to get. Robert Redford has offered you one million dollars for a night with your partner. Fair offer, in his mind. If yours is a moral issue, it may have to be a matter of life or death before you are prepared to negotiate. You might say something along the lines of: 'If you promise not to drop/harm my partner, you can spend the night with them.'

For the more morally flexible, it would be something along the lines of: 'If you pay me two million, you can have my partner for one night.' You are giving Robert what he wants *and* getting what you want in return.

3. Persuade, or 4. Argue

If you were not happy with Robert's offer, you might try to convince him that his proposal violates every fibre of your being, that your fidelity is sacred, that you understand his loneliness and you will find him a worthy partner, or that as a billionaire it is his responsibility to be a role model in society. Think he would buy it? Me neither.

5. Surrender

'Sure. No problem.' Think it will end after one night? Not a chance.

6. Conquer

'Go ahead and drop 'em. I wanted a new partner anyway.'

Or how about, 'No. I will rather have her sleeping in the gutter than spend the night with you'? Would *she* want to live on the street?

This more or less happened to a friend of mine. He wanted to go fishing with my husband in the Zambezi Valley, but his wife didn't want him to go. He went. When he got home 10 days later, his key no longer worked. He figured it must have rusted on the river, and so he scaled the wall. On peering through the windows, he yelled, 'I've been robbed!' You guessed it. His wife had left, taken everything and changed the locks. She never came back.

7. Postpone

You could try to avoid making a decision, hoping your luck will turn, or that Robert gets distracted by another woman, or he forgets (or dies). If you postpone in the scenario we're examining, you will probably end up on the street.

8. Compromise

You resort to the King Solomon solution. Cut her in half. If you have no idea what I'm talking about, King Solomon was a wise ruler in ancient times who had to judge a case in which two women were arguing over which one of them was the mother of a baby. 'Cut the baby in half,' was Solomon's suggestion. The way in which the women responded helped him to identify the real mother. Which half of your partner do you want? Compromise murders deals.

There is an amusing, allegedly true, story about Sir Winston Churchill (British prime minister and Nobel laureate, 1874–1965) in this vein.

Churchill: Madam, would you sleep with me for five million pounds?
Socialite: My goodness, Mr Churchill ... well, I suppose ... we would have to discuss terms, of course ...
Churchill: Would you sleep with me for five pounds?
Socialite: Mr Churchill, what kind of woman do you think I am?!
Churchill: Madam, we've already established that. Now we are haggling about the price.

9. Problem-solve

Robert wants your partner. You solve the problem by suggesting that *you* spend the night with him, or he doesn't touch your partner, or he can have her when you get divorced (because she won't live on the street anyway). Does this get you, or him, or your partner, what you want?

11. Gamble

This is what got you into the mess in the first place. You came to Las Vegas to bet all your money and try to save your house. You lost. Gambling, or taking a bet, works when there is an element of chance, but you have to be pretty certain that the odds are in your favour. What bet could you take? 'I bet you don't have any fun'? Or, 'I bet she says no'?

12. Walk away

You could walk away, but you will be walking straight to the homeless shelter.

13. Deadlock

Deadlock is similar to postponement, but with deadlock the status quo is maintained and the relationship potentially damaged. Would deadlock get you a deal? Only in the way postponement would, in this case.

14. External options

Who you gonna call? The casino manager? Would he be a decent third-party mediator or arbitrator? Can you afford to sue? Assuming you could find a lawyer prepared to work pro bono, on what would you base your case? An indecent proposal?

15. Neutral options

Are just that – neutral. They aren't of any use whatsoever in this scenario.

Although the *Indecent Proposal* case might be a slightly frivolous example, it illustrates two important points. Firstly, a skilled dealmaker recognises that everything can potentially be open to a deal. Secondly, he or she needs to choose which of the alternatives is best for the situation.

Sometimes the personal price may seem too high and you will want to say no. A competent dealmaker very seldom, if ever, says no (more about this in Secret #48). They just keep asking for something in return. The more outrageous the demand, the more outrageous their price.

SECRET #5 Everything is open to a deal

An expert dealmaker recognises that everything can potentially be open to a deal, but the art is in choosing the correct alternatives for each situation, and ensuring that you get the appropriate value in return for any concessions you might need to make.

DEVIL #5

Thinking you are selling your soul if you need to be flexible in a deal is how the unskilled operate. Take off the 'yes' and 'no' blinkers, and ask yourself: 'What are the conditions under which I can agree to this deal?'

SECRET #6
NO ONE IS ABOVE THE LAW OF DEALMAKING

So far, we have established that there is an art and a process to being a skilled dealmaker. We have also seen that there is only a slight difference between selling and being a Lothario, and between negotiating and being a hooker. This may be leading you to assume that dealmaking, somehow, is a bit dirty as a profession. Dr Peter Drucker (Austro-Hungarian management theorist and author, 1909–2005) would not agree. This is his view on the subject: 'I will tell you a secret: dealmaking beats working. Dealmaking is exciting and fun, and working is grubby.'

Although I am quoting Dr Drucker slightly out of context, he believed that dealmaking was at the high end of the work scale – the glamorous and enjoyable end – rather than at the drudge end. The top 20 names on Forbes's The World's Billionaires list for 2011 are all dealmakers. Further down the list are a few sheiks and heirs who inherited their lot, but even they still thrive by doing deals.

What do you think? Is there anyone, or any entity, that is so powerful or important that they do not have to do deals? If I ask this question when I am lecturing, I frequently get the answer 'the revenue service'. Okay, we all have to pay taxes, but it may surprise you to learn that you can negotiate discounts on penalties that the revenue service is levying on you, or negotiate payment methods, or even the period over which you pay tax. 'Death' is another answer I get to this question. Yes, we are all going to die at some point, but you can cheat death to a certain degree with lifestyle, medicines, prayers, affirmations.

An article I recently read, written by 'expert mediator' Robert D. Benjamin, claims that 'negotiation carries a taint of being immoral and sinful'. He cites Satan as being the 'archetype of evil' whose 'modus operandi is to tempt, persuade and negotiate', while 'John Wayne, an American cultural icon', would not be prepared to negotiate (gotta love those mixed metaphors!).

John Wayne (American film actor and director, 1907–1979) famously said, 'If you've got them by the balls, their hearts and minds will follow.' A classic 'conquer' strategy. But if you look at the Politics section of his www.wikipedia.com entry, you will see that he did deals with some right proverbial devils in his time!

Countries, governments, corporations, unions, bosses, employees, customers, suppliers, wives, husbands, parents, children ... you name it, they must all do deals. Even Robert Mugabe. How do you think he's been able to cling to his despotic presidency for as long as he has? Even Chuck Norris is a dealmaker.

SECRET #6 No one is above the law of dealmaking
The world's richest and most successful businesspeople are first and foremost dealmakers. Every person and organisation on the planet needs to be able to close deals to survive, never mind succeed.

DEVIL #6
Do not presume that the more power you have, the less you need to do deals. The opposite is true – the greater your power, the more you will need to do deals to retain that power.

SECRET #7
EVERYONE HAS THE POTENTIAL TO BE A DEALMAKER

An advert for a negotiation seminar recently proclaimed that 'Negotiators are not born. They are made.' Rubbish. Ask almost anyone living with children between the ages of four and eight if they think their little ones are born negotiators or not. Kids are also consummate manipulators. What are tantrums and sulking designed to do if not get the child what he or she wants? These are sales tools for juniors!

We are all born with superb dealmaking instincts and potential.[1] They just need a bit of tweaking. Two of the skills central to dealmaking are selling and negotiating, skills that virtually every six-year-old possesses in abundance.

Some of us may have lost our superpowers as we got older, but the point is that we had them to start. How we get them back is the question.

If you don't believe that *you* were a born salesperson or negotiator, just ask your parents (if you are lucky enough to still have them around) or someone who has known you since you were a small child. They will tell you that you started exhibiting selling skills aged two (screaming your head

1. Approximately 1 to 3 per cent of the world's population is born mentally disabled and thus completely unable to communicate (definitions and statistics differ from source to source). The assumptions above are based on children born with communication abilities.

off in the trolley at the supermarket to encourage them to sign the order, i.e. buy you a chocolate). At age three, you could persuade (or beg, as in 'Pleeeease can I have a chocolate?'). By four years old, you were a master manipulator (more selling skills – 'I love you, Mom, please can I have a chocolate? If I was the mommy I would buy a chocolate for you!').

And at the age of five, you were already a negotiator ('If you buy the chocolate for me, I will share it with you.'). Aged six, you were an expert negotiator ('If you take me to the park on Saturday, I will [go to bed early, eat my peas, not pull my sister's hair, be good, not embarrass you in front of your friends, stop kissing the dog, not throw stones] ...'). By eight, you were persistent, creative and flexible, with the glimmer of a dealmaker who could sell and negotiate all in one transaction.

Children peak as potential dealmakers between the ages of five and eight. Try getting a six-year-old to go to bed if this is not what he wants to do. He can think up endless reasons for why he needs to stay up, or he might nag for five more minutes, or he will ask for a vast range of rewards in exchange for going to bed.

How do adults deal with these brilliant young minds? They say, 'Go to bed now, or else' (or 'Because I said so'). Is this the best a grown person can do? Usually, yes. Why is it that a child, whose cognitive development is not yet complete, can often outmanoeuvre an adult? Especially when you consider their almost complete lack of power?

Here is a list I put together for *Deal Diva*, identifying the traits that make children brilliant early dealmakers:

1. They tell you what they want – they live by the old adage: 'If you don't ask, you don't get.'
2. Children are incredibly creative – they have lots and lots of ideas and alternatives with which to play.

3. They are infinitely flexible – they are willing to offer alternatives if they get a 'no'.
4. They do not apply associative logic to getting what they want – they will happily link bedtime with the lion park, or bathing to ice cream, or being quiet to no vegetables.
5. Kids are ruthless little traders – they continually push their luck.
6. They don't care about ego and 'losing face' – if you say no, they simply try again. And again.

If you look closely, you will see these same qualities in the world's leading dealmakers and in the Forbes list of billionaires.

If we are all born with dealmaking potential, why, and when, do we lose it? Youngsters let go of their persistent negotiating and persuading during primary school. For children to adapt to school life, and because of their initial natural willingness to please and listen to their teachers, they start to conform to 'the system'. And when they unwittingly buy into 'the system', they lose their inherent trading skills – they stop expecting to get something in return for giving the other person what they want. By the time they meet the next real 'system', commonly called 'business', their dealmaking abilities are long gone.

A few children don't lose their skills; they keep developing them. Here is how it works. Imagine you were born with a talent for tennis (or when you were a baby, your father hung a tennis ball in your cot). You were really good at tennis when you were a child and you played every day until you left primary school. Then, for whatever reason, you didn't play tennis for 10 years. How good would you be compared to the kids who had continued to play? Plenty of international tennis champions have been in their teens.

Dealmakers should approach deals like children – with lots of alternatives and lots of variables in their back pockets. If your proposal is rejected, pull out a new one. It's not rocket science – your average six-year-old knows how to get what they want.

SECRET #7 Everyone has the potential to be a dealmaker

Some people retain the dealmaking instincts and potential with which they were born; others lose them. As selling and negotiating are innate abilities, it is not difficult to recapture and develop these life skills.

DEVIL #7

Do not buy into the bull that negotiators or salespeople are made – just look at the average six-year-old. They are demon junior dealmakers.

SECRET #8
VERBAL COMMUNICATION OPERATES ON TWO LEVELS

This book's very first secret mentions the words I would *not* like to see removed from the definition of a dealmaker. One of them is communication. Without the ability to communicate effectively – in whatever form – a dealmaker loses a lot of their power.

Communication seems to mean different things to different people, and a look at dictionary definitions (other than www.urbandictionary.com) is not awfully elucidating, which I find ironic in itself. Proof positive is www.thefreedictionary.com, which defines 'communication' as '1. The act of communicating; transmission' (*yes, really*), and '2. **a.** The exchange of thoughts, messages, or information, as by speech, signals, writing, or behaviour. **b.** Interpersonal rapport'. Along with the definition was a video advert for Scientology. The following, from www.urbandictionary.com, is far more enlightening: 'Person A emits verbal tones in the form of sentences while Person B utilizes sense of hearing to transmit exact words to brain, which in turn re-creates the sentence to fit their own agenda and re-emits into a new and improved, yet rarely accurate, statement'.

Communication is, to my mind, the imparting or exchanging of information either verbally or non-verbally. *Verbal* communication is concerned with words, including speech, sign language and writing, whereas *non-verbal* communication is wordless interaction through gestures, body language, posture, facial expressions, eye contact and telepathy (yes, really).

To make the subject of communication as uncomplicated as possible, it has been divided into two segments – Secret #8 dealing with verbal communication (conscious and unconscious), and Secret #9 covering non-verbal communication (body language, micro-expressions and telepathy).

Verbal communication works on two levels – what we say *consciously* and what we say *unconsciously*. With *conscious* verbal communication, you are cognisant of the words you are choosing and using. *Unconscious* verbal communication is when you include words without being aware that you have actually said them. They are usually simple, descriptive words.

1. Conscious verbal communication

(what we are aware of saying)

The most common form of communication is unquestionably *conscious verbal communication*, and because of this, I'm going to be pedantic about the mindful choice of words in dealmaking. Negotiators, in particular, need to consider what they want to say and how best to say it. Think about hostage negotiators – one wrong word and someone could lose their life. In business, using precise wording is also important. An incorrect word could be the death of your deal. Success does lie in semantics.

The word 'verbal' does not only refer to spoken communication. Verbal is the use of words – whether in the form of speech, writing or sign language. 'Flipping the bird' qualifies as verbal communication. And it's no use saying 'the devil made me do it' – it is conscious verbal communication.

Think before you speak (and before you write) *and* pay careful attention to what the other person is saying. Thinking about what you want to say does mean that you need to consciously plan the exact words you intend to use. The upside of this is that when you think carefully about your words, you are less likely to say something you'll regret.

Carefully chosen words help to increase the control you have in a deal, particularly when you are selling or negotiating. Choosing your words does slow you down, which is good news. Slow is best when you are doing deals, especially if there is tension or conflict.

In Secret #4, I explore arguing as an alternative you could use in dealmaking, but the accompanying warning is that arguing can damage relationships, especially if something is said in the heat of the fracas that could later be cause for regret. Think about the last couple of arguments you had with your parents, partner, children, staff, boss, whomever. As the argument got more heated, the tempo would have increased, allowing more and more unconscious words to slip in. The slower the conversation, the less likely this is to happen.

One Fred W. Householder (American linguistics and classical studies professor, 1913–1994) proclaimed: 'Nothing can be so clearly and carefully expressed that it cannot be utterly misinterpreted.' What you say and what the other party hears might not be the same thing, so in addition to choosing your words diligently, you must check that the other person understands exactly what you mean.

To ensure that you are being correctly understood, you need to ask questions, listen to the answers, summarise and confirm. Doing this properly makes certain that no crazy assumptions or misinterpretations have crept into the discussion. In Part 2 of this book, you will see that questioning, listening and summarising all feature very strongly.

Secret #3 revealed that there is one word used continuously in negotiation: the word 'if'. Huge power is held in this little word because, contained in just two characters, is trading. Trading is giving to get. In giving the other party what they want from a deal, you are far more likely to get what you want.

When you say, 'If you do this for me, then I will do that for you,' you communicate clearly with the other person. This is a much more reliable and honest way of interacting with someone than giving and hoping they will return the favour. Or giving and manipulating them after you have made your 'generous' gesture.

Most people (killjoys excluded) prefer to give good news as opposed to bad. The danger, though, in saying, 'I am going to do this for you,' and then adding, 'but ...' (or leaving out the 'but') is that as soon as the other person hears the offer part, they are already thanking you for your generosity.

A colleague of mine, Holger Morhart, tells the story of when, as a junior in a company, he managed to get his boss to agree to a discount for a customer that would enable him to close a big deal. Holger phoned the customer and proudly announced that he could offer the discount, but before he could add 'in return for a 10 per cent increase in volumes', the customer had thanked him and rung off. The customer was just arriving at the airport for a holiday abroad, and Holger had to wait for two agonising weeks to tell the customer that there was a condition attached to the discount.

Saying, '*If* you do this for me, *then* I will do that for you,' allows you to elucidate your conditions before you make any offers. It does mean putting the 'bad news' upfront, but that is the essence of good dealmaking.

2. Unconscious verbal communication

(what we're not aware of saying)

During verbal communication (bear in mind that this can be spoken, written or signed), clues or cues or signals are dropped into the conversation. No matter how well a person prepares their conscious words, they are unlikely to be able to eradicate all of the *un*conscious communication. With written communication, you have a far greater chance of reducing unconscious signals. This is because you have time to review what you want to say. Not so with direct conversations.

A few skilled dealmakers can control their words to reduce unconscious communication, but the trick is not so much to stop giving clues as it is to start picking up the clues being dropped. Not sure what I'm talking about? Assume you see an advert in the newspaper that reads: 'BMW for sale. £10 000 ONCO.' What is the clue? It's obviously ONCO – Or Nearest Cash Offer – which means that the £10 000 is negotiable.

Here is a less obvious example. You are talking to someone on the phone about a holiday apartment they have to rent out, and you ask them for the daily rate. They will say something like, 'I want in the region of £500 per day,' or, 'It depends on the season, but the average is £500 per day.' Both these statements contain clues, albeit subtle ones. 'In the region of' = negotiable. 'Average' = negotiable. Why, then, do we write down '£500' on our notepads and omit the all-important signals of flexibility?

A classic example from www.urbandictionary.com:

'What are the chances of us getting together, say, 1 in 100?' He smiles.
'More like 1 in 1 000 000.' She grimaces.
'So you're saying there's a chance.' He grins.

A more difficult 'clues' test for you. While my colleague and co-lecturer David Black was in the middle of delivering a programme one morning, a very senior policeman arrived to arrest him. I knew that David had had an altercation with one of the guards at the entrance to the venue earlier, and that David had driven 'through' the boom at the gate. David has a short fuse, so to speak, and I'd expected fallout, but not an arrest.

I asked the delegates to take a break and invited the venue's head of security and the policeman into the room. Keeping one delegate back as a witness, I then asked for an explanation. David and the security head started an almighty shouting match. I stopped them and simply asked the security man what it would take to resolve the issue. 'I want an apology,' the security head replied. I glared at David, who finally said, 'In that case, I would like to apologise.' The security head and the policeman left the room.

Where is the clue?

David said 'I would like to apologise', but under his breath he was muttering 'But I'm damned if I'm going to'. To David's mind, he had not apologised. In the mind of the head of security, he had got his apology.

Clues can range from the blatantly obvious to the David-type obscure. They are woven into communication like the subtitles of a foreign movie. If you are watching a French movie with English subtitles and you can speak French, you will notice that the English subtitles are different from the French being spoken. The combination of the two gives you more information than just hearing the French dialogue.

The trick is to spot the clues rather than to stop yourself from giving them. To recognise clues, you need to increase your awareness and focus on what the other person is saying. Listening for the clues will help you to understand what is important to the other party, and where they are likely to be flexible.

If you pick up a clue, avoid pointing it out to the person who has given it – they could become embarrassed about their transparency and dig in on a position. You need flexibility to close a deal, not intransigence. Simply explore the clue, expand on it and then make a counter-offer.

SECRET #8 Verbal communication operates on two levels

Verbal communication is all about words. To get the most from this in dealmaking, you need to choose your words and phrases *consciously*, and listen for the *unconscious* hints and clues in the language of the other person.

DEVIL #8

Instead of trying to eradicate the unconscious clues from your own communication, concentrate on picking up the other party's areas of flexibility in a deal.

SECRET #9

NON-VERBAL COMMUNICATION CAN BE OBSCURE

To pick up on our thoughts of trains, *verbal* communication is all about words, while *non-verbal* communication is wordless. (Did you spot that the opening words were back to front?)

At the beginning of Secret #8, non-verbal communication was defined as wordless interaction through gestures, body language, posture, facial expressions, eye contact and telepathy.

According to www.wikipedia.com, there are other forms of non-verbal communication, including objects or artefacts (such as clothing, hairstyles or architecture), symbols (icons or graphics) and dance. We are going to focus on body language, micro-expressions and telepathy, as these are the elements most likely to affect a deal. Let's start with body language.

1. Body language

(what we physically suggest without words)

You are sitting at a bar and you see a woman across the room flick her hair and lick her lips while she is looking at you. What does this mean? Do you interpret this as an act of flirtation? The books on body language suggest this assumption could well be correct. What if you decide to go over and offer to buy her a drink? How is she likely to respond?

If the woman is trying to seduce you, you might be okay. If she is just getting the hair out of her eyes, licking the margarita salt off her lips and happened to be looking in your direction at the same time, you could be in a spot of bother.

The cliché of the girl in the bar giving off physical signs of seduction is, like much of body language, subject to variations in culture. To complicate matters, to interpret body language successfully, you need to know the person's normal behaviour, observe the change in their behaviour, and then decode that change. Plus, skilled operators can manipulate their body language to give off the signals they want you to receive.

Body language is strongly tied to culture, gender and generational differences, among others, which suggests that it is a learnt, not a reflex, behaviour. Although I'm no body-language expert, I know that relying on body language in dealmaking is about as effective as relying on it when playing poker. You can far too easily be misled.

Proponents of body language believe that a huge percentage of communication happens via this medium. Interestingly, reliable research to support this opinion can't be found. My view is that other unexplained forms of communication take place that are easier to ascribe to body language than something freaky like instinctive, telepathic or intuitive communication. Body language is not reliable. If you have a choice between body language and verbal communication in dealmaking, trust the latter.

Two books to read on the subject of body language are *Kiss, Bow or Shake Hands* by Terri Morrison and Wayne A. Conaway, and *When Cultures Collide* by Richard D. Lewis. Both books focus on the role of culture in body-language-based communication.

2. Micro-expressions
(what we instinctively suggest without words)

Did you watch the fabulous television programme *Lie to Me*, an American series that ran on the Fox network? If you did, you will know exactly what is meant by micro-expressions.

Micro-expressions are brief, involuntary expressions, usually on the face, indicating emotion. Unlike regular facial expressions, micro-expressions are difficult to fake, as they are recognised by tiny changes such as pupil dilation or contraction, muscle twitches, blushing or blanching (not unique to Caucasians), changes in pulse rate, and similar.

While body language in the main appears to be learnt, this is not the case with micro-expressions. They are instinctive and reflexive. Even though micro-expressions are extremely hard to read, they are a valuable form of non-verbal communication.

In *Lie to Me*, Dr Cal Lightman (played by the gorgeously sleazy British actor Tim Roth), through his ability to detect minute changes in expression, is in effect a human lie detector. As they only last $1/15$ to $1/25$ of a second, very few of us (about one in 400 people) have the conscious ability to observe micro-expressions. I do believe, however, that we pick up these signs at the unconscious, non-verbal level.

People in the Western world tend to have been conditioned to reject that which can't be explained by science or ascribed to a superior being. The net effect is that we have tuned out many abilities that work on the intuitive plane. Interestingly, it was also for reasons of survival that we shut down our alternative communication systems. If we had not, the *Malleus Maleficarum* would have had us burnt at the stake.[2]

Back to the present. The seminal research into micro-expressions has been conducted by Dr Paul Ekman (American psychologist, named one of *Time* magazine's 100 most influential people in 2009, 1934–). The character Dr Cal Lightman from *Lie to Me* is based on Dr Ekman. It would seem,

2. The *Malleus Maleficarum* was the original witch-hunter's handbook written in 1486 by the Dominican friars Heinrich Kramer and Jacob Sprenger. This is not recommended reading.

though, that Dr Ekman's research is not terribly popular with the establishment and that he is, like the witches of yore, being somewhat persecuted by his peers. Maybe not so much 'back to the present' after all.

Back to the point. While we might have tuned out or shut down a lot of our intuitive abilities, they still function at a primordial, unconscious level. From a dealmaking perspective, it would be more helpful if they were accessible to our conscious minds, but to ignore them, as already mentioned in Secret #1, is to ignore the basic dealmaking skills with which we were born.

It is possible to learn to interpret the clues that micro-expressions offer. Dr Ekman's institute offers training programmes for this. For a quick online example of micro-expressions, see http://www.cio.com/article/facial-expressions-test. To start the test, press the number 1 at the bottom of the graphic of the television screen.

3. Telepathy

(what we intuitively communicate without words)

If reading micro-expressions is the interpretation of tiny, instinctive reflexes that form part of non-verbal communication, what is telepathic communication? Have you ever had a distinct feeling about a deal or a person? Did you follow what your intuition was telling you, or did you ignore it? What were the consequences?

When it comes to communication, there is a dimension that goes beyond the verbal and non-verbal, and takes us into the murky realm of the esoteric. Telepathic communication is the ultimate form of intuitive communication. Whether you want to call it telekinesis, feminine intuition, sixth sense, psychic transmission or extrasensory perception, it all means more or less the same.

As a sceptic, I find it easy to reject this form of communication out of hand, but I've had a few experiences that are hard to dismiss with a wave.

My company recently appointed a new distributor in the United Kingdom. The two principal members of the new distributor and I were spending time, over dinner, getting to know one another better. The one principal, let's call him Josh (he is, in real life, a character in a James Patterson novel), had said nothing about his private life in the five days we had been together. I was curious. Looking him directly in the eyes, I asked him a very personal question (see Secret #18 for details on how best to do this). No sooner were the words out my mouth, than I knew the answer. I had somehow read Josh's mind and was hugely embarrassed to be 'looking' into his private life. He did not, however, give me as much detail in his verbal answer as I had picked up in the telepathic moment.

Another incident was with my husband Simon's boss. A bunch of us, including Simon and the boss, were having drinks one evening when I suddenly 'saw' what Simon's boss was thinking. No, it wasn't about sex. I felt confused, almost drunk, until my brain had processed what I had sensed. I was confounded when, the next day, what I'd picked up telepathically came to pass. I asked my enigmatically profound friend Chris van der Walt for his opinion of the incident, and he offered the following philosophical explanation: I was not reading the boss's mind, as such. Thoughts fire in the synapses of the brain, creating energy sparks. I had, for a brief moment, been able to connect to a spark from someone else, which my brain later translated into my conscious thoughts.

Sigmund Freud (Austrian neurologist and founder of psychoanalysis, 1856–1939) called telepathy a regressive and primitive faculty, mostly lost in evolution. It was lost for reasons of surviving manic monks too, I suspect, but my theory is that it has only been lost to our *conscious* minds.

Scientists tend to carry out research into telepathic communication with tribal societies. Is this because the scientists know that the further a group is from Western 'civilisation', the less likely its members are to have been conditioned by scientific and religious radicalism? Moving on swiftly...

A fascinating study of telepathy was conducted with a remote Aboriginal community in Australia. The scientists, after establishing that this group of Aboriginal people had never tasted certain tropical fruits, gave one person a banana to eat. The banana eater had to communicate the *taste* of the banana to his tribesmen telepathically. His compatriots were then presented with a selection of fruit, which none of them had tasted before. On the strength of the telepathic message, the rest of the group was asked to identify the banana. They scored 100 per cent.

Before you reject the idea that telepathic non-verbal communication actually exists, do a little research, read a few books, be open to the possibility that *you* can communicate through energy. Pay attention to what you intuit and sense.

SECRET #9 Non-verbal communication can be obscure
Although non-verbal communication is less reliable than conscious verbal communication, this does not mean it should be ignored. The power of insight is remarkable, so learn to interpret non-verbal messages.

DEVIL #9
You will not get burnt at the stake for opening your mind to forms of communication that go beyond that which can be explained. Don't be afraid to broaden your mind.

SECRET #10

PEOPLE AND DONKEYS ARE NOT THAT DIFFERENT

An expert dealmaker is someone who uses their inborn selling, negotiating and communicating instincts and skills to find leverage and power in order to get what they want, while satisfying the needs of the other party. A dealmaker understands the alternative ways in which deals can be closed, and that there are no holy cows or untouchable people when it comes to dealmaking. So getting the deal should be relatively simple, right? Wrong.

The factor that skews the whole equation is the human one: the lack of skill, the abundance of emotions, of ego, wants, needs and greed. *How*, then, do you get someone to behave sensibly and do a deal with you? The answer lies with carrots, or incentives, if you prefer.

Have you read *Freakonomics: A Rogue Economist Explores the Hidden Side of Everything* by Steven D. Levitt and Stephen J. Dubner? Although a bit passé now, *Freakonomics* is not your typical boring business book. Firstly, the authors don't try to impress you with big words and convoluted text – it is an easy and fun read. Secondly, it explores fascinating ideas, such as why drug dealers live with their mothers and the folly of conventional wisdom.

One of the most interesting aspects of the book is the assertion that '[i]ncentives are the cornerstone of modern life'. The authors go on to say that '[t]he typical economist believes the world has not yet invented a problem that he cannot fix if given a free hand to design the proper incentive scheme'. In other words, if you give someone something that excites them, you can get what you want from them in return. Give a carrot to get a carrot. It is only when this age-old trading system is corrupted by greed that problems begin. Look at the avaricious bankers who broke the global economy.

The reality is that people become far more flexible when you dangle a juicy, fat incentive or two in front of their noses. The more carrots you have that they want, the greater your power. To stop greed in its tracks, though, carrots must come with conditions.

There are two types of incentives or carrots – *big* carrots, which relate to the key issues, and *small* carrots connected to the secondary issues. These two types of issues will be covered in Secrets #26 and #27, but for the moment, we will look at the broad use of carrots in getting someone to engage in a deal with you.

Two important factors to be considered when a dealmaker uses incentives are the relevance of the carrots, and a fair trade or exchange of value.

Let's start with relevance. The carrot must address the other party's issues, needs and wants. Understanding what is important to the other person, and how you can give them what they want, will save you time, effort and money. This means asking questions and *listening to the answers*. All too often in dealmaking, one party does not listen to the needs of the other party, and thus makes proposals that have no value to the other guy. What is the point of offering a carrot to a lion? The lion is more likely to eat you than the carrot, so offer him a chunk of impala instead.

This carrot-to-a-lion example is inextricably linked to understanding value. I'm a rabid vegetarian, so carrots are of much greater value to me than meat. If I go into a deal and the other party offers me rabbit stew, they may think it's a big concession from their side, but it holds zero interest or value to me. I won't bite, even if I am really hungry.

The best way to get what you want in a deal is by offering the other party what will satisfy their needs. If, however, what they want is out of line with the value you are expecting from them, the deal will not close satisfactorily. Selling or trading value for value is crucial to a successful deal.

Case in point, the following story from http://riotwineblog.com:

> Sally was driving home from a business trip in Northern Arizona when she saw an elderly Navajo woman walking on the side of the road. As the trip was a long and quiet one, she stopped the car and asked the Navajo woman if she would like a ride. With a silent nod of thanks, the woman got into the car. Resuming the journey, Sally tried in vain to make small talk with the Navajo woman. The old woman just sat silently, looking intently at everything, studying every little detail, until she noticed a brown bag on the floor. 'What in bag?' asked the old woman. Sally looked down at the brown bag and said, 'It's a bottle of wine. I got it for my husband.' The Navajo woman was silent for another moment, then speaking with the quiet wisdom of an elder, she said: 'Good trade.'

In giving the other side what they want, offer them the carrots *they* value, not the ones you want to give away. In this way, you can leverage tremendous power in a deal. The more value-based incentives you can find to entice the other party, the more interest they will have in doing the deal with you.

SECRET #10 People and donkeys are not that different
A successful deal is one in which you get the incentives (or carrots) you want, and the other party gets the carrots that satisfy their needs. To maximise your deal, trade what *they* value for that which you value most highly.

DEVIL #10
There is not a person on the planet who is not receptive when offered the incentives they desire. Carrots provide leverage and power.

SECRET #11

DEALS NEED TO FOCUS ON VALUE, NOT PRICE

In the business days of yore, i.e. the 1980s and 1990s, people used to talk about win–win. In simple terms, it meant that when a deal was done, both sides needed to feel happy with what they had got from the transaction. The precursor to win–win was win–lose, where only one party or person was supposed to come away with what they wanted (think trade-union negotiations in the 1970s). Lose–lose was when nobody was happy with the deal. The era of win–win is now (or should be!) gone.

The deals of today are all about value. In exchanging value for value, both sides should benefit from the deal. Have another quick look at the definition of a dealmaker in Secret #1. The problem I have with win–win is that it's not necessarily measurable, so it is easy, after the fact, for one party to forget the happy 'win' feeling inside and slide into a win–lose (or 'I've been fleeced') mindset. Value for value is sustainable and measurable and thus promotes long-term relationships.

The simplistic view of the value–value process is that you get something you value, while the other party gets what they value in exchange. Got it?

The classic example is a client who goes to a lawyer for legal advice. The client explains the problem to the lawyer, the lawyer consults a textbook and makes a copy of the textbook page for the client, and the lawyer then invoices the client. Does the lawyer charge for the photocopy, or the time-based value of her advice?

My organisation works with executives and their teams to help them increase revenues and improve profitability. We happen to use training programmes as the means to achieve these outputs, but the executives don't particularly care if it's training, holographic repatterning or chasing their team around a field with a stick. All the executives want are the results. Do we charge only time and materials? No. We charge for the underlying knowledge and intellectual property of the programmes, the expertise of our facilitators, the value of our interventions in driving organisational results, an upside/downside bonus, as well as for direct costs such as venues, catering, taxes, etc.

If a customer is not happy with our fees, we recognise that we have not sold the *value* of our interventions properly. Typically we engage with C-level executives, as they will see the benefit of our programmes on their revenue or profit lines. Occasionally we interface with human resources professionals, but they are more inclined to measure us on compliance, accreditation, charge per training day, that sort of thing. We find it harder to show the human resources people the value we add because their measure of success is different.

I said that C-level executives don't care how we get the results, just that we do. The 'how' is far less important than the value, and the higher up they are in the decision tree, the lesser the importance. If they are not concerned with the how, do you think, if we illustrate value properly, they care much about the price?

What one groups sees as value is not the same as another – lions and carrots. How do you know what the other person will value? Ask questions and *listen to the answers*. Find out what business needs and personal drivers they have. More about this later.

When you start a deal, you will usually begin with selling – persuading the other party to give you what you want. Even if you're in procurement, you start with persuasion. A buying team typically tries to convince suppliers to give them discounts and favourable terms on account of the buying company being reputable, powerful, offering long-term relationships, and so on.

The next move, depending on the situation and alternatives, will frequently be negotiation. The buying team will then ask for a concession, and the supplier will start trading – 'If you want *y* discount, you need to give us *x* volume' and 'If you want 90 days' credit, I need a minimum number of orders placed per month.' The tango begins – backwards and forwards, back and forth. With each step, value is exchanged for value.

Back to the start, for a moment. How often do you think it happens that someone effectively persuades another person to accept a deal without going into negotiation or one of the other alternatives? It depends on the skill of the person doing the selling. And the most powerful way in which anyone can persuade another party is through Value Propositions.

Can you define 'Value Proposition' in a sentence or two? The most useful definition I've found is in an article by Jill Konrath titled 'How to Write a Strong Value Proposition' from www.sideroad.com. Here is the edited version: 'A Value Proposition is a clear statement of the tangible results the other party will get from your proposal, products or services. The more specific your Value Proposition, the better.'

Did you spot the Value Proposition that my company uses? Here it is again: 'My organisation works with executives and their teams to help them increase revenues and improve profitability.' It is short, sharp and answers the question: 'So what?!'

When we first started working with a leading global information technology customer, their sales team insisted that one of their company's Value Propositions was along the lines of: 'We offer the best software in the world to our customers.' *So what?* Where is the value to their customers? Eventually they came up with: 'Our world-leading software enables customers to control their expenditure/stock/manufacturing process in the shortest possible time, thereby making their operations more efficient.' One can now easily see the value of their solution – customers get control over expensive processes quickly, which means that they're able to manage their business results far more efficiently.

A Value Proposition is your or your company's unique selling point, a differentiator. It's the compelling reason why someone would give you what you want. It is *always* stated from the other party's perspective.

Human nature being what it is, we are continually striving to try to get a better deal – to get a discount, or more for the same price, or something for nothing. This means that negotiation often follows persuasion, especially in business.

In the corporate world, the easiest way for a buyer to strip value out of a deal is to try to commoditise the product or service they are buying. They play the 'I can get this cheaper' or 'The other guys include that in their pricing' games. If you are selling a commodity, your price had better be the lowest. For the rest of us, those working with differentiated offerings, it is essential to show the value of the service or product to the other party. The value you offer is the compelling reason why someone will give you the premium you want. The same rules apply when you are selling yourself, by the way.

Warren Buffett (American investor, industrialist and philanthropist, 1930–) had this to say on the subject: 'Price is what you pay. Value is what you get.'

When negotiation comes into the picture, you need to focus on the value of the items you are trading – the value of what you get relative to how the other party perceives the value of the concessions they are receiving. Something that may not cost you much may be of great value to the other person. Value and cost are *not* the same thing – as you will find out in the next secret.

SECRET #11 Deals need to focus on value, not price

In dealmaking, value is more important than price. If you are able to show the other party the *value* for them in the deal, you are far more likely to get what you value in return.

DEVIL #11

A Value Proposition is not some slick statement that a salesperson is able to spout. Value Propositions show the other person that you understand what they want and need, and that the deal is not just about you.

SECRET #12

DO NOT CONFUSE VALUE WITH COST

Secret #11 showed how you could avoid some of the issues around price by emphasising value. As I said, human nature being what it is, though, people often can't help but engage in a bit of a haggling.

Trading during a deal is fine, and expected; but you need to make sure that you are exchanging value for value, and not just giving carrots and getting nothing in return. We'll explore this further, but the saying, 'If you give a man an inch…' doesn't come from nowhere.

Secret #12 is about the cost of value, and how something that may not cost you much could be a huge concession to the other person. Here's a personal example.

I mentioned in Secret #1 that I am a terrible cook and that Simon, my husband, does all the cooking in our house. Not having to think about cooking saves me time, wasted effort and guilt. My guilt is reduced because I don't have to feel like a terrible wife serving up burnt offerings or two-minute noodles every night. Don't think for one minute that Simon doesn't know how much this is worth to me.

Simon has a demanding corporate job. He often comes home at night stressed out from his day. Before he has even taken off his suit, he's into the kitchen with the carving knife, chopping and dicing and slicing and ranting and raving. Cooking not only brings him great pleasure and a sense of achievement, but it's also an important stress reliever. My contribution is to pour us each a glass of wine, put on the music, and fetch and carry.

Being a savvy man, Simon understands how much I value him doing the cooking, so he trades carrots with me. 'If you expect me to do the cooking,' says Simon, 'you need to keep up your end by doing the grocery shopping.' Now Simon loves cooking. And he uses it to unwind at the end of a day. And if he didn't cook, he wouldn't get fed. So why does he negotiate with me? He would cook whether I did the shopping or not, but just because he was going to cook anyway doesn't mean he should underestimate the value it has for me.

In business, it's just as easy to fall into the trap of giving something away for nothing because it doesn't cost you or your company anything.

Think of a situation in which you have been with a customer or supplier and they have asked you for a 'favour' – something they knew wouldn't be much trouble for you. You probably gave it the most cursory of thoughts before you said, 'Sure, no problem.' If you were challenged on this by someone afterwards, you would have explained the gesture away by saying that it wasn't a big deal, it cost you nothing, or that you were doing it in the interests of the relationship. You would be able to justify the 'gift'. However, the fact that the other party was asking for it *meant that it had a value to them*.

The problem with giving something away for nothing is that if the other person sees how easily you made the concession, not only do they not value what you have given them, but they are inclined to think 'there is plenty more where that came from', and they keep asking. A favour here, a favour there, and then when you say 'no more' because the cost of the favours has mounted up, they are 'disappointed' that you don't value the relationship, that you are so mean-spirited.

The golden rule is: If somebody asks you for something, determine what the concession is worth to the other party. If it is of big value to them, get a carrot in return that has a high value to you, but ideally at a low cost to them. They will be far more willing to give you what you want if it doesn't cost them too much.

Am I suggesting you trade every single little thing? Of course not. You need to use your judgement, but the slippery slide down to unconditional giving is a swift and expensive ride.

SECRET #12 Do not confuse value with cost

Just because something doesn't cost you much doesn't mean this has a low value to the other party. Trade items that cost you little but that have high value to the other side for items that you value but are low-cost to them.

DEVIL #12

If you think the fuss over distinguishing value from cost is a waste of time, you will often end up paying much more for what you want than is necessary.

SECRET #13
EVERYTHING IN DEALMAKING IS INTERCONNECTED

Did you ever read either of the Dirk Gently books by Douglas Adams (English writer and dramatist, author of *The Hitchhiker's Guide to the Galaxy*, 1952–2001)? When Douglas Adams died, aged only 49, my biggest sadness was that there would be no more Dirk Gently books – written by Douglas Adams, at any rate.

Dirk Gently (who has a Wikipedia page, although he is a fictional character) is a 'holistic detective' who makes use of 'the fundamental interconnectedness of all things' to solve crimes. Take 'Zen navigation', for example. It would be impossible to use this system of finding where you want to go without believing in interconnectedness. Here is how Zen navigation works (extracted from the Dirk Gently novel *The Long Dark Tea-Time of the Soul*):

> A few turnings later and I was thoroughly lost. There is a school of thought which says that you should consult a map on these occasions, but to such people I merely say, 'Ha! What if you have no map to consult? What if you have a map but it's of the Dordogne?' My own strategy is to find a car, or the nearest equivalent, which looks as if it knows where it is going and follow it. I rarely end up where I was intending to go, but often I end up somewhere that I needed to be. So what do you say to that?

I believe the same about dealmaking – everything is interconnected (although I would recommend navigating a deal with a back-up map!).

Dealmakers rely on the collective abilities that instinct, expertise and processes offer them. They are able to close deals using selling, negotiating and many other alternatives, moving seamlessly around these options. The alternatives are the cars they choose to follow – their version of the Zen navigation system, if you will. Dealmakers are also good communicators who understand, and can leverage, power. And all of these intertwined talents mean they can get what they want, usually satisfying the other side in the process. They are to closing deals what Dirk Gently is to solving crimes.

SECRET #13 Everything in dealmaking is interconnected
World-class dealmakers approach deals holistically. They assess what they need to do to close a deal. They then weave these into a plan to get what they value in exchange for giving the other party the value they want.

DEVIL #13
Having a one-dimensional, disjointed strategy is going to cost you dearly. Not only will the other side get the better of you, but they will think you are a bit thick in the process.

PART 2

THE POWER OF POWER

The most common way people give up their power is by thinking they don't have any.

Alice Walker (American writer, poet and activist, 1944–)

SECRET #14
PLANNING IN ITSELF CREATES POWER

What is your deep-seated attitude towards power? Are you more of a 'power corrupts' or a 'power empowers' kind of person? Alice Walker, who won the Pulitzer Prize for Fiction in 1982 for her book *The Color Purple*, knows that of which she speaks. The biggest disservice anyone can do to themselves is to take away their own power.

A dealmaker is a powerful person, someone 'able to leverage or adjust the balance of power to bring closure to transactions'. The power we have directly impacts our ability to close deals. What fascinates me about power in dealmaking is that while there is obviously power intrinsic to certain situations and positions, power is a frame of mind; and, more importantly, power can be created.

The objective of this section of the book, which is about the secrets of power, is to look at how you can create more power for yourself as a dealmaker. It is not about power for power's sake; it's about finding the leverage you need in order to get what you want from a deal.

In real life, we don't always go into a deal with lots of power – we may have less positional power than the person with whom we are engaging; for example, we might be more junior or have less knowledge and experience; or our company could be in a compromised or weak position relative to the other party. Power, though, can be adjusted.

You have already been given five ways in which to create more power:

1. Persuasion is a compelling and cheap way to get what you want, and the most powerful way in which anyone can persuade another party is by using proposals based on Value Propositions.
2. Having alternative strategies for each deal gives you power. The more time you spend preparing and analysing the costs and benefits of all available options, the stronger your power will be in a deal.
3. If you believe that the balance of power may shift in your favour, postponing can give you an advantage.
4. There is no person or entity on the planet so powerful or important that they do not have to do deals. As Lord Michel de Montaigne (French writer and essayist, 1533–1592) said, 'Even on the highest throne in the world, we are still sitting on our ass.'
5. The more carrots you have that the other party wants and values, the greater your power. Presenting your carrots as Value Proposition–driven proposals maximises this power and reduces the emphasis on price.

Sure, sometimes you are going to have to dig deep to find the power, but here you have a whole chapter dedicated to ideas on how to create, find and leverage power. Keep in mind, though, the immortal line from *Spider-Man*: 'With great power comes great responsibility.'

How planning creates power

There are hundreds of decent definitions of, and thousands of worthy quotes about, planning and preparing. We are not going to get into the semantics of planning versus preparing, so it is fine if you want to use the terms interchangeably (I prefer planning). What is crucial, however, is the inherent power in both planning and preparing.

Planning allows dealmakers with the lowest levels of skill or the weakest imaginable positions to find power. It is the actual process of sitting down and planning that makes you aware of the potential strengths and weaknesses you have in a deal. It is not by chance that I mention strengths and weaknesses here. Do you know what a SWOT analysis is? If not, here is a short, edited extract from Wikipedia to bring you up to speed:

> SWOT analysis is a strategic planning method used to evaluate the Strengths, Weaknesses, Opportunities and Threats involved in a project or in a business venture. It involves specifying the objective of the business venture or project, and identifying the internal and external factors that are favourable and unfavourable to achieve that objective. The technique is credited to Albert Humphrey, who led a convention at Stanford University in the 1960s and 1970s using data from Fortune 500 companies.
>
> *Strengths:* internal characteristics of the business, team or person that give an advantage.
>
> *Weaknesses:* internal characteristics that place the business, team or person at a disadvantage relative to others.
>
> *Opportunities:* external chances to make greater sales, profits or deals in the environment.
>
> *Threats:* external elements in the environment that could cause trouble for the business, team or person.

If you have no idea where you should start your planning for a deal, a SWOT analysis is an uncomplicated tool to use. There are lots of SWOT models available on the Internet (so you don't have to start from scratch), but the clarity a SWOT plan gives you in terms of power is remarkable. Don't be put off by its simplicity – some of the most sophisticated businesspeople I know use a SWOT analysis as a planning mechanism.

Part 3 is dedicated to the secrets of planning, but in the context of power, the process of planning is vital to understanding the intrinsic control you have going into a deal. Once you have a view of this, you can look at all the options available to you to increase your power.

SECRET #14 Planning in itself creates power
The actual process of planning makes you aware of the potential power you have in a deal. A SWOT analysis is a valuable planning tool that highlights potential strengths and weaknesses, opportunities and threats.

DEVIL #14
Waiting to see what happens when you are faced with a situation leaves you completely unprepared and exposed. Even if it is an 'information-gathering' mission, plan what you want from the interaction.

SECRET #15
CONTROLLING INFORMATION PROVIDES STRATEGIC POWER

You've probably heard the expressions 'information is power' and 'knowledge is power'. Which one do you think is correct?

Technically, they are both right, but as with power for power's sake, information for information's sake is pointless. It is how you apply the information you have, how you use it in the context of closing the deals you want, that is important.

Having information available to you but not knowing how to use it is much the same as a parrot being able to 'talk'. The parrot can repeat the words it has learnt but has no knowledge of what the words mean. It is through understanding the relevance and importance of the information that it transforms into knowledge. Knowledge then gives you power, and underpinning knowledge is information.

This takes us back to information again, but not just for information's sake. There are many juicy aspects to information in dealmaking, so the subject won't (and shouldn't) be covered in one bite. The next few secrets are all about information.

Dealmakers are able to control information in a multitude of ways. Mastering these tactics helps to convert information into knowledge, which is what gives you power in a deal. You must be able to give and get information. To do this, ask questions and listen to the answers. You also have to check that the assumptions you are making are correct, and that the other party has the same understanding of the detail as you. The devil is, after all, in the detail.

The getting and giving of information, as well as questioning and listening, are covered later, but for now, let's concentrate on ways in which a dealmaker can *control* information. There are three key points of control: summaries, debate and testing.

1. Summaries

Skilled dealmakers employ a tactic called summarising or recapping. It is so vital that when they have the opportunity to use a team, they will often assign one person responsibility for the summarising. This is pretty much all that this person will do. My organisation calls it the Vice Captain role, and it is covered in more detail in Secret #29. If they don't have a team, dealmakers will do it themselves, but it is never left out.

So what makes summarising so critical in a deal? Summaries are like milestone markers or road signs. Pretend you are driving across a country, from City A to City B. There are sections on the trip where there are no petrol stations for hundreds of kilometres. If you don't know how far you've got to go to the next petrol stop, you may well run out of fuel. Not something you want to do, say, in the middle of the night.

Dealmaking is the same. If you don't use summaries to check where you are, you might find your deal spluttering because nobody took stock of how far you have come or how far you've got to go. Don't rely on the other party to recap – if you keep the markers, you keep control of the discussion.

Summaries need to be made regularly throughout the deal – from the beginning to the close. It is better to summarise a summary than to leave one out. It is so easy to lose your way in a deal, particularly one rich in detail, that you need to check your markers continually.

A very important point: Summaries must be objective. If you summarise in your favour, it becomes a form of persuasion and the other person may feel the need to counter-persuade. Summaries are meant to help move your discussions forwards, to stop you from going round in circles, and to make sure that everyone has the same understanding of where you are in a deal. When the other party trusts your summaries – and they need to be objective to be trustworthy – summaries really become worth their salt.

Summaries help to:

- give structure to the discussions;
- ensure everyone's clarity and understanding;
- maintain focus on the most important issues;
- check what has been discussed and what still needs to be discussed;
- confirm areas of agreement and what still needs to be agreed;
- identify the markers – the milestones – in your discussions; and
- make sure everyone agrees on the final deal.

2. Debate

When we explored the concept of 'argument' in Secret #4, this was as a subset of selling or persuading. We identified two types of argument – verbal sparring and presenting a case.

In talking about 'argument' as part of the control of information, it is better to refer to it as 'debate', as this helps to differentiate it more clearly from the conscious use of persuasion. Debate is extremely useful in deal-making as a platform for exchanging information and ideas and opinions, but it can slip into the realm of negative point-scoring terribly quickly. If you find the debate getting a bit heated or personal (someone's mother starts getting a mention), use a summary to get the discussion back onto safe ground.

Much more time in dealmaking is spent in debate or discussion than in the actual process of closing the deal, which means the Pareto principle, also known as the 80/20 rule, will raise its head. Eighty per cent of the deal time will be spent in debate, leaving only 20 per cent to close the deal. This might *seem* fine because we know that exchanging information is essential, but the point of a deal is to close it, not to have a little boy's 'let's see who can pee the furthest' competition.

Don't be lulled into thinking that a dealmaker meets with the other party, they have a discussion and a few summaries, and then they close the deal. A deal can take years to bring to closure.

An acquisition I was driving in Germany took two years to close. First came the planning, then there were the initial meetings with the chaps selling their company, then more meetings and the start of negotiations, then consultations with everyone's lawyers and accountants and financiers and advisors, then more debate and negotiation with the sellers, more meetings, further meetings, and finally the lawyers were brought in to draft the agreement.

Just when we thought the deal was closed, the lawyers got into a pissing contest and almost lost us the deal. We had to throw the lawyers out of the room, put the deal back on track, and let the lawyers back in once they were ready to behave. I recently asked a world-renowned lawyer about the propensity of the legal profession to meddle unnecessarily in closed deals, and he explained that I needed to see it from a lawyer's perspective – in their eyes there are only 'f*ckees' and 'f*ckors'. He was being facetious, but it was a light-bulb moment for me.

Debate is great, but it can be fraught with danger. Not only does it waste valuable negotiating and closing time, but if you have a weak position, you could be setting yourself up for failure. The longer you spend in discussion, the greater the opportunity for the other person to find out that you are on shaky ground. Here are a couple of examples from my book *Deal Diva*.

Let's say you are a salesperson selling cars, watches, software, hardware, cooking appliances, whatever – and you are aware that a new model is going to be coming out some time in the near future. Your company will not let you off work (or your sales target) until the new product becomes available, so to keep your job, you have to continue selling the old product. The longer you spend chatting to any potential buyer, the greater the chance they will question you about future offerings. Even though you might not know the details, any disclosure around the new model may result in them wanting to delay their purchasing decision. So, you need to meet with the prospective buyer, put your proposal on the table, give the buyer a compelling reason to buy (perhaps a really attractive offer), and leave with the order. This is not the time to get into a detailed conversation.

Another dangerous debate would be when you agree with the other party's point of view. Imagine your company has failed to deliver something crucial to a customer. Your company blames the customer for the mistake, but you believe your company was actually in the wrong. The longer the conversation you have with the customer, the more likely they are to discover that you think they are right. They may well use your sympathetic position to get leverage for compensation, or whatever else they want from your organisation. Again, present your proposal to rectify the problem, give the customer a good reason to accept the proposal, and leave with the agreement.

Here are a few more situations in which you need to limit or control debate as much as possible, and focus on closing the deal:

- Time constraints – debate consumes time without necessarily moving the deal forwards. Negotiation is what usually closes the deal.

- Conflict or tension – the more time spent in debate, the greater the opportunity for conflict to develop or increase. Summaries are objective and thus help to reduce tension.
- Opinions being expressed – this often leads to competitive behaviour in discussions, which in turn can result in escalated emotion and conflict. You can't negotiate an argument, you can only win an argument – which is actually win–lose.
- Hostile or abusive people – those wanting to make or score points enjoy debate as it provides them with the ideal platform from which to launch their abuse. Summaries help to deflate their stage.

3. Testing

One of the benefits of having argument and debate in dealmaking is the chance to get information that can help you to close the deal more effectively. You should have done your planning before you go into any meeting, but it may well happen that in the course of the face-to-face conversations you find out that certain assumptions you had made, or details you had collected, are wrong.

If you do get information that substantially changes the position or strategy you are taking, throw out all the hard work you have done and start again. It is infinitely better to postpone or adjourn the meeting and go away and rethink everything than to carry on with a deal you know will fail. If you ignore the new information and stick stubbornly to your original but now irrelevant plan, you may not get a second chance when it all goes to the dogs.

The time you spend in discussion, or debate, with the other person is the perfect opportunity to make sure that they appreciate what *you* want. Equally essential is that you check your understanding of what *they* want.

SECRET #15 Controlling information provides strategic power
Information is only power if you understand its importance to the deal as a whole. Being in control of the information will give you power, and the three essentials of control in a deal are summaries, debate and testing.

DEVIL #15
If you use information as power in order to compromise the other party, or achieve win–lose deals in your favour, no one will want to share information or do deals with you.

SECRET #16

THE GIVING OF INFORMATION NEEDS TO BE PLANNED

Should you tell or shouldn't you? Silence is golden? The tenets to which we are accustomed in life may or may not work in dealmaking. You need to decide consciously what information you are going to give, and get, in dealmaking.

Disclosing information is an art. The rules that apply to one deal may be inappropriate for the next. For example, should you disclose your profit? Believe it or not, there are times when showing your profit to someone can be particularly helpful in protecting your margin. Obviously, if you are making huge profits, the last thing you want to do is open your books, but if your margins are tight, it could be the best possible strategy.

To get power (and this section is all about power) from the *giving* of information, there are a few guidelines you can follow. And, without further fanfare, here they are.

1. Don't invent information

What happens if you 'invent' information and the other party finds out you have been telling porkies?[3] Your credibility, and your power, go to hell in a

3. Useless piece of information for you – 'porkies' comes from the English Cockney (as in East End of London) rhyming slang expression 'pork pies' or 'lies'.

handbasket. Being caught out in a lie makes the other party mistrust everything you have said or will say.

People tend to fib because they think it will increase their power. Lying may give you a short-term advantage – if you don't get found out – but in the long term, 'the truth will out'. It does not matter if you are lying to yourself or to someone else: nobody respects a liar.

2. Use information to set expectations

The intelligent use of information is a wicked source of power.[4] When you set expectations, you get the other person thinking in the way *you* want them to think. You can pass information to them directly, or drop little clues. You can tell them what you want, hint about when you want it, and signal where you are and are not flexible.

An example: Think of an expensive or exclusive brand. Look at the words used in their advertising campaigns. Do you see the mention of 'cheap' anywhere? No, it's more like 'luxury', 'quality', 'exclusive' or 'for the privileged few'. One of my favourites is a BMW advert, which opens with the line: 'What do you say to compromise?'

3. Disclosing and withholding information is an art

The best way to illustrate this is with a story. Earlier, I said that under certain circumstances, you might want to disclose your profit. This happened to me recently.

I was in discussions with a large, long-term customer about the implementation of a development academy. The customer put me through three rounds of negotiation and finally raised a purchase order for the deal. I then

4. More useless information – 'wicked' from contemporary English slang meaning 'excellent' (nothing to do with the devil).

got a call from someone in their centralised buying department (on another continent), who wanted to 'look at reducing the invoice'. There was obviously still margin in the deal, but not a huge amount.

After much toing and froing, I offered to show the buyer my profit on the deal. *Caveat emptor* (which is Latin for 'let the buyer beware' – I know, I know, I am using it out of context). Of course, I would never have offered to do this if my profit margin was fat, but in disclosing my profit, I was able to show that the customer was already getting a very good deal. The moral of the story is, beware of people who are happy to show you their profit – they are using it to defend their position, not to give you ammunition!

What should you do, though, if you don't want to disclose information? Do you know how to divert attention away from sensitive subjects, or from questions you would rather not answer? Simply blocking questions by making statements such as, 'I'm not prepared to share that,' is considered obstructive and will not necessarily increase your power.

Besides, saying 'I am not prepared to answer' gives far too many clues to the asker about the possible answer. Here's how the clue works: If someone asks you for your profit margin on an item and you say, 'I am not prepared to disclose that,' they will assume that your profit is high, because if it was low, you would probably share the information.

So how do you avoid disclosing information that you don't want to give? If you are thinking, 'Ask *them* a question,' you are right on target. Here are a few classic deflection questions:

- Why do you need to know that?
- Why is this information important to you?
- What is your reason for asking the question?
- Can I ask *you* a question? What ...? And ask them a personal question, if possible. The irony is that people are flattered when you are interested in

them – and it is the easiest way to distract someone from the information they wanted from you.

One size does not fit all when it comes to giving information in dealmaking. How you direct one party's thinking in a deal may differ completely in the next transaction, but it is within your power to choose consciously how you want to use information.

SECRET #16 The giving of information needs to be planned

The giving of information can range from direct, unambiguous statements to subtle hints and suggestions. Deciding what information to give or withhold, and how best to do this, can put plenty of power in your hands.

DEVIL #16

Withholding information does not automatically benefit you. Not only will you be seen as obstructive or obtuse, but you may lose the opportunity to improve your position through the tactical use of information.

SECRET #17

THERE IS NO EXCUSE FOR NOT GETTING INFORMATION

Your plan for *getting* information is just as key as your strategy for giving information. How can you extract information that people are willing, or not, to share? Asking *direct* questions is one of the best ways, and that is covered in Secret #18, but there are other really effective methods of getting information to increase your power.

When you were a youngster and hadn't done your homework, what was your excuse? The dog ate it? Just as not doing your homework for school was unacceptable, not getting the information you need for a deal is equally unacceptable. The dog story just won't hack it when you have access to the Internet, websites, magazines, periodicals, newspapers, books, libraries, specialist clubs, professional associations, annual reports, analyst reports, newsletters, company noticeboards and plenty of other useful sources.[5]

Despite all the information available to us, there are still people who don't or won't go out and get the information they need to close their deals. It's typical 'head in the sand' and 'what I don't know can't hurt me' behaviour. There are three main reasons why people don't get information.

---

5. Google had over one billion hits in the month of May 2011 alone.

1. What if the answer is not the one I want?

People habitually don't seek out information because they are afraid of what they might hear – that they won't like the information they are given. Getting this bad news might mean that they have to start their planning from scratch, or that the deal on which they have been working is of no interest to the other party.

If you don't believe me, take a look at the sales pipelines of any salesperson – there will be deals listed that have been there forever, but that with one or two qualifying questions could be moved on or out. Removing these deals from the pipeline will mean that the pipeline empties – something sure to get the salesperson into trouble with their sales manager. My team and I (blush) are just as guilty.

This is much like the myth of Socrates and his wife. Socrates, being the noble philosopher that he was, would not partake in any idle gossip. One day, an acquaintance cornered Socrates and announced he had important information to share. Socrates stopped the man from speaking and asked that, before he continue, the man checks the information against three filters – was it true, good and useful? The man was unsure, so Socrates would not let him finish. And this is why Socrates never found out that his best friend was sleeping with his wife.

2. Which information is important?

Another reason why people don't bother with getting information is that they are not sure which information is important and which is not. They prefer a strategy of flying by the seat of their pants. Poor dealmakers justify this lack of planning by saying, 'Well, I needed to wait and see what came up during our discussions.' Why are they then so surprised when they get outmanoeuvred?

You do have to *think* about the information you need – apply a bit of grey matter. It's not difficult. Look at the most important issues in your deal and decide what information you need to help you to close on these issues. Then make a list of the questions you need to ask, and ask them. Hardly nuclear physics.

3. But wait, there is more I have to say

The third reason why people don't get information is that they are too busy talking to think about asking questions or listening to what the other side is saying. You probably know a good few people who love the sound of their own voices. Are you one of them?

The top dealmakers, even the egocentric ones, always make sure they get the information they need. And how do they do this? They ask intelligent, well-prepared questions.

SECRET #17 There is no excuse for not getting information

Having the right information helps to facilitate the deal and close it more quickly. Getting meaningful information gives you leverage and power around your most important issues, which helps you to understand what is of significance to the other side.

DEVIL #17

People can sense when you want information for nefarious purposes. If they pick up that your intentions are not good, they will tell you very little. Check your integrity when working with other people's disclosures.

SECRET #18
PLAN AND EXECUTE QUESTIONS WITH CARE AND LOVE

Which is the best and most reliable way of getting information? Asking the person concerned for the information directly. It's that simple. In a conversation, two thirds of the time is meant to be spent listening, and half of the time that's left should be used to ask questions. The majority of people really do like being asked questions – especially if it gives them the opportunity to talk about themselves.

As with the disclosing of information, there is an art to asking questions and extracting information. And don't underestimate the power of face-to-face questioning. When you ask someone for information directly, you have the opportunity to pick up the nuances and subtleties that accompany their answers aurally *and* visually – the 'clues' they give you.

Here are three ways in which to maximise the use of questions to increase your power.

1. The quality of your questions determines the quality of the answers

Poor-quality questions result in vague and unclear answers, but quality questions seldom happen by chance – they need to be prepared in advance.

One of my favourite examples to show the consequences of poor questions is from the Peter Sellers movie *The Pink Panther Strikes Again*. In the movie, the Peter Sellers character, Chief Inspector Jacques Clouseau, is standing at the reception desk of a hotel and sees a dog lying next to the front door. 'Does your dog bite?' asks Inspector Clouseau of the man at the desk. 'No,' answers the man. Inspector Clouseau bends down to pat the dog, which promptly growls and sinks its teeth into his hand. Shocked, he exclaims, 'I thought that you said your dog does not bite!' '*Oui*,' responds the man, 'but that is not my dog.'

The whole point of asking questions is to explore the boundaries of the deal (what we will later refer to as the 'Ball Park') and to find out what the other person wants and needs from a deal. Asking quality questions that are well constructed and carefully considered is a whole lot smarter than asking vague, poorly anticipated questions.

2. Do not feel uncomfortable asking for sensitive information

When was the last time you asked someone for the date by which they would be making a decision, or the amount of their budget, or how much another supplier had quoted? Most of us are guilty of avoiding this type of question, partly because we might not want to hear the answer, but also because we are uncomfortable asking for sensitive information.

To my mind, there is an arrogance in not asking for sensitive information. The person asking the questions decides, on behalf of the person being interviewed, whether the interviewee will be comfortable answering a question. This is how adults tend to treat children! Give the other person the choice as to whether they want to answer a question or not.

If you know *how* to ask questions correctly, there is very little another person – even a complete stranger – won't tell you. My colleagues and I experiment with this all the time, and we are continually shocked by what people will disclose if they are questioned properly.

Can you imagine having the power to ask anyone anything and know that they will answer you honestly? It's not as hard as you might think. The skill is in *how* you ask the difficult questions, and here's how:

- The question must be absolutely clear and not longer than one sentence.
- Use direct, plain language – do not clarify, expand or explain.
- Look the person directly in the eyes when you ask the question.
- If they repeat the question to you or rephrase it, just nod.
- *Wait* for them to answer – do *not* elaborate, look away, fidget or even blink.
- Give them up to one minute to answer.
- If they do not offer you an answer, repeat the question and wait another minute.
- Thank them for their openness once they have answered.
- If they choose to deflect or not answer the question, respect their choice.
- Avoid interrogating them, whether they have answered or not.
- Move straight on to the next subject – one that is less contentious.

Even if the person you are questioning has read *Deal Diva*, where I first shared this technique, they will still answer you. The psychology behind this questioning style is interesting. When you ask the question, the other person (presumably) knows the answer, and it is the pressure of your directness and the discomfort of the silence that encourages the answer to pop out of their mouths.

Be wary of using this procedure with your loved ones. Firstly, if you think someone you love is hiding something from you or lying to you, no matter how you ask the questions, they will not tell you something they do not want you to know. The reason is that they will consciously already be blocking this disclosure, so they're unlikely to let anything slip. Secondly, do you really want or need to know what is going on in the minds of those nearest and dearest to you? Let them have their privacy. They will share when they are good and ready.

From a dealmaking perspective, you owe it to yourself to ask the difficult questions – let the person you are asking decide whether they want to answer or not.

3. Interesting people are interested

Think about the last event you attended where you did not know everyone, and try to remember whom you found most interesting. Think about your interaction with that person. Fifty bucks says they asked you lots of questions about you – and listened to the answers!

Asking, 'So what do you do?' is possibly the most inane question anyone can pose. Does it matter? Are people not more interesting than the work they do? If someone asks this of me, even at a networking event, I quickly move along. There is no way that someone who asks this question will be interested in me (or anyone else), or interesting to talk to, or well connected, for that matter.

People are, in the main, surprisingly intriguing. Try to find out something interesting about everyone you meet from now on. What you will discover is that suddenly everyone wants to know more about *you*.

Ask questions along the lines of:

- If you were a superhero, who would you be?
- Which is the best or worst place you have ever visited? Why?
- If money was no object, what would you be doing with your life?

- Do you have a 'life list' (or 'bucket list')? What is number one on your list?

Thinking up the questions is half the fun!

If you are in doubt about the effectiveness of asking interesting, direct questions, the following research proves the point. In his fascinating book *Quirkology*, Dr Richard Wiseman cites a study that he and two academic colleagues did in association with the Edinburgh International Science Festival to find the best chat-up lines. As with many of his projects, this one was conducted in the real world, and revolved around a large-scale, experimental, speed-dating event. A few months before the event, Dr Wiseman and his team issued a media appeal for single people wanting to participate in a study exploring the science of seduction. They received about 500 replies, and invited 100 arbitrarily selected participants (50 men and 50 women) to what Wiseman called the 'love laboratory'.

Here is the study (edited):

> The event took place in a ballroom at one of Edinburgh's most palatial hotels. At the start of the evening our one hundred participants arrived, and were randomly seated at one of five long tables. At each table, men were seated on one side, and women on the other.
>
> Each person was asked to chat to the person opposite them. Three minutes later, their time was up and everyone was asked to rate their potential beau. Did they find them physically attractive? What was the level of 'chemistry' between them? Would they like to meet the person again? A few moments later, everyone was paired up with a different person, and the entire procedure was repeated.
>
> Two hours, and ten speed dates later, the experiment was over. The following day we entered more than 1,500 pages of data into a giant

spreadsheet. Wherever two people had indicated that they would be happy to meet again, we sent them each other's telephone numbers. Around 60 per cent of those attending walked away with the contact details of at least one other person. Some people did really well, with about 20 per cent getting the details of four others. Women proved to be about twice as picky as men, but the top-rated man and woman of the evening had a 100 per cent success rate, with all of their dates wanting to meet them again.

To uncover the best chat-up lines, we compared the conversations of participants rated as very desirable by their dates with those seen as especially undesirable. The most memorable line from the top-rated man was: 'If you were on *Stars in Their Eyes*, who would you be?', whilst the top-rated female asked 'If you were a pizza topping, what would you be?'[6]

The worst chat-up lines? 'Do you come here often?', 'I have a PhD in computing', and 'My friend is a helicopter pilot'.

Are the two top-rated questions not infinitely more interesting than, 'So what is it that you do?' or, 'Where do you work?'

Being a skilled questioner will not only help you to close better deals, but will make you luckier in love. How about that?

6. In case you are wondering, *Stars in Their Eyes* is a British television programme in which contestants impersonate a show-business celebrity of their choice.

SECRET #18 Plan and execute questions with care and love
Planning which questions you want to ask and how you are going to ask them, and being direct and interested, will get you the information you need for a deal. The intelligent use of this knowledge provides you with the power to close a favourable deal.

DEVIL #18
Firing off a string of questions in the hope that some of them will hit the target and extract the information you need is not good use of your opportunity to ask questions of the other party. Badly planned questions encourage clams.

SECRET #19
LISTENING AND SILENCE REVEAL THE TRUTH

What is it about business – and life – today that so much is said and so little heard? Have we forgotten how to listen, how to *hear* what the other person is saying? To what extent is it the responsibility of the person speaking to grab and hold the attention of the person to whom they are talking? Is it all about ears, or can you listen with your eyes, or your intuition?

In their definition of 'communication', www.thefreedictionary.com makes no mention of the word 'listening'. Neither does www.oxforddictionaries.com. If you search www.amazon.com for books on listening, there are 15 476 results. That seems like a lot, until you search for books on communication (255 727). And most of the books on communication, selling and negotiation I scanned seem to be missing their chapters on listening.

What is the impact of listening, or not listening, on dealmaking? A dealmaker is supposed to be a skilled communicator able to bring closure to a deal, usually to the benefit of all parties. How can we possibly know what the other party wants unless we ask them, and then listen to what they have to say?

When we don't listen properly, the whole communication process goes to the hounds. We don't pick up the clues and signals we need to assess the other party's flexibility and issues. This means that our ability to make proposals and close the deal is compromised. Why not just listen in the first place? Surely this is easier than trying to figure out what is going on afterwards?

To make matters worse, research shows that the average listener understands and retains about half a conversation, and that this retention rate drops to 25 per cent after two days. The implication is that when we don't (or can't) listen properly, our ability to recall a conversation that took place more than 48 hours before is incomplete and unreliable.

Listening is not as automatic as you would think. To listen, to really hear, what is being said and suggested, you need to be fully present in the conversation. Not just in body, but in mind! You should not be wondering if you locked your car, or thinking about what you want for dinner. Being a good listener does require practice.

You need to be fully engaged in the conversation, or 'in the moment' in New Age language. Don't just go through the motions of listening. Listen to the words being used, and to their context. Listen to what is *not* being said, watch the person's expressions and body language, their eye movements.

This does not mean that you are passive in the listening process. You should be showing the person with whom you are talking that you are listening – nod, ask questions, encourage them to continue – without interrupting their flow.

Never underestimate the power of silence. Carry on listening when nothing is being said. Don't feel that you need to fill a space with words, or that you must ease any tension created by silence. Learn to be comfortable with silence.

In Secret #18, you were given tips on how to extract information, even sensitive information. One of the points is *keep quiet after you have asked a question*. When you do this, you will find that the other person will start talking, mostly because they're uncomfortable with the silence – and out will come the information you need.

Mark Twain (American author and humourist, 1835–1910) famously said, 'If we were supposed to talk more than we listen, we would have two mouths and one ear.'

SECRET #19 Listening and silence reveal the truth

Question. Listen. Pause. Think. Speak.
Repeat.
Repeat.
Repeat until you know what you need to do to close the deal.

DEVIL #19

Passive listening – in one ear and out the other – is just as pointless as not listening at all. Practise active listening – keeping quiet but being fully involved in the conversation.

SECRET #20
LONG-TERM RELATIONSHIPS CAN BE COSTLY

While on the subject of power, we are going to move away from information for the moment and concentrate on the importance of relationships.

Any idea what the acronym TINSTAAFL means? If you guessed 'There is no such thing as a free lunch', well done. It is a popular old adage (so popular that it has its own acronym) and means it is not possible to get something at absolutely no cost. Apparently, the 'free lunch' refers to the nineteenth-century practice in America of offering free lunch to entice drinking customers into bars. From what you have read in this book so far, you should realise that nothing has been said that contradicts this old chestnut. The renowned economist Campbell McConnell believes that TINSTAAFL is 'at the core of economics'. The authors of *Freakonomics* would no doubt agree.

It is possible to persuade someone to give you what you want with no anticipation of a return, or for you to make concessions and demand nothing back. But, at an unconscious level, the giver believes the receiver is indebted to them in some way. This could be as simple as expecting gratitude from the other person, or perhaps a sense of self-fulfilment from the gesture.

Much has been said about the power of relationships in business books. There is no doubt that having a good relationship with someone can help to smooth the path of business, but do not for one moment think that these relationships do not cost you anything. TINSTAAFL, after all. The subject of *what* motivates different people is discussed in Secret #34, but there are a multitude of reasons *why* people revere relationships.

Think about this relative to your own life and the individual business relationships that you value. What is it that makes them important to you? Could it be that you get what you need from the other person (orders, stroking, connections, companionship, information, mentoring – the list is endless)? Can you honestly say that you expect nothing from the relationship? Why, then, do you have the connection? Drill down deeper and you will find that you *are* getting value from the relationship – even if this is just that it makes you feel good.

If you are uncomfortable with acknowledging this about yourself, perhaps in the same way the *Indecent Proposal* example pressed buttons in Secret #5, it's time to take a reality check. Every single human being, even the Mother Teresas of the world, is motivated by a personal need – it is this motivation that makes us human. Our compassion, need for approval, self-respect, whatever it is, makes us feel better about ourselves. For some of us, it might be material reward, such as driving an Aston Martin, while for others it could be emotional, like doing community service. Regardless of how this satisfaction is achieved, our primary motivation is self-esteem-related. If you have any doubt about this, read one of the books or papers by Abraham Maslow (American professor of psychology, 1908–1970) in which he postulates his hierarchy-of-needs theory.

Recognising the return you get from a relationship does *not* make you a 'bad' person, it makes you a 'human' person. Now, in the same way as you value your relationships with others, people will value their association with you. It is through these mutual relationships that people feel connected to the world and to each other.

One of the seminal works on relationships in business is *The Trusted Advisor* by David Maister, Robert Galford and Charles Green, in which the theory of being a 'trusted advisor' in business is seen as the definitive affiliation, particularly with regard to customers. A trusted advisor is supposedly someone who is selfless in the input or feedback they offer (as in, you may have to advise against your own product – try telling your team that you told a customer *not* to buy!), a concept that is perhaps a bit naive and idealistic, and potentially expensive.

Let's assume, though, that 'trusted advisor' represents the ultimate relationship in business. What about the lesser relationships? Do these not count? Of course they count. There are lots of levels of relationship – from trusted advisor to fleeting acquaintance. The question is, though, how does the quality of your relationship affect your ability to close a deal with the person concerned?

By nature, I am a generous person. Whether I learnt to be generous because I see it as a good quality, or I justify my generosity on the basis that it is a good quality, is irrelevant. I am happy to give – it is one of my Love Languages (to understand this concept, read Gary Chapman's enlightening book *The Five Love Languages*). What I find, however, is that the closer I am to someone, the more generous I'm inclined to be – I move away from the principle of giving to get.

If I am completely and brutally honest with myself, I suspect that my generosity stems from a desire to be appreciated and favoured. So, I *do* get some value at an emotional level. Being generous is directly linked to my return on the free lunches offer.

This, however, does not always serve me well in business. I make unnecessary concessions to those to whom I am attached or with whom I have long-term relationships. No doubt many trusted advisors do the same thing, which does not make for good dealmaking. It is thus easier for me to close a deal with and get tangible value in return from someone I don't know very well.

In being brave and baring my soul, the point is not just to show you how dumb I can be – it is to encourage you to find the same chinks in your armour when it comes to dealmaking and relationships. What is your Achilles heel? Where do you lose the plot?

So, is there value and power in a long-term or trusted-advisor relationship? There are two answers – a quick one and a more complex one.

The quick one – if you have a *mutually beneficial and respectful* relationship, there will inherently be a willingness to co-operate and look after one another. If this is not happening, bad news: the relationship is one-sided and needs to be re-evaluated.

The more complex answer? To maximise the return on the investment you make in a long-term or trusted-advisor relationship, you need to take a holistic view (think Dirk Gently). Research shows that you *are* more likely to get more business for a longer period of time if you have a relationship built on mutual trust, but this does assume you will make concessions and offer 'free' lunches along the way. If you find that you are offering up lots of carrots, but you're seeing little in the way of returns, again the relationship is lopsided in terms of value and power, and needs to be relooked. The essence of dealmaking is that both parties, ideally, get what they want from a transaction.

When it comes to closing deals by getting what you want through giving the other person what they want, relationships can be a liability. Firstly, as a trusted advisor, you are sometimes expected to go against your human nature – which is to look out for number one. Secondly, as a generous or kind person, you could be inclined to just give and give and give. Thirdly, if you are someone who avoids conflict, you probably offer concessions without making any demands on the other party in the relationship. These three behaviours are the same as those displayed by *un*skilled dealmakers.

To stop the negative return and to get the relationship onto a level playing field, you need to trade value for value. In a strong relationship, where the return could be over a longer period, both parties still need to understand that there is no free lunch, that a *mutually* respectful relationship is based on quid pro quo.

What about personal relationships? Should you be extracting value when you give your partner a birthday present? All will be revealed in Secret #50.

SECRET #20 Long-term relationships can be costly

Not all long-term relationships are necessarily beneficial. You need to ensure continually that there is a mutual and fair exchange of value within a medium-term time frame. If this is not happening, you need to adjust the power by changing your dealings with the relevant party to explicit value-for-value exchanges.

DEVIL #20

Don't let the vanity of being a trusted advisor keep you in a one-sided relationship. There is no way the other party will respect you if they can play you.

SECRET #21
NOT ALL NETWORKS ARE EQUAL

Still on the subject of relationships, let's talk about your business network. You have no doubt been taught that it's not what you know, it's who you know. Do you agree with this sentiment? Does this mean that if you have lots of friends on Facebook, you have a good network?[7]

Before you rush off to celebrate how popular you are because you have 200 Facebook friends, there is a big difference between social-media networks like Facebook and Twitter, and even LinkedIn, and the real people (not avatars) with whom you have regular face-to-face contact.

While the textbook and online definitions of 'networking' make no distinction between the virtual and real people in a network, in dealmaking there is a significant difference. You may well get information about a deal from your online friends, but it is through direct contact that you will be able to change the course of a deal.

The three burning questions people tend to ask about networks in dealmaking are the following: Why is networking so important in dealmaking? How many people should be in a real-life network? Who should be in a network?

1. Why is networking so important in dealmaking?

If you had to hazard a guess, what would you answer? Dirk Gently would have seen it as Secret #15. It's all about the interconnectedness of information, and the power that information and knowledge generate.

7. According to www.facebook.com, the average user in 2011 had 130 friends.

Knowing the issues and concerns of the other party in a deal allows you to understand what they are likely to want from a transaction. First prize is always to ask the person directly for this information, but they may not be willing, for whatever reason, to share this with you. Second prize is to ask someone close to them for the information. And if they won't tell you? You have to spread your questioning circle a bit wider – to your network. Yes, you could ask your LinkedIn contacts, but are they likely to share what could be personal or confidential information with you in a public forum? *Non.*

The more people with whom you are personally connected, the more likely you are to know someone who has the information you need. And the whole point of getting information is so that you can meet the needs and wants of the other person in the transaction. If you know what these are, you can often address their issues in a way that costs you a lot less time, money and effort.

2. How many people should be in your real-life network?

The answer to the first question should give you insight into this question. The more the merrier is the obvious answer, but quantity does not equate to quality. Also bear in mind what has already been said about relationships, particularly long-term relationships. They are not a one-way street. If you use your network to get information but you do not service your network or share information from your side, your network will slowly die.

Having a big network is a powerful benefit. People can connect you with the decision-makers you need to know to get the deals you want; they can give you information vital to your success (or which protects you from failure); and they can support you and promote your products or services. But there is a reciprocal responsibility attached to a network: TINSTAAFL.

A network is all good and well, but it is the substance of your network that counts. When you start developing your network, you may not be able to differentiate between a contact and a valuable contact. That's fine – don't give up. As your network grows, you will learn to distinguish between who is nice to know and who you need to know to help you in your business and your deals. Valuable contacts tend to become part of your life in general.

To build your network, look at your personal relationships, your business contacts, your colleagues, customers, suppliers, people you meet at networking events, book clubs, golf clubs, wherever. It does take time and effort, but having a strong network will serve you well.

3. Who should be in your network?

Should your network only comprise people who have power and influence? The truth is we don't always know the real extent of a person's sphere of authority. I have met plenty of executive assistants who had significant – and I mean *huge* – influence over the person to whom they reported. So be careful of excluding someone on the basis of their job title. As we already know, people are far more interesting than the work they do.

My rule of thumb for choosing my real-life network is 'like-minded and interesting people'. This is pretty arbitrary because it is hard to measure and define. For me, it means people who (as far as I can ascertain) have a common approach to business, have similar values, are prepared to share, are people I have actually met (no strangers), people I think I can trust (if they disappoint me on this, they are *so* off my birthday-card list), people with whom I am happy to share a lunch … you get the picture. You need to determine your own criteria for selecting and maintaining your real-life network – whatever works for you.

You may have noticed that, when it comes to my real-life network, I do not distinguish between a business network and a private network. Networks are face-to-face personal relationships, which means that business and personal inevitably become intertwined. I find it difficult to keep them separate. But that is me – and the same for the like-minded people in my network. Incidentally, I do not have a Facebook profile, although I do have one on LinkedIn. I would rather invest my time in meeting with real people.

The book *999 Legendary Selling for the 21st Century* by Australian author Terrie Anderson is one of the most insightful publications on people (and selling) I have read. My company gives so many of these books away that we now print the title under licence. In her book, Terrie talks about the power of the face-to-face encounter. It is really worth a read. Making sustainable human connections will start with a first impression and should grow into a supportive professional relationship that can last a whole career.

By now you are probably wondering how building a network differs from building relationships. Your network is made up of lots of personal (not cyber) connections. These relationships occur at different levels of maturity, trust and intimacy – some are long-standing and close, others new, and several tenuous.

There is a saying about relationships that goes: 'People come into your life for a reason, a season or a lifetime.' The same can be said about networks. They are dynamic, they grow and die, mature, and are replenished. Relationships are at the heart of a network.

Do you have a small reservation that using a network is tantamount to abusing other people? Using your network and not reciprocating is abusing people, but don't worry too much about this, because if you take and do not give anything back, you will soon have no one in your network.

If you are still a Doubting Thomas, read any books written by or about the best business leaders in the world. Each and every one of them will espouse the value of having a big and wide-ranging network.

SECRET #21 Not all networks are equal
A large network of well-connected people with whom you have direct, personal relationships is a powerful resource. Use your network to get the information you need to optimise and close your deals.

DEVIL #21
Networks need to be mutually beneficial and nurtured. If you are not the sharing kind, don't be surprised when your network shrivels up and dies.

SECRET #22
TAKING TIME TO THINK IS NOT A WEAKNESS

A Funny Thing Happened on the Way to the Forum (a stage musical by Stephen Sondheim, based on the book by Burt Shevelove and Larry Gelbart), philosophically speaking. Somewhere, somehow, people started thinking that if the other party called an adjournment or timeout on the way to the deal, they had the adjourning side on the run. Strangest notion this, because taking the time out to think strengthens your position rather than weakens it.

Professional dealmakers make extensive use of adjournments. Interestingly, the higher up the organisational tree someone is, the more they make use of adjournments. It is at the middle-management level that people seem to hold the distorted view that taking time to catch one's breath is a weakness.

A timeout allows you to reconsider your position. It offers you the opportunity to pause and reflect, the time to think, to calm down if necessary, to consolidate, to consult, to re-strategise, and to check your agenda. As you can see, there are plenty of benefits to an adjournment. The downside to the person calling the timeout? None that I can think of other than if it is too long, it becomes a postponement as opposed to a timeout – which is not really a negative (see Secret #4 for the implications of a postponement).

What are the circumstances under which you may want to adjourn? Firstly, you could have received information during a meeting that significantly impacts your deal. Carrying on regardless with your pre-prepared strategy, or ignoring the information because you have not anticipated it, is simply dumb. Time and again, I see this brainless behaviour in the smartest of people.

Secondly, someone may make you a proposal that you need time to consider (maybe to do the calculations, or consult with other members of your team). Again, you need to withdraw.

Thirdly, if someone is putting pressure on you, or resorting to bullying tactics or aggressive behaviour, removing yourself from the situation will serve you well. Also, when situations get emotional, it is far better to 'get the hell out of Dodge' than to stick around.

Breaks can take the form of a brief caucus, a timeout, an adjournment, a postponement, rescheduling and many other variations. The point is that one (or both) of the parties needs to stop the meeting or proceedings for a while. This 'while' could be anything from a few moments on the other side of the room to another meeting at another time and place.

Taking a break can be a formal or an informal activity. There might be specific allowances made in an agenda, or an impromptu halt to the meeting – maybe coffee or pressure breaks, a respite overnight or agreeing to resume on a different date. You need to choose the format appropriate to the situation in which you find yourself. Regardless of what you choose, get out as and when you need to.

There should not be a limit to the number of timeouts you take. Use them as you need them, even if it means that you feel a bit like a jack-in-the-box, jumping up and down every few minutes. It is better to have a quickie than nothing.

How you call an adjournment is up to you, but it usually depends on the tone of the meeting. It may be a casual suggestion, a formal request or an unequivocal demand. How long it lasts also depends on the situation, but take as long as you need. Timeouts are powerful, so you don't want to compromise them by cutting short your breathing space.

The side that calls the timeout usually leaves the room, as they know how long they need to be gone. If this means that you leave someone in your office, be aware that they may read your papers. Even if the intention is not to snoop, people are curious, or they get bored, so be careful.

There are a few 'clever dicks' who will try to prevent you from taking a break. They might threaten that if you leave their office, you leave forever, or that if you leave they will take it as a sign of bad faith. The best possible response on your part is to leave respectfully, or, at worst, take a vow of silence for the remainder of the meeting – which is a mini timeout in its own right!

Staying in the meeting when you need a break is dangerous. Think about when you have been suckered into going to a timeshare sales pitch (I say 'suckered', because most people I know have gone unwittingly or been misled). The spell the salesperson casts is broken if you leave, so they do everything they can to keep you at the meeting. Simon and I nearly bought timeshare in Mexico – something we were unlikely ever to use on account of us living on the other side of the world – because we fancied the 'free' breakfast. There we were, hungry and trying to save our pitiful travelling allowances, but on the verge of buying a share in an apartment that we didn't need or want, and most certainly couldn't afford.

Of course this has never happened to you, because you do understand the power of timeouts and you would never have gone for the 'free' breakfast in the first place!

SECRET #22 Taking time to think is not a weakness

Giving yourself the opportunity to think about information and proposals during a deal will always serve you well. A timeout has similar power to a postponement. Use as many timeouts as you need.

DEVIL #22

Sales magicians and devilish dealmakers will try to pressure you into making a decision before you have the opportunity to think everything through. Delay your decision until you are sure of what you want.

SECRET #23

POWER CAN BE CREATED FROM VERY BASIC SOURCES

In dealmaking, one of the most obvious – and most overlooked – sources of power is knowing what you want. You would be alarmed to learn how many people go into a deal not having the foggiest idea of what they want to achieve or how they are going to get it. You may have your own system of defining what you want to accomplish in a deal, but just in case you would like to see a particularly effective tool, this is covered in Secret #27.

Over and above knowing what you want, it is possible to make power from next to nothing. A lot of people just don't know where to look. It might be right before their eyes but they can't see it. It's a bit like me and cooking. My talents in this area are deeply buried. I look in the cupboard and see nothing to eat. Simon will look in the same cupboard and see endless possibilities.

There are lots of ways to make power from a seemingly empty cupboard in dealmaking. The ones we have not yet considered are the four below:

1. Get your mind around quid pro quo.
2. Who really needs the deal?
3. Perceptions of you – your authority, legitimacy, knowledge, credibility and appearance.
4. Language and word power – if, if, if…

1. Get your mind around quid pro quo

How many times have I mentioned negotiating or trading or giving to get or quid pro quo or 'if you don't ask, you don't get' or 'ask and ye shall receive' in some form or another? To be a powerful dealmaker, you must embrace the principle of 'give to get' as if you were a six-year-old child.

The childlike mindset of being flexible, creative and relentless is crucial when you are battling to establish your power in a deal, or when you are in a genuinely weak position. The weaker your position, the more you will need to focus on trading – offering incentives (carrots) to get what you want in return. There is inherent power in the trading process, and trading is driven by proposals. To be a brilliant dealmaker, you need to make proposals and to respond to proposals – and this means having a lot more than only one or two carrots with which to negotiate.

The skilled dealmaker, like a kid, will always come to the table with lots of variables and options. The trick, of course, is to think about your incentives *before* you start the deal, as even an expert dealmaker will struggle to think up variables on the spot.

2. Who really needs the deal?

What does it say about your level of power if you can't walk away? Fundamental to power is establishing which side needs the deal more. It obviously stands to reason that the side really needing the deal is in the weaker position. Sometimes there is little you can do to change this situation, so if it is *you* who needs the deal more than the other party, you should spend as much time as you can looking at all the ways in which you can increase your power.

For example, consider whether you are prepared to take a risk or not – high risk, high reward? Taking a risk might pay dividends, but don't rush in – weigh up the pros and cons and then take a calculated risk. Doing something different can give you the edge.

When it comes to monopolies, we often have no choice but to do business with them. They have all the power, so they get to dictate the terms. Monopolies, like cartels, are renowned for holding their customers – and business partners – to ransom. It's the same with sole suppliers, whose power is the fact that their product is not available anywhere else. What happens to the monopolies and sole suppliers when the tide turns and competition enters the market? Power does shift. Think back to the Mexican drug-war example and how the power is shifting from the one cartel to the other.

The opposite of the monopoly is someone who can choose from any number of suppliers and who then proceeds to play one supplier off against the others to drive down price or improve the terms of the deal. To increase your power, are you able to use sole supply or competition? This may not seem fair, but it is used every single day by companies and individuals alike to strengthen their positions in their deals.

3. Perceptions of you

Whether you like it or not, your personal authority, legitimacy, knowledge, credibility and appearance influence your power. The more authority and legitimacy you have – as recognised by the other party – the greater your power. Perception is reality, so if the other party does not see you as having the necessary level of authority or influence, your power is undermined.

Credibility and appearance are also significant factors in influencing personal power. If you don't look and act the part, if your credentials are not up to scratch, your power is damaged. It might be okay for Sir Richard Branson to pitch up at a meeting in his gardener's work togs, but until you have his legitimacy, you need to make the best of your physical appearance. You are what you wear. You are how you look. Like it or not, if you want to be taken seriously, you need to communicate this through your appearance.

People have lost deals, job offers, sales, contracts and more because they didn't polish their shoes.

Regarding credibility, can you see the connection between power and self-promotion? Do not be too modest in establishing your credentials, but be careful of puffery and self-importance. As with liars, nobody enjoys a self-opinionated, pompous git, but a bit of well-positioned self-marketing can be very valuable. Even better, get someone to recommend you to the other party (think networking).

The most effective way in which you can positively impact your personal authority, legitimacy, credibility and appearance is through your knowledge. People respect someone who actually knows what they are talking about. Those who take the time and trouble to get the appropriate information are respected, as are the people who invest in their knowledge base. Your knowledge is well within your power to improve.

4. Language and word power

You might think it logical that words are *less* important when you are doing deals across culture and language boundaries, or that in society today, where it's okay to say 'gr8' rather than 'great', words are losing their significance. Not so. Until we master telepathic communication, words rule.

Words and semantics (the meaning of words) will always hold power, especially when you are communicating with someone who does not share your mother tongue. The words you use can have a direct effect on those you wish to influence. Think about Martin Luther King Jnr's (American clergyman, activist and leader, 1929–1968) 'I Have a Dream' speech, or Winston Churchill's 'We Shall Fight on the Beaches' speech, or, more recently, Barack Obama's (44th American president, 1961–) 'A New Beginning' speech in 2009.[8]

8. There's an excellent list of the world's great speeches on www.wikipedia.com.

In dealmaking, the most important word is 'if'. We dealt with this in Secret #3, but to summarise: 'if' suggests conditions, 'if' suggests trading, 'if' is the centre of all power when you are negotiating or trading. Don't leave home without it.

A power summary

When you are negotiating from a position of weakness, you need to do as much as you can to increase your power. Here is a recap of ideas we have already examined, as well as a few new ones, to help you find power in your cupboard. Any improvement in your position is going to help you when it comes to closing the deal.

1. Persuasion is a potent and cheap way of getting what you want, especially if you use proposals based on Value Propositions.
2. Having alternatives gives you power. The more time you spend preparing and analysing the costs and benefits of all the options in a deal, the stronger your position. Having choices is Zen navigation at its best.
3. If you believe that the balance of power may shift in your favour, postponing can give you an advantage. And don't hesitate to use timeouts as mini-postponements. They allow you to consolidate before you move forwards.
4. No one on the planet is so powerful or important that they do not have to do deals. Everyone has reasons for wanting to close (or avoid) deals.
5. Children, who have no real power, get what they want through being flexible, creative and persistent.
6. The more carrots you have that the other party wants, the greater your power. Value Proposition–based proposals maximise this power.
7. Use a SWOT analysis to assess and improve your position and your power.
8. Information is power, and converting information into knowledge is

even better. Controlling information, through giving and getting and questioning and listening, enables you to use information to close your deals.

9. Beware of too much debate when you are in a weak position. Avoid arguments and stick to trading when the other party holds more power than you.
10. It's not all what you know, it's also who you know. Relationships and networks give you access to information and power.
11. Get your mind around trading and negotiating. Just giving, or just getting, does not make for sustainable deals.
12. The more you need the deal, the less your control – and vice versa. When you really need the deal, you have to work hard to find ways of adjusting your power.
13. How others perceive you affects your power. This is influenced by your authority, legitimacy, knowledge, credibility and appearance. A little self-promotion goes a long way.
14. Choose the words you use carefully – and remember that 'if' is a deal-maker's 'power word'.
15. Do not multitask when you plan for a deal. Give your preparation your complete and undivided attention. Multitasking reduces your IQ points.
16. Playing baroque music (Mozart, Vivaldi, Albinoni, Handel) in the background enhances your memory, improves creativity and stimulates concentration and comprehension.
17. Stay emotionally detached – do *not* let the deal get personal. Personal ≠ power.

SECRET #23 Power can be created from very basic sources

Power can be used to gain an unfair advantage, so go for it. As a dealmaker, you need to check your position of power continually. Think like Simon the *cordon bleu* cook, and not Kim the noodle queen, when your cupboard appears to be empty of power. Go back to *The Basics*.

DEVIL #23

Buying into the belief that you have no power, or no means to adjust your power, is the Conan the Destroyer of the power you *do* have. Luckily there is a manipulative, wicked six-year-old inside all of us.

PART 3

THE PLAN

By failing to prepare, you are preparing to fail.

Benjamin Franklin

(American founding father and inventor, 1706–1790)

SECRET #24
STRUCTURE MUST FOLLOW STRATEGY

While Secret #14 focused on using planning as a means to create power, this chapter is dedicated to *how* to plan for a deal.

When a skilled dealmaker sets out to get what they want, they have a plan. They have thought through their strategy and the information they need to obtain for the deal. They have decided what their key issues and priorities are, where their opening position and bottom line need to be, and how to make the first move. They've determined who will be on their team (and figured out the other party's likely team), prepared arguments and proposals, and practised conversations with the other party in their head. They have even contemplated how they are going to close the deal.

Sounds like a lot of work, doesn't it? It can be, but it doesn't have to be. Are you familiar with the KISS principle? Keep It Simple, Stupid. I'm an avid believer in the power of KISSing. Why overcomplicate things? Why have convoluted models and theories when simple ones will achieve the same objectives?

If a process is too complicated or time-consuming, people tend to avoid it or not do it properly. Planning is really, really important and the consequences of avoiding it or cutting corners can be disastrous. So, in an effort to take the pain out of planning, we are going to look at the easiest possible ways in which you can plan for a deal – even for the deals that are a matter of life and death.

Where should one start when planning a deal? When I said skilled dealmakers have a plan, the next words were that they have thought through their strategy. But why start with strategy? Surely you need to know what you want before you can formulate a strategy?

Author and leading consultant William E. Rothschild provides insight into this dilemma. Here is his advice: 'What do you want to achieve or avoid? The answers to this question are objectives. How will you go about achieving your desired results? The answer to this you can call strategy.'

Why structure must follow strategy

Plenty has been written about strategy by much more illuminated and academic minds than mine. My frame of reference is the rough, tough world of business and of deals. So I have tried, in the interests of KISS, to simplify the subject of strategy and keep it focused on dealmaking.

A good place to start is with historian Dr Alfred DuPont Chandler Jnr (American academic and author, 1918–2007), who won a Pulitzer Prize for his work *The Visible Hand*. Dr Chandler was the first to suggest that structure follows strategy, based on his case studies of four American conglomerates that dominated their industries from the 1920s onwards. The companies he researched were Du Pont (chemical), General Motors (automobile manufacture), Standard Oil of New Jersey (energy) and Sears Roebuck (retail).

Dr Chandler showed that strategic shifts, driven by new technologies and market changes, required these companies to restructure. In simple terms, he found that one should only decide how something should be structured – whether this is a company, a battle plan, a deal, an argument, whatever – after the strategic objectives have been identified.

Assume you are starting a brand-new technology company. You have decided, because of your Microsoft skills and contacts, that you are going to set up a Microsoft Partner business. You are going to take off-the-shelf business solutions from Microsoft and customise these solutions to meet specific customer requirements. Where do you start?

Your first conversation obviously needs to be with Microsoft, to ensure that they will give you a partner licence. And the first thing Microsoft is going to want from you is a business plan. What do you want to achieve – your vision, mission and goals? How are you going to achieve your objectives? And what structure will you put into place to make this happen?

If your starting point is, 'Well, four of us have decided that we want to have our own business and we know Microsoft really well,' Microsoft is hardly going to be jumping up and down with excitement. They are more likely to interpret what you are saying as you and your three mates are rebellious mavericks but don't have a business brain between you. You have started with structure (the four of you) rather than strategy.

As a strategic thinker, you would say, 'Well, four of us have decided that we want to start a Microsoft value-add business because we know Microsoft very well. We will offer shorter development times than the industry norms, but through strict adherence to Microsoft's standards, our solutions will integrate easily into existing IT environments.' Which team would you pick as a business partner?

Visually, this is how your Microsoft Partner business plan might look:

STEP 1: Business strategy
(e.g. defined market, products, services, etc.)

↓

STEP 2: Sales strategy
(e.g. external 'go to market' sales force)

↓

STEP 3: Sales execution and tactics
(e.g. internal systems and processes)

↓

STEP 4: Negotiation strategy
(e.g. external pricing policies, etc.)

↓

STEP 5: Negotiation execution and tactics
(e.g. internal systems, team structure, etc.)

↓

STEP 6: Closed deals

↓

STEP 7: Implementation

When you go into any deal, you also need to have a strategy – one that outlines what you want, how you are going to achieve it – and then you look at your tactics and team, and so on.

Let's make the example with which we are working more relevant to your real life. Imagine you wanted to buy property – it could be an established house, a vacant stand, a game farm. The major factors in this deal are likely to be location, size, price and suitability. You will then set about looking for the property and engaging with the sellers.

The reason you need to consider these major factors for the deal (location, size, price and suitability) is because they form the basis of your strategy. You must have these in mind, otherwise you won't know what strategy to set. You must know that you are buying a property, not a boxing gym or a mobile home. You need to know that your company will be a Microsoft Partner business, not a hamburger joint.

If you had to draw a diagram for the strategic steps for your property, it would be surprisingly similar to the one above. Your big picture (business strategy) would define the price, location and size of the property. Your sales strategy and tactics could be along these lines: as you are in no urgent hurry to buy, you will take a long-term view of the market, watch which properties don't seem to be selling, wait for the seller to have (assumed) time constraints, and then go in with a cheeky offer.

Your negotiation strategy may be to start with a very low offer, without putting yourself too far out of the Ball Park, and then to move up if you have no choice. Your negotiating tactics would be that every time you have to increase an offer, you will ask for something to improve your deal – such as the seller leaves all their farm implements behind, or they include the existing wild game in the deal, or they pay the water and lights for an extra month or two.

Your 'closed deal' should, ideally, end up with you owning a property you want at a good price – your reward for planning properly. The implementation step is your actual occupation of the farm.

SECRET #24 Structure must follow strategy

When you go into a deal, you need to start with a strategy that outlines what you want and how you are going to achieve your objectives. Only once this is in place do you consider the structure of the deal and the team.

DEVIL #24

Do not be tempted to develop your strategy around an existing structure. This is like buying a pair of shoes you like, but which are the wrong size, and trying to squeeze your feet into them. You will never be able to walk properly.

SECRET #25
FOLLOW SIMPLE STEPS TO DEFINE THE DEAL

You now have a strategy to buy your game farm (I'm assuming it is a game farm-cum-sanctuary, as that's what I would want), based on the major factors or key issues you identified for the deal (location, size, price and suitability).

It is time to look at how you will achieve your objectives – you need to define your deal in detail. For the purpose of showing you an easy way to define a deal, let's stick with the game farm/sanctuary example.

The process of defining your deal has three steps. Nothing could be simpler.

1. Step One: the Issues
2. Step Two: the Ball Park
3. Step Three: the Players

We are going to cover these three steps in the next three Secrets, but here is a big-picture view.

1. The Issues

In Secret #10 we spoke about two types of incentives or carrots – big ones that relate to key issues, and small ones linked to secondary issues. When you start defining your deal, you will divide everything you want and need into critical (Key) issues and less important (Secondary) issues.

The other side, of course, also has Key and Secondary Issues, though they might not have clearly thought through this differentiation. The problem is that when you are working with an unskilled dealmaker, they may well deadlock or break the deal over an issue that is not terribly important. It will be up to you to help unskilled dealmakers to distinguish between their priorities.

2. The Ball Park

Earlier I referred to an effective tool that would help you to define what you want to accomplish in a deal. This is covered in detail in Secret #27, but for the moment, just bear in mind that you will need a Likely, a Bottom Line and an Opening position for each of your Key Issues. You also need to try to figure out these positions for the other party's Key Issues.

3. The Players

This is more about structure than strategy, but we will look at the composition of our team in Secret #29, and the roles of the other parties' group members in Secret #30. Who should we take along to help us to close the deal? Who would it be better to leave in the office and out of harm's way? What will the roles of each person in the team be?

We already know about a Vice Captain and their summarising responsibilities from Secret #15, but what about everyone else? Having a properly structured team when you do deals is a godsend.

SECRET #25 Follow simple steps to define the deal

Having an easy-to-use tool will make planning for a deal much easier. The three recommended steps are:

Step One: the Issues
Step Two: the Ball Park
Step Three: the Players.

DEVIL #25

Mike Tyson (American boxer and former undisputed heavyweight champion of the world, 1966–) said, 'Everyone has a plan – until they get punched in the face.' In defining the deal clearly, we can at least anticipate a lot of the punches.

SECRET #26
STEP ONE IS TO IDENTIFY AND PRIORITISE ALL ISSUES

Ready or not, we are going to start defining the Ball Park, using the two types of issues: Key and Secondary.

The *first task* in Step One is to identify *all* the Issues that would be relevant to this specific deal. The major factors (location, size, price and suitability) form part of this. In our game-farm example, I've added all the other Issues that I could think of without too much effort below. They are not in any specific order – just written down as they occurred to me. This process is called brainstorming.[9]

If you are doing a list for one of your real deals to practise this process, firstly, good on you, and, secondly, I recommend that you follow the same methodology.

1. Location (country, region)
2. Price
3. Size of property
4. Subdivisible?

9. In the United Kingdom, the word 'brainstorm' is considered politically incorrect because it could be offensive to epileptics. The British are required to say 'thought shower' or 'mind shower'. The people with epilepsy whom I canvassed for an opinion on this found it either hilarious or ridiculous, so I'm going to stick with 'brainstorm'.

5. Accommodation on property
6. Size of main dwelling
7. Conditions of buildings
8. Safety and security
9. Existing enclosures (game capture, release, etc.)
10. Existing facilities (clinic, hatchery, etc.)
11. Equipment included
12. Game included
13. Natural wildlife in area
14. Prior use – farming, commercial, sanctuary?
15. Quality of grazing
16. Power supply
17. Limitations around power
18. Access to water
19. Agreements in place re water
20. Water rights on property
21. Extent of fencing
22. Quality of fencing
23. Proximity to road
24. Roads on property
25. Access rights and limitations
26. Proximity to nearest:
    a. town
    b. neighbours
    c. airport or landing strip
27. Legislative restrictions
28. Government land-grab policies
29. Mining rights on land

30. Hunting permits in place
31. Obligations to existing staff
32. Cheetah-friendly
33. Storage space
34. Occupation date
35. Occupational rent

This is the list of Issues that came easily to mind. As you can see, I got to 35, but with a little application, I could probably reach 50 Issues.

The *second task* in Step One is to rank and prioritise the list, and you do that by picking out the Key Issues – those that are most important to you. Depending on the deal, the number of Key Issues can range from two or three to about five or six. Try to avoid having only one Key Issue. You are far more likely to clash swords or get into deadlock if you focus too closely on a single Issue.

The Key Issues are often the ones you thought of first – those that are front of mind. You will know when you have identified your Key Issues because there will be a big gap between the last Key Issue you think of and the next most important one. The Issues that are left are called the Secondary Issues. Put the Secondary Issues aside for the moment and let's go back to the Key Issues.

Below are what would be my Key Issues if I were looking for a game farm. I have also put them into order of priority (the original number from the list above is in brackets behind each item).

1. Location (1)
2. Price (2)
3. Size of property (3)

4. Accommodation on property (5)
5. Access to water (18)
6. Power supply (16)

Once you have identified your Key Issues (still parking the Secondary Issues for the moment), you are ready to enter the Ball Park. You could, at this stage already, start trying to work out the other party's Key Issues.

SECRET #26 Step One is to identify and prioritise all Issues
The *first task* in Step One is to identify all your Issues for a specific deal. The *second task* is to prioritise this list. You should have around three to five Key Issues. The balance of the list (which will be long) forms your Secondary Issues.

DEVIL #26
Resist the temptation to rush through this step. The more Issues you can identify during the planning stage of the deal, the easier it will be when it comes to engaging with the other party.

SECRET #27

STEP TWO IS TO KNOW THE LIMITS OF THE BALL PARK

Although you have your Key Issues in hand and your Secondary Issues safely parked, you are not quite ready to press the 'start' button on your deal. You first need to decide on your Ball Park.

The Ball Park is where you set the Likely, Bottom Line and Opening positions for each of your Key Issues. In our game-farm example, the Ball Park for the price would be the highest price you are prepared to pay for a property versus the lowest offer the seller will accept. This defines the boundaries within which the deal will be struck on that Issue. The Secondary Issues serve another purpose, so they will be positioned using a different format in Secret #28.

In the real world, you generally do not know the other person's high or low limits, so you have to focus on your own Ball Park. You should, however, try to 'best-guess' the other party's Ball Park. This is not very scientific, but dealmaking is a large part art and a small part science.

Determining the Ball Park takes time. You need to conduct research and give each Issue thought. In our example, you will need to know the price of similar game farms in the area, understand the market trends (e.g. are farm prices dropping because of land invasions or planned fracking, or are they increasing because of scarcity or an upswing in the economy?), guess at the urgency or reluctance of the seller, identify your own financial expectations and limits, and so on.

To define your Ball Park, you need to prepare the following positions for *each* of your Key Issues:

1. *Likely.* This is your target, or what you realistically expect to get (or pay, in the case of the game farm). Always start preparing your Ball Park using your Likely position.
2. *Bottom Line.* Prepare this second. It is your walk-away position, the point beyond which you will not go, your limit or minimum/maximum.
3. *Opening.* Do this one last. It is the best possible position you could imagine (i.e. the lowest possible price you would expect to pay for the farm). It still needs to be realistic, or you could find yourself 'outside the Ball Park'.

It is easiest to draw up your Ball Park in a five-column table format. Here is a basic example for the game farm.

Key Issues	**#**	**Opening** (do this last)	**Likely** (do this first)	**Bottom Line** (do this second)
Location	1	Karoo, South Africa	Karoo, South Africa	Karoo, South Africa
Price	2	R4 million	R5.5 million	R7.5 million
Size of property	3	5000 hectares	3000 hectares	2000 hectares
Main dwelling	4	Excellent condition	Good	Liveable
Access to water	5	Own water rights	Unlimited	Unlimited
Power supply	6	Grid and solar	Grid or solar	Solar

Try to draw a few conclusions about the table above, and then check your observations with the comments below.

1. *The Opening and Bottom Line positions must make sense.* You need to be able to substantiate where you open and where you walk away. In the example, I am pushing my luck at R4 million already, so opening lower would probably be outside the Ball Park and a waste of everyone's time. I also won't spend more than R7.5 million, as that is the highest price anyone has paid for a similar farm in the area.
2. *The range of 'location' is not flexible.* Position is my primary priority and I do not want any location other than the one I have chosen. Even if a fabulous farm becomes available elsewhere in the country, I would not be interested. I will keep looking in the Karoo until I find a suitable farm. Based on this, my Opening and Bottom Line positions are the same for location.
3. *The chance of all of the Opening Issues being achieved is not likely.* In my dreams would I find a game farm of 5 000 hectares for R4 million in the Karoo.
4. *Settling on all the Bottom Line items would be a terrible deal.* If I paid R7.5 million for 2 000 hectares in the Karoo, and achieved only my minimum on the other Issues, the deal *as a whole* would be a poor one. Going below my Bottom Line would mean I was compromising, which is unacceptable.
5. *The deal I am most likely to get will be a mix of my Opening, Likely and Bottom Line positions.* If I found a game farm in the Karoo for R5 million that had lovely accommodation and its own water supply but is only 2 000 hectares in size, I would be okay with the deal.

On average, the total value of your deal should be somewhere between your Opening and Likely positions. Your Likely position is your realistic expectation, so anything you can close that exceeds this is a good deal.

If you manage to get everything in the Opening column of your Ball

Park, you probably could have set higher goals. The Opening position is meant to test the limits of the Ball Park without breaking the deal. An analogy would be putting your house up for sale and getting your selling price immediately. You most likely didn't ask for enough money.

SECRET #27 Step Two is to know the limits of the Ball Park
For each Key Issue, you need to set a Likely, Bottom Line and Opening range. Your Opening position is the deal you would get in a perfect world, while Bottom Line is where you would walk away. Any deal *as a whole* that is higher than your Likely position is a good one. Less than your Bottom Line is an unacceptable compromise.

DEVIL #27
Unskilled dealmakers can easily destroy a deal by focusing on Issues that are not of prime importance, or by getting stuck on a single Issue. You need to stop this from happening by sticking to the Key Issues and considering the total value of the deal.

SECRET #28
USE MARBLES TO MAINTAIN THE BALL PARK

Even when you are armed with a broad strategy and a Ball Park for your Key Issues, you are not yet ready to start engaging with the other party. What about your long list of Secondary Issues?

A quick recap – the Key Issues in a deal equate to the big and important carrots, and the Secondary Issues to the smaller carrots. The Key Issues are the must-haves, and the Secondary Issues are the nice-to-haves.

Deals can be won or lost over the Key Issues, but the Secondary Issues should not be deal-breakers. If the other side is unskilled, they can mess up the deal by getting stuck on a Secondary Issue or by having only one Key Issue. Secondary Issues bring elasticity into the deal.

The Secondary Issues are variables that my organisation calls Marbles. The reason we chose the word 'marbles' is because it evokes almost everyone's childhood. And the more you can think like a six-year-old, the better you are going to be able to play with your Marbles. Marbles give you your flexibility, creativity and resilience. We will get to *how* to play with your Marbles shortly, but there is a baby step we need to take first, and that is to convert your Secondary Issues into Marbles.

Again, it is easiest to work with a table format, but for Marbles you have only three columns.

Secondary Issue	Marbles to get	Marbles to give

To make Marbles from the Secondary Issues, all the items that are still left on the list on pages 135 and 136 (all 29 of them) are used as a guide. Sort of like using carrots to bake a cake. Carrots on their own do not create a cake, but when combined according to a recipe, you get carrot cake. So, take the items from the list, apply a little creative thinking, and you end up with Marbles you can *get* from the other party and Marbles you can *give*, if need be.

This is how it works. Let's use 'Safety and security' (which was Point 6 on our brainstormed list) as the example. It's no good putting 'Safety and security' verbatim on the Marbles list, as there is not much the seller can do about this Issue. 'Guaranteed safety' is also meaningless. Note how I have used 'Safety and security' in the table below. Here's another one – 'Natural wildlife in area'. Again, the seller can't change the biosphere or fauna of thc region, but the concept 'Natural wildlife in area' can trigger some creativity on my side.

I have only done a few samples. Try to do the rest of the list yourself for practice. Be as outrageously creative as you can.

Secondary Issues	Marbles to get	Marbles to give
Safety and security	• They leave alarm system in buildings; or • Install alarm system in main house; or • Pay for radio alarm for three months after sale	• Take alarm system with them; or • You pay for radio alarm prior to ownership

Natural wildlife in area	• They source existing studies • They conduct or pay for a new study on natural rehabilitation	• Offer copy of studies you do (or source) to them
Subdivisible?	• They apply for subdivision before sale • They pay for subdivision • Sale subject to subdivision • If not subdivisible, price offered drops	• You apply for subdivision • They keep a piece of subdivision at discounted price • If subdivisible, price you offered increases
Existing enclosures	• Need to be built before occupation • Repairs done before sale is concluded • At their cost	• Can take materials with them • You pay for repairs or building • You wait until occupation to build

Have you got the idea? Practice makes perfect – even when it comes to creating lists of Marbles. (As an aside, you can usually increase an offer on a property, but seldom can you reduce it.) It is always a good use of time to try to figure out what Marbles the other party would like to see included on the list.

Now to the *how*. In an ideal world, you would be able to convince or persuade the other party to give you what you want – they get the product or service you are offering and you get your asking price. As you probably know from experience, deals tend not to close this perfectly. The other side often wants to negotiate with you – to get your price down, or for you to include more in the offer at the same price.

It is during negotiation, or trading, that your Marbles will come into play. There are three guidelines that you need to observe.

Firstly, always try to trade your Key Issues with their Key Issues, and only use the Secondary Issues and Marbles when you need to find additional value in the deal. If you are happy with the deal you strike on the Key Issues, leave your Marbles off the table.

Secondly, Marbles are there to give you negotiating leverage – they allow you to massage the deal into a package that offers you the value you want from the total transaction.

Thirdly, the power in getting what you want in a deal lies in giving the other side the value they want. This means that apart from your own agenda, you have to work with Key Issues and Marbles *they* value but that don't cost you too much, not the ones you want to concede.

Putting it back together

This is the practical application of what using the Key and Secondary Issues would look like, relative to our game-farm example.

A farm has come up for sale in the Karoo at R5.6 million. It is 1 800 hectares in size, has a main dwelling that is in an acceptable condition, does not have its own water source (just a loose arrangement with a neighbour), and has a generator that supplies power. If you compare this to your Likely position, it is not a terribly good deal. You need to improve it.

You counter-offer R4.7 million on condition that they put in *x* solar panels to boost the power, and that they pay for and get signed a legal agreement with the neighbour for unlimited water, which your attorney will approve. Or (and it can be an either/or proposal if you want) you offer R4 million for the farm as it stands. There is nothing either party can do about the land size, so you leave this out of the equation, but do include it in your arguments.

They may come back to you saying that at R4.7 million they will agree to the solar power, but not the water, and you must pay cash (i.e. the deal is not conditional on you getting a mortgage). The fact that a cash offer is required probably means that this is a Key Issue for them. Maybe they are cash-strapped?

You could counter their offer again by saying that water is a critical issue and you are not happy to pay R4.7 million without guaranteed water rights. If they can't get the water guaranteed, you want the power supply to be upgraded to solar *and* grid, and that for the transaction to be done in cash, you need a lower price. They then tell you the power company is not giving grid power to any more farms in the area. You say fine, but then the price drops to R4.25 million cash with only solar power. They counter that, over and above the purchase of the farm, you must buy the farm implements at book value, payable as soon as the deal is signed. *You can see you are now into trading Marbles.*

You might find that acceptable, on condition that the implements are in working order and you pay a price based on an independent valuation, and you want them to supply a study of the ecological biosphere of the area. They say that if you fund the study, you've got a deal. You finally accept on condition that you pay no occupational rent before you take ownership. They agree. *Resist the temptation to keep trading Marbles*, because at some point, one side will get greedy or unreasonable. Quit while you're in control.

Once you have a deal, you *must* summarise to make sure you have agreed to the same deal as the other side.

It may seem like a lot of effort to develop Secondary Issues and lists of Marbles when you might not use them in the end. But this is never a waste of time. Your Marbles are your protection against getting a raw deal. Your Marbles defend your value. Your Marbles give you flexibility. And you shouldn't need to postpone every time a deal moves off Key Issues so that you can go and prepare Marbles. Not only will you look clueless, but the power could, in the interim, shift against you.

SECRET #28 Use Marbles to maintain the Ball Park

The Key Issues are your must-haves, and the Secondary Issues your nice-to-haves. Trade your Key Issues with their Key Issues wherever possible, and only get into the Secondary Issues and Marbles should you need to adjust the value of the total deal.

DEVIL #28

Beating the other team up with your logic will not get you the deal. Think like a kid. Toss out logic and link unrelated Marbles – let them keep their tractor in exchange for buying you a cheetah.

SECRET #29

STEP THREE IS TO CHOOSE YOUR PLAYERS CAREFULLY

You got a sneak peak at the Players in Secret #25. The questions already raised were: Who should we take along to help us close the deal? Who would it be better to leave in the office and out of harm's way? What will the roles of each person in our team be?

My bold statement was that it is a godsend to have a properly structured team when you do deals. If your group does not know what it is doing, a complete nightmare will ensue. There are positives and negatives to being part of a team versus doing deals on your own, but having carefully structured and disciplined support does give you an advantage. This means, though, that you have to choose the most appropriate Players (as my organisation calls them).

Your choice of Players can have a dramatic impact on your power. The right people can positively affect the authority and legitimacy of your team. They can bring credibility and knowledge. They can, of course, also damage your deal.

Once we've looked at the structure of, and roles in, a team, we'll examine the upside and downside of going into deals on your own.

Firstly, when you go in with a team, be sure to select the group most appropriate to *that specific deal* – teams can and do change from deal to deal. If you are negotiating with the chief executive of a large organisation, you may consider taking your senior person along with you. Be warned: the top dogs like to be in charge, so even if they promise to sit quietly in the back and behave, in no time at all they will be running the show.

Similarly, if it is the monkeys and not the organ-grinders at a meeting, you may want to hold your big guns back to use at a more opportune time. If the other side brings in experts, such as lawyers or accountants, you should consider doing the same. Just a word on experts: they are so important that they have a secret all of their own (see Secret #31).

Irrespective of whether you are on your own or playing in a team, there are certain tasks that need to be performed in the deal. If you are on your own, these tasks don't disappear. You need to make sure that *you* execute all of them. If you are in a team, you can share these responsibilities with the other Players.

Cast your mind back to the Spanish squad that won the 2010 FIFA World Cup. They are also, incidentally, referred to as *La Furia Roja* (The Red Fury) or *La Roja* (The Red One). In the line-up, there were people with distinct responsibilities. There was Captain Iker Casillas, Vice Captain Carles Puyol, Coach Vicente del Bosque, and the Spanish national team selectors (Management).

No one tried to do the other person's job, except in the case of the Coach Vicente del Bosque, as he was also a selector. We did not, however, see Vicente del Bosque running onto the field to have a kick. We did not see Carles Puyol take over as captain because he thought he could do a better job than Iker Casillas. Maybe the selectors interfered, but as I said, that is what the bosses do.

In a dealmaking team, there are roughly five sets of tasks. As you read each one, think of the football or rugby squad. Obviously they are not exactly the same, but the association with a sports team will help you to define the responsibilities more easily. Here are the general tasks:

1. Captain (the dealmaker, leader or chief negotiator)
2. Vice Captain (the translator, summariser or controller)
3. Coach (the guide or observer)
4. Manager (the strategist or power base)
5. Expert Advisors (subject-matter authorities)

And here are their specific tasks.

1. The Captain

The Captain is like the queen on a chessboard. The Captain can really do pretty much what he or she wants, but this needs to be within the confines of the mandate. Unless they are Captain *and* Coach *and* Manager, they need to adhere to the outlines laid out by the Coach and/or Manager.

The Captain's main purpose is to lead the team in the deal. The Captain:

- leads the discussions and the deal as a whole;
- persuades and trades;
- makes proposals and responds to proposals;
- gives information and engages in debate; and
- closes the deal.

As the queen, the Captain has a fair amount of power, but as with chess or football, the Captain still operates within the designated role. If the Captain goes rogue, the consequences for the team can be disastrous.

Here is an example of bad captaincy from the 2010 FIFA World Cup, in an extract from an article titled 'World Cup 2010: Why Cristiano

Ronaldo is failing as Portugal captain' by Thomas Wood, written for www.guardian.co.uk:

> Ronaldo is an artist, a selfish player who enjoys the limelight. When an opportunity for a backheel arises where a simple pass would do, he would choose the former. Too often when tackled he is riled and will argue with the referee, leading his team to often follow his example. In 2006 when substituted at an away game for Manchester United at Benfica, Ronaldo replied to the fans' booing of him with the middle-finger salute. Later in the same year Wayne Rooney and England were the victims of his protestations.

No matter how talented the Captain might be as an individual, he or she needs to be able to lead the side, to motivate, discipline, guide and set an example to the team.

2. The Vice Captain

The Vice Captain is the wingman. He is Anthony Edwards's 'Goose' to Tom Cruise's 'Maverick', Tonto to the Lone Ranger, Robin to Batman. The Vice Captian is number two, the sidekick. The Vice Captain is not an attention-seeker, but without one, you figuratively get shot out of the sky. The Vice Captain is trustworthy and reliable.

One of the key attributes that the Vice Captain needs to display is objectivity. A Vice Captain is usually the voice of reason in the room (or on the field). If the other side doesn't have a Vice Captain and the deal is a tense and tough one, the danger of issues getting emotional or irrational is high. An objective Vice Captain helps to ensure that this does not happen.

The Vice Captain has three specific duties:

1. *Controls the process.* The more tightly the Vice Captain controls the

structure and processes of the deal, the less likely it is to go off track. Also, a systematic approach helps to take the emotion and tension out of a situation. The agenda is one of the procedures the Vice Captain controls.

2. *Asks the questions.* Although the Captain decides whether to *give* information or not, the Vice Captain is tasked with *getting* the information the team needs. This means that he or she must be sure that questions have been prepared before the meeting and that they actually get asked, and answered.
3. *Recaps and summarises.* Have another look at Secret #15 for the concepts of recapitulation and summarising. Summaries are intended to help move discussions forward and stop everyone from going round in circles. But for them to be meaningful, summaries have to be objective.

Summaries are intended to:

- give structure to the discussions;
- ensure the clarity and understanding of everyone;
- maintain focus on the most important issues;
- check what has been discussed and what still needs to be discussed;
- confirm areas of agreement and what still needs to be agreed upon;
- identify the markers – the milestones – in the discussions;
- buy the captain thinking time;
- calm down any tension – be the voice of reason; and
- make sure that everyone agrees on the details of the final deal.

Does the Vice Captain share information? No, the Captain does that. Does the Vice Captain make or respond to proposals? No, the Captain does that. Does he or she summarise proposals already on the table? Absolutely.

The Vice Captain does about a third of the talking for his or her side, which is about one sixth of the total talking. The Vice Captain's role is thus an active one, and he or she has to know what is going on, despite the gunfire rattling in his or her ears.

3. The Coach

The Coach is critical, vital and fundamental to the success of any team. Choosing the best possible Coach is often the difference between a winning side and a bunch of losers.

The sporting world understands this; the business world not so much. Have a look at what the world's top five sports coaches earn. This is an edited extract from an article by Tomas Aglinskas, published in 2010 on http://en.beterz.com:

The Top 5 Highest Paid Sports Coaches in the World

1. Luiz Felipe Scolari = US$24.05 million
   You take a legendary Brazilian soccer team to a World Cup win. The industry rewards you with a management position at Chelsea FC, one of the world's best clubs. What to do for an encore? Go coach in Uzbekistan, of course. Just imagine how much $24 million is worth there.
2. José Mourinho = US$16.3 million
   Mourinho is one of the most controversial and talented club managers in the world. He took Inter Milan's lower pay offer, but still turned them into a Chelsea-capable team. He will still be cussing at the refs in three different languages.
3. Fabio Capello = US$12.9 million
   When you manage the English national team, you get national kind of money. Capello guided the team to 2010 World Cup qualification. To the Brits, that is worth double the money.

4. Phil Jackson = US$10.3 million
   Jackson has coached the greatest players in the world (Jordan, Kobe) while managing to control the craziest players (Rodman, Shaq). He also navigated his way to nine NBA championships. Heck, he might deserve that $10 million per year – not that the 'Zen Master' cares about money.
5. Sir Alex Ferguson = US$10.2 million
   This legend has coached Manchester United since 1986. His team has won 11 Premier League, five FA Cup, three League Cup and two Champions League titles. Ferguson is widely considered one of the best football managers in the world.

The Coach is literally tasked with guiding the team. To do this effectively, he or she must watch and interpret the game, as well as the players on both sides, but resist the temptation to rush onto the field and play. The Coach is the ultimate active listener.

The problem is that the more the Coach observes, the more he or she knows about what is really going on in the game, so it is imperative to get the Coach's feedback – and this should be done during the timeouts or planning sessions. Having the Coach run onto the field diminishes his or her power – as soon as the Coach gets involved in the fray, the Coach's ability to observe is lost.

In dealmaking, the Coach listens carefully to the verbal communication, watches for the signals and clues, and observes the body language. He or she tries to figure out the other party's issues, needs and concerns. If the Coach can guide the Players to see what the other side needs, the team will be in a position to offer what the other guys truly want – which is often cheaper than guessing and then throwing carrots.

Incidentally, you can have more than one Coach. From a dealmaking point of view, the more people you have guiding you through the maze of a deal, the easier it will be for you to close the deal.

4. The Manager

Where the Coach is the guide, the Manager is the power behind the throne. The Manager does not always attend the meetings. As I said earlier, you need to decide when you want to include the big shots in your deal.

Although the Manager may not attend the meetings, he or she is involved in every deal, mostly from behind the scenes. The Manager ultimately decides strategy; selects, hires and fires the team members; determines the mandate (in other words, the Ball Park – where you open and where you walk away); and puts up the money or finds the budget.

While the Captain is the leader in the dealmaking encounter itself, the Manager still holds the final authority. If the Manager comes into the meeting, he or she usually expects to lead the meeting. This can put the Manager and the Captain in conflict. The Manager is not necessarily a very good player, and can easily mess up the Captain's carefully laid game plan. Even worse, the Manager can undermine and damage the Captain's credibility.

If you bring the Manager into a meeting, he or she must be carefully briefed so that they know what is expected of them and how you want them to behave. Use the five-column Ball Park document as the tool to brief the Manager.

5. The Expert Advisors

Being able to use Expert Advisors effectively is like managing a tightrope walker. One wrong move on their part and you could end up with a dead deal. In dealmaking, experts hold real sway over the balance of power. To do justice to their role, they are discussed in detail in Secret #31.

Whenever you have the luxury of using a team, jump at it, but choose your Players wisely. Your team members must understand the tasks they need to perform and be disciplined enough to stick to them. There is nothing more unsettling for the Captain than having talking Coaches, or a Vice Captain who takes over, or a Manager who interferes with or changes the mandate. A team is only valuable if they play the roles they're meant to play.

If you are the only member of your 'team', you need to be Captain, Vice Captain, Coach, Manager and Expert Advisor. You can't leave out a task just because you are alone. If ever you get the opportunity to practise one of the tasks on its own, take it. This is the best way to get to grips with each function that is required during a deal.

If there are two of you, maybe you and a partner or colleague, split the tasks between you – in a way that makes sense! You can't make the Coach, which is supposed to be a non-speaking role, the same person as the Captain, who does most of the talking. Consider doubling the Captain up as Manager, and merging the roles of Coach and Vice Captain. Whoever is the subject-matter authority can be the Expert Advisor.

When there are 12 of you, you should have one Captain, one Vice Captain, one Manager, as many Expert Advisors as you need, and everyone else can be a Coach. The Coaches are key people in the team, as they are the ones with the knowledge of what is really going on in the deal.

Decide who will play which role early on in the deal cycle – before the planning even begins, if possible. Being able to prepare, knowing that you are Captain or Coach or whatever, significantly changes your focus.

If the other party has a team and you are on your own, don't be put off – and don't be intimidated by a big group. It's an excellent opportunity to play divide and conquer with the other side. A disorderly team is a far greater liability than being on your own.

The other team in a deal is often just a collection of people rather than a well-oiled machine. They all talk, few listen, and – wonder of wonders – they contradict each other in the process. This is good news for you, as it provides you with information and pointers about the deal they might want, and lets you know who's who in the zoo.

SECRET #29 Step Three is to choose your Players carefully

There is comfort and strength in having a well-disciplined, properly briefed team with you when you go into a deal. Your power can be diluted, though, if the players don't stick to the roles they are meant to perform.

DEVIL #29

Taking the boss along to a deal can be a hazard. Not only do they want to be in charge of the proceedings, but they can destroy the Captain's credibility and give away tightly fought ground with a word or a wave of the hand.

SECRET #30

THEIR PLAYERS DO NOT PLAY BY THE SAME RULES

While it is helpful to know who is playing what role – Captain, Vice Captain, Coach or Manager – in the other side's team, this is not as important as you might think. Generally, the teams you come across in dealmaking are not particularly well structured.

The information that makes all the difference to your ability to control and close the deal is an understanding of the level of power and influence that each person in the other group exerts over the deal. Even if you don't know the other chaps well, there will be enough clues in their behaviour to give you this vital information.

You need to be able to sort their monkeys from their king of the jungle. To make this easier to do, I have divided the other side's team into Decision Centre roles (salespeople tend to call this a 'buying centre'). If you can figure out who has the ultimate power, who can say no but not yes, who holds a rubber stamp, and so on, you can direct the relevant aspects of your proposals to the most appropriate people. You will then be able to close your deals far more quickly and effectively.

There are two groups of people in the Decision Centre – the *Decision-makers* and the *Influencers*. These two groups are divided further by the roles played. Here is a summary.

There are two types of *Decision-maker*:

1. The Highlander (he or she who decides)
2. The Rubber Stampers (those who endorse the Highlander).

There are five types of *Influencer*:

3. The Gatekeepers (they block, judge and scrutinise)
4. The Users (they implement or use the end solution)
5. The Expert Advisors (the mama in the cupboard)
6. The Pro-Coach (he/she loves you)
7. The Anti-Coach (he/she loves you not).

Let's take a look at each of the seven roles in more detail. The focus will be on how to spot the responsibilities that each person has relative to the deal.

1. The Highlander (or decider)

Did you see the cult movie *Highlander*? It is a fantasy action movie, released in 1986, starring Christopher Lambert and Sean Connery. The film depicts the climax of an age-old battle between immortal warriors. The film's tagline is 'There can be only one'. The same applies to dealmaking.

There will be only one person who is the ultimate decider. Even though you might be told 'it's a board decision', the Highlander holds the power to make or delegate the decision. It is essential for you to identify the source of the power. The problem is that the Highlander has an aversion to lesser mortals, and actively avoids salespeople and negotiators. This is usually because they are busy, and don't want to be pestered when they have people around them who can take these meetings.

The Highlander is powerful. He or she can create budget and reallocate it, they can accept pricing or reject it. Even in our example of buying a game farm, you need to know where the power base lies. Is it the wife? Or the husband? Or the bank?

The most important characteristic of a Highlander is that they have veto power. They can say yes when everyone else says no, and no when everyone else says yes. The beauty of knowing this is that if you are struggling with a deal or about to lose it, the Highlander can – should they so wish – reverse the decision. There are, of course, ramifications of going over the heads of their generals to access this higher authority, but sometimes that is what you have to do to win the deal.

You will find the Highlander high up the corporate tree if you are in business, or holding the purse strings if you are not. They can, and do, delegate decisions, but ultimately they hold the power.

When you get in front of the Highlander, the Value Propositions you present must centre round measurable value – return on investment, impact on the top or bottom lines, increases in productivity, or reduction of costs. Don't waste their time with a friendly chat or technical detail; you'll have your head taken off.

What you need to be asking yourself continually is: 'What do I need to do to get this person to sign off on the deal?'

2. The Rubber Stampers (or endorsers)

There can be several Rubber Stampers involved in a deal. They are appointed to keep the process honest – like judges or referees, if you prefer. Think board of directors or tender committee.

Rubber Stampers are not present in every deal. You are only likely to come across them if you are doing a deal with a large corporation or government institution. In the main, you don't know who they are, as they operate behind the scenes. If you do identify them, they are unlikely to give you a meeting.

The Highlander might be one of the Rubber Stampers, but he or she will have more power than the others – remember, 'there can be only one'. The Highlander is like the pigs in *Animal Farm* by George Orwell (British writer and journalist, 1903–1950). The Rubber Stampers do not have the power of veto, but they do have the power of postponement – they can delay a deal until they are sure they are endorsing a decision with which they are comfortable.

As with a lot of committees, the Rubber Stampers can be frustrating. If they are obfuscating your deal, only the Highlander can help. They are considered to be Decision-makers rather than Influencers because they don't really influence the deal in any way, but they do play a direct role in the decision.

3. The Gatekeepers (or evaluators)

While Rubber Stampers are endorsers, Gatekeepers are evaluators. You will probably come across numerous Gatekeepers in a business deal. They are appointed to evaluate the 'technical' aspects of your proposal – legal, financial, performance, specifications, compliance, whatever.

You will normally know who they are because they need to engage with you to get technical information and input, so they'll be prepared to spend time with you. They may well tell you that they are the Decision-makers. They say this for one of two reasons: because they have had this responsibility delegated to them by the Highlander, or because they can actually say *no* to you on the basis of a technicality.

What is interesting about Gatekeepers, though, is that they can say no, but they can't give you a final *yes*. They can only make a recommendation. Who makes the final decision? The Highlander, that's who.

Don't underestimate the power of Gatekeepers. They can be like Cerberus, the three-headed beast guarding the gates of Hades. If they say no and you have no access to the Highlander to overrule them, goodbye deal.

If you are dealing with an individual or small business, someone might be the Highlander and the Gatekeeper all rolled into one. In bigger companies,

Gatekeepers can be people from different divisions, but all with some specific technical agenda.

4. The Users

There are typically many Users in a deal. The Users are the people who are affected by the outcome of the deal – they will have to live with the product or service you sell, or the financial implications of a bad deal, that sort of thing. So, they want to be involved in the deal as early as possible, even though they can only influence the choice and not make the decision.

They might want to meet with you to understand the outcomes of the deal and the impact on them and/or their people. They essentially 'own the problem'. Although they can't say yes or no, if they are senior they can influence the decision. Their real power lies post-deal – they can make your life easy or impossible. In our game-farm example, a typical case would be the existing farm manager.

5. The Expert Advisors

As you know, Expert Advisors are so special that they are covered separately in the next Secret.

6. The Pro-Coach (he loves you)

Are you experiencing déjà vu? You should be. One of the most important people on your team is your Coach. The Pro-Coach is the same, but not. The Pro-Coach is a member of the other party's side but they want you, for whatever reason, to get the deal.

Sound suspicious to you? I was deeply distrustful of these people when I first encountered them in business. *Why* did they want to help? Just because the Pro-Coach supports you doesn't mean that they don't support, or are disloyal to, their own team.

One of my long-term customers is the chief executive officer of a large information-systems company. He moves companies every three years or so and, wherever he goes, he gives me business. I met him through business nearly 20 years ago. We are not house friends, we have never been intimate (in case you're wondering), he is an extremely ethical man, and I have never worked for him. And I am not blackmailing or bribing him. Let's call him Connor (as in the hero of *Highlander*).

Why, then, does Connor give me business? Firstly, he likes me, as I do him; but secondly, I have never failed him. He knows he can rely on me to deliver results and that I can make him look good. So, Connor is my Pro-Coach – he calls me in whenever there is a deal in the offing. He gives me all the information I ask for about the deal (without ever disclosing a competitor's bid to me), and tells me whom I need to woo and who is already on my side.

Connor is also usually the Highlander in the companies he runs, but he expects me to win the deals on merit. He does, however, allow me the inside track. This is the upside of long-term relationships. Connor is my trusted advisor, and I am his. We do not take advantage of one another.

Your Pro-Coach can be on the other side's team, in your own organisation or external to both (a consultant, or an ex-employee, for example). Regardless of where they belong, they need to have influence over, or access to, information that helps *you* to close the deal. Be wary of 'nice guys' who give you information but give it to everyone else, too. They are just 'nice guys', not Pro-Coaches. Also be careful of people who give you information on which you can't rely. You might make a wrong move based on this faulty information.

A Pro-Coach wants you to get the deal because they like you, they like your company or your boss, they have designs on you, you make them look good, you are reliable, you are fun or interesting, they owe you or your father, you have a friendship or went to school together ... whatever. The point is that they support you. They might never tell you why, but you can measure their support by their actions.

A couple of years back, my husband, Simon, wanted to buy a new car. I tagged along. We went into a BMW dealership and Simon asked the salesperson to show him the new 3 Series. Simon is a big guy. I knew (as I should after 20 years) that he would soon feel claustrophobic, and bored, with a mid-sized sedan. When Simon went off to the loo, I called the salesman aside and discreetly told him that Simon could afford a bigger car than the 3 Series. My motivation in acting as Pro-Coach to the salesman was to save Simon money in the long term.

Simon was talked out the 3 Series but then bought a very expensive two-seater Porsche. That was *not* the plan.

You seldom have a formalised relationship with a Pro-Coach – you're not likely to approach someone and ask them to guide and coach you with a deal. Although you generally have to develop the relationship actively, your would-be Pro-Coach might be alarmed or suspicious if you asked directly for inside intelligence. Take your time to nurture these relationships, but don't forget that they need to work both ways. Something for you; something for them.

The more Pro-Coaches you can develop, the better. And create relationships with as many people as you can for each deal. The function of the Pro-Coach, in terms of dealmaking, is to help you to get your deal closed. As you can guess, the Highlander makes the perfect Pro-Coach. And if you are coming from a zero base (i.e. no existing relationship), it is near impossible to make a Rubber Stamper your Pro-Coach.

My organisation and I are often asked about bribery. What if someone offers to guide you or give you a deal, but they want something in return that could be perceived as a bribe? In Secret #4, we explored the subject and asked the question: 'At what point does negotiation become bribery?'

A bribe in one person's eyes may not be a bribe in another's, but my advice is always the same: If what you do will get you into trouble with the law, your company, your family or friends, your customers or colleagues – it is probably the wrong side of moral business.

7. The Anti-Coach (he loves you not)

What sort of relationship do you imagine Connor, my Pro-Coach, has with anyone I am competing with in a deal? He would be a dastardly double agent if he was their Pro-Coach too. He is effectively their Anti-Coach. He may not actively block them from getting the deal, but he will do what he can to help me win.

Some Anti-Coaches are far more antagonistic than others. You can literally feel the negative energy flowing towards you. The Pro-Coach is on your side, for whatever reason. The Anti-Coach is against you, for whatever reason. It might be that they have a strong relationship with someone else, or they just detest you, or they don't like your religion or your mother, or you have let them down in the past, or they despise your company or products, or they are vegetarians or feminists or misogynists and you represent what they abhor. Who knows?

Just as your Pro-Coach guides you, your Anti-Coach (or cockroach, as I prefer to call them) might be guiding someone else. The point is that they don't want *you* to get the deal. It's personal, so don't think you can sweet-talk them into seeing the error of their ways. The best you can do is to strategise around them and try to minimise their negative influence.

If the Highlander in a deal is your Anti-Coach, what should you do?

Well, if the Highlander is not actively involved in the deal, you may be okay if you have a decent Pro-Coach and you stay under the radar. But when the Highlander is very involved in the deal, consider your alternatives (have another look at Secret #4). My suggestion would be to walk away. You could try to replace yourself with another person from your team in the deal, but if the problem is your organisation, you don't really stand a chance, so don't waste your time or energy.

A few years ago, a close friend of mine was the CEO and Highlander of a big software company. Although he thought I had good products, he would not allow me to do business with his organisation. He said it would be perceived as favouritism. I disagreed. My company eventually closed some business with his organisation, but I personally kept well away from the deal, and his team kept the deal out of his sight. I took solace in the fact that our products did help his team. He found out what had happened after he left the software company and made me repay him. In beer. For a long time.

The software company and I now have an open affiliation, but just recently, one of the Pro-Coaches with whom I have a long-standing relationship called me. She needed me to discount one of our invoices that her company had already approved. There is a price to long-term relationships.

To summarise, here are a few important points to remember about the other team's players:

- In a small company (or when dealing with an individual), one person can perform six out of the seven roles. Why only six? Well, one person can't be your Pro-Coach and your Anti-Coach.
- Three of the roles are present in every deal – the Highlander, at least one Gatekeeper and at least one User.

- Decision Centres can, and often do, change with each deal.
- If you have no clue who's who in the zoo, ask your Pro-Coach.
- See as many people within the Decision Centre roles as you can, especially the Gatekeepers.
- You must be able to present a Value Proposition that addresses the needs and wants of each person in each role.
- Neglecting the Highlander is a mistake. If you have competition in a deal and they see the Highlander but you do not, don't be disappointed when you lose the deal.

Understanding the role someone is playing helps you to close the deal more quickly and effectively. Not everyone who can influence the deal will necessarily be involved in the face-to-face transaction, so you need to do a lot of work behind the scenes to increase your likelihood of getting the deal.

SECRET #30 Their players do not play by the same rules
Understanding which of the seven roles each person in the other camp plays gives you important insight into their individual levels of power and influence. For you to be successful in closing the deal, the two most valuable roles to you in a deal are likely to be the Highlander and your Pro-Coach.

DEVIL #30
Counter the Anti-Coach with a Pro-Coach and/or the Highlander. If the Highlander is the cockroach, consider qualifying out of the deal.

SECRET #31

EXPERTS AND ADVISORS CAN MAKE OR BREAK A DEAL

When I started my negotiating career, I had no idea that there was a difference between a negotiator and a dealmaker. As a pretty proficient negotiator, I assumed I could do the job of a dealmaker. It was only when I was working as executive director of strategy for a listed information technology company that the distinction began to form in my fuzzy brain.

In the process of buying, selling, merging and financing companies, I learnt a few painful lessons. One was obviously the significant difference in expertise between a negotiator and a dealmaker. Another was how to use Expert Advisors, and that they could facilitate or annihilate a deal faster than I could say Jack Rabbit. How does an Expert Advisor differ from an expert and an advisor, both of whom I have already mentioned several times?

Let's start with 'expert'. According to www.thefreedictionary.com, an expert is 'a person with a high degree of skill in or knowledge of a certain subject'. The anarchists at www.urbandictionary.com see an expert as 'someone who thinks they knew how to do something but actually just screwed everything up', and 'someone who goes into a serious explanation of doing something fairly simple or unimportant, like how to drive a bumper car'. Enough said.

The word 'expert' has been used liberally throughout this book. There is nothing that needs to be added to the thefreedictionary.com explanation for our purposes.

Now on to 'advisor'. The definition from www.thefreedictionary.com is 'one that advises, such as a person or firm that offers official or professional advice to clients'. This is a little too specific, to my mind. An advisor is essentially someone who offers advice, not so? A quote to which I relate wholeheartedly is from Erica Jong (American author and teacher, 1942–) who said, 'Advice is what we ask for when we already know the answer but wish we didn't.'

Either way, in combining the two concepts to form 'expert advisor', there is no specific definition as such, so can we assume it's someone who gives expert advice? Good. Expert Advisors can be accountants, shareholders, lawyers, engineers, technicians, bankers, financiers, and so on.

In Secret #20, we covered the concept of a trusted advisor, who is supposedly someone who gives you unbiased feedback or input. An unworldly view in my opinion, as human nature is seldom this unselfish – just cast your eye back to Secret #15, where I told the story of how two lawyers, supposedly trusted advisors, nearly destroyed an acquisition in Germany. For this reason, and the fact that you don't always have a strong relationship with the expert giving you advice, I prefer the term 'expert advisor' to 'trusted advisor' when looking at the different roles people can play in a deal.

You may have noticed that in the five tasks your team defines, there is an Expert Advisor. There is also an Expert Advisor in the seven roles of the Decision Centre in the other party's team. These functions do overlap. It is one of the motives for separating Expert Advisors from the other players into a discrete secret. It may happen, for example, that another party in a deal uses a brilliant Expert Advisor whom you want to use for your next deal.

Your Expert Advisor is someone who has a specific proficiency that you need for a deal. Knowing when to wheel the Expert Advisors in and out, however, is a talent. I likened this to being a tightrope walker's manager – if they put one foot wrong, it could really hurt your deal.

Fatti's & Moni's is a popular South African brand of dried pasta. In one Fatti's & Moni's advert, an Italian mama is taken out of storage in a kitchen cupboard. As soon as she has cooked up a fabulous assortment of Italian dishes, she is tucked away again in the cupboard with the brooms. This is how you should use your Expert Advisors in dealmaking. Wheel them in when you need them, and wheel them out again when you are done with them. If you don't think you will find the advert offensive (I enjoy it, but then I'm not PC), see www.youtube.com/watch?v=T1RsdRN5Qjg&feature==related.

A property developer on one of my organisation's programmes told me the story of a local town planner he had brought in to meet with the Italian financier of a development project. Instead of advising on the project regulations, the town planner proceeded to tell the Italian about the corruption in the council, the inefficiency of the local authority, and how much he despised the mayor. All this was hearsay, of course, but the net effect was that the Italian developer got on an aeroplane, never to be seen again.

That said, having a competent Expert Advisor on your team is invaluable. This is one of the key differences between negotiators and dealmakers. Dealmakers know how to use Expert Advisors to best effect.

There is a school of thought (advocated mostly by lawyers) that believes the negotiating team should be a separate group to the rest of the people involved in a deal. Maybe they believe that negotiation should be left to the 'experts'. Negotiation, like selling, is a life skill – one that every single person has and needs. Yes, lawyers could be used as Captains, but disrupting the continuity of a deal by separating out negotiation makes little sense to me. I prefer to use lawyers as Expert Advisors rather than as negotiators.

Expert Advisors are often brought in from outside your own company to assist with a deal. This does not make your role in managing them easier or harder. Ask any salesperson you know and they will have a story to tell about how a technical person 'screwed up the deal'. Ask any technical expert you know and they will tell you a story about how a salesperson sold the customer something that didn't exist.

The trick to using Expert Advisors successfully is to brief them very carefully and very specifically. Then wheel them in, let them give their input and wheel them out when you are done with them.

If the other side brings in an Expert Advisor, say, for corporate finance advice, you may want to do the same. This helps to keep a level playing field. Sharing an Expert Advisor can work, but you need to bear in mind that they will be loyal to whoever is paying their bill. They are guns for hire, after all.

Expert Advisors do, because of the respect they command, influence the deal. So, when you look at the other side's Decision Centre, be aware of who they are using as Expert Advisors. If you can get a meeting with one of their Expert Advisors, great, but they are unlikely to agree to see you without their party being present.

Keep any conversations you have with an Expert Advisor focused on their area of expertise – whether they are acting for you or not. Don't forget the case of the town planner and the Italian developer. Encouraging Expert Advisors to give opinions or feedback in other areas is not a terribly good idea – unless you know them and trust them not to fall off the rope.

I have said much about the dangers of using Expert Advisors, but without them, there is no way I would have been able to conclude any of the deals

I was undertaking when I was a negotiator doing a dealmaker's job. Expert Advisors can be invaluable resources and allies. Using them judiciously will give you a vital tactical advantage.

SECRET #31 Experts and advisors can make or break a deal
Expert Advisors are an invaluable resource, but knowing when to wheel them in and out is a talent. It is the knowledge of how to utilise and manage Expert Advisors that differentiates the dealmakers from the negotiators.

DEVIL #31
Expert Advisors, when they have the floor or an audience, can run amok. When someone recognises that they are considered to be an expert, there is often the danger of their ego going haywire. Keep them on a tight leash.

PART 4

THE ENCOUNTER

**Be careful what you pretend to be
because you are what you pretend to be.**

Kurt Vonnegut (American writer, 1922–2007)

SECRET #32

WANTING AND NEEDING ARE NOT SYNONYMOUS

This is probably the part you have been waiting for – the face-to-face encounter. It's a lot like going on a date. You've selected the person you want to date (the target deal); you've decided where to go; you have an escape plan 'just in case' (the strategy); you know what to wear and how much money to spend (the plan); and now you are ready (the encounter).

Much like a date, there are a few secrets to a winning encounter. Before we get started, three broad principles.

Firstly, no magic wand is required for doing deals – it's a matter of skill and process. As a small child, did you wish for a pony or a new bike or whatever? Do you still make wishes? Although I subscribe to the laws of attraction, the universe does not always give you what you want in the way you expect it. If you need to bring certainty into your deals, you should follow the secrets in this book rather than *The Secret* by Rhonda Byrne.

Secondly, success lies in your power (Part 1), the quality of your planning (Part 2), getting the face-to-face encounter right (Part 3) and closing down the deal properly (Part 4). All the tactics, tricks or ploys in the world will not help you if your foundation is weak. I'm not a great fan of negotiation or selling 'games'. It is far better to play your deal straight. You've seen 'good cop, bad cop' being used on television, right? The problem with these sorts of schemes is that they only really work on TV.

Thirdly, you do need to go beyond the obvious to get the deal. You should be able to predict whether the other party will or won't do the deal, and understand what motivates them at a business *and* a personal level in a deal. You need to recognise their behaviour, and how they are likely to receive and respond to you and your proposals. It is acting on these nuances that converts good dealmakers into brilliant dealmakers.

Lastly, to get what you want in the face-to-face engagement, you need to tell the other party what *you* want, let them know that they can get what *they* want in return, listen to their counter-proposals, find flexibility in your Key and Secondary Issues, and then take your game up a notch or two. Make. It. Personal.

Wanting and needing are not the same thing

Any deal or transaction involves at least two parties. Sure, you can do deals with yourself, but this is not that kind of book. Superficially speaking, a skilled dealmaker essentially gets what they want by giving to get.

Although you might have found the title of Secret #10 a bit uncouth (People and donkeys are not that different), you have presumably accepted that if you want someone to do a deal with you, you need to offer them carrots (i.e. incentives). The bottom line is that people do deals because there is something in it for them – and they will do a deal with *you* if you have what they want.

Don't you wish it was that simple? Complications arise when people can get what they want from you, or from somewhere else. You know that you can differentiate yourself from the pack by offering carrots that are relevant (lions need meat), and that are value-based. You also know that the best way to present this value is in the form of Value Propositions.

Incentive-driven Value Propositions are only your foot in the door. They help you to get onto the shortlist. They represent the compelling reason for the other person to engage in the deal. But what if your competitor has done the same – presented value-based incentives? How can you differentiate yourself further?

The first step is to add an element of Secret #20 to the carrots. Lost? In Secret #20, we looked briefly at Maslow's hierarchy of needs. We touched on the fact that every human being, even the Mother Teresa type, is motivated by a need or a want of some sort. It is now time to distinguish the Needs from the Wants – to link big carrots to business Needs, and smaller carrots to personal Wants. (Yes, the use of capitals is intentional from now on.)

The step thereafter is to differentiate the types of Needs, and then we can delve into what the other party Wants from the deal. This may sound like splitting hairs, but in a competitive transaction, this could be the difference between winning and losing the deal.

If you are beginning to suspect that Needs are linked to Key Issues, and Wants to Secondary Issues, you are a genius.

SECRET #32 Wanting and needing are not synonymous

People buy from people, not faceless companies. Being able to distinguish between someone's individual business Needs and personal Wants is important in dealmaking, especially when it comes to competitive deals. The carrots you use to incentivise Needs are different from those you use to address Wants.

DEVIL #32

Before you decide that business Needs and personal Wants amount to the same thing, think about the most extravagant gift you have ever bought (for yourself or someone else). Why did you do it? This is the difference between needing and wanting something.

SECRET #33

A BUSINESS NEED MUST EXIST FOR RESULTS TO BE ACHIEVED

You may have noticed in Secret #32 that a connection was established between business + Needs + Key Issues, and personal + Wants + Secondary Issues. The reason specific words have been chosen and linked is to keep things simple.

Up until now, no real distinction has been drawn between Needs and Wants, but when it comes to the face-to-face encounter in a deal, the difference between the two becomes very important.

Wants, or Hot Buttons if you prefer, are covered in the next secret, so the focus for now is going to be on Needs. When I talk about Needs, I am referring to the specific business results and outcomes that the other party requires from a deal – assuming the Needs are recognised, of course.

A company does not make a decision. A decision on a deal is made by the individuals, led by the Highlander, who make up the Decision Centre. For the deal to exist, however, these individuals have to recognise that there is a Need. If they don't see a Need, the results and outcomes are redundant, and there is therefore no need for a deal.

The challenge is that not everyone sees the Need in the same way. Getting your mind around how each individual involved in the deal perceives the business Need helps you to determine your next steps. To make this analysis easier, four categories of Need have been identified.

1. Need driven by business growth or opportunities
2. Need driven by business problems or threats
3. Indifference about a Need
4. Rejection of a Need.

1. Need driven by business growth or opportunities

This is always good news. If people within a company decide that they want to make changes to facilitate or accommodate business growth and opportunities, a Need exists. And if a Need exists, there is a strong possibility of a deal.

The only problem with growth-driven Needs is that time is on the other party's side, so the urgency to make a decision is moderate. The Value Propositions for growth-based Needs should focus on how the deal will support the growth and maximise the opportunities.

2. Need driven by business problems or threats

This is even better news. When individuals in a company decide they must make changes to overcome or circumvent problems and threats, there is a strong possibility of a deal.

Individuals perceiving trouble in a company have an urgency associated with their Needs, so time could be on your side. Value Propositions in this situation would be directed at how the deal makes the problems go away or wards off the threats.

3. Indifference about a Need

These individuals can't see a Need, which means they have to be convinced that one exists. They are not going to block a deal if others perceive a Need, but they will not motivate it either.

Time to bring in the FUD: fear, uncertainty and doubt. FUD is a useful tool, widely used by computer company IBM in the 1970s to build market share, which casts a shadow of uncertainty over the indecisive and indifferent ones. When used positively, it can make people double-check their apathy and question their vacillation.

Another way in which to move people from indifferent to interested is by pressing their Hot Buttons. Hot Buttons = personal Wants. Coming up shortly.

4. Rejection of a Need

Have you ever gone into a deal in which someone resolutely refused to acknowledge that there was a problem? Or lived in a fool's paradise? Or was overconfident, or simply arrogant, about their position? You walked into their office, and there they were, leaning back in their chair, feet up on the desk, arms folded behind their heads, having kept you waiting for at least half an hour?

If this person is the Highlander, watch my lips – *you will not get the deal.* Qualify out now, before you waste more of your precious time. Resist the temptation to do anything you might regret, though. The problems and threats will come, but not for this deal.

So, the first step in the encounter is to check the recognition of a Need. Are there enough people who see the Need? If the answer is no, then there is no compelling reason for them to do the deal and you should invest your time and energy elsewhere. If it's yes, it's time to dig deeper into the Needs.

While the perception of a Need can differ from person to person, the various groups of Decision-makers and Influencers base their decisions, to a large extent, on your ability to give them certain business outcomes and results from the deal. The different types of groups look for more or less common results or outcomes. Like what, you ask? Here are a few general examples for each category in the Decision Centre.

1. *The Highlander.* It's all about measurable value – return on investment, impact on top or bottom lines, increases in efficiency or productivity or sales, reductions in cost, smoothed cash flow, low cost of ownership.
2. *The Rubber Stampers.* They are compliance junkies. Was there good corporate governance in the decision? Did the deal fulfil the criteria as agreed by this, that and the next thing? Does the deal meet the pre-determined specifications or tender requirements?
3. *The Gatekeepers.* Their role is to scrutinise, judge and block if necessary. They want to know about match to specifications, timeous and continuous delivery, payment terms, best-of-breed technicalities, human resources and corporate-responsibility practices, pricing and discounting, Service Level Agreements (SLAs), terms and conditions, contractual and legal requirements.
4. *The Users.* Ease of implementation, increased efficiency, opportunity to upgrade skills, do the job better or faster or easier, versatility, service excellence, simple to learn and manage.
5. *The Expert Advisors.* The person/group they are advising makes the right decision, opportunity to share knowledge, personal recognition, to be valued for their contribution. As you can see, these are more personal Wants than business results.
6. *The Pro-Coach.* They want you to get the deal – for whatever reason. This is personal, so it stands to reason that their motivation is more driven by Wants than Needs. See Hot Buttons (coming up now).
7. *The Anti-Coach.* They want you *not* to get the deal. Again it is personal. Refer to the Hot Buttons once more.

Presenting the business outcomes in the form of a Value Proposition, prepared for each person in the Decision Centre, will give you the edge. People are inherently self-serving. The more you can acknowledge their individual Needs, the closer the connection they will draw between the deal you are offering versus that of a competitor.

SECRET #33 A business Need must exist for results to be achieved
Only if someone sees a business Need will they show interest in a deal. The perception of a Need can differ from person to person, but the various groups of Deciders and Influencers have a collective view of the business outcomes and results they want from a deal. Use Value Propositions to show each person how their specific Needs will be addressed.

DEVIL #33
People who refuse to acknowledge that a Need exists are essentially Anti-Coaches. Prepare a strategy to minimise their impact on the deal. If this is the Highlander, it is best to qualify out of the deal.

SECRET #34
IGNORE PERSONAL HOT BUTTONS AT YOUR PERIL

Now, on to the interesting part of the hypothetical date we are planning. The next step of the encounter is finding out what is beneath the exterior, so to speak.

Many (mediocre, I might add) dealmakers believe that considering what someone wants from a deal at a personal level is a waste of time. A fundamental truth about dealmaking: If you understand what makes the other person tick – their Hot Buttons, in other words – you are far more likely to develop a relationship with them and will thus be able to give them what they want in a deal.

Relationships are important, so wanting to operate at a purely business level is both naive and arrogant. The dealmaker who invests in their relationship with another person will close the deal. What about people who are, in their customary behaviour, cold and unapproachable (or 'Drivers', as I call them)? Behavioural peculiarities are covered in Secret #35, but everyone has to develop connections in one form or another.

How do you find out what is important to someone at a personal level? You could, of course, ask them, but they will not always be prepared to tell you. Why not, you wonder? In Devil #32, I asked you to think about the most extravagant gift you've ever bought and why you bought it. You can email your answer to me, but you're unlikely to tell me the truth. Here's why, and it is personal.

A few years ago I bought myself a Breitling watch. It was expensive (there's no such thing as a cheap Breitling). If you asked me why I spent so much money on a watch when I could have got one from the local electronics discount warehouse for a fraction of the price, I would tell you that I bought the Breitling 'because it is an investment'. I would probably proceed to justify this to you, but I would be giving you my business reason (Need).

Why did I buy the Breitling and not a Rolex or a Cartier? Because it looked good on my wrist, and it is an unusual watch for a woman. Breitling watches are generally made for men. You are possibly reeling at the superficiality of my wanting to look good and be different. Being a Driver, I don't really care what anyone thinks of me, but the point is that people don't disclose their Wants or Hot Buttons for fear of looking shallow or selfish. What, deep down, was the real reason for *your* extravagant purchase? Was it to win favour with someone, or to look good? Whatever your reason, it's okay. Humans are, at a fundamental level, motivated by self-interest.

When my colleagues and I raise Hot Buttons during a course, there are always a few people who resolutely refuse to acknowledge their humanness. They do not want to believe (or show) that they are self-serving. They are wannabe martyrs. My question to them is then: 'Do you do any charity work, whether giving time, money or old clothes?' They are extremely proud (hah!) to say that they do. 'Why?' I ask. The answers are usually 'To give something back' or 'To help those less fortunate'. When I drill down on this, the bottom line is that serving others in some way makes them feel appreciated or useful or good about themselves. And what is wrong with that? Nothing. What is wrong with me feeling good about myself because I enjoy having a beautiful watch? Nothing.

Back to finding out someone else's Hot Buttons. They will usually be disinclined to tell you the real reason for wanting to do a deal for fear of being branded as selfish, so how do you find out? Look around for clues – what pictures do they have in their office, which watch do they wear, what kind of car do they drive? What does the flash car tell you? What does a family claptrap tell you? It's a lot like being a very smart detective.

There is a better way to find out someone's motivators than playing detective. Ask. Your. Pro-Coach. This might be another executive in their company, or their personal assistant, or their significant other. Best not to ask, 'Why does Patrick have such a bling watch?' You might rather ask, 'What do you think motivates Patrick?' or 'What are Patrick's hobbies or passions?' I can tell you why Patrick wears a bling watch – it's because his wife gave it to him. She thinks he deserves a fantastic watch, and she is his passion, the centre of his universe.

Personal Wants spill over into deals. Whether the other person's Hot Button is to spend more time with their family, or look good in the eyes of their colleagues, or get a promotion, or make life easier for themselves, your role as a dealmaker is not to judge – it is to facilitate. How does your deal give them what they want at a *personal* level?

Hot Buttons differ widely from person to person. They are more a factor of character than the role someone is playing in a Decision Centre. So, while the business Needs for a group might be collective, the personal Wants are individual.

Here are 20 from hundreds of examples of Wants or Hot Buttons:

1. More family or leisure time
2. More time to play golf or cook or travel
3. Do the best for their children
4. Attract potential partners or dates
5. Keep someone off their back

6. Reduce their stress
7. Increase their responsibility
8. Improve personal level of skill
9. Improve self-esteem
10. Look good or impress someone/others
11. Get recognition or promotion
12. Help or serve others
13. Remain in power or control others
14. Material gain – a fast car, lifestyle, apartment, etc.
15. Avoid losing credibility
16. Take the safe road or feel secure
17. Boost own or someone else's ego
18. Have choices
19. Improve social status
20. Be seen as a thought leader

How can your knowledge of personal Wants be used in dealmaking? Is it ethical to be pressing these Hot Buttons?

Deals *should* be won on the battlefield of business Needs and results, but this does not tend to happen. People make decisions (like me and my watch) that are not always logical. They do deals with people they like (or don't do the deal because of a personal issue), they pay more when they could get something for less, they walk away from good deals for reasons known only to themselves.

In the human world, people are not one-dimensional. Factors other than logic and objectivity influence the way in which they make decisions about deals. If you can understand someone's underlying personal motivators and you show them how this will be addressed by choosing your deal, you are actually serving them – and giving yourself a tactical advantage over a competitor in the process.

It is not manipulative to press someone's Hot Buttons. You are meeting their personal issues. The fact that you benefit in the process, that your personal Wants are also met, does not make it unethical. The dishonesty, or arrogance, in the process comes in when you neglect someone's Hot Buttons because *you* want to feel a certain way – that *you* are doing 'the right thing'. Give people what they want at a business *and* a personal level. This is what makes expert dealmakers successful.

There is a fine art to pressing Hot Buttons. People are sensitive about their private drivers. They prefer not to acknowledge that they have self-interest. Their immediate reaction to a question like 'Why did you buy that car?' is more likely to be 'Because it retains its resale value like no other' than 'Because I think I look smokin' hot in it.'

When dealing with people's humanness, it is better to be subtle than to use the direct questioning technique of Secret #18. Gently test the water. You might want to comment on the appeal of the car, or how *you* would feel driving it. Sharing a personal view or experience encourages the other person to be more open. Whatever you do, *avoid being insincere*. Most people can spot a phoney at a hundred yards.

Are you starting to sense a connection between personal Wants and general behaviour? Coming up next.

SECRET #34 Ignore personal Hot Buttons at your peril

Hot Buttons are personal motivators that have significant influence on how an individual's decisions are made. Understanding and meeting another person's Wants or Hot Buttons helps to develop the relationship and can be a vital differentiator in deals that are closely competed.

DEVIL #34

Ignoring someone's personal Wants is naive and arrogant. 'Naive' because deals are closed on factors other than the obvious and logical. 'Arrogant' because relationships are important in deals, and ignoring another's personal issues smacks of conceit.

SECRET #35

IDENTIFY BEHAVIOURAL STYLES TO BUILD RELATIONSHIPS

Are you curious to know what a Driver is, or have you assumed it's someone who makes a living from being a chauffeur? The next move in our encounter process is to look at behaviour and how this impacts a deal.

People often ask the question: 'What role does personality play in dealmaking?' I'm always curious to know their reason for asking this. Is it because they believe personality predetermines an outcome? Or that understanding personality makes it easier to close the deal? Or that if you know someone's personality, you can press their Hot Buttons more effectively?

'Some' and 'none' is the answer. Personality, as such, is not something on which I focus in dealmaking. Broadly speaking, someone's personality is defined by their character, and to really get a grip on this, one needs to have more than a passing grasp of psychology. Far more relevant to dealmaking is *behaviour*. Personality does drive behaviour to an extent, but behaviour in itself is observable, measurable, mostly predictable and manageable.

For a dealmaker, the ability to connect the dots between a person's behaviour and their personal Wants (or Hot Buttons) is a potent aid in building a relationship. The dealmaker who invests in understanding the other party gets the deal.

To fully appreciate the impact of behaviour on a deal, it is necessary to identify the major behavioural styles using a basic classification system.

The intention here is not to profile; it's simply to make sense of a complex subject.

A common tool used to do this is the DISC behavioural model, developed in the 1920s by Dr William Moulton Marston (American psychologist and theorist, 1893–1947). The fact that so many people have copied or modified Dr Marston's original work suggests that there must be merit in his system. In Dr Marston's classification, the 'D' stands for drive, the 'I' for influence, the 'S' for steadiness and the 'C' for compliance. We will develop our own categories and definitions.

For the people reading this book who have already read my books *Work Diva* and/or *Deal Diva*, I have kept the general terminology and concepts in this book as similar as possible to what you already know.

If you have done a social styles (or similar) course, you will know that there are two axes along which a person's behaviour is generally measured. Dr Marston defined the first axis as 'Assert vs Yield'. This axis is also referred to as:

- A-type vs B-type
- Competitive vs Cooperative
- Tense vs Easy-going
- Dominant vs Passive

For the purposes of dealmaking – which includes a person's selling, negotiating and communicating styles – I tend to describe this axis as 'Aggressive vs Agreeable'.

The second axis identified by Dr Marston is the 'Antagonised by vs Allied with' range. This axis is alternatively known as:

- Extravert vs Introvert
- Impulsive vs Considered

- Warm vs Cool
- Spontaneous vs Self-controlled

Relative to dealmaking, I prefer to use the words 'Sceptical vs Receptive' to describe this axis.

When plotted as one vertical axis and one horizontal axis crossing each other in the middle, the two axes form four quadrants or blocks. In a diagram, they look like this:

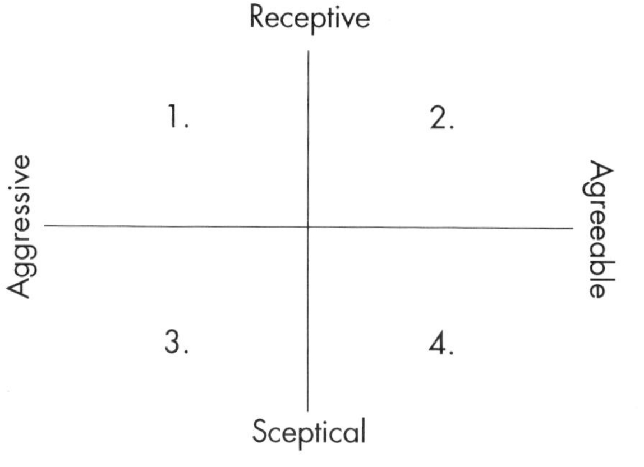

Each of the four quadrants is labelled, typically with a word that describes the behaviour defined by that quadrant. For example, a person falling into Quadrant 1 (the Receptive/Aggressive quadrant) is commonly referred to as an Expressive, or something similar. A person in Quadrant 2 (Receptive/Agreeable) is usually called an Amiable. Collectively, the Expressives and Amiables are the Warm people.

The Quadrant 3 (Aggressive/Sceptical) person is known as a Driver and the Agreeable/Sceptical individual of Quadrant 4 is an Analytical. These are the Cool guys.

Grouping the Expressives and Drivers together will give you the A-type personality, whereas the Amiables and Analyticals are B-types.

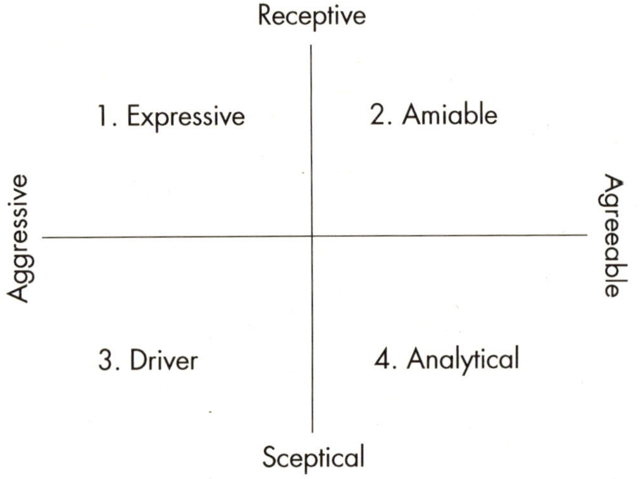

The purpose of these categorisations is to help us to make sense of the factors that govern individual social behaviour. There is obviously a great deal more theory behind an intricate concept of this nature, but for our purposes, simple is good.

Which behavioural style are you? Try to figure it out before we go any further. Are you more Aggressive or Agreeable? And more Receptive or Sceptical? Choosing one word on each axis will identify the primary quadrant that best describes your *general* behaviour. A little about *un*general behaviour later.

What is the relevance of the behavioural styles to dealmaking? When you are meeting a person for the first time, you can try to figure out into which quadrant they would fit – and the majority of the time you'd be on the money. Of course, if you are already familiar with someone, you will have a pretty good idea of which behavioural style best describes them. Once you have determined the person's quadrant or style, you can decide how best to deal with them.

In dealmaking, the most important axis is the Aggressive vs Agreeable alignment. People who are Aggressive (A-type) are inclined to be competitive, decisive, dominant and distributive. These characteristics increase the potential for tension and conflict in a deal. The Agreeable people (B-type) are typically passive, easy-going, cooperative and collaborative, which means they are less confrontational but also less conclusive when doing deals. As you can see, neither style is good or bad, just different.

Here are a few guidelines to assist you in indentifying the four quadrants, interacting with them and determining their Hot Buttons. Be careful, though: there are exceptions to every rule. Constantly test your assumptions.

1. Expressives ♦

Description

Expressives are confident, sociable, enthusiastic, energetic, impulsive, creative, charming, persuasive, supportive, flighty, manipulative, competitive, lacking in detail, undisciplined and overreactive, to name a few of both their positive and negative traits.

If Expressives were birds, they would be peacocks. If they were animals, they'd be lions. If a suit from a deck of cards, the diamonds.

A classic Expressive is Rod 'Show me the money' Tidwell, the character played by Cuba Gooding Jnr in the movie *Jerry Maguire*. In real life, Dennis Rodman, Jennifer Lopez, Liberace and Bill Clinton.

Interaction

When dealing with an Expressive – who is Receptive yet Aggressive – you need to keep the meeting light to avoid confrontation and ensure that you hold their interest. Expressives want to be excited by the master plan, not bored with the minutiae – and they do bore easily. As they are expressive, you will know where you stand very quickly. These are enthusiastic people who will often show a positive initial reaction to a deal, but they also tend to change their minds.

Expressives are aggressive, so they can get nasty if you push them or irritate them. The best way to deal with an Expressive is to excite them with what they will get out of a deal and then go for the close. Tie the agreed deal down in writing as soon as you can.

Hot Buttons

The diamonds? What do you think? Patrick with the bling watch (see Secret #34) is an Expressive. Expressives generally enjoy life in the fast lane. They love glitz, glamour and excitement. Fabulous food, sparkling champagne and travel to exotic locations. They are socialisers of note and inclined to be inveterate name-droppers. Although they can be rather flashy and materialistic, the excitement they seek may be in the form of attention. Attention Seekers Anonymous (ASA) was invented for Expressives, as were Drama Queens United (DQU) and Ritalin.

If you are an Expressive

People will gravitate towards you because you are charismatic and engaging, but because of your love for showmanship, others may not take you seriously. And watch that ego!

2. Amiables ♥

Description

Amiables are friendly, kind, people-orientated, sympathetic, considerate, willing, supportive, dependable, respectful, conflict-averse, unstructured, indecisive and sensitive.

Amiables are the doves of the bird world, and the giraffes of the animal kingdom. In a card deck, they are the hearts.

Beyoncé is a typical Amiable, as are Sandra Bullock, John Cusack, Tom Hanks and characters played by Meg Ryan.

Interaction

The Amiables, falling into the Receptive/Agreeable quadrant, are the 'nice guys' of the world. Amiables do not want to disappoint anyone, so when you are dealing with them, they can unwittingly send you the wrong signals. As a result of their inclination to be kind, they do not like to say no. This makes it difficult to gauge how they really feel about a deal.

Dealmakers continually fall into the trap of thinking that an Amiable's not saying 'no' means a 'yes'. You need to ensure that you understand their issues and concerns. Once you can show that your solution addresses their problems, they will be happy to give you a 'yes' answer. Like Expressives, Amiables are Warm people, so you need to tie the deal down quickly.

Amiables are happy – even if they don't know you awfully well – to chat about their interests, hobbies, families, pets and even their personal lives. They will also show a genuine interest in your life.

Hot Buttons

Relationships, especially with family and friends, are extremely important to Amiables. They love that other people love them, so they go to great lengths to keep this affection. They want to be included – parties, socials, charity or celebrity events – and they like to know what is happening in the lives of others. They also want to keep the peace, so harmony is important to them. Lost causes and underdogs are their thing, and they are happy to be the shoulder on which others cry. An Amiable is the ultimate queen of hearts.

If you are an Amiable

Others love you, but in business they are inclined to leave you because they perceive you as being unable to make decisions. A bit more directness, albeit in your own kind manner, will serve you well. Watch out for being a martyr – other people will take advantage of you.

3. Drivers ♣

Description

Drivers are direct, independent, organised, determined, focused, pragmatic, loyal, results-orientated, demanding, critical, pushy, harsh, aggressive and competitive.

Drivers as birds would be hawks. As animals, great white sharks. Their card suit is clubs.

Jethro Gibbs, played by Mark Harmon in the television series *NCIS*, is a Driver. So are Simon Cowell, Madonna, Hillary Clinton and Sir Alan Sugar.

Interaction

If you are dealing with someone who is Aggressive and Sceptical, you will be dealing with a Driver. They will be cynical about what you are saying, and because they are forceful by nature, conflict and confrontation are never far away. They are comfortable with this kind of discord, but if you are not a Driver, it could make you uneasy. They will drive a hard bargain, but do not allow them to bulldoze you. Equally, avoid fighting fire with fire, as all hell could break loose. Hold your position in a firm but non-confrontational way, and use logic to convince them of the merits of your case.

You need to be fully prepared with the facts and figures. Drivers want to be able to measure value for value, so be sure you can show what they will get and what you expect in quantitative terms. At a personal level, try to behave unemotionally and assertively. This will help to keep the meeting constructive and to reduce tension. On the upside, Drivers are decisive. Of all the behavioural styles, the one who will give you a direct answer, and is most likely to honour that decision, is the Driver.

Do not talk to Drivers about their families, dogs, private lives or anything personal until you have formed a decent relationship.

Hot Buttons

It can be hard to tell with a Driver, because they are low on emotion and expression. They are very driven, so career progress, results and recognition are usually important. Drivers like to get their own way, or be seen to be getting what they want. Like Expressives, their egos are big, so they can be materialistic and drawn to celebrity. I'm a Driver and look at my watch, my car, where I live. Unlike Expressives, quality is more important than the brand. They enjoy more subtle statements of success – art collections, fine wines, tailored clothes. Extremely competitive, they relish the opportunity to prove themselves in any area in which they excel.

If you are a Driver

If your behavioural style is that of a Driver, pay attention to the pleasantries of the meeting, the feelings of the other people in the room and guard against appearing arrogant. As I mentioned, I am a Driver so I need to be careful of coming across as a rude, humourless git.

4. Analyticals ♠

Description

Analyticals are respectful, tactful, listeners, obedient, persistent, industrious, logical, systematic, orderly, deliberate, organised, detailed, consistent, cautious, tedious, and somewhat anal and stubborn.

Analyticals as birds are owls, and as animals they are badgers, and in a deck of cards, they are the spades.

Real-life Analyticals are Bill Gates, Condoleezza Rice, Keanu Reeves and (no more, unfortunately) Princess Diana. Mac Taylor, played by Gary Sinise in *CSI: New York* is an Analytical, but the Horatio Caine character in *CSI: Miami* is an Expressive posing as an Analytical.

Interaction

As Agreeable and Sceptical, Analyticals are cautious and will want a lot of detail and information from you. They need time to consider all facets of the deal, especially the value they will get in exchange for the value you expect. Include as many facts and figures as possible. Analyticals need to be sure that they are making a decision that is fair and well thought out. This takes time, which you may not always have.

To get an Analytical to engage with you and give you a decision, you need to check actively if they need more information and if, they do, provide it. You should be gentle but firm if they are disappearing in a puff of detail. Push gently for an answer, as pushing too hard will provoke their stubborn side. Explain and quantify, if you can, the importance of their making a decision.

Hot Buttons

As with Drivers, it can be hard to ascertain an Analytical's Hot Buttons because of their high level of self-control. But because they are easy-going, it is far easier to engage with an Analytical than with a Driver. Any strong interests they have should come to the fore quite quickly, as they can tend towards obsessiveness. When talking about their areas of interest or hobbies, Analyticals can be surprisingly animated. All you need to do is probe them on a subject they know and then encourage them to talk.

Analyticals are not usually showy, but this does not mean that they are not high achievers. They are just more subtle than the other three styles in expressing what they have achieved and what they want.

If you are an Analytical

If you're Analytical, you need to feel personally comfortable with the people you deal with, but, as with Amiables, try to communicate your decisions more openly. Watch out for that stubborn streak – it makes you irrational.

There is no right or wrong behavioural style. Each has its positives and negatives, its yin and yang, dark and light, good and bad. And it is not possible to categorise people absolutely accurately.

You will find that even if individuals belong to the same behavioural category, there will be substantial differences between them. People also change when they relax, socialise or are under pressure – a Driver may become more Amiable or Analytical, or an Expressive more like a Driver, and so on. This is what I referred to earlier as *un*general behaviour.

When I am lecturing, I become quite Expressive. If I've had a few glasses of champagne, I'm a complete Amiable. If I'm under huge pressure, I become absolutely Driver. Yet I am most comfortable working with Analyticals.

We all have a bit of each style in us, and we have a 'primary' behavioural style and a 'secondary' (or *un*general) style. But I'm going to avoid getting into the secondary styles, as that level of analysis requires a lot more detail

– and we have enough information with just the four primary behavioural styles to press Hot Buttons and close deals more effectively.

SECRET #35 Identify behavioural styles to build relationships
There are four behavioural styles into which people can generally be classified. Understanding someone's primary style guides you on how to approach that person and build a relationship. Hot Buttons can be more easily ascertained if you know a person's style.

DEVIL #35
Resist the temptation to play amateur psychologist. Being a careful, smart detective is a far more productive pursuit in dealmaking.

SECRET #36
MODIFY YOUR BEHAVIOUR TO GET THE DEAL

Knowing someone's behavioural style will help you to build a relationship with that person, and it will offer a guide to their probable Hot Buttons. There is an even better reason to understand behavioural styles, and this is so you can present the deal to each person in the manner to which they are most likely to respond positively.

As in any other areas of their lives, people want to be treated as individuals, for their specific Needs and Wants to be addressed, in a deal. Avoiding the 'one-size-fits-all' mindset will serve you well in dealmaking. You need to modify your approach and your proposals to meet each person's unique requirements.

Not for one minute am I suggesting that you change who you are when dealing with the different behavioural styles. You must always be true to yourself. What you do need to adjust, however, is the way in which you interact with each individual. Be you, but be more animated with an Expressive, more personable with an Amiable, more direct with a Driver, and more detailed with an Analytical. We all have a little bit of each style in us, so it is not a huge stretch.

You should know from experience that it is impossible to change someone else – only they can control or decide whether they want to change or not. What you *can* change, though, is *your* behaviour. Adjusting your behaviour to accommodate someone else's style is *not* selling out. Adjusting your behaviour to make sure you get the deal you want is playing smart. Talking to people in their own behavioural language gives you power.

What is the optimal way of presenting proposals to, and discussing deals with, each of the behavioural styles?

1. Expressives ♦

Have you ever heard the expression 'the easiest person to sell to is a salesperson'? Expressives are naturally persuasive, so you should always first try to convince an Expressive on the merits of a deal. This is best done by keeping a presentation or discussion animated, interesting and focused on the big picture.

If you need to move into negotiating, keep your conditions neutral, but make the upside sound exciting and entirely about them. Pressing Hot Buttons works very well with Expressives.

Enthusiastic by nature, Expressives will probably respond positively to what you are saying, but can soon lose interest or fail to follow through on their promises. They make quick decisions, but this can also be a ploy to get you out of their office. Without being too pushy – remember, Expressives are dominant so they can be quite aggressive if cornered – get the deal signed and sealed as soon as you can.

If an Expressive does not like something, you will know about it. The problem is that an aversion can be accompanied by loud theatrics. Let them vent and rant and rage. Avoid interrupting if you can, do not correct them, and do not bring in any detail. Wait until the tirade is over and say 'you know, you are right, and…' and then tell them something that will distract and interest them. Even if it completely contradicts what they have just said.

When it is important for the deal that you get into the details, point out the salient issues to the Expressive, check that they are following, and close each item as quickly as you can. Their low boredom threshold makes this difficult for them, so help to ease the pain.

2. Amiables ♥

Dealing with an Amiable is both a blessing and a curse. They are warm and easy to get along with, but they do not like making decisions, especially not quick ones. They will listen encouragingly to any proposals or persuasive arguments, but you can't assume that just because they have been supportive, you will get the deal.

When it comes to negotiations, deals often fail because people become intransigent and dig in on a position. Amiables have a useful knack for finding alternatives and solutions to obstacles or deadlock.

Negotiation, however, is frequently linked to conflict, and this is where Amiables struggle. They tend to make needless concessions, which can cost dearly. If you see that an Amiable is willing to throw carrots to keep the peace, be careful of pushing your luck. One-sided deals destroy relationships.

The major problem with Amiables in dealmaking is their indecision. Amiables are archetypal postponers – 'if I leave it for long enough, it will go away'. Postponing can exacerbate conflict, or people with interesting deals on offer may take them somewhere else.

To get an Amiable to make a decision, you can use gentle pressure and press their Hot Buttons. One of their Wants is good relations, so you can point out that if they don't give you a decision by *x* date, the relationship will be damaged, or you will get into trouble, or *y* person will suffer. Make it personal. Amiables need to understand that sometimes the wrong decision is better than no decision.

3. Drivers ♣

The key to a successful deal with a Driver is structure, process and forthrightness. Forget the smarmy snake-oil sales routine. Drivers do not respond terribly well to persuasion, unless it has a base in logic. They want to know about measurable results and specific outcomes. They are usually opinionated, so appealing to their ego or sense of superiority can work, but you have to tread cautiously when hitting these Hot Buttons. If they get a hint that you are trying to schmooze them, you and your deal will be dismissed without ceremony.

The Driver's playing-card suit should give you a clue to their deal-making style – they will club you about the ears until they get what they want, but don't let them intimidate you. They are direct and demanding, but this does not mean that they are more unreasonable than any other style. Drivers intrinsically understand that to get what they want, they need to tell the other party what they want. They don't, however, always remember to give something in return. Make sure, when negotiating, that the Driver knows the value you expect from the transaction.

The joy in dealing with a Driver is that they are decisive. They can't be bothered to play cat and mouse with you, so they will give you their decision once it has been made. If the decision in a deal goes against you, though, it is hard to turn this around. You will need to act quickly. Presenting them with further compelling evidence of the return on investment may buy you a lifeline.

4. Analyticals ♠

You know that I am going to say that when dealing with an Analytical, you have to present lots of facts and figures and information. Well, you do. Skimming over the detail will not hack it with an Analytical. A persistent and detailed approach is essential.

Analyticals are cynical about persuasion, although not immune to it. Your efforts to convince them must be supported by facts and statistics (a few diagrams will also help). Pay careful attention to what they find interesting and focus on that area. Like Amiables, Analyticals are not quick to make decisions. They can resort to Seymour tactics to stall a deal or avoid you. Seymour? See more – the incessant requesting of additional information – hence the spades suit (dig, dig, dig).

Getting to a negotiated agreement with an Analytical can be difficult, as the perpetual need for detail is not always constructive. Their propensity for stubbornness can also create obstacles.

When someone irritates an Analytical, they tend to dig in their heels and become impassive. The phrase 'passive-aggressive' was invented with Analyticals in mind.

If you believe an Analytical is using Seymour to avoid making a decision about a deal, start trading information for information – 'If you give me this information (or decision), I will get you the detail you want.'

Generally, Analyticals are rational people and you should be able to appeal to their sense of reason and fair play to move deals forward. They respond cautiously to their Hot Buttons being pressed, and finding their personal drivers can make all the difference.

The opposite behavioural style to an Analytical is an Expressive. Combining the two styles into the same negotiating team is sound practice, providing the individuals respect each other. Think carefully, though, about sending an Analytical in to close a deal with an Expressive on the other side of the table. And vice versa.

The opposite style to an Amiable is a Driver. An Amiable may aggravate the Driver, while a Driver is almost sure to wound the Amiable. Again, putting these two styles opposite one another in a deal can be tricky, although putting them on the same side does bring balance to the team.

The way in which you approach the behavioural styles can give you a distinct advantage over the competition but, just as importantly, it helps you to close your deals more quickly.

SECRET #36 Modify your behaviour to get the deal
Discerning a person's behaviour will help you to build a relationship with that individual, but the point of the exercise is for you to be able to present your deal in the manner to which they are most likely to respond positively.

DEVIL #36
Modifying the way in which you approach the different styles does not mean you should pretend to be what you are not. Insincerity brings out the best in no one, so be true to the real you.

SECRET #37

YOU SHOULD MAKE THE FIRST PROPOSAL

Are you more of a hard facts (Driver or Analytical) than a touchy-feely (Expressive or Amiable) kind of person? If so, you'll be pleased to know that we are moving away from the 'soft' side of dealmaking. The next few secrets cover the less emotional aspects of dealmaking.

That said, the whole point of the last three secrets was to help you maximise a deal by leveraging other people's Hot Buttons and behavioural styles. Not addressing these soft issues diminishes your relationships and power, and thus your critical differentiators in any deal.

In Part 2, The Power of Power – specifically Secret #23 – I mentioned that to be a brilliant dealmaker you need to make proposals and to respond to proposals. If proposals are so powerful, you may be wondering why I didn't include the power of proposals in the power section.

Before you can plan effectively, you need to understand your power base. Only once you have assessed and considered ways to adjust your power can you start on your strategy, Key and Secondary Issues and Ball Park. Then you start to move into the encounter phase – the Players, their Needs and Hot Buttons, and their behavioural styles. Only when all this has been considered are you ready to start making proposals.

Going back to the dating analogy, you are now ready to start getting involved, making longer-term commitments. Up until now, your relationship has been loose and casual. Who should make the first move?

When I ask the question, 'Who should make the first proposal?' of accountants, they invariably say 'the other guys'. Same with Analyticals. 'Why them?' I ask. 'Because we want to see what they have to say – to see *their* Ball Park first.' Drivers and lawyers are the opposite. They believe that you need to tell the other chaps what you want.

Amiables and human resources people say 'it depends', while Expressives (if they don't forget the question before they get around to answering) shout: 'Me!' This is not unexpected if you look at the Aggressive–Agreeable continuum. Dominant people generally want to assert their authority. When it comes to making proposals, this is the right way in which to behave.

If you're not sure into which camp you fall – the 'me first' or the 'let me hear first' – answer this question: When you meet (or met) someone and you realise you are in love, do you wait for them to say 'I love you', or do you jump in, boots and all? You know the definition of love, of course – it's when your heart turns upside down and pumps the shite to your brain.

I've been a student of dealmaking for nearly 20 years, and while recognising that I still have a lot to learn, I'm confident my guidance is correct when I say *you* should go first. What makes me certain? The school of hard knocks.

Many people are reluctant to make the first move. What if we say 'I love you' and the other person doesn't reciprocate? Will we feel like a fool? Or is it a lack of confidence or not being certain or hoping someone better will come along that stops us from going first?

Actually, the biggest reason people don't want to make the first proposal is the last point – hoping someone or something better will come along. We have already spoken at length about human nature being self-serving, and this is no exception.

In dealmaking, our elementary motivation in *not* making the first proposal is that we are hoping that if we ask the other person to 'make us an offer', they will offer us *more* than we wanted. People don't go first because they are greedy. Protest as much as you like, it does not change the truth. We want to hear the other person's offer just in case it would be better for us than the one we would have made.

The problem with letting the other person make the first move is that they make it on *their* terms, they ask for what *they* want. This is seldom a better deal than we would have wanted for ourselves.

Maybe you spotted my use of the word 'seldom'. I'm not sure what the exact statistics are, but from research I have conducted, the *huge* majority of people are disappointed with the offer they get when they let the other person make the first proposal. Maybe eight or nine out of 10? I certainly don't like those odds, so although one in 10 times I will miss out on a better deal, I'd rather get what I want 90 per cent of the time.

Experiment with this if you like, but I know I'm right. Be brave, tell the other person what you want from a deal.

The issue, irrespective of who makes the first move, is that once the first number is on the table, it becomes the de facto starting point of the deal. It is difficult to move a person up from a low-ball position without making them look like they are being greedy (which we know they are), or without them losing face. Think back to the David Black and the head of security example in Secret #8. Neither man wanted to lose face. Face is a much bigger issue than you can imagine, especially when you are doing deals in East Asia.

We will talk about *where* you open in the next secret, but for the moment, start accepting that you need to make the first move. Sure, you may be rejected, but at least your intentions will be on the table. It's like the game noughts and crosses: the person who makes the first mark usually wins.

Let's assume you are a woman who really wants to get married. Disclosing this before the appropriate stage of the encounter could have your potential beau heading for the hills, but why mess around with someone who has no intention of settling down? You could be hoping to convert him over time, but others tend not to respond well to people who want to change them. *Sic biscuitus disintegratum.*

There are two exceptions to the 'you must make the first proposal' rule. The first is when you have absolutely no idea how much something is worth. Even then, I suggest you do your homework and try to find out. If you are genuinely unable to establish the value of something, wait to hear what the other person has to say first, postpone, do your homework, and then respond to their number.

The second exception is when you have screwed up. Let the other person tell you what they want you to do to put things right. Sometimes they will want an apology, and other times it will be compensation. At least with compensation you can negotiate around giving them what they want, without blindly throwing carrots at them. Customer research shows that it costs about six times as much to attract a new customer than it does to keep an existing one. Even if the unhappy party makes fairly outrageous demands, it might be cheaper to pay this than to find a new deal.

SECRET #37 You should make the first proposal

People resist going first because they are hoping the other party will make them a good offer. This seldom happens, so be bold and make the first move. Even if your proposal is rejected, it will probably be used as the base point from which the deal will be struck. To get what you want, you have to tell the other party what you want.

DEVIL #37

If you let the other person make the first move, and then hope you can move them from their position, you are hoping against thunder.

SECRET #38

OPEN AS HIGH AS YOU CAN WITHIN THE BALL PARK

So, now you have got your mind around making the first move. The next question, of course, is *where* should you open? Hint – there are three positions you prepare in your Ball Park for the Key Issues – the Likely, the Bottom Line and the ... *Opening*! That is exactly where you start.

Deals, however, do not always go according to plan. You will sometimes get to present your Opening proposal as a package, sometimes in chunks, and other times line by line. Use your judgement to decide which is the most appropriate for each situation. A small warning: dumping your whole Opening package on the table can be daunting for the other side, and even though it might be within their range, they may balk. Sometimes, slowly slowly catchy monkey; at other times, you need to go for broke.

This step of the encounter in our dating comparison would be whether you ask the other person to marry you, or to move in with you. If the other person is a bit commitment-phobic, marriage might frighten them off.

I've been encouraging you to push the limits of the Ball Park but not exceed them. How is one supposed to know what is asking too much? It comes back to planning.

The first position you prepare for your Ball Park is your Likely position. This was described in Secret #27 as your realistic expectation of the deal.

Once you know what you can realistically expect to get, the Opening becomes more obvious. Using your Likely as the base point, your Opening position is the best you could expect for each Key Issue. If you are too far from the Likely, you will probably be outside the Ball Park.

Nowhere in this book have you been encouraged to be greedy. John Paul Getty III (American industrialist and richest person in the world in 1966, 1892–1976) agrees that scalping a deal is not a good idea – 'My father said: You must never try to make all the money that's in a deal. Let the other fellow make some money too, because if you have a reputation for always making all the money, you won't have many deals.'

Bear in mind that when you put your proposal on the table, the other party is in all probability going to want you to move, so starting at your Likely position means that you will get pushed towards your Bottom Line. Opening as high as is reasonably possible gives you maximum flexibility. Remember, though, that you need to keep the total value of the deal in sight.

SECRET #38 Open as high as you can within the Ball Park
Using your Likely position for each Key Issue as the realistic base from which to start, open as high as you can while still being reasonable. Decide whether you are going to present your Opening position for a deal as a package or in smaller chunks.

DEVIL #38
Greedy little pigs get eaten by the big bad wolf.

SECRET #39
THERE ARE GUIDELINES FOR GIVING PROPOSALS

When you make your Opening proposal, it is important to use the 'If you … then I' format. The other party is probably going to want you to change some elements of your proposal (even the whole proposal), so using this conditional phrasing makes it clear from the beginning that there are going to be conditions attached to any moves you make.

Having a pre-prepared Ball Park and lots of Marbles means that moving should be a breeze, but it does not mean that you just move. Any movement on your part is a concession, so for each move you make, there needs to be a condition attached: 'If you want me to move on *x*, then I need you to move on *y*.' This is difficult to do without those Marbles.

There are a few tips and techniques for giving and getting proposals that will help to make the most of the proposals on the table. Here are the three key guidelines for when you are *making* proposals.

1. Choose your words carefully.
2. Present your proposal in a structured manner.
3. Be specific when stating your conditions and offers.

1. Choose your words carefully

As you know, the specific words you choose and use in dealmaking, particularly when you are making proposals, are critical. Success *is* in the semantics. Giving careful consideration to your conscious verbal communication, especially when selling or negotiating, goes a long way towards keeping the deal and its various components manageable.

Using the 'If you … then I' format in your proposals helps to increase your control over the trading process, but to maximise the impact of this format, the structure in which you use this phrase also needs attention.

2. Present your proposal in a structured manner

For your proposal to have maximum impact, it needs to be comprehensible but concise. The proposals you make should follow something like the five-step plan structure outlined below (which reminds me of the 'Five Point Palm Exploding Heart Technique' from the *Kill Bill* movies).

STEP 1: Set the scene
(Give context to your proposal)

↓

STEP 2: Make the proposal
(Using 'If you … then I' trading terminology)

↓

STEP 3: Discuss the proposal
(Summaries, explanations, clarification, persuasion, justification, testing assumptions, asking questions, summarising again, etc.)

↓

STEP 4: Try to close
(Get input on your proposal or a counter-proposal)

↓

STEP 5: Repeat
(Steps 1 to 4 are repeated until the deal closes)

Step 1 is important because if you rush in with an 'If you marry me, I will make you happy for the rest of your life', the other side is going to be a bit overwhelmed. Choose the restaurant, the wine, the moment. Pre-empt what you are going to say with 'I love you so much' – that sort of thing.

Try not to muddle up Steps 2 and 3. Keep Step 2 short and sharp by saying 'If you do this for me, then I will do that for you'. Then move to Step 3 with a segue along the lines of 'Let me explain/summarise/clarify …' Use your Vice Captain, if you are lucky enough to have one, to handle Step 3 for you. Step 3 is an interactive one – encourage the other person to ask questions so that you can check their understanding.

In Step 4, you test the water to see how the other party feels about your proposal. A good way to do this is with a Test Close (see Secret #45 for details). Be sure of the other person's position – you don't want to be phoning Mom to tell her you're getting married if the love of your life hasn't given you a definitive answer.

You might be able to seal the deal in Step 4, but if the other person wants to counter-propose, you go back to Step 1 or Step 2 and go through the cycle again – until the deal is closed.

3. Be specific when stating your conditions and offers

Although Step 2 above is short and sharp, do not skimp on the details. Ensure that the conditions you want, and the concessions you're prepared to make, are very clear – 'If you give me a discount of 12.3 per cent and 30 calendar days within which to pay, then I will sign the order next week Tuesday.'

Avoid being vague and avoid being too wordy. Getting the balance between being specific, being concise and giving details is a delicate one. Following a structure helps to manage and maximise your proposals.

SECRET #39 There are guidelines for giving proposals

When you are *making* proposals, be sure to choose your words carefully, present your proposal in a properly structured way, and be specific when stating your conditions and offers. And keep the other party fully involved in the process.

DEVIL #39

Being laissez-faire when you give a proposal dilutes the power and impact of your proposal. Keep the structure and wording of this step in the encounter tight and controlled, and make sure that you are clear on the other party's position.

SECRET #40
THERE ARE GUIDELINES WHEN GETTING PROPOSALS

Something for something, quid pro quo, trading, negotiating, selling, deal-making – all of these imply giving and getting. When you make proposals, expect the other party to make them too.

Back to the dating game. You have now asked your one true love to marry you. Hopefully they say yes, but they might have a counter-proposal ('let's live together first') or a few conditions attached. When I unexpectedly accepted my husband's proposal (we had been together for thirteen years, and he had been proposing every week for the last ten years), I had three conditions – 'It's today, you pay, and I want a ring and a honeymoon.' When I said, 'It's today', it took him a while to realise I meant that very same day. But that's another story.

Just as there are guidelines for making proposals (see Secret #39), there are guidelines for when you get proposals. Here are the three major principles to follow for *receiving* proposals.

1. Do not interrupt a proposal.
2. Listen, check your understanding and ask questions.
3. Invite them to go dancing with you.

1. Do not interrupt a proposal

Never underestimate the power of silence. When someone is making you a proposal, be as quiet and as still as you can. Pay attention to *what* they are saying and *how* they are saying it. You've been encouraged to choose a Coach for your team (who is silent during the face to face) to listen and observe, but this is one time when the whole team needs to be absolutely quiet.

Wait for the other person to finish, and continue to keep quiet. Not only does this give you time to think, but the other guys may try to wake you up by throwing a carrot or two at you. This happened to a colleague of mine, Paul Keates. Paul went into a meeting to discuss a long-term contract, and after the customer had finished making a proposal on pricing, Paul kept quiet. This unnerved the customer, who immediately upped his offer. Paul was speechless. The customer increased his offer again. Silence certainly was golden in this case.

By keeping quiet and letting the other person finish speaking, you get to see the whole proposal, rather than the proposal only up to the point at which you interrupted. Do not allow them to interrupt your proposal either. Ask them to hold their questions and comments until you have finished. In this way, a lot of misunderstanding can be avoided, and time and frustration saved.

2. Listen, check understanding and ask questions

The lost art of listening was covered, along with silence, in Secret #19. If you've forgotten about the power inherent in being quiet and paying attention, read Secret #19 again.

By listening carefully to the other person's issues and concerns, and not just throwing arbitrary carrots at their Needs and Wants, you can save yourself a whole lot of money in a deal. Also, a vigilant listener is far more likely to pick up any clues the other side may drop.

It is imperative in dealmaking that you fully comprehend any proposal you receive. Be sure to test your assumptions, validate your interpretations, understand the conditions and the value, and get the full picture. Ask as many questions as you need – it is better to be thought of as a fool than to accept a proposal you don't understand and be proved a fool.

3. Invite them to go dancing with you

Has this got you wondering? Paying careful attention to the words and structure you use for your proposals, and listening to what the other party says and means, should enable you to move around the Ball Park with the ease and grace of a dancer.

Are you John Travolta, or more William H. Macy doing the sprinkler dance, in the movie *Wild Hogs*? Help is on the way.

SECRET #40 There are guidelines when getting proposals
When you are *receiving* proposals, ensure that the whole proposal is on the table and that you understand exactly what you are being offered. Do not move forward until you have all the detail you need regarding the other side's proposal.

DEVIL #40
Interrupting a proposal, or allowing your proposal to be interrupted, leads to confusion and frustration in a deal. Be still like broccoli.

SECRET #41
FEEL THE RHYTHM OF THE DEAL

Did you ever watch the television programme *Strictly Come Dancing*? If not, here's a brief description of the show. A celebrity is paired with a professional dancer, and the dancer has to teach the celebrity to tango, foxtrot, waltz, rumba, you name it. Every week the dancer–celebrity couple has to perform for a panel of judges, and the couple with the lowest number of votes from the judges, the audience and the phone lines gets thrown off the show. There is more often than not a remarkable improvement in the non-dancers' performances each week.

I have only watched the BBC version, and my absolute favourite 2009 dancer was former boxing champion Joe Calzaghe. He looked like he had an ironing board strapped to his back and a carrot stuck up an interesting place.

The relevance of this to dealmaking? When you are doing a deal, you and the other party should be moving backwards and forwards with the effortlessness of a professional dance team. You make a proposal, there's a bit of cha-cha-cha, they make a counter-proposal, then a rumba, you make a counter-proposal, a few side steps, and they counter-propose once more. There is a rhythm to dealmaking.

If your deal is not moving around easily, somebody is doing it wrong. The problem is that when this happens, the skilled dealmaker (the professional dancer) has to wield the unskilled dealmaker (the boxer) around the room.

You need to take the boxer in your arms and literally manoeuvre his or her body into the rhythm. This takes time and considerable effort.

You give them your proposal (your move), and they interrupt, or immediately reject your proposal, or sulk, or start to argue (their clumsy move). They are supposed to be listening and then making you a counter-proposal (their smooth move). When this does not happen, you need to guide them (you take them in your arms and move them) – ask them to hear you out, ask them for a response, ask which aspects of your proposal they find acceptable, ask if they want time to think, or for the conditions on which they would be prepared to accept the deal (so you both look good).

The trick for not getting thrown off the show is to make the unskilled dancer look good, to move with the rhythm of the deal. In real life, this means that to get the deal, you need to help the unskilled dealmaker to get what they want without making them look stupid or feel inept. There is more on dealing with unskilled (and difficult) dealmakers in Secret #42.

Your unskilled dealmaker is a lot like the person who immediately says no to the indecent proposal (see Secret #5). It is your job to be John Travolta and to show them how to dance, to lead them to the next step they should be taking. Every time they stumble awkwardly, you must guide them into a more graceful movement. It is impossible to do this without a pre-prepared Ball Park and lots of Marbles.

SECRET #41 Feel the rhythm of the deal

If there is no rhythm to your deal, you will struggle to move it to closure. You must patiently but firmly manoeuvre the other party into the steps that keep the deal moving forwards.

DEVIL #41

Do not yield to the temptation to take the 'kill' in 'unskilled' literally. It is up to you to make the bad dealmaker look good by using the momentum inherent in a deal.

SECRET #42

TEACH DIFFICULT OR UNSKILLED DEALMAKERS TO DANCE

Dancing with an unskilled dealmaker takes a lot more time and effort than dancing with a skilled person. You might be thinking that you'd rather do a deal with someone who is unskilled because you'll get a better deal, but this is not generally what happens.

The essential difference between a skilled and an unskilled dealmaker is that the skilled dealmaker gets what they want by giving you what you want (well, most of it, at any rate). An expert dealmaker will not set out to take advantage, whereas an unskilled person tends to try to get the better of you. The only time a skilled person pushes the deal to their advantage is when it is a once-off, short-term transaction.

There is not a huge difference between someone who is difficult and an unskilled dealmaker. You can spot the difficult and unskilled people in a heartbeat because they:

- are unaware of the rhythm in a deal;
- are often aggressive or bullying;
- don't seem to want to do a deal;
- keep saying no;
- make unreasonable demands;
- get bogged down in non-critical issues;
- see trading as 'acting in bad faith';

- try to take advantage of the other party;
- appear to pursue a win/lose strategy;
- use negotiating tricks like 'good cop, bad cop'; and
- go around in circles and eventually disappear up Joe Calzaghe's bottom.

Secret #41 suggested that you guide the unskilled dealmaker/dancer, take them in your arms and show them the rhythm and the steps. This will take you a lot longer to get the deal than if you were dancing with a partner who knows the moves.

It is frustrating trying to close a transaction with someone who seems not to want the deal. The temptation to tell them to 'stick it' is high, but if you do this, you'll be behaving no better than they are. You have to find ways to 'encourage' them to dance with you.

Here are a few dance moves you can use to help them look good and not get thrown off the show:

- Adopt a neutral, non-confrontational style.
- Try not to be defensive or get irritated.
- Say less and listen more.
- Use lots of summaries and make notes.
- Understand what they really want – their concerns, expectations, Issues, Needs, Wants, Hot Buttons.
- Ask questions to find out where they could be flexible.
- Make proposals based on the answers you get.
- When making proposals, do not allow them to interrupt you.
- Meet their demands with clear conditions.
- Separate, in your mind, the person from their behaviour.
- If the clash is personal, consider changing Captains and/or environments.
- If they are ego-driven, they will want to 'win'.

- Allow them to save face, but move the deal forward in exchange for this.
- Tie down the details in the deal.

Skilled dealmakers know the rules of the game, while difficult or unskilled dealmakers are amateurs. If you can't choose to do a deal with a skilled person, you'll need to show the inexperienced party how to behave like a professional.

SECRET #42 Teach difficult or unskilled dealmakers to dance
Difficult or unskilled dealmakers appear not to want the deal. When you are dancing with someone who is an amateur, you need to allocate far more time to the deal. Take the lead and do not react to what appears to be intransigent behaviour. You will surreptitiously be teaching them how to dance.

DEVIL #42
Try not to lose patience with someone who does not know what they are doing in a deal. This is challenging when they are being arrogant or pushy, but bite your tongue and be the professional.

SECRET #43

DEADLOCK DOES NOT HAVE TO MEAN THE END

There are times in a deal when you hit a brick wall – you can move no further. The brick wall is an impasse, a sticking point in the deal. It is an issue on which neither party can, or will, move. Your deal has become deadlocked.

Many people are afraid of deadlock. Even the threat of deadlock is enough to get them whirling around the dance floor like a dervish. Deadlock is not good news, but if you can understand the reason for the deadlock, you can often save the deal from destructing.

Deadlock occurs when one party (or sometimes both) does not want to proceed with the deal on the table. It can be intentional or unintentional. The first step is to establish if the objections are genuine, tactical or attributable to a lack of skill. Let's tackle *unintentional* deadlock first.

Inadvertent deadlock is usually the symptom of one party being unskilled or difficult. Sometimes they do not want to concede a point, and the only way in which they know how to stop this from happening is to say no. Other times they get stuck without Marbles, which means they have no manoeuvrability or flexibility. On other occasions they are digging in on an issue (at times not even an important one) or just being pig-headed. And amateurish dealmakers can be inclined to get their knickers in a knot over relatively minor issues.

In Secret #42, lots of moves were recommended for use with less skilled dealmakers. These are just as effective with deadlock, but the most important one here is: 'Ask questions to find out where they could be flexible.'

The questions you ask must be specifically focused on what it will take to overcome any obstacles. Here are a few examples of questions you can use:

1. What do I need to do to get you to (sign the order, move from your position, park that issue for a moment, etc.)?
2. Under what circumstances would you be willing to (be flexible, consider making this move, give me what I want, and so on)?
3. What are the conditions on which you would be prepared to (agree to increasing *x*, taking less than *y*, etc.)?
4. Just suppose I was to …, would you …?

When working with the inexpert or difficult, *expect* them to be petulant and reply 'none' or 'no' to your questions. Just keep probing, give them ideas for Marbles, and dangle carrots in front of them. Once you have answers or clues, make proposals to address their issues. Yes, it may cost you a few more concessions, but you need to decide if making the concessions is less costly than losing the deal altogether.

If deadlock is *intentional*, it is typically because one party has a genuine problem, or deadlock is being used as a tactical ploy.

When it comes to *genuine objections*, someone is going to have to save the deal by being flexible and presenting proposals that overcome the stalemate. What gives you flexibility? Marbles, that's what.

Concerns that are normally legitimate are:

- the cost of doing the deal is becoming too high;
- there is a lack of value in the transaction;
- 'face' or ego may be lost in agreeing to a deal;

- the deal is going beyond one party's Bottom Line;
- there is no mandate to continue discussions;
- it is cheaper to maintain the status quo than to negotiate; and
- someone is looking for an opportunity to postpone a decision or deal.

No matter what the reasons are, use Questions 1 to 4 on the previous page to test the objections, and then make a call. Is it cheaper to give them what they want, or for you to allow the deadlock to continue, or to lose the deal completely? When deadlock raises its head, there are always going to be ramifications. These can be financial, time-related, precedent, face or ego, social and political factors.

An example that illustrates the costs associated with deadlock perfectly is the British firefighters' strike of 2002/03.

The dispute began when the UK firefighters' union (the Fire Brigades Union or FBU) voted to strike when their demand for a 39 per cent pay increase was rejected by the UK Fire Service (funded from the government public services budget). The increase would have brought the average firefighter's wage up to around £30 000 per annum.

Initially, despite the size of the FBU's demands, public support was with the firemen, who were recognised as risking their lives every day to save others. The British armed forces had to provide emergency cover during the strike, using vintage Green Goddess fire engines. Public support for the firemen began to waver when reports of people dying in fires due to the strike began to increase.

The FBU refused to abandon its 39 per cent increase demand, until a publically released study showed firefighting to be only the 23rd-most dangerous profession, and another report revealed that there were roughly 40 applicants for every firefighter position advertised (suggesting that pay rates were sufficient).

Losing the support of the public was pivotal in getting the FBU to be flexible. Almost seven months after the strike began, a 16 per cent increase over three years, linked to changes to working conditions, was accepted. If the FBU had settled earlier, they would have got a more favourable deal at far less cost to themselves and the fire victims.

There are many interesting facets to the costs of this deadlock – the length of the strike, the role of public pressure, the social issues around the preventable loss of life, the cost to the FBU of strike pay for the firefighters, the perceived greed associated with the pay demands and the armed forces winning public favour for the employer.

This brings us to the *intentional tactical* use of deadlock. My view of the UK firefighters' strike is that the excessive demands of the FBU showed that they were staging a show of force against the government, using the firefighters and the fire victims as pawns in their game. The power they would have gained, had they not lost public support, would have been staggering.

Intentional deadlock is not found only in the public services domain. It is also very common in business. Here are a couple of cases in point.

A large motor-car manufacturer needed to shut down a plant to retool for a new model car. This meant having the production workers on paid leave for six weeks while output from the plant was zero. The manufacturer waited until the annual wage negotiations, drove the negotiations into deadlock, and retooled the plant while the workers were on strike on a no-work, no-pay basis.

Obviously this was a morally questionable action, but then again, the manufacturer had been on the receiving end of destructive strikes from the workforce for many years.

In another instance, a large and powerful retailer demanded that a supplier substantially drop the margin on its best-selling perishable consumer product, or have its product delisted (taken off the shelves). The supplier could not offset this discount against any other merchandise lines, as it is a one-product company. The cost of agreeing to the discount would have been catastrophic for the supplier, so they had no choice but to drive the negotiations into deadlock. Their product was delisted.

Soon enough, the retailer was losing 'baskets' of sales due to the supplier's product not being available in rural supermarkets. Populations with low literacy levels tend to shop by the basket, and if one of their preferred products is not available, they leave the whole basket and shop elsewhere. The retailer begrudgingly asked the supplier to relist at the old price. The supplier refused. They maintained the deadlock until the retailer *increased* their profits.

The intentional use of deadlock is usually linked to power and money. Even if this conjures up images of the Mafia for you, do not judge deadlock too harshly. Before you use this tactic, though, you do need to calculate the costs and benefits of deadlock versus doing the deal. Weigh them up carefully. Deadlock plays havoc with relationships, and if you have to work together in future, this strategy takes its toll.

You can use the dance moves you've learnt from dealing with unskilled dealmakers to *break* deadlock. Also bring some persuasion into play – highlight the costs of the deadlock to the other party. Gauge them in financial and non-financial terms, and then make proposals to move the deal forward.

Just as there are techniques to break deadlock, there are ways in which you can *create* deadlock. Again, look at the list of identifiers from Secret #42 describing how to spot difficult or inexpert dealmakers, and use a few of those less-than-desirable techniques. Be warned, though: intentionally provoking conflict always carries a price.

SECRET #43 Deadlock does not have to mean the end
Deadlock can be intentional or unintentional. Establish whether the objections are genuine, tactical or attributable to a lack of skill. Each one requires a different approach. Be comfortable with breaking and creating deadlock, but be mindful of the consequences.

DEVIL #43
Do not shy away from deadlock. It can be a useful means of postponing a deal or maintaining the status quo. It does come at a price and more often than not damages the relationship.

PART 5

THE CLOSE

People get caught up in wonderful eye-catching pitches, but they don't do enough to close the deal.

Donald Trump (American business entrepreneur, 1946–)

SECRET #44

VALIDATE THE FINAL PROPOSAL AND CLOSE DATE

This part is the shortest in the book, but do not misinterpret this as meaning that the close phase is the least important aspect of a deal. It is not – it is the *most* important.

Dr Peter Drucker was quoted in Secret #6 as saying that dealmaking is exciting and fun. But it is all too easy to get swept up in the euphoria of the moment and neglect the detail of the deal. This can be disastrous.

To get a large or complex deal to finality, you would have invested huge amounts of time and energy – looking at the alternatives in the deal, evaluating your power base, defining the deal, identifying the various individuals involved in the decision, building these relationships and understanding what each person expects from the deal, making and receiving proposals, and dancing around the room with the other team. Do you leave it there and hope it comes to fruition? Of course not. You need to protect your investment – you can't afford to relax yet.

Closing is my *bête noire*, the element of the deal that is anathema to me. I do not avoid it because I'm afraid someone will say no at the end of a deal, or because I lack the confidence to go for the close. I avoid it because as soon as I think the deal is done, I want to find something else to excite me.

In traditional selling definitions, there are two kinds of salesperson – the hunter who chases new business, and the farmer who looks after existing accounts. In dealmaking it is no different. As a classic hunter, once I have 'caught' the deal, I need the thrill of a new conquest. The problem is that I look for the new deal before I have closed down the details of the last one.

There is a well-known aphorism of which I continually remind myself – 'The devil is in the detail'. Warren Buffett (American investor, industrialist and philanthropist, 1930–) is credited with having first made this proclamation, but the original source was supposedly Ludwig Mies van der Rohe (German architect, 1886–1969) who said, 'God is in the details.' Regardless as to which end of the theological divide it belongs, it is good advice. I've lost more deals than I care to admit because I did not tie down the details properly. This happens most frequently in deals that benefit me personally – commission, profit share, stock. I assume the other party will do good by me. When am I going to learn that people can be pretty greedy?

The devil in the deal is in the detail – in the close; at the end; the vinegar strokes, in a manner of speaking.

The final proposal and the close date

You are now almost sure that your deal is ready for closing – you have persuaded the other party on the merits of the deal, negotiated the Key Issues with them, and are fiddling around with minor Secondary Issues or Marbles. How do you move the deal to close?

Here are five tips to help you check that your deal is actually at the end point, that when you go for the close you will meet with little resistance:

1. *Have a target close date.* You need to be working towards a date by which the deal will be signed. This can't be a date that suits only you – it *must* be one with which the other party is also comfortable.
2. *Measure the support you have from each player.* Remember the Decision Centre – all the other party's players you needed to get on your side to

progress the deal towards finality? The people whose business Needs, personal Wants and behavioural styles you spent time getting your head around? Once you have a feel for the close date, actively solicit support for this date from each person in the Decision Centre. In doing this, you can simultaneously flush out any remaining issues and concerns.

3. *Agree the deal with the Highlander.* Whenever possible, get the Highlander to tacitly express their support for the deal and, equally importantly, the close date. If you are able to get the key decision-maker aligned, the rest of their team will follow far more readily.
4. *First prize is a group close.* Once you are confident that you have the Highlander's endorsement, try to get all the Decision Centre players into one room and get a collective 'yes' to your final proposal. If you can achieve this, you don't have to 'herd cats', and you can contain the threat of the Anti-Coach scuppering your deal – all in one move.
5. *Listen to your gut feel.* If your gut is telling you that something is wrong with the deal – if you feel anxious or worried or uncomfortable – then there is sure to be a problem. You are close to the end now, so you don't really want to start at the beginning, but you have to identify what is unconsciously bothering you. The best way to figure this out? Get coaching from your Pro-Coach.

SECRET #44 Validate the final proposal and close date
Before you rush in to close the deal, make sure that everyone involved in the deal is in favour of your final proposal, especially the date by which you plan to sign the deal. Getting the buy-in of the entire Decision Centre in one meeting is first prize.

DEVIL #44
One of the biggest mistakes that dealmakers are inclined to make is to set a close date that suits their own requirements. The other party must agree to the close date, or the deal will be a pipe dream.

SECRET #45
TEST-CLOSE THE DEAL BEFORE YOU COMMIT

It is almost time to close the deal, to consummate the relationship. But. Before you make the deal final, you may want to be absolutely certain that there are no hidden-agenda items, or any last-minute problems or concerns that could derail the transaction. The best way to test that the deal is ready for final signature is by using a trial close, or what is better described as a Test Close.

The term 'trial close' is usually associated with selling, but the ways in which a salesperson and a dealmaker employ this technique are different. The *Monash Marketing Dictionary* describes a trial close as:

> [a] technique used in selling to assess the buyer's readiness to make a purchase decision. A trial close usually takes the form of questions that ask for decisions on minor selling points; if the salesperson gets favourable responses to these questions, he or she can more confidently attempt to close the sale.

The literal translation of this definition is the following, an edited definition from the website www.changingminds.org (use this site with caution – I was spammed after looking at it):

A trial close is not a normal closing technique but a test to determine whether the person is ready to close. Use it after a presentation or after you have made a strong selling point. Use it when you have answered objections. Ask questions that assume they have already bought the product:

It looks like you really like this. Is that true?
If you took it home, would you be proud to own this?
Do you prefer the larger or smaller version?
How would it look on the shelf back at home?

Although this smacks of insultingly obvious manipulation and 'timeshare' sales techniques, do not discount the value of the trial close as a whole when used properly. There is no need to stage-manage the other party when all you want to do is close the deal.

You know when the deal is ready to close – you have negotiated the Key Issues, settled the Secondary Issues, and are now into fine-tuning your final proposal. In dealmaking, though, it is prudent to ensure that nobody plans to take last-minute advantage as the deal reaches finality.

I used to be part of a dealmaking team in which one very senior person in our group could not help but twist the deal in his favour just before it closed, or add something just after it had been agreed. This destroyed many a good deal, but what I learnt is that some people just can't help themselves – they can't control their inner piggy.

Before you sign, you need to confirm that the other party is also ready to put pen to paper. The Test Close allows you to check the other party's position without fully committing to close from your side. The best way to do this is to use supposition questions such as:

- Before we sign, is there any last issue you need to raise?

- If you have nothing more to add, are we ready to close?
- Is there any reason you can't sign the deal as it stands?
- If we can agree on these items, will you then be satisfied with the deal?
- Just suppose I was to accept the deal, would that be everything from your side?

These are closed questions – they require a yes-or-no reply. It is extremely difficult for the other person to answer these questions without revealing their hand.

Even if you are happy with the Test Close, you still need to make absolutely sure that everyone has the same understanding of the deal to which they are agreeing.

SECRET #45 Test-close the deal before you commit
A Test Close is used in dealmaking to check that all the agenda items have been agreed, and that there is nothing under the table that could derail the deal at the last minute. Use supposition questions to flush out any surprises before you sign.

DEVIL #45
The trial close used by a salesperson is not the same as the Test Close of the dealmaker. A trial close can be seen as a blatant attempt to manipulate the other team, and could blow your deal.

SECRET #46

TAKE THREE MORE SMALL STEPS BEFORE CLOSING

You have set up the close of the deal by validating your final proposal and you've done a Test Close or two. Even if you and your gut are happy, don't sign quite yet – you still have three little moves to make. You need to compare the final deal to your Likely position; make absolutely certain that everyone has exactly the same understanding of the deal to which they are agreeing; and agree on the implementation plan.

1. Compare the deal to your Likely position

Before you shake hands, compare the deal you are about to sign to the Likely position of your Ball Park. If you realise that you've made a mistake or need to adjust something, now is the time to do it. Do not try to sneak the item into the agreement at a later stage, as you will probably ruin the whole deal *and* damage the relationship – rather say to the other side that there is 'one last thing I need to discuss' and put it on the table. Be aware that this is liable to reopen the negotiations, but it is preferable to signing a deal you will regret.

This is also the point at which you may need to bring in the Expert Advisors once more (usually the lawyers, to draw up the final contract) and perhaps the Highlanders of both sides (if you need their input or approval). Including the latter to test and validate the deal can be extremely useful, but the danger is that 'there can be only one'. They might destroy your deal while trying to prove who is cock-a-hoop.

Tie down the detail and close any loopholes – you do not want surprises later. If you are bad with detail (you are probably an Expressive or Amiable), get someone to help you with this – a trusted Vice Captain, or a team member who is an Analytical.

2. Check that you are signing the same deal

When you are sure that everything is now on the table and that no further adjustments need to be made, check the understanding that both parties (yes, double-check yourself too) have of the deal. This is vitally important when you are working with different cultures or languages. Two people can glean completely different meanings from the same word.

How should you check? Summarise their side, summarise your side, summarise the whole deal and summarise again. If you get bored in the same way as I do with the close, get someone to do this part for you. Just because you don't want to do the detail doesn't mean it shouldn't be done. Closing is the stage at which you thank the heavens for Analyticals.

3. Agree on the implementation plan

One last consideration before you sign: to make sure the deal does not disappear into the woodwork after it is signed, you need to agree on the implementation plan – who, what, when and where. You may think this should be discussed after the deal has been closed, but the issues that implementation pre-empts often mean that a bit more negotiation and fine-tuning becomes necessary.

SECRET #46 Take three more small steps before closing

Before putting pen to paper, compare the final deal on the table to your Likely Ball Park position, make sure that both sides have exactly the same understanding of the deal they will be signing, and agree on the implementation plan. Then summarise the final summaries of the deal.

DEVIL #46

The deal may have taken longer than expected. Don't be tempted to miss these three steps. Doing so could delay the deal further or even take it backwards.

SECRET #47
CLOSE THE DEAL IN WRITING

Finally, it is time to close the deal. You have validated your final proposal and summarised the deal to within an inch of its life. You've worked hard to get the deal to this point, so don't go messing it up! There is a temptation at the close to sweeten the deal a bit for yourself, but being greedy is often the final straw.

Picture your deal as a delicious meal – appetisers, soup, salad, the main course with side dishes, dessert, cheese and biscuits, and even coffee and *petits fours*. You are satiated, but you still demand a mint. If you are a Monty Python fan, you will know what happens to the glutton who eats the mint – he literally explodes.[10] Keep your inner pig under control.

On the flipside of this, if you realise that the other party has made an unintentional mistake, don't just sign the deal anyway. When, rather than if, the other party realises what has happened, you will have a problem. You need to point out the mistake, make a proposal about what should be done to correct it (maybe get yourself a small carrot in the process), and then move to the final deal.

Now you can close the deal. Ideally, you want to sign the deal while everything is fresh in everyone's mind. Get the deal in writing as soon as

10. The Monty Python sketch in which the glutton eats a wafer-thin mint is called 'Mr Creosote'. Although generally a Monty Python fan, I find the sketch quite revolting and do not recommend you look for it unless you are extremely tolerant and have a strong stomach.

possible. It does not matter if this takes the form of minutes, Heads of Agreement, a contract or a handwritten piece of paper. Leave nothing out and even less to chance.

SECRET #47 Close the deal in writing
When the deal finally closes, put it in writing as soon as you can. Deals, especially the details, go to hell in a handbasket far too easily if the specifics are not recorded promptly.

DEVIL #47
A deal is not really closed until you have the money.

SECRET #48

REJECTION HAPPENS TO EVERYONE

The deal is now signed and sealed. Why, then, are there still three more secrets? These are all about *you.*

One of the biggest challenges you will face in dealmaking is when someone says 'no' to your deal. There will be times when no matter how hard you persuade, no matter how well you prepare, no matter how expertly you negotiate, the other party will reject your proposal. Unless you have the hide of a rhinoceros, it is extremely difficult not to take this personally. Think about a marriage proposal. There you are, making yourself vulnerable, and the object of your affection rejects you. People banish themselves for less.

When you feel as if you have been kicked in the teeth, here are a few pointers to keep in mind.

1. It is not always about you

Try to find out *why* the other party is saying no. Is it about them, or about you?

If it's you, accept that people are reluctant to come straight out and say as much. They will sidestep you, invent problems or bald-facedly lie. Back to the wedding proposal being rejected (or if this is not something to which you can relate, think about breaking off any relationship). 'It's not you, it's me.' Is it really them, or are they just sparing your feelings? Or if they can't bear to blame themselves, they might pick a fight with you – provoke you until you walk away.

Seldom will you meet someone who is horribly heartless, brutally unkind or completely honest. While an open rebuff is hard to handle, *not* being told the issue means you don't know what to fix. It will serve you well to remember that there is nothing you can do to change the way someone else behaves; you can only change your own behaviour. Loosen up on being a control freak.

When you are uncertain about whether the 'no' is about you or them, the best approach is to ask questions. Below is a list of quick questions you can use, but also have another look at the questions suggested in Secret #43.

- What do I need to do to get you to agree to …?
- What must I change to make my proposal acceptable to you?
- Exactly what is it in my proposal that you find unacceptable?
- Under what conditions would you give me what I want?
- Can you give me a detailed response to my proposal?
- What if I was to change *x* in my proposal?
- Just suppose I was to offer you *y*, would you …?

You might still not know if it is you or them, but at least you will have tried to find out. It is not always personal. The other party may have restrictions or issues about which you know nothing, and which they may not be at liberty to share with you. Then again, they might be an immovable force taking a stand. There is nothing you can do about that.

2. Before you give up …

Before you throw yourself dramatically to the ground and weep over the rejection, give the deal another try. Look at Secret #4 once more, and explore the alternative choices available to you. Follow another car using the Dirk Gently–inspired Zen navigation technique.

The first stop is always persuasion. Try to change their minds by persuading them how it will benefit them to shift their position. If you are not able to convince them to move, try negotiating. 'If you do *this* for me, then I will do *that* for you.' Go through all the alternatives if you must, or try teaching them to dance (Secret #42). They might just be unskilled or difficult.

One more port of call is to check the Bottom Line of *their* Ball Park. Ask the question directly – 'Is this beyond your mandate?', or 'Am I offering too little?' It may lead you back to wondering if it is you or them, but at least you tried to shake the 'no' loose.

3. Pick yourself up, dust yourself off

Very rarely have I seen an expert dealmaker say 'no'. Even if the other person wants something completely outrageous, the expert makes sure they get something equally ridiculous in return. This usually has the effect of seeing off silly demands, but sadly, not everyone is skilled. Accept that sometimes you are not going to be able to shift the 'no'.

Pick yourself up, dust yourself off, put your underpants on the outside, and deal with it. You can't win 'em all.

SECRET #48 Rejection happens to everyone

Rejection is disheartening but it happens to us all. Try everything you can to shift the 'no', but also recognise when you are just not going to win and accept the rejection with as much dignity as you can muster.

DEVIL #48

Practise not taking rejection to heart. If you can do this, you will be able to bounce back far more quickly, be happier and live longer.

SECRET #49

HAVE A VERY GOOD REASON TO WALK AWAY

Although walking away is one of the alternatives you need to consider in dealmaking (see Secret #4), it is not one you should consider lightly. Good deals are lost because someone could not be bothered to persevere (they're lazy), or they throw in the towel when the going gets rough (they're a wimp), or they quickly exit for fear of being rejected (they're an egotist).

We all believe that we're *not* lazy or wimpy or egomaniacs? But, think back to how you have conducted your relationships. I hate to admit it, but I have been guilty in the past of running before I could get dumped.

Distinguish between when you need to walk away and when you are making excuses for giving up (lazy, wimp, ego) on a deal. If you have good reason for quitting, don't be too hard on yourself – but make sure you have *good* reason.

As I mentioned in Secret #48, very seldom have I seen an expert dealmaker walk away, but there are a few situations in which you may not want to continue with the deal.

1. Your values are being compromised

In the *Indecent Proposal* exercise (Secret #5), I encouraged you to see flexibility in everything, including your values and morals. I did say, though, that this depended on the price you would have to pay to get what you want. The point of this exercise was to help you realise that deals are not black and white – or negotiable and not negotiable. As a dealmaker, your knee-jerk reactions need to be overridden. You must be able to ask yourself 'Under what circumstances could I agree to that?' rather than responding with an immediate 'yes' or 'no'.

In real life, unless it is a matter of life or death, don't sell your soul. Be true to who you are and what you believe. If someone is asking you to do something that goes against every fibre of your being, ask yourself 'Under what conditions ...' and then reply. You might find that 'none' is the answer in your heart, and that you're not just an unskilled dealmaker making a clumsy move.

Selling out on who you are, and what you hold dear, carries a terrible price. Been there, done that. It takes an age to recover from betraying yourself in this way. No deal is worth the sacrifice.

2. You are going below your Bottom Line

When someone else, like your boss or life partner or whoever, has set the mandate and determined the Bottom Line of the Ball Park, you can't simply drop below this limit. If the other party wants you to exceed the limit, you need to renegotiate your mandate or walk away. If the boss (or whoever) agreed to your Marbles beforehand, you can usually stay above the line.

If it is a self-determined Bottom Line, again ask yourself: 'What are the conditions under which I could agree to this?' Expert dealmakers do not walk away – they put a price on the demands being made of them. They have a bag full of Marbles, and understand the exact value of each Marble going into the deal. No Marbles = no flexibility.

3. Use your judgement

If doing the deal with the other party is excruciating, and every single move is a struggle, and you're not sure you want to do a deal with people you can't respect or don't trust, then walk away. It is *very* difficult for someone who has the deal in their sights to stop and take stock, but this is exactly what you might want to do if your alarm bells are ringing.

It may be expensive to walk away, but doing business with someone who has shown dishonesty, or who is vengeful and mean, or has the capacity to renege on what has been agreed, is sure to be a nightmare.

There are people with whom I choose not to engage, as I feel we do not share a common set of values – and as you have probably figured out, my morals are not so conservative. I'm just not prepared to do deals with people who foul my soul.

SECRET #49 Have a very good reason to walk away

Good deals are lost because someone could not bother to persevere, or throws in the towel at the first sign of trouble, or exits for fear of being rejected. Being Mr Lazy, a scaredy-cat or an insufferable egomaniac are not excuses for walking away. Only let go of a deal if your values, the Bottom Line or your judgement scream warnings at you.

DEVIL #49

Walking away is easy. Staying the course is far more difficult. If you quit too soon, you'll never get the high of a deal well done. But don't sell your soul for a shot of euphoria.

SECRET #50

RELENTLESS DEALMAKING CHASES AWAY LOVED ONES

How to Win Friends and Influence People by Dale Carnegie (American writer, lecturer and self-help expert, 1888–1955) is acknowledged to be the first ever self-improvement book. It has sold 15 million copies since it was first published in 1936. Being contrary, I prefer *How to Lose Friends and Alienate People* by Toby Young (British journalist and author, 1963–). I must admit to not having read the book, but the movie is hilarious.

The quickest way to 'lose friends and alienate people' in real life is to start treating everything as a deal. Your six-year-old son wants a new bike for his birthday? If you say, 'Well, keep your room tidy until you leave home and we'll talk about it,' you are sure to alienate your loved ones. Your wife wants to take you out for dinner for your anniversary? You would be ill-advised to value this in your eyes and announce, 'If you promise to cook every night for the next year, I will grace you with my presence.' Some things are best given as gifts.

As with walking away from a deal, you need to be honest with yourself when it comes to giving presents and being of service to others. If you are giving something away and getting nothing in return under the guise of 'because I love them' or 'I am a generous soul', you deserve to get your backside kicked. Give because it is from the heart, and walk away only if you have no choice.

Generosity breeds greed, not gratitude. The more you give, the more people expect. There are hundreds of sayings and proverbs about this. My husband's favourite is: 'Give her an inch and she'll think she's the ruler.'

People are always moaning to me about how advantage is being taken of them in their family and business lives. They complain continually about being unappreciated. So who is to blame? A line has to be drawn between gift-giving and mindless gifts. And there is no time to start like now. If you feel you are being used and abused, put a stop to it. Put a condition on the demands being made of you. When you start trading with the people in your life, they will be surprised – even outraged – if what you gave in the past now has a price tag attached. They will test you for a while, but luckily people learn quickly – the exploitation will stop or move away.

You now have the power to get exactly what you want from deals. Don't become a jerk just because you can. Be kind to those around you. The line, 'Don't confuse kindness with weakness', from the 2001 movie *Swordfish*, starring John Travolta, says it all for me. And according to *The Second Coming* by controversial author John Niven (Scottish writer, 1968–), 'Be kind' is the one true commandment.

SECRET #50 Relentless dealmaking chases away loved ones
Decide when to give unconditionally, and when you want value in return. With loved ones, you may want to give out of the generosity of your heart. This is fine, as long as it is a conscious choice on your part and not because you are a dog of a dealmaker.

DEVIL #50
If you give and give, don't be surprised or disappointed when people take and take from you. Or tell you to 'sod off'.

PART 6

SUMMARY

If we're looking for the source of our troubles, we shouldn't test people for drugs, we should test them for stupidity, ignorance, greed and love of power.

P. J. O'Rourke

(American political satirist, journalist and author, 1947–)

50 SECRETS AND DEVILS IN SHORT

In my Introduction, I made the statement: 'Dealmaking is the lifeblood of business.' Dealmaking is actually much broader than this. There is not one aspect of our existence that it does not touch.

Being a skilled dealmaker makes for a far easier path through life. What, again, is a dealmaker? 'A person skilled in using instinct, processes and expertise in primarily negotiation, selling and communication, and able to leverage or adjust the balance of power to bring closure to transactions that usually benefit all parties' (© The Dealmaker Programmes Company).

Through sharing my successes and failures with you, I intended to strip naked all the nonsense around the subject of dealmaking. *The Devil in the Deal: 50 Secrets to Successful Dealmaking* has hopefully given you insight into the 50 key Secrets and dastardly Devils that make and break deals. You should now be an expert dealmaker.

And here, something for nothing, is a summary of all 100 lessons.

The 50 Secrets

SECRET #1 Dealmakers use specific skills to get what they want
Stripping down the definition of a successful dealmaker into a basic single sentence, this is how it reads: A dealmaker is someone who is able to get what they want by using a finely tuned set of skills.

SECRET #2 Selling is not a swear word
Selling often allows you to get what you want using just the power of persuasion, making it an essential dealmaking process and tool.

SECRET #3 Negotiation is the world's oldest profession
Negotiating is about giving to get – you trade something of value to the other party in exchange for getting what you want and value.

SECRET #4 There is power in having alternatives
There are lots of alternatives a dealmaker can use to get the deal, but they all have a cost – choose the most appropriate one for each situation, but keep other options in your back pocket for leverage and to adjust power.

SECRET #5 Everything is open to a deal
An expert dealmaker recognises that everything can potentially be open to a deal, but the art is in choosing the correct alternatives for each situation, and ensuring that you get the appropriate value in return for any concessions you might need to make.

SECRET #6 No one is above the law of dealmaking
The world's richest and most successful businesspeople are first and foremost dealmakers. Every person and organisation on the planet needs to be able to close deals to survive, never mind succeed.

SECRET #7 Everyone has the potential to be a dealmaker
Some people retain the dealmaking instincts and potential with which they were born; others lose them. As selling and negotiating are innate abilities, it is not difficult to recapture and develop these life skills.

SECRET #8 Verbal communication operates on two levels
Verbal communication is all about words. To get the most from this in dealmaking, you need to choose your words and phrases *consciously*, and listen for the *unconscious* hints and clues in the language of the other person.

SECRET #9 Non-verbal communication can be obscure
Although non-verbal communication is less reliable than conscious verbal communication, this does not mean it should be ignored. The power of insight is remarkable, so learn to interpret non-verbal messages.

SECRET #10 People and donkeys are not that different
A successful deal is one in which you get the incentives (or carrots) you want, and the other party gets the carrots that satisfy their needs. To maximise your deal, trade what *they* value for that which you value most highly.

SECRET #11 Deals need to focus on value, not price
In dealmaking, value is more important than price. If you are able to show the other party the *value* for them in the deal, you are far more likely to get what you value in return.

SECRET #12 Do not confuse value with cost
Just because something doesn't cost you much doesn't mean this has a low value to the other party. Trade items that cost you little but that have high value to the other side for items that you value but are low-cost to them.

SECRET #13 Everything in dealmaking is interconnected
World-class dealmakers approach deals holistically. They assess what they need to do to close a deal. They then weave these into a plan to get what they value in exchange for giving the other party the value they want.

SECRET #14 Planning in itself creates power
The actual process of planning makes you aware of the potential power you have in a deal. A SWOT analysis is a valuable planning tool that highlights potential strengths and weaknesses, opportunities and threats.

SECRET #15 Controlling information provides strategic power
Information is only power if you understand its importance to the deal as a whole. Being in control of the information will give you power, and the three essentials of control in a deal are summaries, debate and testing.

SECRET #16 The giving of information needs to be planned
The giving of information can range from direct, unambiguous statements to subtle hints and suggestions. Deciding what information to give or withhold, and how best to do this, can put plenty of power in your hands.

SECRET #17 There is no excuse for not getting information
Having the right information helps to facilitate the deal and close it more quickly. Getting meaningful information gives you leverage and power around your most important issues, which helps you to understand what is of significance to the other side.

SECRET #18 Plan and execute questions with care and love
Planning which questions you want to ask and how you are going to ask them, and being direct and interested, will get you the information you need for a deal. The intelligent use of this knowledge provides you with the power to close a favourable deal.

SECRET #19 Listening and silence reveal the truth
Question. Listen. Pause. Think. Speak.
Repeat.
Repeat.
Repeat until you know what you need to do to close the deal.

SECRET #20 Long-term relationships can be costly
Not all long-term relationships are necessarily beneficial. You need to ensure continually that there is a mutual and fair exchange of value within a medium-term time frame. If this is not happening, you need to adjust the power by changing your dealings with the relevant party to explicit value-for-value exchanges.

SECRET #21 Not all networks are equal
A large network of well-connected people with whom you have direct, personal relationships is a powerful resource. Use your network to get the information you need to optimise and close your deals.

SECRET #22 Taking time to think is not a weakness
Giving yourself the opportunity to think about information and proposals during a deal will always serve you well. A timeout has similar power to a postponement. Use as many timeouts as you need.

SECRET #23 Power can be created from very basic sources
Power can be used to gain an unfair advantage, so go for it. As a dealmaker, you need to check your position of power continually. Think like Simon the *cordon bleu* cook, and not Kim the noodle queen, when your cupboard appears to be empty of power. Go back to *The Basics*.

SECRET #24 Structure must follow strategy
When you go into a deal, you need to start with a strategy that outlines what you want and how you are going to achieve your objectives. Only once this is in place do you consider the structure of the deal and the team.

SECRET #25 Follow simple steps to define the deal
Having an easy-to-use tool will make planning for a deal much easier. The three recommended steps are:
Step One: the Issues
Step Two: the Ball Park
Step Three: the Players.

SECRET #26 Step One is to identify and prioritise all Issues
The *first task* in Step One is to identify all your Issues for a specific deal. The *second task* is to prioritise this list. You should have around three to five Key Issues. The balance of the list (which will be long) forms your Secondary Issues.

SECRET #27 Step Two is to know the limits of the Ball Park
For each Key Issue, you need to set a Likely, Bottom Line and Opening range. Your Opening position is the deal you would get in a perfect world, while Bottom Line is where you would walk away. Any deal *as a whole* that is higher than your Likely position is a good one. Less than your Bottom Line is an unacceptable compromise.

SECRET #28 Use Marbles to maintain the Ball Park
The Key Issues are your must-haves, and the Secondary Issues your nice-to-haves. Trade your Key Issues with their Key Issues wherever possible, and only get into the Secondary Issues and Marbles should you need to adjust the value of the total deal.

SECRET #29 Step Three is to choose your Players carefully
There is comfort and strength in having a well-disciplined, properly briefed team with you when you go into a deal. Your power can be diluted, though, if the players don't stick to the roles they are meant to perform.

SECRET #30 Their players do not play by the same rules
Understanding which of the seven roles that each person in the other camp plays gives you important insight into their individual levels of power and influence. For you to be successful in closing the deal, the two most valuable roles to you in a deal are likely to be the Highlander and your Pro-Coach.

SECRET #31 Experts and advisors can make or break a deal
Expert Advisors are an invaluable resource, but knowing when to wheel them in and out is a talent. It is the knowledge of how to utilise and manage Expert Advisors that differentiates the dealmakers from the negotiators.

SECRET #32 Wanting and needing are not synonymous
People buy from people, not faceless companies. Being able to distinguish between someone's individual business Needs and personal Wants is important in dealmaking, especially when it comes to competitive deals. The carrots you use to incentivise Needs are different to those you use to address Wants.

SECRET #33 A business Need must exist for results to be achieved
Only if someone sees a business Need will they show interest in a deal. The perception of a Need can differ from person to person, but the various groups of Deciders and Influencers have a collective view of the business outcomes and results they want from a deal. Use Value Propositions to show each person how their specific Needs will be addressed.

SECRET #34 Ignore personal Hot Buttons at your peril
Hot Buttons are personal motivators that have significant influence over how an individual's decisions are made. Understanding and meeting another person's Wants or Hot Buttons helps to develop the relationship and can be a vital differentiator in deals that are closely competed.

SECRET #35 Identify behavioural styles to build relationships
There are four behavioural styles into which people can generally be classified. Understanding someone's primary style guides you on how to approach that person and build a relationship. Hot Buttons can be more easily ascertained if you know a person's style.

SECRET #36 Modify your behaviour to get the deal
Discerning a person's behaviour will help you to build a relationship with that individual, but the point of the exercise is for you to be able to present your deal in the manner to which they are most likely to respond positively.

SECRET #37 You should make the first proposal
People resist going first because they are hoping the other party will make them a good offer. This seldom happens, so be bold and make the first move. Even if your proposal is rejected, it will probably be used as the base point from which the deal will be struck. To get what you want, you have to tell the other party what you want.

SECRET #38 Open as high as you can within the Ball Park
Using your Likely position for each Key Issue as the realistic base from which to start, open as high as you can while still being reasonable. Decide whether you are going to present your Opening position for a deal as a package or in smaller chunks.

SECRET #39 There are guidelines for giving proposals
When you are *making* proposals, be sure to choose your words carefully, present your proposal in a properly structured way, and be specific when stating your conditions and offers. And keep the other party fully involved in the process.

SECRET #40 There are guidelines when getting proposals
When you are *receiving* proposals, ensure that the whole proposal is on the table and that you understand exactly what you are being offered. Do not move forward until you have all the detail you need regarding the other side's proposal.

SECRET #41 Feel the rhythm of the deal
If there is no rhythm to your deal, you will struggle to move it to closure. You must patiently but firmly manoeuvre the other party into the steps that keep the deal moving forwards.

SECRET #42 Teach difficult or unskilled dealmakers to dance
Difficult or unskilled dealmakers appear not to want the deal. When you are dancing with someone who is an amateur, you need to allocate far more time to the deal. Take the lead and do not react to what appears to be intransigent behaviour. You will surreptitiously be teaching them how to dance.

SECRET #43 Deadlock does not have to mean the end
Deadlock can be intentional or unintentional. Establish whether the objections are genuine, tactical or attributable to a lack of skill. Each one requires a different approach. Be comfortable with breaking and creating deadlock, but be mindful of the consequences.

SECRET #44 Validate the final proposal and close date
Before you rush in to close the deal, make sure that everyone involved in the deal is in favour of your final proposal, especially the date by which you plan to sign the deal. Getting the buy-in of the entire Decision Centre in one meeting is first prize.

SECRET #45 Test-close the deal before you commit
A Test Close is used in dealmaking to check that all the agenda items have been agreed, and that there is nothing under the table that could derail the deal at the last minute. Use supposition questions to flush out any surprises before you sign.

SECRET #46 Take three more small steps before closing
Before putting pen to paper, compare the final deal on the table to your Likely Ball Park position, make sure that both sides have exactly the same understanding of the deal they will be signing, and agree on the implementation plan. Then summarise the final summaries of the deal.

SECRET #47 Close the deal in writing
When the deal finally closes, put it in writing as soon as you can. Deals, especially the details, go to hell in a handbasket far too easily if the specifics are not recorded promptly.

SECRET #48 Rejection happens to everyone
Rejection is disheartening but it happens to us all. Try everything you can to shift the 'no', but also recognise when you are just not going to win and accept the rejection with as much dignity as you can muster.

SECRET #49 Have a very good reason to walk away
Good deals are lost because someone could not bother to persevere, or throws in the towel at the first sign of trouble, or exits for fear of being rejected. Being Mr Lazy, a scaredy-cat or an insufferable egomaniac are not excuses for walking away. Only let go of a deal if your values, the Bottom Line or your judgement scream warnings at you.

SECRET #50 Relentless dealmaking chases away loved ones
Decide when to give unconditionally, and when you want value in return. With loved ones, you may want to give out of the generosity of your heart. This is fine, as long as it is a conscious choice on your part and not because you are a dog of a dealmaker.

The 50 Devils

DEVIL #1 (Dealmakers use specific skills to get what they want)
Assuming that a dealmaker is a salesperson or a negotiator will not only inhibit your ability to close world-class deals, it will leave you unprepared and vulnerable when you do meet a proficient dealmaker.

DEVIL #2 (Selling is not a swear word)
Believing that you have limited sales capabilities, or that selling is for lesser mortals, completely undermines your potential to be a brilliant dealmaker.

DEVIL #3 (Negotiation is the world's oldest profession)
Prostitution or not, every competent dealmaker is able to negotiate and trade with ease, and without compromising their position.

DEVIL #4 (There is power in having alternatives)
Going into a deal relying on only one closing strategy is a big mistake – if the other side plays a game for which you have not prepared, you will be outmanoeuvred – even if you can think on your feet.

DEVIL #5 (Everything is open to a deal)
Thinking you are selling your soul if you need to be flexible in a deal is how the unskilled operate. Take off the 'yes' and 'no' blinkers, and ask yourself: 'What are the conditions under which I can agree to this deal?'

DEVIL #6 (No one is above the law of dealmaking)
Do not presume that the more power you have, the less you need to do deals. The opposite is true – the greater your power, the more you will need to do deals to retain that power.

DEVIL #7 (Everyone has the potential to be a dealmaker)
Do not buy into the bull that negotiators or salespeople are made – just look at the average six-year-old. They are demon junior dealmakers.

DEVIL #8 (Verbal communication operates on two levels)
Instead of trying to eradicate the unconscious clues from your own communication, concentrate on picking up the other party's areas of flexibility in a deal.

DEVIL #9 (Non-verbal communication can be obscure)
You will not get burnt at the stake for opening your mind to forms of communication that go beyond that which can be explained. Don't be afraid to broaden your mind.

DEVIL #10 (People and donkeys are not that different)
There is not a person on the planet who is not receptive when offered the incentives they desire. Carrots provide leverage and power.

DEVIL #11 (Deals need to focus on value, not price)
A Value Proposition is not some slick statement that a salesperson is able to spout. Value Propositions show the other person that you understand what they want and need, and that the deal is not just about you.

DEVIL #12 (Do not confuse value with cost)
If you think the fuss over distinguishing value from cost is a waste of time, you will often end up paying much more for what you want than is necessary.

DEVIL #13 (Everything in dealmaking is interconnected)
Having a one-dimensional, disjointed strategy is going to cost you dearly. Not only will the other side get the better of you, but they will think you are a bit thick in the process.

DEVIL #14 (Planning in itself creates power)
Waiting to see what happens when you are faced with a situation leaves you completely unprepared and exposed. Even if it is an 'information-gathering' mission, plan what you want from the interaction.

DEVIL #15 (Controlling information provides strategic power)
If you use information as power in order to compromise the other party, or achieve win–lose deals in your favour, no one will want to share information or do deals with you.

DEVIL #16 (The giving of information needs to be planned)
Withholding information does not automatically benefit you. Not only will you be seen as obstructive or obtuse, but you may lose the opportunity to improve your position through the tactical use of information.

DEVIL #17 (There is no excuse for not getting information)
People can sense when you want information for nefarious purposes. If they pick up that your intentions are not good, they will tell you very little. Check your integrity when working with other people's disclosures.

DEVIL #18 (Plan and execute questions with care and love)
Firing off a string of questions in the hope that some of them will hit the target and extract the information you need is not good use of your opportunity to ask questions of the other party. Badly planned questions encourage clams.

DEVIL #19 (Listening and silence reveal the truth)
Passive listening – in one ear and out the other – is just as pointless as not listening at all. Practise active listening – keeping quiet but being fully involved in the conversation.

DEVIL #20 (Long-term relationships can be costly)
Don't let the vanity of being a trusted advisor keep you in a one-sided relationship. There is no way the other party will respect you if they can play you.

DEVIL #21 (Not all networks are equal)
Networks need to be mutually beneficial and nurtured. If you are not the sharing kind, don't be surprised when your network shrivels up and dies.

DEVIL #22 (Taking time to think is not a weakness)
Sales magicians and devilish dealmakers will try to pressure you into making a decision before you have the opportunity to think everything through. Delay your decision until you are sure of what you want.

DEVIL #23 (Power can be created from very basic sources)
Buying into the belief that you have no power, or no means to adjust your power, is the Conan the Destroyer of the power you *do* have. Luckily there is a manipulative, wicked six-year-old inside all of us.

DEVIL #24 (Structure must follow strategy)
Do not be tempted to develop your strategy around an existing structure. This is like buying a pair of shoes you like, but which are the wrong size, and trying to squeeze your feet into them. You will never be able to walk properly.

DEVIL #25 (Follow simple steps to define the deal)
Mike Tyson (American boxer and former undisputed heavyweight champion of the world, 1966–) said, 'Everyone has a plan – until they get punched in the face.' In defining the deal clearly, we can at least anticipate a lot of the punches.

DEVIL #26 (Step One is to identify and prioritise all Issues)
Resist the temptation to rush through this step. The more Issues you can identify during the planning stage of the deal, the easier it will be when it comes to engaging with the other party.

DEVIL #27 (Step Two is to know the limits of the Ball Park)
Unskilled dealmakers can easily destroy a deal by focusing on Issues that are not of prime importance, or by getting stuck on a single Issue. You need to stop this from happening by sticking to the Key Issues and considering the total value of the deal.

DEVIL #28 (Use Marbles to maintain the Ball Park)
Beating the other team up with your logic will not get you the deal. Think like a kid. Toss out logic and link unrelated Marbles – let them keep their tractor in exchange for buying you a cheetah.

DEVIL #29 (Step Three is to choose your Players carefully)
Taking the boss along to a deal can be a hazard. Not only do they want to be in charge of the proceedings, but they can destroy the Captain's credibility and give away tightly fought ground with a word or a wave of the hand.

DEVIL #30 (Their players do not play by the same rules)
Counter the Anti-Coach with a Pro-Coach and/or the Highlander. If the Highlander is the cockroach, consider qualifying out of the deal.

DEVIL #31 (Experts and advisors can make or break a deal)
Expert Advisors, when they have the floor or an audience, can run amok. When someone recognises that they are considered to be an expert, there is often the danger of their ego going haywire. Keep them on a tight leash.

DEVIL #32 (Wanting and needing are not synonymous)
Before you decide that business Needs and personal Wants amount to the same thing, think about the most extravagant gift you have ever bought (for yourself or someone else). Why did you do it? This is the difference between needing and wanting something.

DEVIL #33 (A business Need must exist for results to be achieved)
People who refuse to acknowledge that a Need exists are essentially Anti-Coaches. Prepare a strategy to minimise their impact on the deal. If this is the Highlander, it is best to qualify out of the deal.

DEVIL #34 (Ignore personal Hot Buttons at your peril)
Ignoring someone's personal Wants is naive and arrogant. Naive because deals are closed on factors other than the obvious and logical. Arrogant because relationships are important in deals, and ignoring another's personal issues smacks of conceit.

DEVIL #35 (Identify behavioural styles to build relationships)
Resist the temptation to play amateur psychologist. Being a careful, smart detective is a far more productive pursuit in dealmaking.

DEVIL #36 (Modify your behaviour to get the deal)
Modifying the way in which you approach the different styles does not mean you should pretend to be what you are not. Insincerity brings out the best in no one, so be true to the real you.

DEVIL #37 (You should make the first proposal)
If you let the other person make the first move, and then hope you can move them from their position, you are hoping against thunder.

DEVIL #38 (Open as high as you can within the Ball Park)
Greedy little pigs get eaten by the big bad wolf.

DEVIL #39 (There are guidelines for giving proposals)
Being laissez-faire when you give a proposal dilutes the power and impact of your proposal. Keep the structure and wording of this step in the encounter tight and controlled, and make sure that you are clear on the other party's position.

DEVIL #40 (There are guidelines when getting proposals)
Interrupting a proposal, or allowing your proposal to be interrupted, leads to confusion and frustration in a deal. Be still like broccoli.

DEVIL #41 (Feel the rhythm of the deal)
Do not yield to the temptation to take the 'kill' in 'unskilled' literally. It is up to you to make the bad dealmaker look good by using the momentum inherent in a deal.

DEVIL #42 (Teach difficult or unskilled dealmakers to dance)
Try not to lose patience with someone who does not know what they are doing in a deal. This is challenging when they are being arrogant or pushy, but bite your tongue and be the professional.

DEVIL #43 (Deadlock does not have to mean the end)
Do not shy away from deadlock. It can be a useful means of postponing a deal or maintaining the status quo. It does come at a price and more often than not damages the relationship.

DEVIL #44 (Validate the final proposal and close date)
One of the biggest mistakes that dealmakers are inclined to make is to set a close date that suits their own requirements. The other party must agree to the close date, or the deal will be a pipe dream.

DEVIL #45 (Test-close the deal before you commit)
The trial close used by a salesperson is not the same as the Test Close of the dealmaker. A trial close can be seen as a blatant attempt to manipulate the other team, and could blow your deal.

DEVIL #46 (Take three more small steps before closing)
The deal may have taken longer than expected. Don't be tempted to miss these three steps. Doing so could delay the deal further or even take it backwards.

DEVIL #47 (Close the deal in writing)
A deal is not really closed until you have the money.

DEVIL #48 (Rejection happens to everyone)
Practise not taking rejection to heart. If you can do this, you will be able to bounce back far more quickly, be happier and live longer.

DEVIL #49 (Have a very good reason to walk away)
Walking away is easy. Staying the course is far more difficult. If you quit too soon, you'll never get the high of a deal well done. But don't sell your soul for a shot of euphoria.

DEVIL #50 (Relentless dealmaking chases away loved ones)
If you give and give, don't be surprised or disappointed when people take and take from you. Or tell you to 'sod off'.

REFERENCES

Books

Adams, Douglas. *The Long Dark Tea-time of the Soul.* London: Pan Books, 1988

Anderson, Terrie. *One Minute More: The Human Connection.* Brisbane: Easy Online Portals, 2010

———. *999 Legendary Selling for the 21st Century.* Brisbane: Easy Online Portals, 2010

Campbell, Don. *The Mozart Effect: Tapping the Power of Music to Heal the Body, Strengthen the Mind, and Unlock the Creative Spirit.* London: HarperCollins, 1997

Carnegie, Dale. *How to Win Friends and Influence People.* London: Vermilion, 2007

Chandler, Alfred D. *The Visible Hand: Managerial Revolution in American Business.* Cambridge: Harvard University Press, 1977

Chapman, Gary. *The Five Love Languages: How to Express Heartfelt Commitment to Your Mate.* Northfield: Northfield Publishing, 1995

Fisher, Roger, and William Ury. *Getting to Yes: How to Negotiate to Agreement Without Giving In.* London: Arrow Books, 1981

Jarski, Rosemarie. *A Word from the Wise.* London: Ebury Press, 2007

Leff, Arthur Allen. *Swindling and Selling.* New York: Free Press, 1976

Levitt, Steven D., and Stephen J. Dubner. *Freakonomics: A Rogue Economist Explores the Hidden Side of Everything.* London: Penguin Books, 2005

Lewis, Richard D. *When Cultures Collide: Leading, Teamworking and Managing Across the Globe.* Boston: Nicholas Brealey Publishing, 2005

Maister, David H., Robert Galford, and Charles Green. *The Trusted Advisor.* London: Simon & Schuster, 2001

Maslow, Abraham. *Motivation and Personality.* New York: Harper, 1954

McConnell, Campbell R., and Stanley L. Brue. *Economics: Principles, Problems, and Policies.* Boston: McGraw-Hill/Irwin, 2005

McCormack, Mark. *What They Don't Teach You at Harvard Business School: Notes from a Street-Smart Executive.* New York: Bantam, 1984

Meredith, Kim. *Deal Diva: How to negotiate your way to success without selling your soul.* Cape Town: Zebra Press, 2010

———. *Work Diva: How to climb the corporate ladder without selling your soul.* Cape Town: Oshun Books, 2009

Morrison, Terri, and Wayne A. Conway. *Kiss, Bow or Shake Hands: The Bestselling Guide to Doing Business in More Than 60 Countries.* Avon, MA: Adams Media Corporation, 2006

Ross, George H. *Trump-Style Negotiation: Powerful Strategies and Tactics for Mastering Every Deal.* Hoboken: John Wiley & Sons, 2008

The Basics. Boechout, Belgium: Homarus Cookbooks, 2006

Wiseman, Richard. *Quirkology: The Curious Science of Everyday Lives.* London: Macmillan, 2007

Young, Toby. *How to Lose Friends and Alienate People*. Cambridge, MA: Da Capo Press, 2003

Reference books

Collins Concise Dictionary Plus. Glasgow: William Collins Sons & Co., 1989

Encarta Concise English Dictionary. London: Bloomsbury Publishing PLC, 2001

Magazines, newspapers and articles

Bazerman, Max H., and Deepak Malhotra. 'When Not to Trust Your Gut'. Harvard Business School, July 2006

Benjamin, Robert D. 'Swindlers, Dealmakers and Mediators: A Brief History of Ethics in Negotiation'. *AC Resolutions* magazine, Spring 2004

Maslow, Abraham H. 'A Theory of Human Motivation'. *Psychological Review* 50 (4), 1943

Websites

http://en.beterz.com
http://oxforddictionaries.com
http://whatis.techtarget.com
www.amazon.com
www.beedictionary.com
www.buseco.monash.edu.au
www.changingminds.org
www.chinesenegotiation.com
www.cio.com
www.facebook.com
www.forbes.com
www.google.com
www.guardian.co.uk
www.imdb.com
www.malleusmaleficarum.org
www.riotwineblog.com
www.sideroad.com
www.telegraph.co.uk
www.thefreedictionary.com
www.thinkexist.com
www.wikipedia.com
www.urbandictionary.com
www.youtube.com